LIBRARY OF NEW TESTAMENT STUDIES

638

Formerly the Journal for the Study of the New Testament Supplement series

Editor
Chris Keith

Editorial Board
Dale C. Allison, John M.G. Barclay, Lynn H. Cohick, R. Alan Culpepper, Craig A. Evans, Robert Fowler, Simon J. Gathercole, Juan Hernández Jr., John S. Kloppenborg, Michael Labahn, Matthew V. Novenson, Love L. Sechrest, Robert Wall, Catrin H. Williams, Brittany E. Wilson

Satan, the Heavenly Adversary of Man

A Narrative Analysis of the Function of Satan in the Book of Revelation

Cato Gulaker

LONDON • NEW YORK • OXFORD • NEW DELHI • SYDNEY

T&T CLARK
Bloomsbury Publishing Plc
50 Bedford Square, London, WC1B 3DP, UK
1385 Broadway, New York, NY 10018, USA
29 Earlsfort Terrace, Dublin 2, Ireland

BLOOMSBURY, T&T CLARK and the T&T Clark logo are trademarks of
Bloomsbury Publishing Plc

First published in Great Britain 2021
This paperback edition published in 2022

Copyright © Cato Gulaker, 2021

Cato Gulaker has asserted his right under the Copyright, Designs and Patents Act, 1988, to
be identified as Author of this work.

All rights reserved. No part of this publication may be reproduced or transmitted
in any form or by any means, electronic or mechanical, including photocopying,
recording, or any information storage or retrieval system, without prior permission
in writing from the publishers.

Bloomsbury Publishing Plc does not have any control over, or responsibility for, any
third-party websites referred to or in this book. All internet addresses given in this book were
correct at the time of going to press. The author and publisher regret any inconvenience
caused if addresses have changed or sites have ceased to exist, but can accept
no responsibility for any such changes.

A catalogue record for this book is available from the British Library.

Library of Congress Cataloging-in-Publication Data
Names: Gulaker, Cato, 1979– author.
Title: Satan, the heavenly adversary of man : a narrative analysis of the
function of Satan in the book of Revelation / Cato Gulaker.
Description: London ; New York : T&T Clark, 2021. | Series: Library of New Testament
studies, 2513-8790 ; 638 | Includes bibliographical references and index. |
Summary: "Cato Gulaker employs narrative criticism to explore where the depiction of Satan found
in the Book of Revelation is positioned on the axis of two divergent roles. The literary character of
Satan is commonly perceived to gradually evolve from the first divine agents in the Hebrew Bible,
representing the darker sides of the divine governing of affairs (Job 1-2; Zech 3; 1 Chr 21:1;
Num 22:22, 32), to the full-blown enemy of God of the post-biblical era. However, Gulaker posits
that texts referring to Satan in between these two poles are not uniform and diverge considerably.
This book argues for a new way of perceiving Satan in Revelation that provides a more probable
reading, as it creates less narrative dissonance than the alternative of the ancient combat
myth/cosmic conflict between Satan and God. From this reading emerges a subdued Satan more
akin to its Hebrew Bible hypotexts and Second Temple Judaism parallels - one that fits seamlessly
with the theology, cosmology and the overarching plot of the narrative itself. Gulaker explores the
functions of Satan in a text written relatively late compared to the rest of the New Testament, but
with strong affinities to the Hebrew Bible, concluding that Satan is characterized more as
the leash, rod, and sifting device in the hand of God, than as his enemy"– Provided by publisher.
Identifiers: LCCN 2020033876 (print) | LCCN 2020033877 (ebook) |
ISBN 9780567696502 (hardback) | ISBN 9780567697554 (paperback) |
ISBN 9780567696519 (pdf) | ISBN 9780567696533 (epub)
Subjects: LCSH: Bible. Revelation–Criticism, Narrative. |
Bible. Revelation–Criticism, interpretation, etc. | Devil–Biblical teaching.
Classification: LCC BS2825.6.D5 G85 2021 (print) |
LCC BS2825.6.D5 (ebook) | DDC 228/.066–dc23
LC record available at https://lccn.loc.gov/2020033876
LC ebook record available at https://lccn.loc.gov/2020033877

ISBN: HB: 978-0-5676-9650-2
PB: 978-0-5676-9755-4
ePDF: 978-0-5676-9651-9
ePUB: 978-0-5676-9653-3

Series: Library of New Testament Studies, ISSN 2513–8790, volume 638

Typeset by Newgen KnowledgeWorks Pvt. Ltd., Chennai, India

To find out more about our authors and books visit www.bloomsbury.com
and sign up for our newsletters.

Contents

List of Figures ix
List of Tables x
List of Abbreviations xi

1 Introduction 1
   1.1 Ambiguous Satans and the Issue of Tension 2
      1.1.1 A Monistic Approach to the Character of Satan 4
      1.1.2 A Dualistic Approach to the Character of Satan 11
      1.1.3 Tensions in Revelation 16
      1.1.4 Excursus: Dualism and Monism in Revelation 17
   1.2 Contemporary Research 20
      1.2.1 Publications on Satan 21
      1.2.2 Narrative and Literary Studies on Revelation 24
      1.2.3 Concluding Remarks 29
   1.3 The Scope of This Book 29

2 Theoretical and Methodological Considerations 31
   2.1 Introduction 31
   2.2 On the Nature of Narrative Criticism 32
      2.2.1 Plot 34
      2.2.2 Characterization 35
      2.2.3 Point of View 41
   2.3 Defining the Overarching Plot of Revelation 44
   2.4 Text Selection 47
   2.5 Excursus: The Use of Extratextual References in Narrative Criticism 49

3 Satan in the Messages to the Seven Congregations 55
   3.1 Introduction 55
   3.2 The Literary Frame of the Messages 56
   3.3 The Literary Form and Function of the Messages 60
   3.4 Analysis 64

		3.4.1	Smyrna	64
			3.4.1.1 Plot	64
			3.4.1.2 Characterization	66
			3.4.1.3 Point of View	71
		3.4.2	Pergamum	72
			3.4.2.1 Plot	72
			3.4.2.2 Characterization	73
			3.4.2.3 Point of View	77
		3.4.3	Thyatira	78
			3.4.3.1 Plot	78
			3.4.3.2 Characterization	79
			3.4.3.3 Point of View	81
		3.4.4	Philadelphia	83
			3.4.4.1 Plot	83
			3.4.4.2 Characterization	84
			3.4.4.3 Point of View	85
		3.4.5	Ephesus	87
			3.4.5.1 Plot	87
			3.4.5.2 Characterization	87
			3.4.5.3 Point of View	88
		3.4.6	Sardis	89
			3.4.6.1 Plot	89
			3.4.6.2 Characterization	89
			3.4.6.3 Point of View	91
		3.4.7	Laodicea	91
			3.4.7.1 Plot	91
			3.4.7.2 Characterization	92
			3.4.7.3 Point of View	93
	3.5	Concluding Remarks		94
4	Satan in the Story of the Woman, the Dragon, and the Beasts			97
	4.1	Introduction		97
	4.2	The Literary Context of Revelation 12–13		98
		4.2.1	The Throne Vision	98
			4.2.1.1 The Ethos of John	99
			4.2.1.2 God upon the Throne and His Assembly	100

			4.2.1.3 The Lamb	104
		4.2.2	The Septets of Revelation 6–16	106
			4.2.2.1 The Literary Structure of Revelation 6–16 and Its Relation to Revelation 4–5	107
			4.2.2.2 Intermediary Agents in the Three Septets of Revelation 6–16	111
		4.2.3	Preliminary Conclusion on the Literary Context of Revelation 12–13	117
	4.3	The Literary Form and Function of Revelation 12–13		117
	4.4	Analysis		119
		4.4.1	Plot	119
		4.4.2	Characterization	122
			4.4.2.1 The Satan of Plot A—The Story of the Woman and the Dragon (12:1–6, 13–17)	123
			4.4.2.1.1 Excursus on the Combat Myth and Revelation 12	138
			4.4.2.2 The Satan of Plot B—The War in Heaven	143
			4.4.2.3 The Satan of Plot C—The Beasts of the Sea and the Earth	150
			4.4.2.3.1 The Beast from the Sea	150
			4.4.2.3.2 The Beast from the Earth	157
		4.4.3	Point of View	162
			4.4.3.1 God's Point of View	162
			4.4.3.2 Sympathy, Antipathy, and the Evaluative Point of View	163
			4.4.3.3 The Horizontal/Vertical Point of View	164
	4.5	Concluding Remarks		166
5	The End of Satan			169
	5.1	Introduction		169
	5.2	The Literary Context of Revelation 20		170
		5.2.1	The Whore and the Bride	172
		5.2.2	Vindication/Retribution	174
		5.2.3	Babylon the Great	178
		5.2.4	The Two Suppers	186
		5.2.5	Preliminary Conclusion on the Literary Context of Revelation 20	190

	5.3	The Literary Form and Function of Revelation 20		192
	5.4	Analysis		194
		5.4.1 Plot		194
		5.4.2 Characterization		195
			5.4.2.1 Introduction	195
			5.4.2.2 The Temporary Binding of Satan	198
			5.4.2.3 Deceiving the Nations, from Gog and Magog	210
			5.4.2.4 The Death of Satan	213
		5.4.3 Point of View		221
			5.4.3.1 God's Point of View	221
			5.4.3.2 Evaluative Point of View	223
	5.5	Concluding Remarks		225
6	Conclusion			229
Bibliography				235
Index				247

Figures

1	Monism and dualism in Revelation	19
2	The diegetic levels of the messages to the seven congregations	57
3	The actants of the message to Smyrna	66
4	The actants of the story of the woman, the dragon, and the beasts	122
5	The actants of Revelation 20	196

Tables

1	Text Selection	49
2	Cross-References to the First and Last Sections of the Book of Revelation in the Messages to the Seven Congregations	63
3	Parallels in the Jezebel Stories of 1 Kings and the Book of Revelation	81
4	Parallels in the Presentations of God and the Lamb in Revelation 4 and 5	105
5	Synopsis on the Seals, Trumpets, and Bowls of Revelation 6–16	108
6	Bowls and Trumpets Compared to the Plagues of Exodus	114
7	A Survey of Plot Strands in Revelation 12–13	120
8	Rise and Fall of Adversaries in Revelation 12–20	171
9	The Two Cities	174
10	Outline of the Major Parts of Revelation in Light of the Overarching Plot	179
11	Perspectives on the Plot of Revelation 20	195

Abbreviations

ABRL	Anchor Bible Reference Library
BBR	*Bulletin of Biblical Research*
BECNT	Baker Exegetical Commentary on the New Testament
BibInt	*Biblical Interpretation Series*
BNTC	Black's New Testament Commentaries
CBQ	*Catholic Biblical Quarterly*
CPT	Centre for Pentecostal Theology
CTA	*Cuneiform Alphabetic Texts from Ugarit*
ExAud	*Ex Auditu*
HNTC	Harper's New Testament Commentaries
HSM	Harvard Semitic Monographs
HTR	*Harvard Theological Review*
ICC	International Critical Commentary
JAJSup	*Journal of Ancient Judaism, Supplements*
JBL	*Journal of Biblical Literature*
JETS	*Journal of the Evangelical Theological Society*
JSNTSup	Journal for the Study of the New Testament Supplement Series
JSP	*Journal for the Study of the Pseudepigrapha*
LHBOTS	The Library of Hebrew Bible/Old Testament Studies
LNTS	The Library of New Testament Studies
NCBC	New Cambridge Bible Commentary
NCCS	New Covenant Commentary Series
NICNT	New International Commentary on the New Testament
NIGTC	New International Greek Testament Commentary
NovT	*Novum Testamentum*
PTMS	Pittsburgh Theological Monograph Series
RevExp	*Review and Expositor*
SBLSymS	Society of Biblical Literature Symposium Series
SNTSMS	Society for New Testament Studies Monograph Series
SPCK	Society for Promoting Christian Knowledge
StBibLit	Studies in Biblical Literature (Lang)
SVTP	Studia in Veteris Testamenti Pseudepigraphica
TJ	*Trinity Journal*
TPINTC	TPI New Testament Commentaries
WBC	Word Biblical Commentary
WGRWSup	Writings from the Greco-Roman World Supplement Series
WMANT	Wissenschaftliche Monographien zum Alten und Neuen Testament
WUNT	Wissenschaftliche Untersuchungen zum Neuen Testament

1

Introduction

Making sense of the concepts of good and evil is often considered to be the main issue of the book of Revelation.[1] The author struggles to cope with the apparent suffering of believers in Asia Minor and the prosperity of the persecuting authorities and local unbelievers.[2] How can a just and almighty God retain his position as worthy of trust while his own people are suffering? How can the saints be afflicted, while at the same time their transgressors prosper? In the end, the suffering of the saints raises the question of God's justice (cf. Rev 6:10–11; 18:6–8; 19:1–2).[3] The basic pattern of the answer provided is that everything happens according to God's eschatological plan of salvation of his creation. The horrors and afflictions the churches of Asia Minor are experiencing represent a combination of the divine sifting of humankind and wrath poured upon the inhabitants of this world referred to as the hour of testing which is about to be unleashed (Rev 3:10). The outcome is either salvation or judgment, depending on how one responds to the trials of affliction presented in the visionary section of the book (Revelation 6–20).

Satan is one among many agents actively taking part in this eschatological ordeal. His violent conduct on earth represents a serious challenge to the congregations to be overcome through faithfulness to Christ unto death (Rev 2:10; 13:10, 15). As the rewards for enduring such afflictions by far outweighs the short-term pain in question

---

[1] See Adela Yarbro Collins, *Crisis and Catharsis: The Power of the Apocalypse* (Philadelphia: Westminster, 1984), 152; Steven Grabiner, *Revelation's Hymns: Commentary on the Cosmic Conflict*, LNTS 511 (London: T&T Clark, 2015), 36, 43; and Sigve Tonstad, *Saving God's Reputation: The Theological Function of Pistis Iesou in the Cosmic Narratives of Revelation*, LNTS 337 (London: Bloomsbury T&T Clark, 2006), 15.
[2] According to Adela Yarbro Collins, the tension between what is and ought to be is reflected in the sharp contradiction between the symbols of Revelation. These symbols can be seen, in light of the historical situation of the book, to fulfill the task "to overcome the intolerable tension between reality and hopeful faith" (Yarbro Collins, *Crisis and Catharsis*, 141).
[3] As Meira Z. Kensky has rightly pointed out, the question of Rev 6:10–11 fits in naturally with the element of theodicy embedded in Revelation in that it questions the justice of God. "The way the question is framed actually points to the actions that God is *not taking* in the present, actions that they believed are required and necessary" (Meira Z. Kensky, *Trying Man, Trying God: The Divine Courtroom in Early Jewish and Christian Literature*, WUNT II/289 [Tübingen: Mohr Siebeck, 2010], 244). The question is loaded with expectancy, but it is nonetheless posed as a question, and subsequently creates tension in the reader regarding when, and possibly if, justice will be done (ibid., 242–7).

(12:11; 20:4–5), the plot of the book turns out to be a cosmic version of the now famous "marshmallow test" conducted by Walter Mischel in the 1960s and 1970s.[4] If one abstains from the present momentary bliss of survival and social inclusion (cf. Rev 13:15–17), popular, intriguing, and tempting religious deviations included (Rev 2:6, 14–15, 20), the future rewards will be marvelous and manifold (cf. Revelation 21–22). However, in Revelation, the stakes are raised acutely from mere rewards to the inclusion of dire punishment (cf. Rev 14:9–11; 20:12–15). The function of Satan is central to this eschatological ordeal of sifting the world's population into two categories, and causes several questions regarding the cosmological framework of Revelation to surface. If Satan is functioning as a sifting device in the hands of the divine, to what extent is his malevolent conduct described as his actions and not those of God? To what degree can we speak of subjectivity or autonomy in his cunning deception of the world? Does Satan function literally as a necessary opposition against which the faithfulness of believers is to be measured?[5] Is he partaking in a carefully composed hour of testing in the vein of the renowned trial of Abraham (Gen 22:1–19), the ordeal of Christ in the desert (Mark 1:12–13; Matt 4:1–11; Luke 4:1–13), or perhaps the general acts of testing of believers referred to by Paul in 1 Cor 10:13? Also, if this can be argued to be the case, how does this affect the image of God in the narrative? It is at these crossroads that we encounter the main problem of interest to the present study.

1.1 Ambiguous Satans and the Issue of Tension

According to Jeffrey Burton Russell, Christianity is a semi-dualistic religion with a history of resisting the simpler solutions of dualism and monism. This "tension between monism and dualism has led to inconsistencies in Christian dualism,"[6] which has always been the "weak seam in Christian theology."[7] It is probably from these tensions that the different incompatible concepts of the Devil in the New Testament evolved.[8] The patristic era reveals some struggles in coming to terms with these

---

[4] Walter Mischel, *The Marshmallow Test: Mastering Self-Control and How to Master It* (London: Corgi Books, 2014).

[5] The conclusion of Robert Charles Branden in his example from the story of Little Red Riding Hood (derived from Nicholas Thomas Wright, *The New Testament and the People of God* [London: SPCK, 1992], 69–80) could be a useful comparison to the necessity of the Devil in Revelation: "Without the opponent, the Wolf, not only is there no need for the woodcutter, there is no story because there is no plot" (Robert Charles Branden, *Satanic Conflict and the Plot of Matthew*, StBibLit 89 [New York: Peter Lang, 2006], 8). In other words, in the narrative of Revelation, the Devil constitutes a necessary component in establishing the plot, as he is the main device in making sense of the tribulations of the saints. In time, as Neil Forsyth has pointed out, the character of the Devil turned out to be an important device for early Christianity in explaining and processing evil in light of the merging faith and the forging of doctrine: "If Satan had not already existed, the church would have had to invent him" (Neil Forsyth, *The Old Enemy: Satan & the Combat Myth* [Princeton, NJ: Princeton University Press, 1987], 317).

[6] Jeffrey Burton Russell, *The Devil: Perceptions of Evil from Antiquity to Primitive Christianity* (Ithaca, NY: Cornell University Press, 1977), 228.

[7] Russell, *The Devil*, 222–3.

[8] According to Henry Ansgar Kelly, the biblical texts related to the theme of demonology reveal "the great disparity of source materials and concepts that exists in the scriptures. There is no systematic demonology present; that comes only later, and only at the cost of distorting the biblical data to

tensions as what one say about Satan in turn affects what is said about God:[9] If one accepts the idea of God not being responsible for the suffering of sentient beings in the world, but attributes it to the Devil, then the image of God diminishes to the benefit of two divine entities heading toward dualism.[10] On the other hand, if one retorts with the idea of God in the end being somehow the ultimate sovereign divine force, controlling, utilizing, and forcing the hand of the Devil, then he is ultimately responsible for said suffering—a characteristic of cosmological monism. The New Testament Satans/Devils[11] moved along the axis between these two poles, never fully embracing either, and left it to the church fathers to solve the issue of theodicy from its loose ends.[12] The main task of this reading is to pinpoint where on this axis the Satan of Revelation is to be situated.[13] In the following, I will explain the concept of this axis by giving a few examples from the Scriptures of how tension is created within the Christian tradition by its diverse utilization of various cosmological adaptations and perspectives on the character of Satan from the Hebrew Bible[14] throughout the New Testament. These literary references will be of great hermeneutical value to my exegesis below, as they constitute a wide array of possible interpretational points of reference—the echo chamber of the text and symbolism of Revelation. I have categorized the texts under the

---

Procrustean specifications" (Henry Ansgar Kelly, *The Devil, Demonology, and Witchcraft: The Development of Christian Beliefs In Evil Spirits*, rev. ed. [Eugene, OR: Wipf & Stock, 2004], 23; see also Christopher W. Skinner,"Overcoming Satan, Overcoming the World: Exploring the Cosmologies of Mark and John," in *Evil in Second Temple Judaism and Early Christianity*, ed. Chris Keith and Loren T. Stuckenbruck, WUNT II/417 [Tübingen: Mohr Siebeck, 2016], 101–21, 101–2, 112).

[9] See Susanne Rudnig-Zelt, "Der Teufel und der alttestamentliche Monotheismus," in *Das Böse, der Teufel und Dämonen—Evil, the Devil, and Demons*, ed. Jan Dochhorn, Susanne Rudnig-Zelt, and Benjamin G. Wold, WUNT II/412 (Tübingen: Mohr Siebeck, 2016), 1–20; Russell, *The Devil*, 1; and Kirsten Nielsen, *Satan: Den Fortabte Søn?* (Frederiksberg: ANIS, 1991), 16.

[10] It was on these grounds that Celsus criticized Christianity, that it by identifying pagan gods with devils ended up believing in two powers in the universe rather than one—and thus became dualistic. See Neil Forsyth, *The Satanic Epic* (Princeton, NJ: Princeton University Press, 2003), 44–45.

[11] Διαβολος, meaning "slanderer," is the term by which the LXX translates the Hebrew שטן. In the New Testament, we find that Mark and Paul prefer the Aramaic σατανας when referring to this character, while the other writings use both or none with the exception of the letter of Jude, which uses only διαβολος.

[12] Elaine Pagels, *The Origin of Satan* (New York: Random House, 1995), 112–48; Henry Ansgar Kelly, *Satan: A Biography* (New York: Cambridge University Press, 2006), parts III and IV; and Jeffrey Burton Russell, *Satan: The Early Christian Tradition* (Ithaca, NY: Cornell University Press, 1981), 30–50, provide insight to how the early Christian tradition struggled to cope with the bits and pieces of the biblical texts concerning Satan.

[13] The concept of an implied reader in narrative criticism is a theoretical construct of the scholar conducting the narrative analysis. How one defines one's reader and his/her assumed competence will therefore determine the hermeneutical outcome to a certain extent. The text and the defined competence of one's reader constitute the main premises for any narrative reading, and I believe it is here, between these elements, that one can discern how one narrative/literary reading of Revelation diverges from the other—including this one. I will therefore use the term "reading" in referring to the hermeneutical deliberations of this book because the literary meaning in the narrative sense of the word occurs in such a "dialectical interaction between the words of the text and the scenarios of the reader" (David L. Barr,"The Lamb Who Looks Like a Dragon? Characterizing Jesus in John's Apocalypse," in *The Reality of Apocalypse*, ed. David L. Barr, SBLSymS 39 [Atlanta, GA: Society of Biblical Literature, 2006], 205–20, 212). Cf. Chapter 2 in this reading on method.

[14] I will use the term "the Hebrew Bible" when referring to the holy books from Jewish tradition known by the acronym TaNaKh, in order to distinguish this particular canon from the Septuagint, and its related noncanonical traditions, the Pseudepigrapha.

headings "A Monistic Approach to the Character of Satan" and "A Dualistic Approach to the Character of Satan" (see Section 1.1.4 for the use of the terms "dualism" and "monism" in this book) to indicate which pole the texts are most close to, while at the same time being fully aware that only a few of the texts in question actually reflect such a cosmology to its fullest extent. Subsequent to this, I will point out a few indicators of how this tension is reflected in the text of Revelation. Finally, I will comment on how contemporary research has dealt with these matters before I lay out the scope and approach of this study.

1.1.1 A Monistic Approach to the Character of Satan

Much ink has been spilled on the issue of Satan in the Hebrew Bible. As a great many scholars have contributed informative studies on the development of Satan from the Hebrew Bible and Second Temple Judaism, I will here only present an excerpt from this development to prove my point.[15]

In the Hebrew Bible we have several texts describing both human and celestial agents functioning as divinely sanctioned adversaries in which their adversarial function is either explicit (Num 22:22; 1 Kgs 11:14, 23) or implicit (1 Kgs 22:19–23; Exod 12:23; 2 Sam 24:16). In addition, we have four texts reflecting what could be referred to as the cradle of what in time would become the New Testament Satan by their use of the term שָׂטָן (adversary) as a specific title/name (1 Chr 21:1) or referring to a particular celestial office of prosecution (Job 1–2; Zechariah 3).[16] In these nongeneric references to a Satan in the Hebrew Bible he is characterized as one of the בְּנֵי הָאֱלֹהִים (Sons of God, Job 1:6; 2:1), functioning as a tester and tempter (Job 1–2; 1 Chr 21:1) as well as a judicial accuser (Job 1–2; Zech 3:1–2).[17] Nowhere in the Hebrew Bible do we find any reference to Satan as the enemy of God, but from the sixth century BC, he frequently appears as a facilitator of God's shadier side.[18] As many have suggested, one can easily

---

[15] In their own respective ways I find the following surveys particularly helpful in grasping the conception and initial development of the character of Satan: Derek Brown, *The God of This Age*, WUNT II/409 (Tübingen: Mohr Siebeck, 2015), 21–60; Forsyth, *The Old Enemy*, 105–212; Kelly, *The Devil, Demonology, and Witchcraft*, 11–23; Kelly, *Satan: A Biography*, 17–52; Adam Kotsko, *The Prince of This World* (Stanford, NC: Stanford University Press, 2017); Peter Stanford, *The Devil: A Biography* (London: Arrow Books, 2003), 19–46; Pagels, *The Origin of Satan*, 35–62; Rudnig-Zelt, "Der Teufel und der alttestamentliche Monotheismus," 1–20; and Russell, *The Devil*, 174–220.

[16] See Richard H. Bell, *Deliver Us from Evil: Interpreting the Redemption from the Power of Satan in New Testament Theology*, WUNT 216 (Tübingen: Mohr Siebeck, 2007), 10–11.

[17] In Job 1–2 and Zechariah 3, the term refers to a particular office in the heavenly assembly. This is signaled by the presence of the definite article. According to Elaine Pagels, any member of the assembly could assume this role (Pagels, *The Origin of Satan*, 39). This makes the term in these instances generic in function, yet nongeneric in the sense of a particular office set apart from others. In 1 Chr 21:1 Satan is used as a proper name, indicated by the absence of the definite article—thus nongeneric (see Bell, *Deliver Us from Evil*, 10–11; Christopher A. Rollston, "An Ur-History of the New Testament Devil: The Celestial שׂטן (śāṭān) in Zechariah and Job," in *Evil in Second Temple Judaism and Early Christianity*, ed. Chris Keith and Loren T. Stuckenbruck, WUNT II/417 [Tübingen: Mohr Siebeck, 2016], 1–16, 2–6).

[18] Margaret Baker suggests, "In origin, however, Satan appears to have been an aspect of the LORD himself, insofar as later texts attribute to him what had formerly been described as actions of the LORD" and "Isaiah knew that the LORD created both 'weal and woe' (Isa. 45.7) but this was changed at the beginning of the second temple period, and there appeared an angel whose role was to tempt

perceive this development in the alteration of 1 Sam 24:1 in 1 Chr 21:1 by making Satan an intermediary agent of the deed of deception.[19] Such a development might reflect a distrust or dissatisfaction in the monistic cosmology expressed in texts such as Isa 45:7 and the book of Job.[20] After all, a recurring element in the prophetic literature is the description of the suffering of the people as *just* punishment or chastisement, due to previously unfavorable conduct (cf. Isa 64:5–12; Jer 33:4–5; Ezek 39:23–24; Mic 3:4). However, such a way of dealing with the suffering of the people of God only works if they deserve it.

In the post-exilic period we witness the growth of a body of literature attempting to answer the main problem of Job (cf. Job 9:24; 21:7, 17, compared to 24:12, 18, 19; 22) by means of solving the issue of theodicy through reference to an eschatological future. This development can be seen at play in the third century BC LXX revision of the ending of Job (42:17).[21] According to Alan Bernstein, "apocalyptic literature proclaims a future judgment that will separate the good from the wicked so that they will no longer share the same soil in the underworld."[22] In the apocalyptic vision of Daniel, the cosmic perspective is still monistic as the saints are to be given over to these violent afflictions of the fourth beast for a divinely apportioned time (Dan 7:23–25; 9:24–27; 11:27, 29, 36; 12:6–7). Here the violent conduct of Antiochus Epiphanes IV is described not as much as just judgment of the saints (although possibly, in 9:24), but rather as necessary

---

and oppose" (Margaret Baker, *The Revelation of Jesus Christ: Which God Gave to Him to Show to His Servants What Must Soon Take Place (Revelation 1.1)* [Edinburgh: T& T Clark, 2000], 215).

[19] As Ryan E. Stokes has rightly pointed out, this is not a way of relieving Yahweh free of any charge of wrongdoing (cf. 2 Chr 18:18–22): "Any distance between Yhwh and David's sin created by this substitution is very slight" (Ryan E. Stokes, "The Devil Made David Do It … or Did He? The Nature, Identity, and Literary Origins of the Satan in 1 Chronicles 21:1," *JBL* 128 [2009]: 90–106, 100; see also Sydney H. T. Page, "Satan: God's Servant," *JETS* 50 [2007]: 449–65, 454–6).

[20] According to Othmar Keel, one cannot find in the Hebrew Bible any trace of an "Evil Kingdom" as a self-sufficient entity, but the concept of Satan evolves in the intertestamental period as a solution to separate the elements of reality one did not want to associate too closely with a compassionate God: "Das Böse wird in der Hebräischen Bibel noch weitgehend von JHWH selber resp. seiner nächsten Umgebung, seiner Begleitung, seinem Hofstaat wahrgenommen und verantwortet. Die Satansgestalt wird dann aber in der frühjüdischen Literatur zu einem der Zentren einer von JHWH weitgehend abgespaltenen Welt, einem eigenen dämonsichen Bereich (einer Art Müllhalde, décharge publique), wo alles, was zum immer reineren, moralischeren Gott nicht passt, deponiert wird" (Othmar Keel, "Schwache alttestamentliche Ansätze zur Konstruktion einer stark dualistisch getönen Welt," in *Die Dämonen: die Dämonologie der israelitisch- jüdischen und frühchristlichen Literatur in Kontext ihrer Umwelt*, ed. Armin Lange, Herman Lichtenberger, and K. F. Diethard Römheld [Tübingen: Mohr Siebeck, 2003], 211–36, 229). Moreover, as Susanne Rudnig-Zelt has suggested, even if there was a development in the direction of radical dualism, the monistic affinity of the Hebrew Bible seems to be developed and emphasized in the intertestamental texts as well as in the New Testament, to a greater extent than earlier research has allowed for. Thus, the continued insistence on the supremacy and sovereignty of the one God prevented moderate dualism to develop into radical dualism (see Rudnig-Zelt, "Der Teufel und der alttestamentliche Monotheismus," 16–17).

[21] "And Job died, old and full of days. *It is written that he will rise again with those whom the Lord raises up.*" The italicized words mark the shortest of the three LXX additions to the Masoretic Text of Job 42:27 (see Jeffrey Burton Russell, *A History of Heaven* [Princeton, NJ: Princeton University Press, 1997], 28–9).

[22] Alan E. Bernstein, *The Formation of Hell: Death and Retribution in the Ancient and Early Christian World* (Ithaca, NY: Cornell University Press, 1993), 172.

for the divinely predestined history to unfold.[23] By describing the foreign perpetrator as acting according to the divine governing of time, unknowingly filling up the divine measure of evil, a solution to the momentary affliction can be explained as a necessary rite of passage on the path toward eternal bliss (12:2-3). Daniel 11:32-35 and 12:10-12 describe three types of response to the tribulations: the wise who prevail even unto death (11:33), the sinners and the ungodly who turns to apostasy (11:32a; 12:10a), and the wise who stumble but are refined, purified, and cleansed (11:35; 12:10). The end of affliction will come when the power of the saints is completely devastated (12:7). Moreover, it is by responding wisely to the contents of what is revealed that one can hope to become one of the happy souls having prevailed over the ordeal (12:12). There is no Satan in the book of Daniel, but as these visions constitute the blueprint of Satan and his minions as they appear in Revelation 12-13, their cosmological implications on theodicy will be important to my exegesis below. Moreover, despite the absence of any Satan, the plot of the visionary part of Daniel is similar to that of Revelation.[24]

When turning to the noncanonical literature of Second Temple Judaism, one finds in the book of Jubilees (approx. 150 BC[25]) an implied necessity of adversaries to be the main explanation of the existence of Mastema/Satan (Jub. 10:7-9).[26] Their devious nature and violent conduct are presented as early as the beginning of the book (1:11; 7:26-28), whereas their origins are explained later (10:1-14). After having been confronted and defeated by Michael and his angels in battle, the leader of the demons, Mastema, is granted one-tenth of his demons to continue his work. Important to this reading is the logical thrust of his argument, which apparently tips the divine scale of decision in his favor: "Because if some of them are not left to me, I will not be able to exercise the authority of my will among the children of men because they are (intended) to corrupt and lead astray before my judgment because the evil of the sons of men is great" (Jub. 10:8-9).[27] Thus, according to this tradition, there exists a purpose behind the malignant spiritual forces of Mastema that is grounded in the evil of men *and* their inherent nature—all validated by divine decree.[28] In addition, we have the

---

[23] See the repeated use of the expression לְמוֹעֵד (at the appointed time, Dan 8:19; 11:27, 29, 35; 12:7), to refer to the different fixed points in time where the events in question are revealed to occur.

[24] This means that Dan 12:2-3 is the first explicit biblical mentioning of a promised afterlife to those worthy, and, as is the case with Revelation, this outcome is contingent on the manner one responds to the tribulations revealed.

[25] James C. VanderKam, "The Demons in the *Book of Jubilees*," in *Die Dämonen: die Dämonologie der israelitisch-jüdischen und frühchristlichen Literatur in Kontext ihrer Umwelt*, ed. Armin Lange, Herman Lichtenberger, and K. F.Diethard Römheld (Tübingen: Mohr Siebeck, 2003), 339–64, 339.

[26] Mastema is the main name used to refer to the leader of demons in Jubilees, although Satan occurs in 10:11 and 23:29. The title is probably derived from the Hifil participle form of שׂטם (cherish animosity against) and the noun מַשְׂטֵמָה (animosity, cf. Hos 9:7), which are both fitting epithets reflecting the adversarial nature of his conduct. See Robert H. Charles, *The Book of Jubilees or the Little Genesis* (London: SPCK, 1917; San Diego, CA: Book Tree, 2003), 80.

[27] James H. Charlesworth, ed., *The Old Testament Pseudepigrapha Volume Two* (Peabody, MA: Hendrickson, 1983), 76; see also Charles, *The Book of Jubilees*, 80.

[28] According to James C. VanderKam this aspect of Jubilees represents a dramatic departure from its source, "The Book of Watchers," and further refers to God's response to Mastema's request as "truly surprising" and presenting "the major puzzle regarding the demons in the *Book of Jubilees*" (VanderKam, "Demons in the *Book of Jubilees*," 344). Moreover, it forces a conclusion that Jubilees "found a place for the demons in the post-diluvian world. In that world that are ultimately subordinate to God who allows the satan, the prince of Mastema, to rule them" (ibid., 362). Miryam T. Brand

demons delineating the ethnic borders of Israel, separating them from the rest of the children of men (Jub. 15:30–31).[29] A similar function of corrupting and leading astray that is grounded in divine origins and intent can be found in the various antagonistic characters of the writings from Qumran[30]—Belial in particular.[31] In these writings, the idea of external spiritual forces tugging and tempting the children of light to stray from the path of the righteous corresponds well with their dualistic notion of society, constituting the very means of division. The most famous example of this epistemology is the *Treatise of the Two Spirits* (1QS III, 13–IV, 26), which is, according to Florentino García Martínez, "the most systematic exposition of the dualistic thinking of the community."[32] Still, this notion of dualism must be understood in light of the divine cosmological governing of such evil. Important to this reading is the explicit idea in this treatise of an Angel of Darkness *appointed by God* to humankind, leading the children of righteousness away *according to the mysteries of God and his glorious design*,

---

finds several parallels in Mesopotamian literature in the subjugation of evil spirits under Mastema, and reaches the following conclusion on the role of Mastema to that of the divine in the divine court: "From this point on, the evil spirits are a functional part of the divine system, and do not represent a force independent of God's will or control" (Miryam Brand, *Evil Within and Without: The Source of Sin and Its Nature in Second Temple Literature*, JAJSup 9 [Göttingen: Vandenhoeck & Ruprecht, 2013], 180–1; see also Jörg Frey, "Dualismus: Zur frühjüdischen Herausbildung und zur neutestamentlichen Rezeption dualistischer Weltdeutung," in *Dualismus, Dämonologie und diabolische Firguren*, ed. Jörg Frey and Enno Edzard Popkes, WUNT II [Tübingen: Mohr Siebeck, 2018], 13–14). According to Loren T. Stuckenbruck, the nature of the demons of Jubilees seems to diverge from the one of 1 Enoch 15 in that it "is not expressed as an inherent characteristic" and that "it is not clear that they are evil *per se*" (Loren T. Stuckenbruck, *The Myth of Rebellious Angels: Studies in Second Temple Judaism and New Testament Text* [Grand Rapids, MI: Eerdmans, 2014], 30). If this indeed is the case, such a premise would further support and favor the notion of divine government to that of divine utilization of malign forces in order to accomplish good in spite of inherent malevolent intentions.

[29] See also Bell, *Deliver Us from Evil*, 16–17.
[30] The large number of fragments from the book of Jubilees (remnants from fourteen manuscripts or excerpts), as well as 1 Enoch (possibly as many as twenty-one), suggests some form of authoritative status within the community. The similarities in cosmology regarding the theological understanding of celestial agents of evil should therefore be of no surprise. See Eugene Ulrich, "Our Sharper Focus on the Bible and Theology, Thanks to the Dead Sea Scrolls," *CBQ* 66 (2004): 1–24, 8.
[31] Belial is attributed a wide array of functions in the texts of Qumran, such as being an instrument of God's eschatological cleansing of the world (CD VIII:1–3), which also features an element of testing and deception (CD IV:13, 17–18); bringer of enmity and accusations (1QM XIII, 11–12); a tester and means of purification (1QH VIII, 26–29); finally, Belial and his armies originated in the acts of creation of God (1QS III, 13–IV, 26) and he is made with an eye for his own destruction (1QS XIII, 4–5, 10; cf. 11QMelch XII), which in itself will produce glorification of God in the manner of the fate of Pharaoh in the Exodus (1QM XI, 8–10). According to Stephan Schreiber, "Being tested and purified by Belial provides an explanation of the present suffering from the *yahad*, but in the end originates in God himself, who uses Belial as his instrument and will provide eschatological release" (Stephan Schreiber, "The Great Opponent: The Devil in Early Jewish and Formative Christian Literature," in *Deuterocanonical and Cognate Literature—Yearbook 2007—Angels: The Concept of Celestial Beings—Origins, Development and Reception*, ed. Friedrich V. Reiterer, Tobias Nicklas, and Karin Schöpflin [Berlin: Walter de Gruyter, 2007], 437–58, 445).
[32] Florentino García Martínez, "Apocalypticism in the Dead Sea Scrolls," in *The Encyclopedia of Apocalypticism Vol 1*, ed. John J. Collins (New York: Continuum, 1998), 162–92, 168. See also Jutta Leonhardt-Balzer, who stresses when commenting that 1QS III, 13–IV, 26 (the Treatise) along with 1QS I, 16–III, 12; 4QBerakhot; 4QCurses; and 1QM (the War Scroll) are all dualistic texts central to the community (Jutta Leonhardt-Balzer, "Evil at Qumran," in *Evil in Second Temple Judaism and Early Christianity*, ed. Chris Keith and Loren T. Stuckenbruck, WUNT II/417 [Tübingen: Mohr Siebeck, 2016], 17–33, 18).

constantly seeking to overthrow the sons of light by utilizing his *allotted spirits*.[33] From the function of the treatise as part of the introduction to the Community Rule, and the presence of virtues and the emphasized value of teaching, one can derive an implied possibility of straying from one's path. This adds an element of rhetorical incitement to the treatise, which nuances the explicit and repeated mentioning of the system as an eternal prescribed ordination of God.[34] In any case, it is the ethical conduct of each individual, in turn, determined by which spirit is apportioned to them, which seems to matter in the end—at the time of God's visitation.[35] Paramount to this reading is the idea that the various spirits of the Qumran writings, whether malignant or benign, are considered as "not independent or even divine figures but subject to God, who has created and appointed them (3:17, 25)."[36] In the War Scroll, we find both the cosmic concept of the treatise as well as the character of Belial present, partaking as divinely apportioned means of destruction of the children of Darkness in the final battle (1QM VIII, 10–15; cf. I, 10).[37] The dualism in these writings then seems to primarily function as an indicator of identity (in-group/out-group),[38] leading up toward the endgame—the final battle. It is from this dualism they could determine who would be left standing on the battlefield after the age of eschatological salvation has been ushered through the purging of anything evil.[39] To this purging of the earth, the sifting of the elect, the

---

[33] The emphasized expressions are derived from the translation of Geza Vermes, *The Complete Dead Sea Scrolls in English* (London: Penguin Books, 1998), 101.

[34] According to Jörg Frey, "The teaching is probably to be interpreted as a kind of theodicy, an attempt to explain the experience of affliction and hostility (4:6–8) and the fact that even the pious can go astray and sin (3:21–22), and to ensure the final perfection of the covenant, the purification of the elect and the removal of all evil" (Jörg Frey, "Apocalyptic Dualism," in *The Oxford Handbook of Apocalyptic Literature*, ed. John J. Collins [New York: Oxford University Press, 2014], 271–94, 280).

[35] This ethical paradigm is found present in 4Q544, which, according to Jörg Frey, "is a very early, probably the earliest example of a cosmic dualism of opposed angelic powers dominating the world and struggling for possession over human beings" (ibid., 278).

[36] Ibid., 281; see also Frey, "Dualismus: Zur frühjüdischen Herausbildung und zur neutestamentlichen Rezeption dualistischer Weltdeutung," 20–1; Archie T. Wright, *The Origin of Evil Spirits: The Reception of Genesis 6:1–4 in Early Jewish Literature* (Minneapolis: Fortress, 2015), 170.

[37] See Brand, *Evil Within and Without*, 260–1, regarding the closeness and differences in ideas and terminology between the treatise and the War Scroll. According to Brand, "the emphasis on two opposing but equal domains *ruled* by angelic figures goes much further than other texts in removing God from the struggle between good and evil" (ibid., 261). Moreover, despite that "recent scholarship has recognized that this text is unusual and should be studied independently," she argues "the placement of the *Treatise* indicates that it was significant to the Qumran community or, at the very least, to the redactor of the *Community Rule*" (ibid., 257). To my reading these examples from the Qumran writings attest to an understanding of God as sovereign and in charge of adversarial agents similar to that of Revelation and is thus highly relevant—whether they are to be considered marginal or not.

[38] According to Archie T. Wright, in some Dead Sea Scroll manuscripts the ethical dualism corresponds with the cosmological dualism in that weak human spirits are under the control of Beliar, whereas those led by the will of the spirit of truth are outside his reach. Thus, the external spirits reflect and emphasize the internal spirits of humankind and magnify the duality of good versus evil. In this way "the ethical dualism of the *DSS*, in an effort to delineate a more precise anthropology, draws boundaries that distinguish two classes of individual"—the sons of light and the sons of darkness/ Beliar (Wright, *Origin of Evil Spirits*, 180).

[39] The same kind of ethical dualism can be perceived at play in the Testaments of the Twelve Patriarchs. The children of Israel are divided into two categories according to their adherence to the commandments and virtues of the Lord, or giving in to the schemes of Beliar (T. Dan 5:1; 6:1–8; T. Ash. 1:8). The liquidation of Beliar and his reign is described in a similar manner to that of

Angel of Darkness and Belial are given a clearly subdued function in the divine order of things.[40] This means that if one is to continue to refer to the epistemology of these Qumran writings as dualistic, it must be in a sense that at the same time acknowledges the subordination of agents of evil to a monistic cosmology.[41]

The view that there exists a horde of demons under supervision of a named leader, similar to that of Mastema, Satan as described in the Hebrew Bible, or the Angel/Spirit of Darkness and Belial in the Dead Sea Scrolls, is part and parcel of the cosmology of the New Testament texts. Moreover, we often find traces of the abovementioned subjugation of their conduct to the divine restrictions and governing, as well as a characterization of their functions as "a means to an end." Finally, the eschatological hope of a life without any adversarial forces to be wary of is also present. A few examples from the New Testament will suffice in order to prove my point. The Satan we find in the Pauline tradition is characterized as a deceiver and stumbling block of sinners (2 Thess 2:9) as well as believers (1 Cor 7:5; 2 Cor 2:11; 11:14; 1 Tim 5:15), but is also given a clearly rehabilitative function (1 Cor 5:5; 2 Cor 12:7; 1 Tim 1:20).[42] In light of the apostle's own teaching on the matters of testing (1 Cor 10:12–13) as well as his own experience (2 Cor 12:7–10), it becomes clear that the hardships of being a believer included occasional ordeals of testing and affliction. To this process, Satan is attributed an active function and is thus part of the divinely established order.[43] It is when speaking

---

Revelation: deprivation of power (T. Levi 18:10–12), facing defeat in the final battle (T. Dan 5:10–11), and finally tossed into eternal fire (T. Jud. 25:3). Schreiber, "The Great Opponent," 445–6.

[40] Archie T. Wright is completely in line with this reading when pointing out in his well-written study on the reception of Gen 6:1-4 in early Jewish literature that "the origin of *Mastema* as the leader of the demonic realm began in *Jubilees* and the Qumran literature" (Wright, *Origin of Evil Spirits*, 161, see 160-3) and not in the Watcher tradition of 1 Enoch, as the latter does not mention him as part of the Watcher entourage or grant its Watchers autonomy in their post-incarceration period on/in earth. Moreover, Wright is right in tracing a development from the Hebrew Bible to the New Testament "in the figure of Satan, *Mastema* (*Jubilees*), Belial (DSS) and other designations in the New Testament" (ibid., 161). Finally, I agree completely with his concluding remarks on the matter when he states, "The Watcher tradition was taken up by authors of the Qumran material and was further developed in the cosmic and ethical dualisms of the Scrolls. The evil spirits develop as a group that operates under the leadership of a chief spirit who is known by the names of Belial, Beliar, and Mastema, and who probably evolves into the 'Satan' figure in later Christianity. The evil spirits in the Scrolls seem to be an adaptation of the *Jubilees* Watcher tradition, which places them within the divine economy as instruments of God to punish and test humanity (Jub. 10)" (ibid., 225; see also 163).

[41] As Loren T. Stuckenbruck (*The Myth of Rebellious Angels*, 101) has pointed out, the various writings associated with Qumran are in no way to be considered unison regarding these matters. He notices a difference in the ideas and practices related to demonic beings as reflected in literature connected to the Yahad and the one not, and in writings preserved in Aramaic to those in Hebrew. He locates the crucial period for these shifts to "around the middle of the 2nd century B.C.E., a period of major change not only in the way Jews were responding to the incursions of Hellenistic culture under the Seleucids, but also in the way Jewish groups began to form while openly staking out cultural and religious claims in response to one another" (ibid., 80).

[42] The term Διαβολος occurs predominantly in the Deutero-Pauline or disputed letters and reflects the characteristics of deception (Eph 4:27; 6:11; 1 Tim 3:6–7, 11; 2 Tim 2:26; 3:3; Titus 2:3). The term σατανᾶς is preferred in the undisputed letters (Rom 16:20; 1 Cor 5:5; 7:5; 2 Cor 2:11; 11:14; 12:7; 1 Thess 2:18; cf. 2 Thess 2:9; 1 Tim 1:20; 5:15).

[43] Derek Brown (*The God of This Age*, 186–92) seems to be missing the point when insisting on an anti-divine motivation in the angel of Satan in 2 Cor 12:7. The text is silent regarding any satanic motives behind the thorn, whereas the interpretation of Paul regarding the motives of the Lord for not relieving him from the thorn the Lord gave him is, on the other hand, explicit. The divine

of such hardships that the apostle in 1 Thess 2:18–3:5 refers to such adversarial forces as ὁ πειράζων (the tempter, 3:5), alongside the more common Satan (2:18), as well as the implied earthly facilitators of persecution (3:3–4). Ὁ πειράζων is also one of the titles used for Satan in the temptation scene of Christ (Matt 4:3), an important text to this reading as it casts Christ in a similar rite of passage as that of Abraham (Gen 22:1–18; cf. Heb 11:17)—another key person in the salvific history, tested by God through celestial intermediaries. Moreover, the collaboration of celestial forces in facilitating the event is important to the cosmological perspective of the text: Τότε ὁ Ἰησοῦς ἀνήχθη εἰς τὴν ἔρημον ὑπὸ τοῦ πνεύματος πειρασθῆναι ὑπὸ τοῦ διαβόλου (then Jesus was led into the desert by the Spirit in order to be tested by the Devil, Matt 4:1).[44] As was also the case with Abraham (Genesis 22), Jesus must be proven worthy of and faithful to the task he is given. In Luke 22:31–34, we find the twelve disciples about to face a similar kind of ordeal. Satan has demanded to sift all of the disciples (22:31), and the counter-prayer of Jesus (22:32) reflects an acknowledgment of the validity of the claim by opting to warn the disciples of the coming ordeal rather than retorting to apotropaic prayer.[45] The phenomenon of apotropaic prayer itself may serve as the last example from the New Testament, reflecting a monistic approach to the adversarial forces on earth. In these prayers (cf. Matt 6:13; 2 Cor 12:8), God is perceived as ultimately being in control of the conduct of malignant spirits. In some texts, this aspect is developed even further. For instance, in Matt 6:13a the prayer is not only apotropaic in the usual sense (cf. the Plea for Deliverance [11Q5 XIX, 13–16[46]]; the prayer of Levi [4QTLevi[a] Ar I:17][47]; Jub. 1:20; 10:3–6; 12:19–20) as a plea for protection from/warding off evil spirits, but it goes further by pleading to be spared from a trial similar to that of Christ

---

governing of the elation of Paul is the central point concerning cosmology here, and it leaves no trace of what Brown deems "antithetical agency" (ibid., 189). For the view of a divine governing of the thorn, see John Christopher Thomas, *The Devil, Disease and Deliverance: Origins of Illness in New Testament Thought* (Cleveland: CPT, 2010), 52–5, 62, 296.

[44] Luke 4:1 uses the formulation ἤγετο ἐν τῷ πνεύματι ἐν τῇ ἐρήμῳ (he was led in/by the spirit to the desert) which is a less violent description than the εὐθὺς τὸ πνεῦμα αὐτὸν ἐκβάλλει εἰς τὴν ἔρημον (immediately the Spirit drove him out into the desert) of Mark 1:12 (see Page, "Satan: God's Servant," 456).

[45] I use the term "apotropaic" here as defined by Benjamin Wold: "Essentially apotropaic petitions are directed to God to deliver one from demonic beings … a petition to God to ward off an *evil spirit*" (Benjamin G. Wold, "Apotropaic Prayer and the Matthean Lord's Prayer," in *Das Böse, der Teufel und Dämonen—Evil, the Devil, and Demons*, ed. Jan Dochhorn, Susanne Rudnig-Zelt, and Benjamin G. Wold, WUNT II/412 [Tübingen: Mohr Siebeck, 2016], 101–12, 104, 111).

A similar subjugation of the mandate to test humankind of supernatural agents to divine permission is clearly present in the Apocalypse of Abraham 13:7–14. In this apocalyptic writing from approximately the late first or second century (see James H. Charlesworth, *The Old Testament Pseudepigrapha Vol. 1*. [Peabody, MA: Hendrickson, 1983], 683), Azazel is granted to test humankind in general, but not the righteous. In the end, those of Azazel have been prepared for judgment by God (22:1–5), to which Azazel is himself the means of judgment (31:5–7): For they shall putrefy in the belly of the crafty worm Azazel, and be burned by the fire of Azazel's tongue.

[46] According to Miryam T. Brand, "this prayer … presents a complex view of sin in which internal and external sources of sin combine to cause iniquity. Only God can prevent the rule of these entities, providing the motivation for prayer" (Brand, *Evil Within and Without*, 209; see ibid., 214 regarding her view on the cosmological implications of such prayers: "The ultimate control belongs to God, and demons may only influence humans if they are enabled to do so by the Deity").

[47] Wold, "Apotropaic Prayer and the Matthean Lord's Prayer," 104–9; see also Brand, *Evil Within and Without*, 214.

in the desert: it is a prayer *to* God for *him* not to lead *us* into the evil one/evil.⁴⁸ The cosmological implications of this seem hard to miss.

The texts referred to above reveal the presence of a monistic approach to the function and character of Satan and his likes in Second Temple Judaism and early Christianity. Personified evil is not characterized as the enemy of God here, although it is definitely the enemy of humankind, but rather as necessary in the divine ordering of things. The development of Satan as an effort to relieve the Godhead of its shadier aspects, and the subordination of the character of Satan to reflect the strict boundaries of monotheism by not becoming a celestial subject of his own, makes it less probable to even consider him as something purely evil used by God to do something good. The instrumental aspects of these texts imply little or no degree of autonomy and leave little room for any envious, hubris-laden usurper. In these texts, Satan has yet to become "a real boy," to use a phrase from Carlo Collodi's *Pinocchio*.

1.1.2 A Dualistic Approach to the Character of Satan

To many scholars, the exorcisms of the New Testament represent strong evidence of enmity between Christ (and thereby God) and the demonic powers.⁴⁹ However, upon scrutiny, they seem to represent something of a watershed in these matters by encompassing the imminent inauguration of the kingdom of God as a foretaste of the age of salvation. Do they represent the anticipation of a planned removal of office by the supreme power in charge, or a cosmological war raging on since the dawn of creation between two opposing sides? Both biblical and intertestamental writers seem to favor the former. To the age of salvation the exorcisms represent an anticipation of the long-awaited removal of adversarial spiritual forces—including Satan (see Jub. 23:29; T. Mos. 10:1; 1QS I, 14–15; cf. Rom 16:20; Rev 20:10). Thus, both texts predating the

---

⁴⁸ The second-person aorist subjunctive active form of εἰσενέγκῃς is not permissive, but rather causal and contingent, implying God as the one in charge of the act of leading: may *you* not lead me into temptation. According to Robert Charles Branden, "God's will ... is currently being contested by a host of demons led by Satan in his various guises" (Branden, *Satanic Conflict and the Plot of Matthew*, 150); "the conflict in Matthew is essentially satanic" (ibid., 151); and "the one who ultimately stands opposed to God's plan is Satan" (ibid.); and Branden ends up stating that the essence of the plot is satanic conflict and that there is no part of Matthew's story unrelated to the conflicting kingdoms of God and Satan (see ibid., 114, 150–1). This is problematic when he identifies τοῦ πονηροῦ (evil/the evil one) of Matt 6:13 as Satan (ibid., 24, 48, 68, 111) and thus creates unnecessary tension to his defined plot as it begs the question of what kind of God would lead his believers into temptation of his primary enemy? As Branden rightly points out, the demonologies of Jubilees and Matthew are very close (ibid., 24) and constitute an element which in my opinion would provide Branden with the necessary means of resolving the unnecessary tension mentioned above.

⁴⁹ See Graham H. Twelftree, *In the Name of Jesus: Exorcism among Early Christians* (Grand Rapids, MI: Baker Academic, 2007), 93–4, 135; Todd Klutz, *The Exorcism Stories in Luke-Acts: A Sociostylistic Reading*, SNTSMS 129 (Cambridge: Cambridge University Press, 2004), 109; Nicholas Thomas Wright, *Jesus and the Victory of God* (London: SPCK, 1996), 228–9. Indeed, to Richard H. Bell, the exorcisms of Christ represent an attack on Satan himself: "Through the exorcisms, Satan's kingdom is being destroyed and God's kingdom is being established" (Bell, *Deliver Us from Evil*, 65; see also 10, 90–1). This is of course due to the premise of Bell's endeavors being "the work of Christ can be (indeed must be!) seen as a reversal of the work of the Devil" (ibid., 64; see also a similar argument made by Christopher W. Skinner regarding the Gospel of Mark in "Overcoming Satan, Overcoming the World," 107).

community at Qumran and texts associated with the Yahad seem to have no difficulty in combining exorcisms and war imagery with the idea of God establishing the Angel of Darkness/Belial/Spirit of Injustice to serve their purpose before their final removal (i.e., a monistic approach).[50] This opens up the possibility of the same train of thought being behind the exorcism stories of the New Testament. Moreover, as the temptation of Christ and the final prayer in the Lord's Prayer suggest, the tensions between the intrusion of the coming kingdom and the established order of this one seem to be part of the divine order of things, and not the result of a primordial accident. The liquidation of the satanic office is a future event, but Christ embodies the (God-given) means to this process together with the response of the saints.[51] The exorcisms of Christ are not a marginal activity, but one that largely defines his public ministry.[52] They encompass the purpose of his coming—the ushering of salvation by gradually removing the spiritual shackles of the order of this age. The Beelzebul controversy (Mark 3:22–30; Matt 12:22–31; Luke 11:14–26) reflects such a monistic cosmological perspective by affirming the existence of a malevolent kingdom of Satan and his minions as part of the order of this age. The Christ event represents the long-awaited end of it. Instead of insisting on some kind of inconsistency in this malignant kingdom (i.e., Satan casting out Satan, Matt 12:26), the removal of it must come from the only power superior to it—God.[53] It is from this perspective that the fall of Satan of Luke 10:18 as well as the wishful greeting of Rom 16:20 should be interpreted—a glimpse of the contours of the kingdom at hand. The tables are about to be turned, and the downtrodden will conquer their enemy (Matt 17:20; cf. Rev 12:11), but for now, a period of transition is at hand (i.e., tribulation) that must be overcome. There is an enmity reflected in the exorcism stories between Satan and Christ, but it does not refer to a primordial war, but rather an ongoing event anticipating its future completion. Judging by the words from the legion of demons in Matt 8:29, the existence of a conflict and the awareness of any fronts seem blurry or surprising to at least one of the parties involved: τί ἡμῖν καὶ σοί, υἱὲ τοῦ θεοῦ; ἦλθες ὧδε πρὸ καιροῦ βασανίσαι ἡμᾶς; (What have you to do with us, Son of God? Have you come now, before the time to torment us?). These questions reflect several cosmological implications. Firstly, there exists a timely order for when they are to be tormented, and thus not be doing what they are doing now.

---

[50] On the prominence of exorcisms at Qumran, see John P. Meier, *A Marginal Jew Volume II: Mentor, Message, and Miracles* (New York: Yale University Press, 1994), 405; Cecilia Wassén, "Engler og Demoner," in *Dødehavsrullene: Deres innhold, historie og betydning*, ed. Årstein Justnes (Kristiansand: Norwegian Academic, 2009), 341–54, 350–2.

[51] According to Benjamin Wold, the New Testament testimony bears witness to this ongoing struggle for the believers. Moreover, its consummation lies in the future: "If the early church is instructed how to ward off personified evil and 'evil' is defined as demonic activity, then the final defeat of Satan and demonic beings lies in the future rather than perhaps the past" (Wold, "Apotropaic Prayer and the Matthean Lord's Prayer," 112).

[52] According to John P. Meier, "exorcisms make up the single largest category of healings in the Synoptics" and Jesus saw the exorcisms "as part of his overall ministry of healing and liberating the people of Israel from the illnesses and other physical and spiritual evils that beset them" (Meier, *A Marginal Jew Volume II*, 406–7).

[53] Emphasis is given to God as the source of the efficacy of the exorcism by the fact that this is the first of only four references to ἡ βασιλεία τοῦ θεοῦ (the kingdom of God) in the Gospel of Matthew, as opposed to the more frequent ἡ βασιλεία τῶν οὐρανῶν (the kingdom of heaven). See Branden, *Satanic Conflict and the Plot of Matthew*, 64.

Secondly, they are unaware of what the Son of God is doing there, and why. In other words, if there is a spiritual war going on, this legion is not aware of it. Thirdly, they recognize Christ and exhibit inferior status by their humble approach to him. The sum of this is that the text does not open for any cosmic dualism, much less a primordial one, but seems to reflect a divine ordering of things. One of the main functions of the exorcism stories is to provide a context to the ministry and function of Christ, as he embodies the end of an era and the beginning of another. There is enmity between the demonic sphere and Christ (as in a conflict of interest), between humankind and demons, but not one between demons and God. This cosmology seems very much akin to the one of Jubilees, where the demonic activity reflects the evil of humankind, yet as the lineage of Noah were given the remedy for the malevolence of Mastema and his henchmen (cf. Jub. 10:12–14), so have the children of Israel too been given the means to conquer their adversaries through the Messiah (cf. Matt 17:20). In this way the demons and exorcisms of the Gospels point primarily toward revealing the identity of Christ and the implications of the ushering in of the kingdom of God. However, several texts involving demons and exorcisms do also seem to emphasize a measure of faith and commitment (Mark 16:17; Matt 17:20; Acts 19:13–17; cf. Rev 3:10; 13:8) and thus imply adversarial foes to be overcome.

Although the textual evidence above (see Section 1.1.1) seems overwhelming, there are other texts from this period suggesting an approach to the character of Satan incompatible with the servant/agent imagery perspective. In 1 Enoch 6–11 we find the oldest version of the rebellious angels overstepping their divinely ordained boundaries by descending to earth desiring the daughters of men. This exposition of the rather brief and enigmatic text of Gen 6:1–5 constitutes the main source for Jub. 5:1–11, but where the latter uses this myth as an etiology for the demons granted by God to walk the earth (Jub. 10:9), 1 En. 10:4–13 describes only the violent death of their offspring.[54] In both cases, the Watchers themselves await their final judgment, but the Enochic versions lack any legitimation of demonic activity along with their named leader.[55] The Watcher myth is told three times in this section of the book, all revolving around the themes of sexual impurity, knowledge, and violence (1 En. 7; 8; 9:6–10), although with some narrative dissonance.[56] Even if the various accounts differ in terms of culpability

---

[54] See also the *Animal Apocalypse*, 1 En. 89:6. First Enoch 12–16, a later addition to the *Book of the Watchers*, offers a different account of the fate of the giants, similar to the one found in the Book of Jubilees. First Enoch 19:1–2 (as opposed to 15:8–12) refers to the spirits of the Watchers themselves continuing to lead humankind astray, and not their offspring. See Annette Yoshiko Reed, *Fallen Angels and the History of Judaism and Christianity: The Reception of Enochic Literature* (New York: Cambridge University Press, 2005), 50; Stuckenbruck, *The Myth of Rebellious Angels*, 15–17, 22–3, 34; see also Matthew Goff, "Enochic Literature and the Persistence of Evil: Giants and Demons, Satan and Azazel," in *Das Böse, der Teufel und Dämonen—Evil, the Devil, and Demons*, ed. Jan Dochhorn, Susanne Rudnig-Zelt, and Benjamin G. Wold, WUNT II/412 (Tübingen: Mohr Siebeck, 2016), 43–58, 48–9; Brand, *Evil Within and Without*, 160–2, 166–7.

[55] See VanderKam, "Demons in the *Book of Jubilees*," 344. Loren T. Stuckenbruck (*The Myth of Rebellious Angels*, 15–16, 84) seems to suggest that God allows for the giants to retain a post-diluvian spiritual existence with reference to 1 En. 15:8–9. This would reduce the gap between Jubilees and the Enochic traditions in these matters considerably. However, it is hard to find sufficient evidence for such a reading in the text itself.

[56] See the thematic analysis of the passage in Reed, *Fallen Angels and the History of Judaism and Christianity*, 29–34.

between the Watchers and humankind concerning the entering of sin into the world (the giving of prohibited knowledge or the reception and utilizing of it),[57] it does not reveal any trace of Satan in these matters. However, Satan is mentioned in later parts of 1 Enoch (40:7; 53:4; 54:6; 65:6),[58] when envisioning eschatological salvation without any Satan/Satans and the final judgment. First Enoch 54:6 contains the phrase "messengers of Satan" as a description of the oppressive deeds of Azazel leading astray those who dwell upon the earth. Whether one interprets this figuratively or literally, the association of these deeds and primordial rebellion with Satan and without any reference to any divine utilization of these spirits, we have here perhaps the seed of the notion of personified evil enmity to God deserving of eternal judgment.[59] The primordial nature of this perspective stands at odds with the whole string of texts mentioned above (see Section 1.1.1), where Satan is a necessary byproduct due to the evil of humankind deriving precisely from the event of the Watchers. If Satan is to be equated with Semyaza or Azazel, then he is bound beneath the earth awaiting judgment rather than functioning as prosecuting attorney, responding to the evil of men, rehabilitating members of the congregations of Paul or sifting the disciples of Christ.[60] On the other hand, however, if he is functioning as an ethical label of the deeds of these Watchers, then he is only a description of the wrong path that no man should tread. According to Annette Yoshiko Reed, "The *Similitudes* clearly draw from angelological/demonological traditions not present in The Book of Watchers … The *Similitudes* may preserve an intermediary stage in an interesting development, namely, the gradual transference of traditions about the antediluvian descent of the angels onto the figure of Serpent/Satan."[61] The fusing of traditions seems complete in the harmonization of the traditions of Justin Martyr (*Dialogue*) and the subordination of Azazel to Satan of Irenaeus (*Haer.* 1.15.6). In time the story of the illicit teachings of the Watchers and the demonic deception turned out to be powerful allies in the demonization of heretics in the early church.[62]

The Johannine literature picks up this theme of the primordial evil of the Devil/Satan. The deceptive nature of the Devil is reflected in several texts (John 6:70; 13:2; 1 John 3:10), whereas his oppositional nature is rooted in the beginning (John 8:44; 1 John 3:8; cf. 1 John 3:12, in which the sin of Cain is connected with the evil one). As the purpose of the Son of God is to destroy the works of the Devil (1 John 3:8), a dichotomy between the sphere of God and the Devil seems inevitable.[63] This

---

[57] Ibid., 35–7.
[58] This section of 1 Enoch is usually referred to as *The Book of Similitudes* (1 Enoch 37–71) and dates to approximately the first century BC.
[59] See Matthew Goff and his informative section on development of the character of Satan in relation to the Watchers, Azazel, Gadreel, and the Eden story within the Enochic literature and its reception in ancient Judaism and Christian authors (Goff, "Enochic Literature and the Persistence of Evil," 54–7). According to him, "the development of Satan from an important being in heaven to God's ultimate adversary is to some extent reliant upon older Enochic traditions about angels who flout God's will. In any case, texts written after the 1st century CE clearly show a mingling of Satanic and Enochic watcher traditions" (ibid., 56–7).
[60] See Wright, *Origin of Evil Spirits*, 224.
[61] Reed, *Fallen Angels and the History of Judaism and Christianity*, 115.
[62] Ibid., 166–7; 178; Forsyth, *The Old Enemy*, 310–11.
[63] For the close connection between Satan/Devil and κόσμος, see Skinner, "Overcoming Satan, Overcoming the World," 118–19.

impression is further enhanced by the absence of references to creation and purpose of such personified evil as found present in the texts from Qumran,[64] and the integral dichotomy of the children of God and children of the Devil (1 John 3:10). The sum of these texts indicates an eternal dichotomy between the sphere of the Devil and that of God, rendering the latter one of the sides of the dual relationship rather than governing the events of history by means of it. Perhaps this development was inevitable as the heretical challenges of the early church demanded a more coherent approach to the character of the Devil than the loose ends of the biblical texts involving him and his kind allowed.

The late provenance of the Johannine texts fits well with the literary development of the Devil, from the traditions witnessed in the Hebrew Bible to the dualistic ones of the early church. According to Neil Forsyth, "What was seen as Satan's opposition to Christ in the present was projected backward into the story of his origin. Only thus could the church construct a satisfactory account of the origin of things with which to oppose the many rival myths of the period."[65] It seems that the Johannine School represents an early voice in this development.[66]

---

[64] However, such purpose, if not creation, could be discerned in the use of the title ὁ ἄρχων τοῦ κόσμου (the ruler of this world), which is unique to the Gospel of John. According to Loren T. Stuckenbruck (*The Myth of Rebellious Angels*, 192–3), "in contrast to the terms 'devil' or 'demon' and perhaps even 'Satan'—these terms surface in specific instances of oppositional activity that occurs in particular groups or human beings—the designation 'the ruler of this world' is more comprehensive and wide-ranging" and refers to an organizing power behind the evil works of the world. In the Gospel of John, the use of this title implies that it is in light of the death of Jesus that the ruler of this world will be driven out (John 12:31) and that this future event is anticipated by his present judgment (16:11). However, his rule is perceived as a continuing threat to the followers of Jesus in the time after the death and resurrection of Jesus as indicated by John 14:29–30. The presence of this impending threat seems to be behind the petition of Jesus on behalf of his disciples in 17:15, which reflects a future need for protection from the evil one. This petition is reminiscent of similar petitions and prayers in the New Testament (Matt 6:13; Luke 22:32; 2 Cor 12:8; see also Jub. 10:3–6). The presence of such prayers and petitions reflect a cosmological reality to the believers in question that their adversarial agents are real, governed, and/or allowed by divine decree, but also that said believers possess the means to endure and prevail over such antagonism. The divine reluctance to comply with these petitions and prayers by means of complete removal could thus reflect the necessity of such antagonism, for instance for believers to prove their loyalty.

[65] Forsyth, *The Old Enemy*, 311.

[66] The traditions of Jesus Ben Sira seem largely to side with the monistic approach as the only occurrence of Satan/Devil in the text is probably implying one's inner adversarial voice (Sir 21:27) as part of the good and bad inclination found in any man (33:11–12). However, some form of cosmological inconsistency can be detected in the insistence that this particular sphere of anthropology does not stem from the Creator since he is not to blame for either one's failing to seek wisdom or the subsequent sinning (15:11–12). This is a stance similar to the one found in the letter of James, who admits the existence of a devil (Jas 4:7), maintains considerable focus on the believer's responsibility to one's inner spirituality, yet firmly concludes that God is not testing anyone (1:12–14). Thus, due to the scarce amount of texts concerning Satan/the Devil, one cannot conclude with any certainty regarding where on the axis of tension these traditions adhere. Regarding the similarities and differences between the letter of James and Ben Sira (and Philo of Alexandria) in these matters, see Nicholas J. Ellis, "A Theology of Evil in the Epistle of James: Cosmic Trials and the Dramatis Personae of Evil," in *Evil in Second Temple Judaism and Early Christianity*, ed. Chris Keith and Loren T. Stuckenbruck, WUNT II/417 (Tübingen: Mohr Siebeck, 2016), 262–81, 278–80.

1.1.3 Tensions in Revelation

As the book of Revelation also originated toward the end of first century AD, with its profound interest in evil and its various manifestations, the main question of this reading will be where on this axis of tension the Satan of Revelation is to be located—as counter-principle to and enemy of God, or necessary evil in the divine governing of his creation. Perhaps more to the point is the question of whether he is working *against* or *on behalf of* God. In light of this dichotomy, Satan is characterized in a seemingly ambivalent manner in the book of Revelation, due to its strong affinities to the Hebrew Bible and its dedication to the Jesus movement of its time. Here Satan is both the heavenly prosecutor of man (Rev 12:11) and perhaps being reproached for being so (20:7–10). He who up to now has been an agent of God will, in the end, be rejected, ejected from heaven, and be tormented in the lake of fire for all eternity. As no explicit reason is stated as to why Satan is to suffer this fate, the reader is left to make his/her own conclusions from the text. The traditional reading of biblical texts concerning Satan tends to minimize the "servant of God" aspect of this character and to favor a more "hostile to God" lens of reading.[67] The motivation for doing so seems to be provided by the book of Revelation itself. After all, Revelation delivers the most vivid portrait of the horrific actions of Satan/the Devil in the Bible (cf. 12:1–13:18). He is the main antagonist of humankind, working relentlessly to deceive as many as possible to stray from the path of salvation. He is cast as the opponent of Michael and his angels in a war in heaven (12:7–8). The outcome of this war is expulsion from heaven. Again, the reader is not left with any information as to why this occurs but has to connect the dots in the text of his/her own accord. For many, the reason for the war in heaven, the subsequent ejection, and the fate of the lake of fire is allegedly due to an *anti-divine* trait of Satan—enmity toward God.[68] Yet, nowhere in Revelation do we find an explicit characterization of Satan as the enemy of God. Moreover, in light of the monumental and downright monistic image of God in the narrative (see Revelation 4–5 in particular) derived from its strong affinity to the prophetic traditions of the Hebrew Bible, a cosmic dualistic adversary in the veins of Ahriman in Persian Zoroastrianism would be obviously unfitting.[69] To put it briefly, we might say that the

---

[67] Regarding the use of the term "servant" about Satan, I concur with the following comments of Sydney Page: "One need not be consciously devoted to someone to serve them. The Babylonian king Nebuchadnezzar is portrayed as Yahweh's servant in Jer 25:9 and 43:10. The Persian king Cyrus is portrayed similarly in Isa 44:28 and 45:1, 13. Neither Nebuchadnezzar nor Cyrus intentionally served Yahweh, but the biblical authors represent them as instruments through which he accomplished his will nonetheless" (Page, "Satan: God's Servant," 449).

[68] For instance, many exegetes conclude bluntly that both the throwing of Satan into the abyss and the lake of fire must be seen as punishment often explained in a presumed rebellion against God, thus failing to see the lack of evidence of this in the text itself (see 5.2.2).

[69] As Susanne Rudnig-Zelt has pointed out, it is the ability to create that separates the Ahriman of Zoroastrianism from the biblical Satan: "Die fähigkeit des Gegenspielers Gottes, zu schaffen, könnte somit die Grenze zwischen der biblischen Tradition und einer ausgeprägt dualistischen Religion wie dem Zoroastrismus markieren" (Rudnig-Zelt, "Der Teufel und der alttestamentliche Monotheismus," 16; cf. Frey, "Dualismus: Zur frühjüdischen Herausbildung und zur neutestamentlichen Rezeption dualistischer Weltdeutung," 3–4, 44). In Revelation it is the acts of creation that separate the Godhead from its creation and constitutes the worthiness of receiving worship (4:11), thus establishing his sovereign status to all creation, Satan included.

παντοκράτωρ (almighty/omnipotent one) of the book of Revelation leaves no room for the cosmic dualism that the early Christian tradition was to make out of these texts.[70]

However, even if he is no enemy of God, this does not necessarily make him a servant. As Satan is called neither δοῦλος (servant) nor ἐχθρός (enemy) in Revelation, arguments for either interpretation must be based on other elements of characterization rather than direct descriptions—for instance, events and actions involving him. On the one hand, he is thrown out of heaven, bound and incarcerated, and is to be tortured in the lake of fire for all eternity. Yet, on the other hand, he is apparently given (ἐδόθη) to do all of his endeavors by God, and released from prison by necessity (δεῖ, Rev 20:3; cf. 1:1; 4:1; 22:6) to continue his work after the reign of a thousand years have ended.[71] It seems that Revelation draws material from both poles of the axis of tension above in its characterization of Satan. The main object of this book necessitates an answer to the question of how these seemingly contradictory statements make sense within the narrative.

1.1.4 Excursus: Dualism and Monism in Revelation

Before conducting the main analysis of this study, a few words on the use of the terms "dualism" and "monism" are in order, as they will occur frequently and their ability to sufficiently describe the various points of view of the biblical writings is somewhat disputed. The term "dualism" is modern, but the phenomenon of classifying reality into binary opposites seems as old as human culture.[72] According to Fred L. Horton, "whatever qualifying adjective we use, the New Testament clearly contains dualism expressed in terms of stark oppositions like flesh and spirit, light and darkness, good and evil, heaven and earth, this age and the age to come."[73] To these "terms of stark opposition" Piet F. M. Fontaine adds that the term "dualism" refers to an unresolvable opposition between the terms in question: "It is no longer possible to reduce the terms of the opposition more or less to each other; there are no longer intermediate terms; there is no longer any relationship or connection at all between the terms."[74] This understanding

---

[70] Pagels, *The Origin of Satan*, 112–48; Kelly, *Satan: A Biography*, parts III and IV; and Russell, *Satan: The Early Christian Tradition*, 30–50, provide insight into how the early Christian tradition struggled to cope with the many bits and pieces of traditions in the biblical texts involving Satan.

[71] See also the fitting comments of Jan Dochhorn along the same line of argumentation, in his comprehensive study on the impact of Revelation 12 on the interpretation of Revelation in its entirety (Jan Dochhorn, *Schriftgelehrte Prophetie: Der eschatologische Teufelsfall in Apc Joh 12 und seine Bedeutung für das Verständnis der Johannesoffenbarung*, WUNT 268 [Tübingen: Mohr Siebeck, 2010], 7–8).

[72] See Armin Lange et al., "Introduction," in *Light against Darkness: Dualism in Ancient Mediterranean Religion and the Contemporary World*, ed. Armin Lange, Eric M. Meyers, Bennie H. Reynolds III, and Randall Styers, JAJSup 2. (Göttingen: Vandenhoeck & Ruprecht, 2011), 8–9.

[73] Fred L. Horton, "Dualism in the New Testament: A Surprising Rhetoric and a Rhetoric of Surprise," in *Light against Darkness: Dualism in Ancient Mediterranean Religion and the Contemporary World*, ed. Armin Lange, Eric M. Meyers, Bennie H. Reynolds III, and Randall Styers, JAJSup 2 (Göttingen: Vandenhoeck & Ruprecht, 2011), 186–208, 188.

[74] Piet F. M. Fontaine, "What Is Dualism and What Is It Not?," in *Light against Darkness: Dualism in Ancient Mediterranean Religion and the Contemporary World*, ed. Armin Lange, Eric M. Meyers, Bennie H. Reynolds III, and Randall Styers, JAJSup 2 (Göttingen: Vandenhoeck & Ruprecht, 2011), 266–76, 266.

of dualism is often accompanied by a gradation of the concept of dualism into various subcategories.[75] Regardless of how one describes the oppositional language of the New Testament, scholars tend to agree on the importance of keeping apart the kind of dualism referred to as "moderate" or "monarchical" from the "radical" or "true."[76] This distinction serves to "distinguish between dualisms that recognize no power or god higher than the two competing gods or powers and those that see the conflict of the two cosmic powers as occurring under the ultimate authority of a single divine reality."[77] The scholarly insistence on the presence of dualism in the New Testament, yet at the same time displaying a need to disqualify its more radical expression, constitutes a kind of opposition in itself—possibly reflected in the long ongoing quest for where the dualistic influence on early Christianity came from (Gnostic, Hellenistic, Qumran, and Zoroastrian, to name a few).[78] Quoting Rudolf Schnackenburg, Fred L. Horton concludes that the main roots of New Testament dualistic language are found in Judaism.[79] I find this conclusion sound but remain uncertain as to whether the New Testament writings could be perceived as uniform in their approach to the matter. For instance, the diverging cosmology in Pauline and Johannine literature seems to reflect different takes on dualism. The thorn in the flesh of Paul, characterized appositionally as an angel of Satan (2 Cor 12:7), is more compatible with the idea of the testing, sovereign, monistic God of the Hebrew Bible, than, say, the antagonist in 1 John 3:8, which implies a more cosmic kind of opposition. Using the nomenclature of Fontaine, one might say that the former is more resolvable than the latter.

In the book of Revelation the scholarly consensus on moderate dualism being the dominant view in the New Testament seems to be confirmed by the sovereign image of God (Revelation 4–5) combined with the stark opposition between those written in the book of life (Rev 13:8; 17:8; 21:27) and those marked by the beast (13:16–17; 14:9, 11; 16:2; 19:20; 20:4). This is sometimes referred to as ethical dualism, as it is the choices of men that divide the population into two categories—the good and the evil so to speak. This ethical dualism seems in turn to be the governing principle (in that it constitutes the main plot of the narrative; see Section 2.3) for any trace of cosmic dualism in Revelation, as the various oppositional divine agents relate directly to this separation (i.e., Michael/the dragon, the beasts and Christ, and Satan and the jailor angel, and so forth).[80] However, if any opposition between divine agents can be

---

[75] Jörg Frey ("Apocalyptic Dualism," 272; cf. Frey, "Dualismus: Zur frühjüdischen Herausbildung und zur neutestamentlichen Rezeption dualistischer Weltdeutung," 7–9) lists the following list of categories of dualism found in biblical studies: metaphysical (God/Satan, Belial); cosmic (world divided into two opposing entities); spatial (above/below, heavenly/earthly realms); eschatological or temporal; ethical (good/evil); soteriological (the saved/the rejected); theological/creational (creator/creation, God/world); physical (matter/spirit); anthropological (body/soul, spirit); and psychological (the struggle between good and evil within the human heart or mind).

[76] Horton, "Dualism in the New Testament," 187; and Fontaine, "What Is Dualism, and What Is It Not?," 266–7.

[77] Horton, "Dualism in the New Testament," 187.

[78] Ibid., 187–93.

[79] Ibid., 193.

[80] The same principle also goes for the divine agents not involved in direct conflict with other divine agents but cast on the negative side of conflicts of interest—working against the subjects of the narrative (humankind). Examples of these are Abaddon/Apollyon, Rev 9:11; the four horsemen,

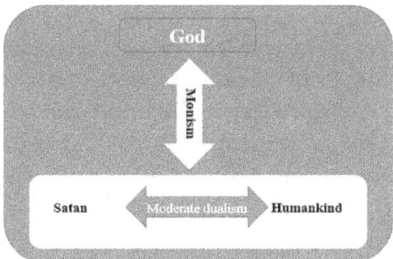

Figure 1 Monism and dualism in Revelation

resolved by subjugating the relation under the divine governing of earthly matters by the sovereign God, should one not deem this cosmology monistic (duality), and not moderately dualistic?[81]

An assumed oppositional relation between Satan and God would blur this distinction of dualism and monism. If this element is even to be considered an element in Revelation, it cannot be deemed radical dualism as Satan obviously does not exist on his own but only through his relation to God. However, can one deem it moderate dualism? In Revelation, the tension between Satan and the saints is resolved by their common subjugation to the agenda of the sovereign God. The resolving through destruction is a mark of dualism, but certainly a moderate one, as none of the oppositional parties exists on their own, but rather as a creation of the creator. This makes the overall cosmology monistic and the opposition between Satan and the saints/humankind moderately dualistic (see Figure 1).[82]

6:1–8; the star Wormwood, 8:11; the unnamed fallen star, 9:1; and the bound angels at the river Euphrates, 9:14–15. Despite cheering for the wrong team and working against the "good guys" of the narrative, their antagonism is resolved by subjugation to the sovereign God. Bearing in mind that this is the main mode of answering the question of theodicy in Revelation, it is no small element in the narrative but rather a crucial one; see Grant R. Osborne, "Theodicy in the Apocalypse," *TJ* 14 (1993): 63–77, 64 and 70.

[81] Piet F. M. Fontaine deems such *resolvable* oppositions "dualities" rather than "dualistic," in order to emphasize the difference. Moreover, he points out that monism is not the opposite of dualism, as they are "products of the same defective view of the world," and that monism in the end can generate dualism (Fontaine, "What Is Dualism, and What Is It Not?," 268). In Revelation, this can be perceived by the presence of both a monistic cosmology (everything is subordinated under the sovereign God) as well as a moderately dualistic one (the opposition between creator and his creation) (ibid., 268–9).

[82] A similar two-level cosmology can be discerned in the development of Zoroastrian thought found in the Young Avesta (first half of the first millennium BC). There, Ahura Mazdâ is characterized as the sovereign creator god, whereas two inferior spirits are ordering his creation: the Life-Giving Spirit and the Evil One. "Thus, already in the *Young Avesta*, we see a merging of the creative functions of Ahura Mazdâ and the Life-giving Spirit," in turn giving way to the heretical thought of identifying the two (Prods Oktor Skjærvø, "Zoroastrian Dualism," in *Light against Darkness: Dualism in Ancient Mediterranean Religion and the Contemporary World*, ed. Armin Lange, Eric M. Meyers, Bennie H. Reynolds III, and Randall Styers, *JAJSup* 2 [Göttingen: Vandenhoeck & Ruprecht, 2011], 55–76, 67–8; see 56, 60–1; see also Fontaine, "What Is Dualism, and What Is It Not?," 269). In Revelation we find a similar event creating tension to the two levels of cosmology in the dual worship of the Lamb and God (Rev 5:12–13).

The thrust of this study is, however, to argue that a hostile opposition between Satan and God seems to be unaccounted for (at least explicitly) in the text, that it adds unnecessary tension to the plot of the narrative, and that it is a stranger to the two-step cosmology of the narrative. Satan does not exist on his own as his existence depends on the will of God, who in turn does exist on his own.[83] This excludes defining the alleged conflict as radical dualism. Moreover, if there is opposition between the two, it must be one-sided on the part of Satan, as God is frequently described as *giving* Satan to do many things in Revelation, utilizing his character to set in motion the sifting of the population of the earth, and finally removing him when he has fulfilled his mission. This monistic government of the forces at play has more in common with the monism of prophetic writings of the Hebrew Bible than a hostile clash of divine beings known from various ancient Near Eastern texts. Remember that the Yahweh of the prophets of the Hebrew Bible raised and aided adversaries of the people to do his bidding, not to oppose or harm himself, but to chastise, discipline, and/or motivate his people (cf. 1 Kgs 11:14 and 23; Isa 9:11–13; Ezek 38). Thus, if the reader is to assume enmity between Satan and God in Revelation (i.e., possibly moderate dualism on the vertical axis), it would make God a self-harmer by proxy, and Satan his delusional opponent, obviously unaware of his inferiority, aiding and abetting the divine governing of the earth, blinded by his own hubris to his incapability to usurp the throne of the sovereign God.[84] Such an uneven relation (dualistic on the part of Satan, monistic on the part of God) seems odd and out of place as it creates unnecessary narrative dissonance. However, as antagonists in narratives often tend to be flat characters, often characterized by a single trait to enhance their oppositional function, this too could be the case with Satan in Revelation. Perhaps he is characterized as a simple, hubristic, and delusional character in order to fulfill his literary function in the narrative? The probability of such a reading must be accounted for in light of other possible readings.

As the dualistic approach to Revelation has dominated scholarly readings of Revelation up to now, resulting in considerable narrative tension as mentioned above, this book will explore another angle—the monistic one.

1.2 Contemporary Research

No monography exclusively devoted to the issue of the function of Satan in the book of Revelation has yet been published. This means that the literature mentioned in this section is only considered in light of its relevance to the topic of this study, and thereby not their respective scopes of deliberation. I have divided this section into two parts, of which the former considers literature devoted to the topic of Satan per se, and the latter

---

[83] See also Frey, "Apocalyptic Dualism," 271: "In Jewish (and Christian) contexts, 'dualistic' worldviews are at least modified by the biblical view of the one creator, so that evil (or Satan) is never thought to be coeternal with the one God."

[84] This idea will be entertained as possible until the textual data has been analyzed, but in light of the many occurrences of the aorist passive in the characterization of Satan and related agents, the active function to the main plot given Satan, and the divine utilization of Satan on earth, I suspect, however, that such a reading will create more tension rather than resolve it.

relevant research on the book of Revelation. The purpose of this part of the chapter is to argue for the need and relevance of a new reading to shed light on an otherwise neglected area of research: How does the diverse scriptural character of Satan function literarily in the text of Revelation?

1.2.1 Publications on Satan

Monographies published on the topic of the Devil/Satan have flourished over the past few decades. Perhaps this is due to what Philip C. Almond refers to as the "re-engagement with the demonic in film, television, literature, and music that has lasted into the twenty-first century."[85] In light of the vast success of movies like *Rosemary's Baby* (1968), *The Exorcist* (1973), *The Omen* franchise (1976–2016), *The Prophecy I* and *II* (1995 and 1998), and *Constantine* (2005), to mention a few, one would be surprised if the question of personified evil did not enter the gates of sermons or seminaries at one point. Another possible reason for the sudden increase in interest in the Devil could be the timeless struggle of trying to cope with the suffering of sentient beings.[86] If this really is what Gottfried Leibniz referred to as "the best of all possible worlds," we must at the same time agree with Voltaire's Candide or perhaps Ivan Karamazov that it is indeed a suffering world, and according to Carl Gustav Jung, "if you regard the principle of evil as a reality you can just as well call it the Devil."[87] Recent decades have witnessed an increased tendency to do just that. P. G. Maxwell-Stuart finds several possible reasons for the increased attention on Satan, besides that of popular culture: in the emphasis on Satan in certain forms of Evangelical Christianity; the combination of attributing both physical and mental illness to the work of evil spirits in certain religious confessions, and the explosion of books promoting these ideas; and the emergence of organizations devoted to the worship of Satan.[88]

With increased attention and belief in the existence of Satan follows an increased need to define his character. As the characterization of Satan differs considerably in these cultural and ecclesial expressions, several of the monographs on Satan explicitly set out to give us *the real* Satan—that is, the Satan of tradition and Scriptures.[89] The main vehicle for providing this Satan has been to tread the history-of-religions approach. Most of these newer monographs on Satan constitute some form of historical survey on this attribution and explanation/rationalization of suffering by means of

---

[85] Philip C. Almond, *The Devil: A New Biography* (London: I.B. Tauris, 2014), xiii.
[86] See Russell, *The Devil*, 17–35; Kotsko, *The Prince of This World*, 1–5.
[87] Russell, *The Devil*, 33.
[88] P. G. Maxwell-Stuart, *Satan: A Biography* (Gloucestershire: Amberley, 2008), 194–9.
[89] The premise for these works is that there is something wrong, missing, or misinformed with the common perception of the character of the Devil, creating the need for a new biography of him. The term "biography" seems to be derived from the historical study of Kersey Graves, *The Biography of Satan or a Historical Exposition of the Devil and His Fiery Dominions: Disclosing the Oriental Origin of the Belief in a Devil and Future Endless Punishment* (Montana: Kessinger, 1865), which is based upon a similar premise of skepticism toward the conventional religious perception and utilization of the character of the Devil/Satan. Henry Ansgar Kelly (*Satan: A Biography*, 1), on the other hand, overtly explains his choice of title as an allusion to Jack Miles and his *God: A Biography* (New York: Knopf, 1995).

personifying it as Satan/the Devil.⁹⁰ Related to these, often equipped with a similar motivation of providing the *real* Satan, we have the academic publications on the Satan of Scriptures.⁹¹

Regarding the relevance of these works on Satan to the scope of this reading, they often appear too broad to offer any substantial contribution to my exegesis of Revelation due to the lack of any in-depth engagement with the texts in question.⁹² However, several of them have proved immensely valuable toward gaining an understanding of the development of the literary character of Satan through history. Moreover, they shed valuable light on the many facets of Satan at play within the biblical texts and thus trigger two important questions relevant to this reading: Which of these traditions do we find at work as implied references within the text of Revelation? Could a combination of said traditions be able to explain the inherent tensions in the characterization of Satan in Revelation? (See Section 1.3 on how these questions relate to the primary research question of this reading.)

With a few notable exceptions, these monographs present a unanimous picture of the Satan of the New Testament in general or Revelation in particular: a dualistic counter-principle to God.⁹³ The tensions between the monotheistic framework of Judaism, from which the character of Satan is derived, and the establishing of a cosmic enemy are frequently commented upon, but not resolved. The functions and characteristics of Satan as found in the New Testament are subsequently described as anomalous,⁹⁴ irresoluble and inconsistent,⁹⁵ enigmatic and

---

⁹⁰ See Almond, *The Devil: A New Biography* (2014); Forsyth, *The Old Enemy* (1987); Maxwell-Stuart, *Satan: A Biography* (2008); Henry Ansgar Kelly, *Satan: A Biography* (2006); Kotsko, *The Prince of This World* (2017); Gerald Messadié, *A History of The Devil* (New York: Kodansha, 1996); Darren Oldridge, *The Devil: A Very Short Introduction* (New York: Oxford University Press, 2012); Pagels, *The Origin of Satan* (1995); Russell, *The Devil* (1977); Russell, *Satan: The Early Christian Tradition* (1981); Russell, *Lucifer: The Devil in the Middle Ages* (Ithaca, NY: Cornell University Press, 1984); Russell, *Mephistopheles: The Devil in the Modern World* (Ithaca, NY: Cornell University Press, 1986); Russell, *The Prince of Darkness: Radical Evil and the Power of Good in History* (Ithaca, NY: Cornell University Press, 1988); Stanford, *The Devil: A Biography* (1996).

⁹¹ Of the more recent publications in this category we find Brown, *The God of This Age* (2015); Michael Tilly, Matthias Morgenstern, and Volker Henning Drecoll, eds., *L'Adversaire de Dieu—Der Widersacher Gottes*, WUNT 364 (Tübingen: Mohr Siebeck, 2016); Jan Dochhorn, Susanne Rudnig-Zelt, and Benjamin Wold, eds., *Das Böse, der Teufel und Dämonen—Evil, the Devil, and Demons* (2016); Ida Frölich and Erkki Koskenniemi, eds., *Evil and the Devil*, LNTS 481 (London: T&T Clark, 2013); Chris Keith and Loren T. Stuckenbruck, eds., *Evil in Second Temple Judaism and Early Christianity* (2016); Jörg Frey and Enno Edzard Popkes, eds., *Dualismus, Dämonologie und diabolische Figuren* (2018); T. J. Wray and Gregory Mobley, *The Birth of Satan: Tracing the Devil's Biblical Roots* (New York: Palgrave Macmillan, 2005); Sydney H. T. Page, *Powers of Evil: A Biblical Study of Satan & Demons* (Grand Rapids, MI: Baker Books, 1995); Brand, *Evil Within and Without* (2013); Bell, *Deliver Us from Evil* (2007); Branden, *Satanic Conflict and the Plot of Matthew* (2006); Armin Lange, Herman Lichtenberger, and K. F. Diethard Römheld, eds., *Die Dämonen: die Dämonologie der israelittisch-jüdischen and frühchristlichen Literatur in Kontext ihrer Umwelt* (2003). Pastoral, homiletical, and semi-academic works on the biblical Satan—often written as a direct response to the often uncritical and unorthodox utilization of the biblical texts on Satan in popular culture—are outside the scope and nature of this reading due to their lack of sufficient argumentation and an often accompanying dogmatic bias, and are thus not considered here.

⁹² See the similar conclusion of Derek R. Brown on the matter in his highly enjoyable study of the Pauline references to Satan (Brown, *The God of This Age*, 4–5).

⁹³ See, for instance, Russell, *The Devil*, 229–30; and Maxwell-Stuart, *Satan: A Biography*, 24–5.

⁹⁴ Russell, *The Devil*, 232.

⁹⁵ Ibid., 242–3.

unprecedented,[96] paradoxical or parodic,[97] even moronic and without purpose,[98] yet few or none of the monographs seems to be able to explain how this figure makes sense within the individual texts in which he occurs. Should we settle for the assumption that the inconsistent or contradictory characterization of the characters in a text is intended, part of the discourse, or due to the incompetence or ignorance of ancient authors? If not, the question begging our attention is how it becomes meaningful for the author of the book of Revelation to combine two such seemingly contradictory features (enemy/servant) in a single concept as Satan/the Devil.

A notable exception to this "trend" of accentuating/attributing an anti-divine trait to the characteristics of Satan at the expense of the servant/divine agent aspect of him (i.e., the monistic features derived from the Hebrew Scriptures) is Henry Ansgar Kelly's *Satan: A Biography* (2006).[99] His main thesis is that the Satan we have come to know and recognize in the Bible is a postbiblical concept (the new biography of Satan), which in turn has been retrofitted onto the Satan of the New Testament (the original biography of Satan).[100] The Devil we know from church history is an invention imposed upon the texts themselves. His agenda is to clarify "exactly what is in the Bible and what has been added to the Bible. And it represents a clear challenge to those who believe that the Bible demands belief in the existence of Satan."[101] Despite the freshness and boldness of his approach, the scope becomes too broad to be able to deliver a credible exegesis of Revelation on the matter. Instead, summaries are offered that miss important exegetical points that could support his thesis.[102] In 2017, Henry

---

[96] According to Neil Forsyth, the limited measure of independence that is given Satan by necessity after his incarceration (Rev 20:3) is caused by unprecedented obligation. However, it is a central rhetorical point of Revelation that nothing happens in human history that is not warranted, supervised, or sanctioned by God. Thus, from the perspective of "an ontological dualism more extreme than anything we have noticed in the Jewish tradition," the necessity of Rev 20:3 becomes the odd one out and is left without a conclusion (Forsyth, *The Enemy*, 257).

[97] According to Adam Kotsko (*The Prince of This World*, 4), the devil is a paradoxical figure: "The fully developed Christian devil is both the ultimate enemy and God's most capable servant, the representative and leader of all who rebel against God as well as the eternal executor of God's will." A recurring element in Kotsko's book is the insistence that God becomes (a mirror image/an exaggeration of) the Devil through his ultimate control/ushering of human suffering (ibid., 56–7).

[98] According to Gerald Messadié (*A History of the Devil*, 252–3, 255, 257), the New Testament authors' diverse utilization of the character of Satan of the Hebrew Bible demanded considerable effort from the church fathers in their struggle to cope consistently with the problem of evil (see also Forsyth, *The Old Enemy*, 257; Russell, *Satan: The Early Christian Tradition*, 30–50).

[99] Sydney H. T. Page, in his article "Satan: God's Servant," has a similar scope and approach to the texts mentioning Satan in the Bible as my reading, but does not consider the text of Revelation. Moreover, as he insists that Satan is the enemy and adversary of God throughout the article, any argument justifying this a priori assumption would be a welcome addition to and strengthen his otherwise sound conclusions.

[100] "Retrofitting" is, according to Henry Ansgar Kelly, the act of interpreting the past in light of knowledge acquired later (*Satan: A Biography*, 2).

[101] Ibid., 5.

[102] The scope of his monograph should be able to provide Henry Ansgar Kelly with the opportunity to settle once and for all what the Bible actually has to say about Satan. Yet it seems to me that he is more interested in tracing the origin of what he calls "the new biography of Satan" (the retrofitted Satan) rather than the old one (i.e., the biblical). He dedicates 171 pages on the biblical and intertestamental Satan, which in itself is far more than most monographies on the matter. Still, the references to the texts remain just that: references to texts. There is no analysis here, only summaries and unsustained conclusions. This is also the case for his chapter on the book of Revelation (Kelly, *Satan: A Biography*, 141–59). As an example, he spends half of this chapter on Revelation 12–13,

Ansgar Kelly published another monograph on Satan, *Satan in the Bible: God's Minister of Justice*. The content and argumentation is largely the same as his first book on the matter, and the publication seems motivated by the apparent scholarly silence to his previous efforts: "All this is prologue to my reminding readers that no one, to my knowledge, has entertained or even noticed my thesis that the Satan/Devil of Job and Zechariah, as presented in the Septuagint, is almost exactly the same character as the Satan/Devil of the New Testament, except for individual variations of each author, or each book, in the canon."[103] It should therefore, perhaps, come as a pleasant surprise then for Kelly to discover this reading as a serious as well as critical consideration of his bold thesis. Sadly, his new book does not improve the impression of *Satan: A Biography* as in dire need of its main argumentation being fleshed out on exegetical grounds.[104] It is generally to be considered a condensed version of *Satan: A Biography*, and where the earlier volume dedicated eighteen pages to the Satan of Revelation, the latter contains twelve. For this reading, this new publication provides little new material to be of any value to the narrative reading below other than what is already mentioned regarding his previous book.

Several of the publications in this section contain highly valuable chapters and articles relevant to this book and thus serve as valuable dialogue partners in the analysis below. However, as none of them are devoted to the topic of evil or Satan in the book of Revelation, or have been able to explain credibly the apparent tensions in the characterization of Satan in the New Testament, the relevance and necessity of this contribution seem obvious.

1.2.2 Narrative and Literary Studies on Revelation

There is one notable exception to the apparent lack of scholarly attention to the literary function of Satan in the book of Revelation in Michael Labahn's essay "The Dangerous Loser: The Narrative and Rhetorical Function of the Devil as Character in the Book of Revelation."[105] As his choice of method coincides with the one chosen for this book

---

yet pays more attention to when in time Satan is supposed to be cast out of heaven than the actual meaning and implications of what a full-scale war in heaven might add to his perception of the biblical Satan. He finds his tension between the "old" and "new biography of Satan," not in the biblical texts as I suggest above. The question of tension is therefore answered in a manner that, in my opinion, does not take all the relevant data into consideration. Why the hostility, and why the harsh treatment? These are aspects of the Satan we find in the book of Revelation that must be compared to and reconciled with the texts with a subordinated servant and tester kind of Satan. Perhaps the dichotomy between the so-called old and new biography of Satan, as defined by Henry Ansgar Kelly, is too rigid for the texts in question?

[103] Henry Ansgar Kelly, *Satan in the Bible: God's Minister of Justice* (Eugene, OR: Cascade Books, 2017), 35. His motivation for publishing yet another monograph on Satan is stated in his introductory chapter: "In spite of the stress that I have laid on this point in my writings, it has not been taken note of or adduced as a position worthy of discussion, let alone of acceptance … I have decided, therefore, to produce this book with the title *Satan in the Bible, God's Minister of Justice*. I pray that it works!" (ibid., xii).

[104] The lack of any references to other scholarly literature on the matter could perhaps suggest that Henry Ansgar Kelly is receiving a corresponding degree of academic attention to that which he exhibits to others in his own work.

[105] In Frölich and Koskenniemi, eds., *Evil and the Devil*, 156–80.

(see my Chapter 2 below), the study is of immense value to the scope of this reading.[106] However, as the essay format is too sparse to expect thorough textual analyses on the texts in Revelation concerning Satan in total, the conclusions of Labahn tend to appear without compelling exegesis to support their claims. In Labahn's reading, Satan appears as a defeated enemy deprived of his powers, "a powerless figure who was rendered impotent by God's power," and "one that can be described as 'the absolute anti-divine power.'"[107] The most important differences between Labahn's reading and this one are probably the view on the degree of autonomy in the characterization of Satan, and the objects of his enmity. He starts his reading in Revelation 12 via chapter 20, before considering and concluding on Revelation 2–3. This enables him by a stretch to establish an anti-divine characterization of Satan, which he utilizes on the messages to the seven churches. The release of Satan in Rev 20:7 is left uncommented, which seems strange as he refers to this as "one of the most surprising and threatening aspects of his portrait in Revelation."[108] Furthermore, that "Satan escapes" (*sic!*) only to be caught once again makes him a "caricature that prepares ultimately for his decisive defeat."[109] I will contest several of these alleged elements of characterization as they appear as unwarranted a priori assumptions. Despite the close to verbatim scopes of Labahn's study and this one, the conclusions are worlds apart.

The narrative commentary of David L. Barr offers a small section on the topic related to the scope of this book under the heading "Characters of Destruction,"[110] whereas that of James L. Resseguie has no such chapter.[111] Both commentaries will of course be conferred with in the exegesis whenever relevant.[112] The same goes for the literary and theological commentaries of Joseph L. Trafton and John Christopher Thomas.[113] As the number of narrative and literary studies and commentaries on Revelation is scarce, studies and commentaries of diverging methodological branches, in turn, constitute highly appreciated dialogue partners to the exegetical analysis of this reading.

Two literary studies that have proved to be important dialogue partners in this study are Sigve K. Tonstad's *Saving God's Reputation: The Theological Function of Pistis*

---

[106] Adela Yarbro Collins, *The Combat Myth in the Book of Revelation* (Missoula, MT: Scholars Press for Harvard Theological Review, 1976), is similarly an important study to be reckoned with, despite the differences in methodological approach compared to this study (historical-critical as opposed to narrative critical), as it constitutes a study fully dedicated to the conflict of Revelation 12 (see my remarks on her hermeneutical premises of interpreting the plot of Revelation in light of the ancient combat myth in Section 4.4.2.1.1, "Excursus on the Combat Myth and Revelation 12").

[107] Michael Labahn, "The Dangerous Loser: The Narrative and Rhetorical Function of the Devil as Character in the Book of Revelation," in *Evil and the Devil*, ed. Ida Frölich and Erkki Koskenniemi, LNTS 481 (London: T&T Clark, 2013), 156–80, 168, 157.

[108] Ibid., 169.

[109] Ibid.

[110] David L. Barr, *Tales of the End: A Narrative Commentary on the Book of Revelation*, 2nd ed. (Salem, OR: Polebridge, 2012), 186–93.

[111] David L. Barr diverges in his view on the character of Satan from my reading by how he defines the plot of Revelation (*Tales of the End*, 15–25). This seems to be the reason for why he finds the necessity of the release of Satan (Rev 20:3, 7) surprising and important (ibid., 244, 248).

[112] Barr, *Tales of the End* (2012); James L. Resseguie, *The Revelation of John: A Narrative Commentary* (Grand Rapids, MI: Baker Academic, 2009).

[113] Joseph L. Trafton, *Reading Revelation: A Literary and Theological Commentary* (Macon, GA: Smyth & Helwys, 2012); John Christopher Thomas, *The Apocalypse: A Literary and Theological Commentary* (Cleveland: CPT Press, 2012).

Iesou *in the Cosmic Narratives of Revelation* (2006) and Steven Grabiner's *Revelation's Hymns: Commentary on the Cosmic Conflict* (2015). Both are literary studies, but only the latter explicitly uses narrative criticism as a method. Although neither of the studies explicitly focuses on the function of Satan, they are both contingent on a particular characterization of Satan in order for their main thesis to be able to stick. Their literary approach to Revelation combined with considerable attention to Satan makes them both highly relevant studies of comparison here. Steven Grabiner attempts to show how the hymns of Revelation are best interpreted in light of a war-in-heaven theme, reflecting a cosmic conflict. In order to do this, he has to establish this conflict as having a prominent role in the narrative of Revelation. The result is an exaggerated characterization of Satan by making his antagonism the narrative's center of attention—constituting the main plot to be resolved. Furthermore, his canonical fusing of this narrative construct of Revelation backward onto texts from the Hebrew Bible is problematic as he perceives this meaning as not only as implied in Revelation. Rather, he uses this alleged implied perspective to argue for the presence of a similar implied perspective in much earlier texts.[114] This way of establishing a cosmic conflict

---

[114] Grabiner (*Revelation's Hymns*, 53–9; and probably also Gordon D. Fee, *Revelation*, NCCS [Eugene, OR: Cascade Books, 2011], 169–70) finds in Ezekiel 28 and Isaiah 14 descriptions of Satan's alleged earlier elevated status in the heavenly assembly, and subsequently uses this assumption to contrast his role as deceiver and accuser in other texts such as Job 1–2 and Zech 3:1–7. From this perspective, the accusatory and deceptive function of Satan can be seen as antithetical to an assumed elevated past. Such readings of these texts allow him to establish this cosmology as an intertextual dialogue partner of the implied reader of Revelation 12. Grabiner states that he is aware of, yet puts aside, the growing number of scholars perceiving the articular השטן (Job 1:8) as not referring to a specific name, but functions as a description of an accusing angel (*Revelation's Hymns*, 53–4, n.73–4). Instead, he argues that "there is a development of the idea throughout the context of canon and that earlier references, in fact, need to be seen in the light of later ones. Naturally this would call into question hermeneutical presuppositions as to what the Bible writers were attempting to communicate, which is beyond the confines of this study" (ibid., 53). In my opinion, this view is problematic for many reasons. Firstly, it is highly unlikely that the Satan, as he is known from New Testament writings (and thus Revelation 12), can be found within the Hebrew Bible, simply because his character is not fully developed at the time when the writings Grabiner cites to support his assumptions were written. (The books of Zechariah, Ezekiel, Isaiah, and perhaps Job are usually considered to have been written between the seventh and fifth centuries BC, a literary period where monotheism with monistic features was at its peak, as in part a response to Israel's political and social reduction in the world from pre- to post-exilic time [see Mark S. Smith, *The Origins of Biblical Monotheism: Israel's Polytheistic Background and the Ugaritic Texts* (New York: Oxford University Press, 2001), 164–5].) I find the hermeneutical presupposition of reading old texts in light of later ones far more problematic than any speculation about what the biblical writers were attempting to communicate. Secondly, the one anarthrous occurrence of שטן with reference to a celestial being in the Hebrew Bible (1 Chr 21:1) is left out in Grabiner's grappling with the Satan in the Hebrew Bible. This text is important as it represents a rewriting of a familiar text with Yahweh as its original subject in 2 Sam 24:15–16, but now with Satan (anarthrous) as the subject of the verb. This is the first occurrence of Satan used as a proper name in the Hebrew Bible, and it represents a theological development from the oldest reference of a celestial being referred to as adversary (Num 22:22, 32) to the latest (1 Chr 21:1), with Zechariah 3 and Job 1–2 wedged in between. It will be argued here that celestial beings referred to as Satans/adversaries (both articular and anarthrous) in the Hebrew Bible must be interpreted in light of their literary and theological context. This context consists of a sovereign God characterized as either overseeing (Job 1–2 and Zechariah 3) or instigating (Numbers 22 and 1 Chronicles 21) the actions of the adversaries, as well as a series of other related references to celestial beings making a negative impact on humankind on behalf of God and/or his divine assembly (see the angels of death and destruction in Genesis 18–19; Exod 12:23; 2 Sam 24:15–16 / 1 Chr 21:15–16; 2 Kgs 19:35 / Isa 37:36; the evil spirit of 1 Sam 16:14; and

where there is none is unwarranted and does not help Grabiner in arguing for the presence of a grand cosmic conflict governing the plot of Revelation.[115]

A similar and related hermeneutical enterprise is found in Sigve K. Tonstad's *Saving God's Reputation*, to which Steven Grabiner is explicitly indebted to.[116] Tonstad's is a comprehensive study of how the faithfulness of Jesus (Rev 14:12) is best understood in light of "God's handling of the reality of evil from its inception to its demise."[117] The method God utilizes in "handling" this is through disclosure of his own character and the unmasking of evil—both of which are accomplished by the function of Jesus as the Lamb. From this perspective, it becomes important to elevate the function of Satan from "merely a shadow in the background, a lifeless stage accessory dwarfed by events playing out on the earthly-historical stage" to "God's leading adversary."[118] The way this is achieved is by appealing to an alleged background of Satan. He criticizes James L. Resseguie for delivering Satan as a "stock character who has nothing to say" but would have had, "if Resseguie had allowed for more room for Revelation's Old Testament allusions in his interpretation."[119] According to Tonstad, he will "pursue leads that

---

the lying spirit of 1 Kgs 22:20–23). Thirdly, I find Grabiner's reading of the book of Job lacking in attention to the importance of the theme of theodicy in the book. He also states that "Job contains the first direct mention of Satan in the Hebrew Bible. Job unambiguously highlights Satan as bringing accusations against God within the context of the council" (Grabiner, *Revelation's Hymns*, 53). The former is simply not the case as here we have yet another articular use of the term and the latter is wrong as it lacks attestation within the book of Job. The answer to why Job is suffering is located in the closing chapters of the book. There God answers Job's implied accusations of unjust punishment, as there seems to be no apparent reason for his misery: the words of Elihu (Job 32–37) and God (Job 38–41) express divine sovereignty efficiently sweeping away any objections against the creator from the created. Job is thus guided toward agnosticism regarding the reason for his suffering (37:23; 42:2–6). The book of Job states that (1) the Satan is one of the sons of God (Job 1:6; 2:1); (2) the Satan is functioning as the "eyes and ears" of God, considering the matters of the earth (1:7–8); and (3) God is explicitly responsible for and is described as the instigator of the sufferings of Job (42:11; see also the delimitations of Satan's actions, 1:12; 2:6).

In short, there is no cosmic conflict present in the texts Grabiner refers to because in these texts Satan is subordinate to the will of God, clearly functioning as commander in chief. Elaine Pagels puts this aptly when she writes, "As he first appears in the Hebrew Bible, Satan is not necessarily evil, much less opposed to God. On the contrary, he appears in the book of Numbers and Job as one of God's obedient servants" (Pagels, *The Origin of Satan*, 39; see also Rollston, "An Ur-History of the New Testament Devil," 16).

For other works supporting the view of this reading in seeing a development in the character of Satan in the Hebrew Bible, from that of an impersonal office to an identified servant of God within the divine assembly, see Pagels, *The Origin of Satan*, 39–40; Forsyth, *The Old Enemy*, 107; Kelly, *Satan: A Biography*, 1–30; Grant R. Osborne, *Revelation*, BECNT (Grand Rapids, MI: Baker Academic, 2002), 472; Russell, *The Devil*, 174; Messadié, *A History of the Devil*, 232–5; Walter Wink, *Unmasking the Powers: The Invisible Forces That Determine Human Existence* (Philadelphia: Fortress, 1986), 11–15; Brown, *The God of This Age*, 21–7; Ryan E. Stokes, "What Is a Demon, What Is an Evil Spirit, and What Is a Satan?," in *Das Böse, der Teufel und Dämonen—Evil, the Devil, and Demons*, ed. Jan Dochhorn, Susanne Rudnig-Zelt, and Benjamin G. Wold, WUNT II/412 (Tübingen: Mohr Siebeck, 2016), 259–72, 267–9; Peggy L. Day, *An Adversary in Heaven: Satan in the Hebrew Bible*, HSM 43 (Atlanta, GA: Scholars Press, 1988), 74–8; Almond, *The Devil: A New Biography*, 16–19; Maxwell-Stuart, *Satan: A Biography*, 20–3; Oldridge, *The Devil: A Very Short Introduction*, 21–3.

[115] See Section 4.4.2.1.1, "Excursus on the Combat Myth and Revelation 12."
[116] According to Steven Grabiner, "certain parts of Tonstad's work have no bearing on this study, but his central claim that the cosmic conflict is an integral part of understanding Revelation clearly is a central aspect of this investigation" (Grabiner, *Revelation's Hymns*, 36).
[117] Tonstad, *Saving God's Reputation*, 3.
[118] Ibid., 3, 8.
[119] Ibid., 13.

fracture these stereotypes," referring to characterizations of Satan in the vein of Elaine Pagels's characterization of Satan as a rhetorical device (*The Origin of Satan*), Hannah Arendt's portrait of Adolf Eichmann as the loyal subject of bureaucracy (*Eichmann in Jerusalem*), or Joseph Kafka's unknowing yet orderly predestined character of Joseph K. (*The Trial*).[120] Tonstad seems to derive his characterization of Satan from the dialectic relationship between the narrative of Revelation and its echoing chamber—the shared perceptions and common ground of the implied reader and the text. As with Grabiner, it is his understanding of the scriptural component of this echoing chamber that separates my reading from that of Tonstad. His canonical approach to the Hebrew Bible allows him to interpret the narrative of Revelation from the perspective of a cosmic conflict between Satan and God/Christ.[121] The characterization of Christ as the Morningstar (22:16) constitutes, according to Tonstad, the antithesis of the bright and shining one in Isaiah 14—a reference to the fall of Satan after the primordial war in heaven. He finds a retroactive element in the war-in-heaven theme of Revelation 12 to provide the best interpretational lens for the entire "main body" of the narrative (4:1–22:5). It is important to notice that his entire hermeneutical enterprise is contingent upon a primordial war in heaven.[122] From this perspective, he reads the narrative as follows:

> War broke out in heaven (12.7); the heavenly council is at a loss to understand the mind of "the One who sits on the throne" (5.1–3); the insistent cry of incomprehension ascends from the victims of injustice on earth (6.9–10); the restraining hand is about to be lifted from the forces of destruction (9.15); and from the mouths of the dragon, the beast and the false prophet demonic spirits go forth "to the kings of the whole world, to assemble them for battle on the great day of God the Almighty" (16.13–14).[123]

God's faithfulness in Christ is the divine response to the saints regarding the progressive unfolding of evil in the world. I intend to pursue the leads of the text that fractures this understanding of the plot of Revelation and its characterization of Satan. I suspect I will find a Satan more akin to the rhetorical device of Pagels, the Eichmann of Arendt, and the Joseph K. of Kafka in the echoing chamber of Revelation than Tonstad has allowed for.

The main difference between the studies of Tonstad and Grabiner from this one relates to the choice of perspective: Where the former two see the conflict in Revelation on a cosmic scale presenting itself on earth, I see the earthly conflict presented through a cosmic lens. The former perceive the main conflict, the overarching plot, as one

---

[120] Ibid., also see 9–15.
[121] See his argument for perceiving the Eden serpent as reappearing at the end of history due to his merits of the beginning of history, in Tonstad, *Saving God's Reputation*, 48–53, and my counterarguments in Section 4.4.2.1.
[122] According to Tonstad, "primordial origin is the inescapable premise of the narrative" (Tonstad, *Saving God's Reputation*, 67). For a brief survey of the chronological premises of his reading, see ibid., 162–3.
[123] Ibid., 193–4.

between God and Satan, the latter as the process of dividing and sifting humankind. To the former, Satan becomes the chief antagonist, whereas to the latter as a means, if rather unwillingly, to an end. In light of these discrepancies, it appears that defining the plot and reader of the narrative is paramount in defining the function of Satan in Revelation (see Section 2.3).

1.2.3 Concluding Remarks

Despite the overwhelming number of studies published on the character of Satan per se, none of them has dealt with the characterization of Satan in Revelation specifically. Moreover, most of these studies are not literary approaches to the text but historically inclined. However, these studies contain valuable information on the conventional meaning behind the various personifications of evil in the period of antiquity and are thus of great value to the process of establishing the cultural point of view of my implied reader (see Section 2.2.3).

The literary and narrative critical readings of Revelation have devoted little or no attention to the character of Satan, whereas those who have diverge considerably from my reading regarding methodological premises and plot definition. Moreover, as for many the function of Satan in the plot of Revelation seems to depend on how one comprehends and interprets his character in light of other scriptural traditions of the Bible, this book will represent a fresh perspective on the matter. Furthermore, as it constitutes the only narrative critical reading of texts concerning Satan in Revelation seen from this particular perspective, it is my hope that it will offer something new in the scholarly discourse on both Satan and Revelation.

1.3 The Scope of This Book

As there seems to be tension in the characterization of Satan in Revelation compared to the biblical traditions of Second Temple Judaism and early Christianity, the focus of this book will be on how this tension makes best sense within the text itself. This focus is thus contingent on the premise that the narrative actually makes sense and can be perceived to do so. Moreover, this text-oriented focus makes a synchronic reading more suitable than a diachronic one, as the object is to explain how this tension makes sense in the narrative per se and not necessarily compared to a historical development of the character of Satan. The focus on the function of a certain character within a text further narrows down the scope to a narrative reading (methodological and theoretical considerations will be thoroughly discussed in Chapter 2). The primary research question will therefore be, *What is the narrative function of Satan in the Book of Revelation?*

In order to be able to answer this question, a series of other questions must be answered by establishing an interpretational context from the narrative framework of texts concerning Satan. If Revelation is a book about God and God's plan with his people, what is the cosmological function of God in Revelation? Also, if Christ is close to but not identical to God, what is his cosmological relation to God/Satan? Finally, regardless of whether Satan is characterized as servant or enemy, how does his function relate to other evil or destructive characters in the book? What is their cosmological function in the divine plan? By answering such secondary questions constituting the background to Satan's activities, I believe the primary object of my reading will become much clearer.

As the majority of scholarly publications on either Satan or Revelation mentioned above tend to read from an anti-divine, cosmic conflict perspective, either deliberately or not, the analysis below will explore the validity of reading with an added emphasis on the "servant of God" perspective in the text. It is a hypothesis of this reading that such an approach could help me get around the ambiguity of the interpretation of the character of Satan present in other readings. Furthermore, the issue of intertextuality seems to separate the different readings of Revelation regarding the understanding of the function of Satan in the narrative (i.e., what intertextual references are assumed to be known to the implied reader in the characterization of Satan?). Therefore, the following questions will need to be addressed in light of the possible implied meaning in the intertextual references in the text: Which of these traditions do we find at work within the text of Revelation? Could a combination of said traditions explain the inherent tensions in the characterization of Satan there?

In the next chapter, I will present and argue for my choice of method and elaborate on how I will make use of it in order to answer my main research question. Chapters 3–5 will constitute the exegetical analysis of the primary texts in their context. Finally, in Chapter 6 I will sum up the findings of my reading and compare it to the current state of research as mapped out above.

2

Theoretical and Methodological Considerations

2.1 Introduction

If the role of Satan seen from the more traditional hermeneutical perspective is described as possibly ambivalent, my aim in this analysis will be to sort out how his literary function makes sense within the text itself. What function is this character assigned in each part of the story? How does this make sense in the overall structure of the book? One possible way of answering this could be to analyze the various writings on and about Revelation in the patristic era, trying to find some clues to how the early generations of Christians understood the author's utilization of this character. One could make use of the results from such an approach to put forth a more probable historical understanding of the interpretation of Satan in the book of Revelation.[1] Yet, in some ways, this has already been done, as shown in the contemporary research section of my introductory chapter. However, due to the rather broad scope of most of the monographs on the subject, none of these have been able to address in a sufficient way the issue of tension in the characterization of Satan. Moreover, they often end up far too general in scope to be of critical use to this reading. In my opinion, a critical diachronic study of the reception of the Satan tradition as found in the book of Revelation is still lacking. However, I doubt if a diachronic approach is the most suitable method for this reading, bearing in mind its scope and nature: What is the function of Satan *in* Revelation? This question is not diachronic in nature. It is not the social history of Satan through the ages I am concerned with here, but rather the Satan of one particular moment in time—of one particular text. This document speaks of a Satan being in some way responsible for the suffering of Christians in seven specified congregations in Asia Minor. This particular Satan is portrayed as an instrument of sifting, testing, and dividing the population of these areas—preparing them for the rewards or punishment in the judgment that is soon to follow. In the end, the removal of this Satan seems to be made on the grounds of him doing what he is apparently "given" to do. This is what the text actually states about Satan, and if we are to assume

---

[1] See Almond, *The Devil* (2014); Kelly, *Satan: A Biography* (2006); Russell, *Satan: The Early Christian Tradition* (1987) and *The Prince of Darkness* (1988); Forsyth, *The Old Enemy* (1987); Maxwell-Stuart, *Satan: A Biography* (2008); Messadié, *A History of the Devil* (1996); and Pagels, *The Origin of Satan* (1995).

that this is to make sense to anyone, it will probably be a good idea to inquire into the mechanisms of the story holding these aspects together.² If the main object is to understand the Satan of Revelation, then it is the text of Revelation itself that first and foremost ought to be one's concern. Texts involving Satan must be analyzed on their own terms to find the functions assigned to him in light of what these elements provide to the story as a whole. Thus, I find the branch of literary criticism known as narrative criticism most suitable for this enterprise.

2.2 On the Nature of Narrative Criticism

The earliest narrative analyses done within the field of New Testament scholarship were performed on the gospels. In time the Acts of the Apostles, the book of Revelation, and even the letters of Paul became objects of proponents of narrative criticism.³ However, it is important to reflect on the degree to which Revelation could be considered as narrative. Monika Fludernik defines the term "narrative" as follows: "A Narrative (Fr. *récit*; Ger. *Erzählung*) is a representation of a possible world in a linguistic and/or visual medium, at whose centre there are one or several protagonists of an anthropomorphic nature who are existentially anchored in a temporal and spatial sense and who (mostly) perform goal-directed actions (action and plot structure)."⁴ The book of Revelation includes all of these elements, with the saints, as the addressees of the book, as perhaps the most prominent protagonists. David L. Barr reaches the same conclusion in his narrative commentary on Revelation, though by a less complex definition. He defines it as narrative simply by appealing to the fact that "writers of apocalypses were attempting to share a story of something that had happened to them … the author is telling this story so others too can share his experience."⁵ Revelation is a story told of connected events, ergo it is a narrative.⁶ Still, the way it is told sets it apart from more familiar narratives of the modern era due to its particular genre and imagery as

---

2 In this book, I will presuppose that it is possible to search for meaning embedded within any text in itself, and from there to argue for more or less probable implied meanings derived from the text. Although I am aware of reader-response criticism's attention to the fact that deriving meaning from a text is largely a subjective enterprise, and deconstructionism with its claim that any text possesses endless possibilities of meaning, I still want to direct attention to the mechanisms in the text itself and how they invite and govern such meanings. On the implications of reader-response criticism and deconstructionism and their view of how texts convey meaning, see Mark Allen Powell, *What Is Narrative Criticism? A New Approach to the Bible* (Minneapolis: Augsburg Fortress, 1990), 16–18; and Edgar V. McKnight, "Reader-Response Criticism," in *To Each Its Own Meaning: An Introduction to Biblical Criticisms and Their Application*, rev. and exp. ed., ed. Steven L. McKenzie and Stephen R. Haynes (Louisville, KY: Westminster John Knox, 1999), 230–52, 231–6.
3 For a survey on contributions from narrative criticism on New Testament writings, see James L. Resseguie, *Narrative Criticism of the New Testament: An Introduction* (Grand Rapids, MI: Baker Academic, 2005), 24–5, nn. 21–6; and Section 2.5 in this reading.
4 Monika Fludernik, *An Introduction to Narratology*, trans. Patricia Häusler-Greenfield and Monika Fludernik (New York: Routledge, 2009), 6.
5 Barr, *Tales of the End*, 1.
6 See also Pierre Prigent: "The book of Revelation is composed of visions, or more exactly of narratives of visions. It is intended, as its author reminds us, to be heard at public readings. We would therefore not be unreasonable at all in analyzing it as one would do with a narrative" (Pierre Prigent, *Commentary on the Apocalypse of St. John* [Tübingen: Mohr Siebeck, 2004], 86).

well as its somewhat complex layers of focalization. This makes it an odd narrative, but a narrative nonetheless.[7] However, having established the validity of considering Revelation as narrative, one must be cautious to the warnings of David E. Aune against overstating the literary unity by means of or under the pretense of doing narrative criticism.[8] Regardless of whether Aune is correct in his assumptions of why there is tension in the narrative unity of Revelation, the tensions must by no means be bent into shape by one's choice of method. Rather, if tensions are discovered in the narrative, the most promising inquiry would be to determine the range of meanings created by it, accompanied by an in-depth consideration of their probability. An obvious consequence of this is a self-imposed restriction from overstating the conclusions when encountering such tensions.

Narrative criticism has been used in biblical studies since the 1980s and is a development from New Criticism, a movement within American literary theory that rose and developed in the middle part of the twentieth century. The term "narrative criticism" is used mainly in the context of biblical studies and was coined by David Rhoads and the publication of his co-written book with Joanna Dewey and Donald Michie, *Mark as Story: An Introduction to the Narrative of a Gospel*.[9] This particular hermeneutical approach presupposes a decisive move away from the traditional search for authorial intent and alleged effect upon readers. The text is thus regarded as an autonomous unity, a world in itself, and it is from the text one can deduce the only author and reader available to us: the implied author and his assumed reader.[10] The sharp focus on the text as the sole proprietor of meaning in narrative criticism leads

---

[7] According to Eugene Boring, Revelation is closely related to the narrative genre on all levels of genre embedded within it (vision, apocalypse, and letter). Both the vision report and the visions themselves are narratives and are therefore not to be considered separate genres from that of the narrative. As apocalypse, Revelation is equipped with a narrative framework that continues throughout the narration of the content of the visions. Finally, as a letter, it belongs to a genre that "may not only contain discursive information, exhortations, or commands, but may also tell stories. Letters are often in the narrative mode, as the letter writer tells a story or reports an incident" (Eugene M. Boring, "Narrative Christology in the Apocalypse," *CBQ* 54 [1992], 702–23, 704). The different genres of Revelation thus include narrative as an "indispensable element in the genre of Revelation" (ibid., 703). The narrative component is also recognized in the broadly accepted definition of apocalyptic literature of the Society of Biblical Literature (SBL) Genres Project, published in *Semeia* 14 (1979): "a genre of revelatory literature with *a narrative framework*" (John J. Collins, *The Apocalyptic Imagination: An Introduction to Jewish Apocalyptic Literature*, 2nd ed. [Grand Rapids, MI: Eerdmans, 1998], 5 [my italics]).

[8] David E. Aune, *Revelation 1–5*, WBC 52A (Dallas: Word, 1997), cviii–cix.

[9] David Rhoads, Joanna Dewey, and Donald Michie, *Mark as Story: An Introduction to the Narrative of a Gospel* (Philadelphia: Fortress, 1982).

[10] Narrator and implied author are to be considered distinct entities in narrative criticism. The implied author is "reconstructed by the reader from the narrative. He is not the narrator, but rather the principle that invented the narrator, along with everything else in the narrative" (Seymour Chatman, *Story and Discourse: Narrative Structure in Fiction and Film* [Ithaca, NY: Cornell University Press, 1978], 148). In narrative criticism, the "implied reader and author" is the imagined reader of the presumed author, deduced from the text itself. "Narrative critics generally speak of an *implied reader* who is presupposed by the narrative itself. This implied reader is distinct from any real, historical reader in the same way that the implied author is distinct from the real, historical author. The actual responses of real readers are unpredictable, but there may be clues within the narrative that indicate an anticipated response from the implied reader ... The goal of narrative criticism is to read the text as the implied reader" (Powell, *What Is Narrative Criticism?*, 19–20). I will use the terms "implied author/reader" here, with the meaning as explained by Chatman and Powell.

to a detailed analysis of the text known as "close readings"—"the detailed analysis of the complex interrelations and *ambiguities* (multiple meanings) of the verbal and figurative components within a work."[11] These close readings encompass certain key elements used to accomplish a thorough narrative analysis, such as plot development, characterization, point of view, structure, rhetoric, setting, time, implied reader, and so on.[12] These elements represent questions asked, and meaning sought when interpreting any given narrative. The vast array of elements utilized in narrative criticism implies that not every question finds its answer in every text. Some perspectives will be of greater interest than others for me due to the rather narrow scope of this study—to focus on the function of one of the secondary characters in the narrative. The elements of plot, characterization, and point of view will therefore be my primary concerns in determining the literary function of Satan in Revelation. However, other aspects of narrative analysis will be taken into consideration along the way if the text requires it.

2.2.1 Plot

Central to any narrative analysis is detecting the plot of the text in question. Regarding a definition of the term, James L. Resseguie puts it this way: "The plot is the sequence of events or incidents that make up a narrative."[13] What story is being told here? What is the main problem being resolved, and how is this unveiled to the reader? The plot is "the organizing force or design, which we see as connecting events into some kind of comprehensible pattern."[14] Events and incidents are thereby the meat and potatoes of a plot, the very things that move it forward. They could be arranged in any number of ways and order, for the narrative to provide the implicit journey toward the resolution of the plot. To this R. Alan Culpepper adds, "The central features of 'plot' are the sequence, causality, unity, and affective power of a narrative."[15] How does the story begin and end, and what happened on the way in between? Is there a conflict in the story somewhere, that drives the plot forward? What events does the story consist of and how do these contribute to the resolution of this conflict? Are these smaller stories part of a larger story, and if so, how do they relate? In our case, the crucial question to each text will be what role Satan is being assigned in each particular plot strand. How do the character of Satan and his actions contribute to the resolution of the conflict— the turn of events? How do the individual parts fit the overall structure and plot of Revelation?

---

[11] Resseguie, *Narrative Criticism of the New Testament*, 24 (quoting M. H. Abrahams, *A Glossary of Literary Terms*).
[12] There is no formal agreement on the number, subdivisions, and order of the components of narrative analysis, yet those listed here seems to recur in several surveys and commentaries (see Resseguie, *Narrative Criticism of the New Testament*, 241–4; Powell, *What Is Narrative Criticism?*, 103–5; R. Alan Culpepper, *Anatomy of the Fourth Gospel: A Study in Literary Design* [Philadelphia: Fortress, 1983], see his introductory chapter as well as the overall structure of his book; Barr, *Tales of the End*, 2–33; and David M. Gunn, "Narrative Criticism," in *To Each Its Own Meaning: An Introduction to Biblical Criticisms and Their Application*, rev. and exp. ed., ed. Steven L. McKenzie and Stephen R. Haynes [Louisville, KY: Westminster John Knox, 1999], 201–29, 201).
[13] Resseguie, *Narrative Criticism of the New Testament*, 197.
[14] McKenzie and Haynes, *To Each Its Own Meaning*, 213.
[15] Culpepper, *Anatomy of the Fourth Gospel*, 80.

In the analysis, it will be of utmost importance to discern how these smaller plot strands—such as those found in the letters to the seven congregations, or the texts about the woman and the dragon of Revelation 12 and 13—are resolved and contribute to the understanding and resolving of the main plot of the book. It follows from this that the understanding of the main plot will be one of the decisive premises any narrative reading depends upon. I will try to define the overarching narrative plot of Revelation below in Section 2.3.

In my analysis of the plot structure of each text unit I will make use of the Quinary scheme of Paul Larivaille as a structural model to identify the different elements of the plot of the narrative: the initial situation, complication, transforming action, denouement, and final situation.[16] This is a convenient model to analyze plots within a narrative, and I will try to utilize it to the extent the text allows me.

2.2.2 Characterization

In the pursuit of the narrative function of Satan in the book of Revelation, it is important to identify how Satan is individualized; in other words, how he relates to and is distinguished from the vast array of heavenly agents in the narrative. The question of his character will thus be central to this reading. According to Mark Allen Powell, "characters are constructs of the implied author, created to fulfill a particular role in the story."[17] In essence, this is what this endeavor of determining the function of Satan in Revelation is all about: How is the character of Satan constructed and molded to fulfill his particular role in Revelation? The plot defines his role, his characterization—"that is, the process through which the implied author provides the implied reader with what is necessary to reconstruct a character from the narrative," and enables him to fulfill this.[18] How is he described? What actions does he take? What attributes—skills, names, epithets, suggestions, and so forth—are being used to describe him? How is he spoken of or treated by other characters? What is implied about his characteristics? What contributions does he make to the resolving of the plot? When asking ourselves these questions about the text, it is also important to note how we find the answers to them. Is the implied author telling us this or is he showing it? Does he create the means to comprehend Satan's characteristics by implying and/or explaining? Having settled the means of characterization, the contents of it—the traits of the character—must be clarified.

A question that will probably arise during the analysis is the question of whether Satan is to be considered a dynamic or a static character. Dynamic characters "may develop within a narrative and undergo an important change either for the better or for the worse."[19] It may seem like this is exactly what is happening to Satan during the course of the narrative. Satan's status as a heavenly prosecutor in the same vein

---

[16] Paul Larivaille, "L'Analyse (morpho)logique du récit," *Poétique* 19 (1974): 368–88, 387; for a more recent application of the model, see Daniel Marguerat and Yvan Bourquin, *How to Read Bible Stories* (London: SCM, 1999), 43–9.
[17] Powell, *What Is Narrative Criticism?*, 51.
[18] Ibid., 52.
[19] Resseguie, *Narrative Criticism of the New Testament*, 122.

as the notorious accuser of Job (Job 1–2) is explained as being "in transit," as his fate is depending on the faithfulness of the believers determined to die for their faith in Christ. The wording of the hymn in Rev 12:10–12, and in particular verse 11, depicts Satan being thrown down on the grounds of the blood of the Lamb and by the words of their testimony. It follows from the context that the subject of the action, the αὐτοί who conquers, is the brethren being accused in verse 10—the faithful and suffering believers in Asia Minor, and the martyrs under the altar in 6:9–11. The διά with accusative indicates the cause of the expulsion of Satan—the means by which it is effectuated.[20] We may conclude from this that Satan's status is not only being declined and rejected, but this is being done due to other characters' actions.[21] We should therefore be alert to the role of other characters in the characterization of Satan. The often-suggested idea of Christ being characterized as the antithesis to Satan may be of contribution in these matters.[22]

Traits to be explored other than dynamic/static are whether the character is to be considered flat or round (complex or "one-dimensional"), stock (is he a cliché in terms of the conventions of the genre in use?), foil (is he the mirror, the contrasting background, that makes jewels appear shinier?), or walk-on character (does he merely serve a function or as a background actor in the narrative scenery with no part or identity on his own?).[23]

In order to differentiate the characters, I find the nomenclature of the actantial scheme of A. J. Greimas highly useful.[24] This scheme is an attempt toward a formalization of the roles in a story and is used to describe the narrative functions of the characters essential to the plot. One important premise of this theory is the principle of subordination of character to the plot, an idea already known from the works of Aristotle and Vladimir Propp. This principle suits the aims of my book here well because the book of Revelation typically displays the characteristics of "non-autonomy of its characters."[25] This is typical for biblical narratives, and the term refers to the construction of "characters within a system which is entirely governed (from

---

[20] Frederick W. Danker, Walter Bauer, William F. Arndt, and F. Wilbur Gingrich, *Greek-English Lexicon of the New Testament and Other Early Christian Literature*, 3rd ed. (Chicago: University of Chicago Press, 2000), 226; and Gregory K. Beale, *The Book of Revelation*, NIGTC (Grand Rapids, MI: Eerdmans, 1999), 664.

[21] See Richard Bauckham, *The Theology of the Book of Revelation* (Cambridge: Cambridge University Press, 1993), 75–6.

[22] For an interesting and somewhat original interpretation of the apparent dichotomy of these biblical characters, see Kirsten Nielsen, *Satan: Den Fortabte Søn?* (Frederiksberg: ANIS, 1991). Here they are depicted as opposing sons with God as their father, in the manner of Cain and Abel, Esau and Jacob, Ishmael and Isaac, and the two sons in the parable of the prodigal son.

[23] Resseguie, *Narrative Criticism of the New Testament*, 122–30.

[24] A short presentation of this scheme, presented as a development of earlier and insufficient models by Vladimir Propp and Etienne Souriau, is found in Julien Algirdas Greimas, *Structural Semantics: An Attempt at a Method* (Lincoln: University of Nebraska Press, 1984), 198–213. (The model itself is presented in brief on page 207.) Greimas invented the term "actant," which allows us to differentiate both the agent and the character. According to Marguerat and Bourquin, "an actant is the one who performs the function needed to bring about the transformation which is at the centre of the narrative" (Marguerat and Bourquin, *How to Read Bible Stories*, 62; see also Branden, *Satanic Conflict and the Plot of Matthew*, 8–9).

[25] Marguerat and Bourquin, *How to Read Bible Stories*, 64–5.

a narrative point of view) by a central agent, God or Jesus."[26] The plot of Revelation is the plot of God, and everything in the narrative is subject to his governing plan. This feature is typically present in apocalyptic literature by the notion of God as the architect of history in constant control of earthly matters. A frequently occurring example of this feature in Revelation is the setting of limited periods of time given by God to allow or intend for unfortunate things to happen (note the limited affliction released upon the congregation of Smyrna for ten days, Rev 2:10). Such an element of an omnipotent God in total control is considered by many as one of the defining characteristics of the genre.[27]

According to Greimas, there are six typical actantial positions in all stories: the *Subject* chasing a valuable *Object*, the *Sender* mobilizing the Subject to do this, and a *Receiver* to whom the Subject in the end must give the Object. In this process, the Subject can be helped by a *Helper*, or obstructed by an *Opponent*. Since the first presentation of the actantial model in *Sémantique structural* (1966), it has been reworked many times over, both by Greimas himself as well as others, due to critique presented over time.[28] The most relevant implications from this reworking to my reading are (1) an actor can embody more than one actantial role; (2) an actantial role may embody more than one actant; and (3) the matching of actants with actors is the result of an ongoing interpretive process and is governed by genres and subgenres in the narrative. It follows then from this that we must abandon the idea of "one size fits all" when approaching the actantial scheme. Instead, I will make use of the actantial scheme of Greimas to draw up an actantial inventory as it is presented within the narrative, to be able to define and sort out the different roles the characters within the narrative are assigned.[29] The actantial scheme is centered on the object of desire aimed at by the subject. This desire is what the helper and opponent act in relation to. I will use this scheme on the various texts mentioning Satan, in order to better be able to identify and make clear what role is being attached to his character in each text per se.

To determine how a character is built within a narrative is to read for the elements within the text that individualize one character from the others. These elements could be characterizing descriptions from the narrator, the words of the character, the words of other characters about the character in question, the actions of the character, actions relating to this character, knowledge of this character assumed known to the implied reader and thus not explicitly stated in the text, and so on.[30] The process of

---

[26] Ibid., 64.
[27] For references to time limitations in apocalyptic literature expressing that the cosmos is controlled by God or other heavenly beings, see Adela Yarbro Collins, *Cosmology and Eschatology in Jewish and Christian Apocalypticism* (Leiden: Brill, 1996), 114–15; David Syme Russell, *Divine Disclosure: An Introduction to Jewish Apocalyptic* (London: SCM, 1992), 86–91; and Ben Witherington, *Revelation*, NCBC (Cambridge: Cambridge University Press, 2003), 40.
[28] In this section I am indebted to David Herman and his clarifying survey on the actantial scheme, elaborating on both its strengths and weaknesses. See David Herman, *Story Logic: Problems and Possibilities of Narrative* (Lincoln: University of Nebraska Press, 2002), 122–33.
[29] For a similar utilization of the actantial scheme of Greimas, see Elisabeth Schüssler Fiorenza, *The Book of Revelation: Justice and Judgment*, 2nd ed. (Minneapolis: Augsburg Fortress, 1998), 174–5; Marguerat and Bourquin, *How to Read Bible Stories*, 62–3; Branden, *Satanic Conflict and the Plot of Matthew*, 8–9; Wright, *The New Testament and the People of God*, 69–80.
[30] According to Steven Grabiner, the implied reader (IR)

connecting all this information to a comprehensible character is often referred to as (re-)construction or building of character.[31]

I will attempt to construct the character of Satan in the following manner: Firstly, I will identify how Satan is individualized in the text. I compare what is said about him and the actions attributed to him with the function he is assigned in the plot of the text in focus. Secondly, the results from this will, in turn, be compared and merged with the results from the analysis of the other texts involving his character. The accumulated results will in the end be compared to his overall role in the major plot of Revelation. And thirdly, due to the book of Revelation being written about an extratextual phenomenon, Jesus and the related movement of the first century AD, the implied reader is presumed to have some prior knowledge of what the narrative is all about. If there is assumed knowledge related to Satan in the narrative, the recognizing of this will be of crucial value to my reconstruction of the character of Satan. If there are indeed gaps in the characterization of Satan indicating such knowledge (the epithets of Rev 12:7–12 would in my opinion be a valid candidate) I will presume the following probable sources known to the implied reader of Revelation: the Hebrew Bible and related Jewish and Christian Scriptures, the Jesus movement and tradition of the first century AD, and to some extent the cultural environment of the Judeo-Christian milieu of the Roman Empire in the first century AD. I will argue briefly in the following for why I perceive these sources as assumed known to the implied reader. Due to the topic of extratextual references in narrative criticism being sometimes considered a controversial issue among some scholars, a more extensive line of argumentation can be found in the excursus of Section 2.5.

Due to the vast number of allusions to the traditions of the Hebrew Bible within the book, it seems likely that the implied author assumes an acquaintance with it.[32] Little or no space is used to explain the vocabulary or theological implications related to this source. This indicates an assumption that this makes sense to the implied

> represents a construct of a reader who would know things not specifically stated within the text (e.g. the worth of a talent) that today's readers might not know without additional research. The IR knows everything the text assumes the reader knows and forgets what the text does not assume the reader knows. From a narrative-critical approach, the actual reader is to read the text from the standpoint of the IR ... one of the purposes of this construct is to understand what is the text demanding of its intended reader. (Grabiner, *Revelation's Hymns*, 16)

> I will use the term "implied reader" in this sense, but here and in the excursus in Section 2.5 I will define a probable competence of the implied reader within a narrative assuming acquaintance with the literary and cultural environment of Revelation in the first century AD.

[31] Cornelis Bennema refers to his new theory of character in the New Testament as character *reconstruction*, whereas John Darr prefers the term "character *building*." The terminology in both cases refers to the process of piecing together the various elements of characterization present and implied in the text to a fully comprehensible description of characters in the New Testament. See Cornelis Bennema, *A Theory of Character in New Testament Narrative* (Minneapolis: Fortress, 2014); and John A. Darr, *On Character Building: The Reader and the Rhetoric of Characterization in Luke-Acts* (Louisville, KY: Westminster John Knox, 1992).

[32] Craig R. Koester mentions studies noting up to three hundred possible allusions to this tradition, depending on how one defines allusion. His section on intertextuality in the book of Revelation confirms my identification of the Hebrew Bible as an assumed known source to the implied reader. See Craig R. Koester, *Revelation: A New Translation with Introduction and Commentary*, Anchor Bible 38A (New Haven, CT: Yale University Press, 2014), 123–6.

reader without any further explanation. The mentioning of τὸν Γὼγ καὶ Μαγώγ ("Gog and Magog," Rev 20:8) is a fitting example of an obvious reference to the Hebrew Bible (Ezekiel 38–39) assumed known to the implied reader and with considerable implications to the literary meaning of the text in question (see Section 5.4.2.3).

The narrative assumes that the reader finds the name and person of Jesus Christ (Rev 1:1–5) meaningful without any further explanation. Moreover, the story of the woman, the boy, and the dragon of Revelation 12 seems to derive its meaning from the infancy and passion narratives known from the Gospel traditions. An assumed acquaintance with the Jesus movement of the first century AD follows from the narrative's own interpretation of Christ in light of the allusions to the Hebrew Bible as well as its vocabulary, theology, and general missiological message—all of which are known from the first-century Christian tradition.

Finally, the book is written within and assumes at least some knowledge of its cultural place of provenance—the Judeo-Christian and Greco-Roman culture. This forms the background to the earthly reality the book orients itself within. It is presumed known to the reader what Rome is and represents in the form of executive power upon pain of death. The identification of the dragon/beast in Rev 17:9–14 as a city seated upon seven mountains presupposes knowledge of Roman geography as well as apocalyptic imagery. Thus, the book is written with the genre conventions used and developed within the scriptural traditions assumed known within the book. The use of apocalyptic imagery, symbolism, prophetic oracles, imperial/royal edicts, and so forth is presumed comprehensible by their very presence within the text.

Having established an implied reader acquainted with the scriptural echoes within the narrative, some comments on the issue of intertextuality should be made. According to Jean Zumstein, in dealing with the issue of intertextuality in narrative criticism—the intertextual dialectic between the hypertext (the narrative) and the hypotext (the reference text)—one must distinguish between quotations, references, and allusions:

> A "quotation" is to be understood as the literal reproduction of a text A in text B. A "reference" is also an explicit form of intertextuality; however, in contrast to a quotation, text B refers to text A without presenting it *in extenso*—we are confronted here with a relationship *in absentia*. In contrast to a quotation, an "allusion" is neither an explicit nor a literal reproduction of text A in text B. Rather, a word or turn of phrase is used so as to call some other well-known text to mind.[33]

In Revelation there are no direct quotations of any known hypotexts, but we do have several references to the Hebrew Bible such as the events of Numbers 22–25 referred to in Rev 2:14 and the τοῦ ξύλου τῆς ζωῆς (the tree of life) of Genesis 3 in Rev 22:2, 19. Still, the major intertextual tool utilized in Revelation is the allusion. Due to the elaborate symbolism of the narrative, the allusions present within the

---

[33] Jean Zumstein, "Intratextuality and Intertextuality in the Gospel of John," in *Anatomies of Narrative Criticism: The Past, Present, and Futures of the Fourth Gospel as Literature*, ed. Tom Thatcher and Stephen D. Moore (Atlanta, GA: Society of Biblical Literature Resources for Biblical Study, 2008), 121–35, 133.

text carry considerably hermeneutical significance to their meaning.[34] Having detected an allusion within the text, the decisive interpretational task when using narrative criticism is to decipher the most probable implied output of this dialectic relationship between texts—the intratextual meaning derived from the recognizing of the intertextual reference within the text. Depending on the (defined) competence of one's implied reader, such an enterprise may result in various readings of the same text. I will therefore argue at length for the probability of the assumed dialectic of meaning from such allusions if proven decisive for the hermeneutical enterprise of my reading.[35] These arguments will in part be contingent on the assumed competence of my implied reader, as defined.

According to Steve Moyise, a side effect of intertextuality is an unpredictable tension created by the juxtaposing of the texts involved. It is in particular when discussing Thomas Green and his fourth category of forms of imitation, dialectic imitation, that Moyise wrestles with the consequences of the open-ended use of allusions in Revelation.[36] How much or little of the connotations of the source text and its context "bleed over" the meaning of the work in question?[37] The extent of influence can be both *over-* as well as *under*estimated. In the analytical chapters below, I will discuss such possible connotations in light of the context of the allusion, and conclude whenever possible or entertain different possible implications if necessary. In the end, "the task of intertextuality is to explore how the source text continues to speak through the new work and how the new work forces new meanings from the source text,"[38] and it "is not so much applying a method as asking certain types of questions and pondering particularly evocative phrases."[39] For a narrative critical reading, such effort is paramount in order for the texts to be able to convey their meaning to any implied reader familiar with the source text involved (see Section 2.5).[40]

---

[34] According to John Christopher Thomas, the relationship between Revelation and the Hebrew Bible is a dynamic phenomenon, one in which an "intersection of OT texts, ideas, imagery, and vocabulary with John's visionary experience results in an intertext where echoes and allusions to the OT (among other things) provide shape and definition of meaning to the vision that is the Apocalypse" (Thomas, *The Apocalypse*, 17). To grasp the literary meaning produced by this literary relation, one has to engage with the question of how the reference context interacts with the new.

[35] In light of the taxonomy of the different kinds of intertextuality of Robert S. Miola, it is only category one (texts mediated by the author into the text) and two (an originary text radiates its presence through intermediaries and indirect routes such as traditions, culture, and expectations) that concern my reading here. The third category (what the audience brings to the text) represents any possible intertextual relation depending on the reader rather than the text/author, and is outside this reading. Since it is the most probable reading of the reader presumed by the text (implied reader) I want to interpret, I will make it a primary effort to argue extensively on intratextual grounds for the probability of any intertextual allusion or reference in the narrative. See Robert S. Miola, "Seven Types of Intertextuality," in *Shakespeare, Italy and Intertextuality*, ed. Michele Marrapodi (Manchester: Manchester University Press, 2004), 13–25.

[36] Steve Moyise, *The Old Testament in the Book of Revelation*, JSNTSup 115 (Sheffield: Sheffield Academic, 1995), 127–33.

[37] Ibid., 135.

[38] Ibid., 111.

[39] Ibid., 135.

[40] Zumstein, "Intratextuality and Intertextuality in the Gospel of John," 134.

2.2.3 Point of View

Point of view represents the way the story is told to us and on which premises. From what angle do we perceive what is being described? This is the somewhat technical aspect of point of view: *How* do we learn about Satan? Is it from the voice of the narrator or do we learn from other characters' testimonies about him or his actions? The Satan of the book of Revelation does not speak himself. We are solely dependent upon what is said and implied regarding his nature, his actions, and his character. The narrator of our text is what we call a first-person narrator, being himself an active part of what is narrated, referring to events from a first-person perspective. For instance, when we read "And I saw a beast coming up from the sea" in Rev 13:1, the "I" in the text is not the omniscient author like the one found in the Gospels but constitutes a narrator that provides authority to what is written by himself being a witness to what is told.[41] This type of point of view will largely be explored in the sections analyzing the literary frame, form, and function of each primary text. This aspect corresponds to what Gérard Genette referred to as the focalization of the narrative—the lens through which the reader perceives.[42]

A second aspect of point of view is the conceptual framework embedded in the text. The worldview of the narrator is sometimes referred to as the evaluative point of view.[43] We must consider the characterization of Satan up against the general evaluative point of view of the implied author. What system of values is assumed in the process of prejudicing the readers toward or against the characters and actions of a text? Does the characterization of Satan orient him toward truth or untruth—toward God or away from him?

It is important to be aware of the fact that the characterization of Satan in Revelation will probably in itself be one of the key elements of the general evaluative point of view of the book, himself being the very element that the believers in Asia Minor are to avoid. Furthermore, when searching for the evaluative point of view in biblical writings, we often find that the narrator has aligned this with what he finds to be God's evaluative point of view.[44] This makes the movement to or away from truth into an ethical evaluation of right or wrong, and in the case of the book of Revelation, it comes with severe consequences. Powell states, "The creation of a narrative world in which God's evaluative point of view can be determined and must be accepted as normative is a powerful rhetorical device … the implied reader will tend to empathize with those characters who express God's point of view and will seek distance from those characters who do not."[45] This is precisely what seems to be the rhetorical thrust of the narrative of

---

[41] Powell, *What Is Narrative Criticism?*, 23–5; and Resseguie, *Narrative Criticism of the New Testament*, 168.
[42] Gérard Genette, *Narrative Discourse Revisited*, trans. Jane E. Lewin (Ithaca, NY: Cornell University Press, 1988), 64–5; cf. his *Narrative Discourse: An Essay in Method*, trans. Jane E. Lewin (Ithaca, NY: Cornell University Press, 1980), 189–94.
[43] Resseguie, *Narrative Criticism of the New Testament*, 169.
[44] Powell (*What Is Narrative Criticism?*, 24) depends on Jack D. Kingsbury in his comments on this phenomenon in the Gospels. The same point may in my opinion be applied to the book of Revelation, due to the insistence on this being a revelation of Jesus Christ given by God (Rev 1:1–2).
[45] Powell, *What Is Narrative Criticism?*, 25.

Revelation: choose to endure and prevail, and you will conquer (i.e., the right thing to do), and do not give in to the temptations of adversarial forces (i.e., the wrong thing to do). However, this is not the narrative plot of Satan, but the plot aimed at the implied readers, and therefore not the evaluative point of view he is to be measured up against. The work of a prosecutor is measured by a different evaluative point of view than the work of a defense attorney. The question of this reading in light of this evaluative point of view must therefore be how and to what degree he fulfills his role or not—to what degree he fits into the plot of God's evaluative point of view. Bearing in mind how it all ends up for our antagonist, it will be of special interest for us to find out if any reasons for this action can be discerned from the evaluative point of view.

A third kind of point of view is what we may call the cultural point of view. The implied reader is a literary construct from a cultural expression of the first century, and thus shares the cultural assumptions present within it. The cultural point of view encompasses these cultural assumptions. As they are assumed known to the implied reader, they are therefore not explained. Examples of such assumptions are language, genre, imagery, as well as cultural, social, and literary references. For instance, in Revelation, there is an assumed correspondence between the world above and the world below.[46] It exhibits the impression of a transcendental reality that corresponds with the immanent reality. This is what we often refer to as an apocalyptic worldview. The common themes in the letters of the seven congregations (see especially the phrasing of 2:10) and the scene depicted in chapter 12 suggest that the latter is the transcendental parallel to the former. It represents the vertical point of view in the apocalyptic genre: the very things being revealed—the truth behind perceived reality. The events on earth are directly related to Michael's actions in heaven.[47] This corresponds well with one particular aspect of John J. Collins's definition of apocalyptic:

> A genre of revelatory literature with a narrative framework, in which a revelation is mediated by an otherworldly being to a human recipient, disclosing a transcendent reality which is both temporal, insofar as it envisages eschatological salvation, and spatial insofar as it involves another, supernatural world.[48]

It is the spatial element that we might see at play in our text. Collins elaborates further on this matter when writing,

> The revelation of a supernatural world and the activity of supernatural beings are essential to all the apocalypses … there is a hidden world of angels and demons that is directly relevant to human destiny; and this destiny is finally determined by a definitive eschatological judgment. In short, human life is bounded in the present by the supernatural world of angels and demons and in the future by the inevitability of a final judgment.[49]

---

[46] Barr, *Tales of the End*, 6.
[47] See Beale, *The Book of Revelation*, 663–4.
[48] Collins, *The Apocalyptic Imagination*, 5.
[49] Ibid., 6 and 8.

Collins relates this way of perceiving reality to the literary function of apocalypses, what he calls the "apocalyptic technique": "All apocalypses address some underlying problem … whatever the underlying problem, it is viewed from a distinctive apocalyptic perspective … it is viewed in the light of a transcendent reality disclosed by the apocalypse." In short, this is the reality that is being revealed.[50] We also find a similar perspective on time. What is being revealed to the seer in real time is often referring to future events by means of symbols and images alluding to the past. This is done to emphasize that what one chooses today implies the outcome of one's future. This is often expressed through an eschatological perspective of prophecy. Apocalypticism and eschatological prophecy are genres of literary expression that the implied author assumes the implied reader understands and is able to make sense of.[51] This is particularly important to be aware of in encountering their extravagant and somewhat awkward symbolism from a perspective of narrative criticism, as it opens up the issue of intertextuality as well as the cultural range of meaning connected to what is being narrated.[52] This posits a hermeneutical challenge to us as modern readers not reading from this cultural or historical point of view. Furthermore, it provides a necessary exception to narrative criticism's fixation on the text itself being the sole proprietor of meaning. This way, meaning is embedded semantically to a world outside the text. We need to address this by identifying these possible allusions in order to get to the meaning assumed as "given" to the implied reader (see Section 2.5). Bearing in mind the vast number of allusions to the Hebrew Bible, along with possible intertestamental Judeo-Christian traditions regarding Satan, we must ask ourselves if it is possible to detect any of these traditions as implied in the characterization of Satan in the narrative itself. If so, it belongs to the point of view of the implied author.[53]

---

[50] Ibid., 41.
[51] As Michelle Fletcher has pointed out (Michelle Fletcher, "Apocalypse Noir: How Revelation Defined and Defied a Genre," in *The Book of Revelation: Currents in British Research on the Apocalypse*, ed. Garrick V. Allen, Ian Paul, and Simon P. Woodman, WUNT II/411 [Tübingen: Mohr Siebeck, 2015], 115–34, 115–21), the book of Revelation serves the function of both defining and defying the genre apocalyptic literature. According to her, the understanding of apocalyptic has grown out of a comparison of texts with Revelation but at the same time recognizing that Revelation itself lacks several of the key features shared by these other books (such as pseudonymity, vision interpretation, and narrative conclusion). It follows from this that the point of reference to the term "apocalyptic literature" should be approached and used with care. See also Russell S. Morton, *Recent Research on Revelation* (Sheffield: Sheffield Phoenix, 2014), 17–28. After a lengthy discussion of the various definitions of "apocalyptic" as a genre, Morton concludes that we should use the term "apocalypse" as "an indicator of visionary literature that is similar to Revelation. We must, however, be flexible in our understanding of what the term means as a genre definition" (ibid., 28).
[52] Powell refers to these as "symbols of ancestral vitality," which derive their meaning from earlier sources, and "symbols of cultural range," which "derive their meaning from the social and historical context of the real author and his or her community" (Powell, *What Is Narrative Criticism?*, 29).
[53] Even to a scholar explicitly dedicated to the principle of not to resorting to extratextual reconstructions such as W. Gordon Campbell, one still has to grapple with the allusions to the Hebrew Bible. Campbell refers to the Hebrew Bible as intertextual in nature to the book of Revelation. "The Old Testament serves as Revelation's sub-text from start to finish" and "it will frequently provide us with indispensable interpretive keys" (W. Gordon Campbell, *Reading Revelation: A Thematic Approach* [Cambridge: James Clarke, 2012], 29; see 22–9, 34).

2.3 Defining the Overarching Plot of Revelation

The book of Revelation is not a narrative about Satan. Its plot does not revolve around him. He is a secondary character existing only to further the plot for the protagonists, who are probably the believers of Asia Minor and/or Jesus. It is therefore important at this point to try to identify and define the main narrative plot if we are to make sense of the implied author's utilization of this character in the story. James L. Resseguie emphasizes an essential premise of literary criticism when stating, "A basic premise of a literary approach is the understanding that the work is a unified whole. The parts cannot be understood without understanding the whole."[54] This is really an explication of the basic principle of interpretation known as the hermeneutical circle: our understanding of the whole of the narrative affects our understanding of its individual parts, and vice versa. However, since I am not going to interpret every individual part of the text of Revelation, a preliminary explication of the main narrative plot will be of crucial value to my analysis of the individual texts concerning Satan. If we are to understand and perceive the book as a unified whole, my close readings will have to be governed by that organizing design. A Satan that does not fit the overarching storyline is likely to be a stranger to the implied author—a fictive Satan expected or invented by us as readers—most likely a result of eisegesis. This methodical rule will therefore be my hermeneutical razor, so to speak: a characteristic of Satan who is not present in or is a stranger to the text is an irrelevant one. Henry Ansgar Kelly's example of how the questionable identification of the Eden serpent in Revelation 12 became the dominant perspective of Satan in the patristic era serves as an exemplary warning of how later culturally contingent readings of a text may disrupt the meaning of the text itself (see Section 4.4.2.1).[55]

Alas, church history is full of examples of this kind of anachronistic or retrofitted reading. This is probably partly due to the secondary role Satan is assigned in almost every biblical text he appears in, and partly because the Devil usually does not figure that often at Sunday sermons, bible studies, or even lessons at seminaries of theology. Satan is beside the point at hand: salvation, the savior, and the saved. People are therefore pretty much left to themselves regarding his whereabouts, merits, characteristics, wits, and preoccupations. This is probably why we are not to be surprised by the ever growing number of incompatible presumptions about Satan over the course of history. Vivid examples of the symbiosis of folklore, congregational expectations, and clerical theology are Dante Alighieri's characterization of Satan in his *Divine Comedy* and the Satan of John Milton's *Paradise Lost* and eventually *Paradise Regained*.[56] The

---

[54] Resseguie, *The Revelation of John: A Narrative Commentary*, 17.
[55] Kelly, *Satan: A Biography*, 148–5, and *Satan in the Bible: God's Minister of Justice*, 133–7. The same point is made by Almond, *The Devil: A New Biography*, 34–5; and Maxwell-Stuart, *Satan: A Biography*, 27. (Although Maxwell-Stuart states that the Apocalypse certainly links the serpent with Satan, he also writes that "St Justin Martyr (died 165 AD) seems to have been the first to make the connection, and yet he does so in an offhand way which suggests that the notion was not his, but had been current for a while"; ibid., 27–8.)
[56] In the *Divine Comedy*, Inferno song 34, verse 28, Satan is referred to as "Lo 'mperador del doloroso regno"—the emperor of the painful kingdom. He is further portrayed as suffering, yet at the same time governing. He chews sinners with his three heads, later identified as Judas, Brutus, and Cassius, and he is equipped with six wings by which he creates three stormy winds that turn everything

protagonist chief torturer now enthroned in Hell is probably as far from the biblical testimony as we could get. Therefore, a strict focus on the text will be paramount in light of the numerous attributes, roles, and epithets attributed to him over history. Such attributions contribute to and broaden one's horizon of understanding, and inform the preconceptions and prejudgments that are brought forth in order to interpret the text. It is important to be aware of these in order to get to the other side—to the meaning embedded in the text itself. I want to know what this particular Satan looks like and to what purpose he serves in the text—this is my object of inquiry.

The book of Revelation is a book about suffering, endurance, and hope—hope that one day all of the horrors of this world will be eliminated. These themes repeatedly occur throughout the book:

Firstly, the main concern for the congregations in Asia Minor is to remain faithful to their belief in Christ while facing their ordeals. The tribulations of the congregations differ in nature, but they all seem to have the same purpose: they point to the same potential outcome, expressed by the returning formula toward the end of each message, attached with a promise of reward referring to the events described in the last two chapters of the book. The element of parenesis in the messages implies that the rewards require some effort to be pursued. From this we may infer a causal connection between the suffering/testing element of the message and the potential rewarding/punishing outcome: If you do *this* you will receive *that*. The result may go either way, depending on the recipients of the message. Hope is directly connected to the outcome of the endurance of suffering.

Secondly, in the three septets of Revelation 6–16, we read about the unfolding of the coming eschatological ordeal of the earth in detail. The purpose of this suffering is to test the endurance of the faithful, invoke repentance, and justify and unleash divine wrath. When reading about the seven seals (Rev 6:1–8:1), our attention is drawn to the implications that these activities must go on until the number of martyrs is completed (Rev 6:9–11). By the end of the ordeal this is accomplished and consolidated by the sealing of the foreheads of the servants of God—the ones who have come out of the great ordeal and are destined for the water of life (Rev 7:3, 13–17.) In chapters 8:2–11:19 we read about the seven trumpets. A recurring element in all three septets is the enabling, delimiting, and utilization of agents of suffering imposed and/or permitted by God upon humanity (see Section 4.2.2.2). Within the septets, we witness a progression and intensification in the severity of the ordeals imposed, from the seals via the trumpets to the bowls. In the case of the seven trumpets, they are described as worse than the seals, but even worse events are yet to come with the bowls of wrath (see Table 5 in Chapter 4). In Rev 9:20–21 we see an element of justification of the punishment and wrath at play:

> The rest of humankind who were not killed by these plagues did not repent from the work of their hands. They did not stop worshipping demons or idols of gold,

around him into ice (verses 46–52, 55–69.) In *Paradise Lost*, book 1, verses 670–98, we witness the building and establishing of the Pandemonium, Satan's parliament, followed by his enthronement of his "throne of royal state" described in the opening lines of book 2.

silver, bronze, stone or wood—which cannot see, hear or walk. And they did not repent from their murders, sorceries, fornication or thefts.

As many commentators have pointed out, the manner of suffering and their reported effect here probably echoes the tribulations of Pharaoh as narrated in Exod 7:14–12:51.[57] This allusion adds another element to the meaning of the tribulations of Revelation—they are meant to point to the glorification and magnification of God as well as to justify the suffering imposed upon the dwellers of the earth.[58] The response to these horrors divides the population of the earth in two (13:9–13). Those aligned with the dragon, the beast, and the prophet are in the end destined for the lake of fire, but the ones who conquer in the face of suffering and death will inherit the new heaven and earth (21:6–8). This sifting of people is the main purpose of the eschatological ordeal and seems to be the governing principle of the entire narrative.

Thirdly, in the last sections of the book we read about how these elements of suffering, endurance, and hope are woven together in a semi-dualistic taxonomy: the final battle contrasting the followers of Christ/God and those of the dragon/beasts (Rev 16:12–16; 19:11–21; 20:7–10); the judgment of the world separating those written in the book of life from the dwellers of the earth (20:4–6, 11–15); and the establishing of the two contrasting cosmological destinations separating the inhabitants of the new heaven and earth from those of the lake of fire (21:7–8). The outcome of the eschatological ordeal thereby determines what category the congregations of Asia Minor will be given. The single most important question in the narrative is therefore this: Who will remain faithful to Christ unto death, and who will give in to the pressure of temptation and chaos (21:6–8; 22:11–15)?

The sifting of humankind by means of inflicted tribulation seems from this to form the overarching narrative plot of the book. This is my starting point, from which I intend to deduce the characteristics of Satan; the point of view from which I seek to find and consider his role; and the plot in which I am to understand the individual texts referring to him. If I am correct in assuming some sort of tension in the characteristics and roles assigned to Satan in Revelation, I suspect that analyzing their respective relation to this overarching plot will be the best way to make sense of this. This approach goes both ways, as the individual parts of the narrative in total both contribute to and are governed by the overarching plot. The overarching plot as tentatively defined here will therefore be continuously revised in light of the results of the close readings of the individual texts along the way, whenever the interpretations of the texts in question deem it necessary.

---

[57] David E. Aune, *Revelation 6–16*, WBC 52B (Nashville: Thomas Nelson, 1998), 499–507; Robert H. Mounce, *The Book of Revelation*, NICNT (Grand Rapids, MI: Eerdmans, 1977), 188 and 291–2; Beale, *The Book of Revelation*, 465–7 and 808–12; Stephen S. Smalley, *The Revelation to John: A Commentary on the Greek Text of the Apocalypse* (London: Society for Promoting Christian Knowledge, 2005), 398–9; Osborne, *Revelation*, 339–40; and Koester, *Revelation*, 445–7.

[58] According to Exod 14:17–18, this is something that Yahweh is doing partly as an act of self-presentation:

> I (Yahweh) will glorify myself (niphal) in Pharaoh and all his army, by all of his chariots and by all of his horsemen." Moreover, "The Egyptians will know that I am Yahweh when I glorify myself in Pharaoh, and his chariots and his horsemen.

2.4 Text Selection

Texts explicitly mentioning the term ὁ Σατανᾶς, the Greek rendering of the Hebrew שָׂטָן, and its Greek equivalent ὁ διάβολος will be the main texts of my analysis. The term ὁ Σατανᾶς and/or ὁ διάβολος can be found in the following texts: the message to the congregation of Smyrna, 2:8–11; Pergamum, 2:12–17; Thyatira, 2:18–29; Philadelphia, 3:7–13; the story of the woman, the dragon, and the war in heaven, 12:1–12; and Satan imprisoned and released, followed by the siege of the beloved city, and the lake of fire, 20:1–10. These will be my primary texts of analysis.

However, the Satan of the book of Revelation has many names and epithets, and if the purpose of the analysis is to find his function in the overall structure of the book, one must take into consideration that there might be more relevant texts involving him beside the texts only referring to him by his primary epithets. Thus, texts indicating an obvious relationship to this character or his function in the plot must be taken into consideration. These will be my secondary texts of analysis.

Several texts seem to fit this second category:

Firstly, although there is explicit mentioning of Satan in only four of the seven messages to the congregations, their common structural pattern, their common themes, and their compositional link to the other parts of the book indicate that the messages to the congregations of Ephesus, Sardis, and Laodicea may also contribute to our understanding. If Gregory K. Beale is right in his assumption that "relationships cohere between the body of the letters and the visionary body of the book" and that "it is in this sense that we can call the letters the literary microcosm of the entire book's macrocosmic structure," then it is plausible that there is a correspondence in theme, function, and purpose between messages mentioning Satan and those that do not.[59] For instance, the Devil will imprison some of the members of the congregation of Smyrna to put them through a test of fidelity (2:10). Another aspect of this testing is mentioned in 3:10 to the congregation of Sardis, yet they will be spared from this hour of trial that God, not the Devil, will send to test the dwellers of the earth. In the message to Thyatira the heretical teachings of Jezebel, referred to as "the depths of Satan," are the very things to abstain from in order to prove one's fidelity (2:24–25). Moreover, in the message to Laodicea, we read that God rebukes and disciplines the ones he loves (3:19). If the messages to the seven congregations follow a common structural and thematic blueprint and share a common relationship to the overarching plot of the narrative, then the non-Devil/Satan texts speak of the same phenomenon seen from the same perspective as the Devil/Satan texts.

Secondly, a key text in identifying other secondary texts is Rev 12:7–12. Here Satan is referred to as (1) ὁ δράκων ὁ μέγας (the great dragon), (2) ὁ ὄφις ὁ ἀρχαῖος (the ancient serpent), (3) ὁ καλούμενος Διάβολος καὶ ὁ Σατανᾶς (the one called the Devil and Satan), (4) ὁ πλανῶν τὴν οἰκουμένην ὅλην (the one leading the whole world astray), and (5) ὁ κατήγωρ τῶν ἀδελφῶν ἡμῶν (the accuser of our brothers). This text connects Satan to a wide array of titles and characteristics with clear allusions to the

---

[59] Beale, *The Book of Revelation*, 224.

Hebrew Bible assumed familiar to the implied reader—hence, no explanation or further description is given. Each of these titles, epithets, and descriptions must be taken into consideration in order to decipher how they contribute to the characterization of Satan. The epithet ὁ δράκων clearly connects Satan as a dragon to the story of the two beasts in chapter 13. This makes the text of chapter 13 highly relevant to my reading, even though the very name of Satan is not mentioned in it.

Thirdly, the dragon/beast that is given its powers and impact from God in chapter 13 is characterized as closely related to Babylon/Rome in chapters 17–18. The association of Babylon/Rome with Satan might shed light on the reasons for this massive political, economic, and religious critique of the Roman Empire (Rev 13; 17–19:8).[60] The vision of God's rule and justice in chapter 4 is the antithesis to the vain self-proclaimed grandeur of the Roman Empire.[61] The faith in the one true God is presented as being incompatible with allegiance to Rome. On the matter, Richard Bauckham comments, "It is a critique which makes Revelation the most powerful piece of political resistance literature from the period of the early Empire."[62] The implied reader is to resist the urge to give in to this tempting/threatening benefactor/malefactor. The connection of Rome to Satan and his activities adds to the element of temptation/test (πειρασμός).

When comparing the primary texts (2:8–11, 12–17, 18–29; 3:7–13; 12:7–9; and 20:1–10) to the secondary texts (2:1–7; 3:1–6, 14–22; 12–13; and 17–18) one notices that most of the secondary texts are located in the same narrative text units as the primary texts. It therefore makes sense to group the material in the same textual units for analysis, and not to treat them as separate entities. This leaves us with the structuring of relevant texts as shown in Table 1.

The primary texts will be my main object of interpretation. The secondary texts will be interpreted as relevant literary context to the primary texts with the notable exception of Rev 12:1–6 and 13:1–18. In Rev 12:9 and 20:2 the dragon is explicitly identified as Satan, thus making Revelation 12–13 in its entirety a primary text in light of the scope of this reading.

The three analytical chapters are limited by the scope of this reading: the narrative function of Satan as derived from his role in the plot, characterization, and point of view. This analysis will be a constant back-and-forth movement from the individual

---

[60] For the idea of locating the primary reason for the critique of the Roman Empire in the political, economic, and religious sphere rather than in the persecution of Christians in Asia Minor, see Bauckham, *The Theology of the Book of Revelation*, 35–41.

[61] The extent to which the heavenly throne room in Revelation mirrors the Roman imperial court is vast and, according to Stephen D. Moore, seldom pursued to its fullest extent by modern exegetes (Stephen D. Moore, "Hypermasculinity and Divinity," in *A Feminist Companion to the Apocalypse of John*, ed. Amy-Jill Levine and Maria Mayo Robbins [New York: T&T Clark International, 2009], 180–204, 186–92). Moore suggests that the reason for downplaying these traits of characterization could be found in the tensions occurring in a reading where the solution to the problems of the oppressed is found in a force mirroring the problem itself: "And yet the theology or ideology of Revelation is anything but simple inversion, reversal or renunciation of the political and social ideology of imperial Rome. Instead it represents the apotheosis of this imperial ideology, its ascension to a transhistorical site" (ibid., 186–7). This way, the violence, grandeur, and awesome might of the God of Revelation become comforting to the narratées and serves, perhaps, as a necessary companion to the exhortation to follow the example of the Lamb in nonviolent resistance unto the pain of death. See Section 5.2.2 for a discussion of the purpose of the violent imagery of Revelation.

[62] Bauckham, *The Theology of the Book of Revelation*, 38.

Table 1 Text Selection

Primary texts	Secondary texts	Textual units for analysis
2:8–29; 3:7–13	2:1–7; 3:1–6, 14–22	2–3
12:7–12	12:1–6; 13:1–18	12–13
20:1–10	19:11–21 17–18	20

analysis of each text in question to the overarching plot, continuously proceeding in a mutual converging hermeneutical spiral.

2.5 Excursus: The Use of Extratextual References in Narrative Criticism

The study of a text as a self-referential aesthetic object is a principle inherited by New Criticism from formalism. It represented an uprising against the practice of the historical hermeneutical approach of its time. Extratextual focus such as authorial intent and audience reception was considered a distraction from the text itself. The assumed external factors could end up governing, and possibly sidetracking, the very understanding of the text. To avoid this, the author and the reader were cut off from the interpretational enterprise altogether. The intentional and affective fallacies were thus considered by some to be avoided at all cost within New Criticism. Yet, giving up the quest for the alleged historical intentions and reception of a work did not involve ignoring every extratextual aspect of a text. This excursus intends to argue first that such considerations have been made all along during the evolution of this branch of literary theory and, second, to propose a method of applying such considerations within narrative criticism.

The terms *the intentional fallacy* and *the affective fallacy* originated in the essays of the same names per se, written by William K. Wimsatt and Monroe C. Beardsley, within the context of an argument for the return to the text and its words as the focal point of interpretation. In the essay "The Intentional Fallacy," they divide the evidence used in making interpretations of a poem into three categories: internal evidence, external evidence, and intermediate evidence.[63] The third category refers to the information assumed known to the reader and may prove important to the critic in his interpretation of the poem: "The use of biographical evidence need not involve intentionalism, because while it may be evidence of what the author intended, it may also be evidence of the meaning of his words and the dramatic character of his utterance."[64] Thus, to grasp the meaning of the words in a poem, one occasionally has to implement this third category in order to be able to interpret the words within the text by utilizing information from outside the text. By noticing this precaution

---

[63] William K. Wimsatt and Monroe C. Beardsley, "The Intentional Fallacy," *Sewanee Review* 54 (1946): 468–88, 477–9.
[64] Ibid., 478.

already present within the early stages of New Criticism, one is not surprised to find the phenomenon of extratextual considerations present in a later development of formalism and New Criticism, namely narratology.[65] Despite being equally fond of viewing the text as the sole proprietor of meaning as their predecessors, narratologists too must take into consideration what Mieke Bal refers to as the "so-called extratextual situation."[66] On the one hand, she sets out to restrict any investigation of character not presented to us in the actual text in order to avoid any form of flattening of characters due to preconceived expectations.[67] On the other hand, she has to admit that the issue has to be addressed at some point, since this element of constructing an image of character may contribute significantly to its meaning. It is in regarding these matters that she writes the following:

> The so-called extratextual situation creates yet another ambiguity. This concerns the influence of reality on the story, in so far as reality plays a part in it. Even if we do not wish to study the relations between text and context as a separate object of analysis, we cannot ignore the fact that direct or indirect knowledge of the context of certain characters contributes significantly to their meaning … The influence of data from reality is all the more difficult to determine since the personal situation, knowledge, background, historical moment, and so on of the reader are involved here.[68]

She urges to include rather than censure or ignore such elements in the text. It is important to do so in order to be able to discuss them with insight, which in the end may benefit the analysis. It is also important not to take such frames of reference at face value. Even if an expectation is evoked from the occurrence of a historical name, or the mentioning of social conventions of its time, within the narrative, it still is the text as it is written that determines if this expectation is met or not. It is therefore equally important to pay attention to *how* the narrative makes use of these extratextual components, as to acknowledge their presence.[69]

---

[65] For a convenient clarification on the relation between the terms "New Criticism," "new formalism," "narratology," and "narrative criticism," I am indebted to Andy Chambers and his book, *Exemplary Life: A Theology of Church Life in Acts* (Nashville, TN: B&H, 2012), 23–5. On the difference between the latter two, he states, "Although narratology and narrative criticism are closely related, they differ at an important point. Both seek to understand narrative texts, but narratology is more concerned with developing theories of how narratives work, while narrative criticism uses the theories of narratologists in the work of exegesis" (ibid., 25).

[66] Mieke Bal, *Narratology: Introduction to the Theory of Narrative*, 3rd ed. (Toronto: University of Toronto Press, 2009), 119.

[67] Ibid., 114.

[68] Ibid., 119.

[69] According to Steve Moyise, a work attuned to allusions and scriptural echoes "must do more than simply point out their presence, for an allusion is not simply a footnote to a previous work. By absorbing words used in one context into a new context or configuration, a metaphorical relationship is established" (Moyise, *The Old Testament in the Book of Revelation*, 110). This metaphorical relationship carries meaning from its source text by "bleeding over" the new work, a terminology derived from Richard B. Hays and his *Echoes of Scripture in the Letters of Paul* (ibid., 115). Moyise concludes his chapter on Revelation and intertextuality by quoting Harriet Davidson when stating, "Meaning in Revelation 'is in the tension between its previous contextual definition and its present

This means that for both new critics and narratologists, it is possible and sometimes necessary to confer with the world outside the text in order to understand the meaning within the text. This is not considered a devaluation of the autonomy of the text or a relapse into the intentional or affective fallacy. It is a prerequisite to being able to understand the text in a meaningful way. It should therefore be of no surprise to find the same precautions at work within narrative criticism as it is a development of these two strands of literary theory applied on biblical exegesis. In fact, restricting one's literary analysis only to the text itself has over the years been challenged within narrative criticism on the grounds of the danger of missing out on essential meaning within the narrative by neglecting the possibility of implied extratextual references.[70] The use of symbolism, allusions, and metaphors within a narrative is of special concern in these matters since occurrences of such elements in a text presuppose knowledge assumed known to the implied reader regarding their meaning. They could, on the one hand, derive their meaning from either a universally accepted context (shepherds as caretakers and light as opposition to darkness) and/or from within the narrative itself. Given that a universally accepted context of meaning two thousand years ago is the same as today, these categories could readily be interpreted within the narrative as a self-contained unit. Yet if, on the other hand, their referential meaning is derived from the social and historical context of the real author, his or her community, or earlier sources, then their meaning cannot be found within the narrative itself.[71] It is an assumed known reference within the text, signifying an object external to the text. By restricting ourselves to only the text in itself, we are thus in danger of ignoring the meaning and thereby the function of the word at stake, simply because its meaning is regarded by the narrative itself as given. According to Mark Allen Powell, this is where historical criticism and narrative criticism cross paths: "If modern critics are to read the narratives as the implied reader they must at this point rely on insights gained from historical criticism."[72]

No text comes into existence within a void. Even though we read and interpret the text as an autonomous literary unit, it presumes the existence of other writings.[73] From

---

context'" (ibid., 138). It is in this tension that the question of the scope of this "bleeding over of connotations" presents itself.

[70] Powell, *What Is Narrative Criticism?*, 29, 97; Resseguie, *Narrative Criticism of the New Testament*, 29–30, and 32, 39; Resseguie, *The Revelation of John*, 18; Culpepper, *Anatomy of the Fourth Gospel*, 8–11; Darr, *On Character Building*, 17–23; Bennema, *A Theory of Character in New Testament Narrative*, 63–72; Barr, *Tales of the End*, 11–15; Grabiner, *Revelation's Hymns*, 16; David Rhoads, Joanna Dewey, and Donald Michie, *Mark as Story: An Introduction to the Narrative of a Gospel*, 2nd ed. (Minneapolis: Fortress, 1999), 5–6; Marguerat and Bourquin, *How to Read Bible Stories*, 106–11; Branden, *Satanic Conflict and the Plot of Matthew*, 9–10; Francis J. Moloney, *The Resurrection of the Messiah: A Narrative Commentary on the Resurrection Accounts in the Four Gospels* (New York: Paulist, 2013), x–xii; as well as several literary-oriented works on Revelation: Thomas, *The Apocalypse*, 16–17; Tonstad, *Saving God's Reputation*, 17–38; and Trafton, *Reading Revelation*, 3–13. The authors mentioned here do not restrict themselves to the text as a self-containing autonomous unit in their literary approach to the text, and several of them show no obligation to justify their hermeneutical choice of considering extratextual material in their interpretation.

[71] See Powell, *What Is Narrative Criticism?*, 29; and Philip Wheelwright, *Metaphor and Reality* (Bloomington: Indiana Fortress, 1962), 99–110.

[72] Powell, *What Is Narrative Criticism?*, 29.

[73] Zumstein, "Intratextuality and Intertextuality in the Gospel of John," 122.

this point of view, it is possible to construct an implied reader from such extratextual elements by pointing to the fact that the text assumes this information known to the reader it has in mind. From the book of Revelation, we may deduce a reader well acquainted with certain books of the Hebrew Bible. This follows from the numerous allusions to this particular tradition within the narrative itself. The point of reference remains outside the narrative, yet the utilization of it can only be derived from an analysis of the narrative in which it is found. If narrative analysis is performed in order to fully appreciate the meaning expressed within a narrative, this meaning depends in such cases on the consideration of the external contribution in the occurrence of allusions, as well as of symbolism, irony, and intertextual references.[74] In close readings of biblical narratives, the issue becomes particularly evident, due to the fact that these writings seem to be more or less governed by theological presuppositions typical of their culture of provenance. The ignorance of literary criticism to the benefits of historical criticism and the historical nature of the Gospel of John is one of R. Alan Culpepper's objections to the venture of narrative criticism.[75] He suggests the necessity and fruitfulness of both approaches to the text. According to Culpepper, to a literary critic:

> Appeals to general historical considerations regarding the age of the story, the culture it assumes, and the meaning of the words with which it is told are, of course, necessary if one is to understand the dynamics of the narrative, but using historical data as aids to interpretation is quite different from using the gospel story for historical reconstruction.[76]

To Culpepper, then, these considerations are "of course, necessary," and I agree. If not taken into consideration, such presuppositions within the narrative may, in some cases, prevent the interpreter from understanding the narrative as implied by the author.

In his book *A Theory of Character in New Testament Narrative*, Cornelis Bennema suggests a possible explanation for why we are dependent on extratextual knowledge in interpreting New Testament narratives as well as how this can be resolved hermeneutically. According to him, ancient characterization is often indirect as well as sparse, leaving gaps for the reader to fill by inference from the text in order to reconstruct character.[77] Such a reconstruction of character through "filling the gaps," an idea derived from the works of Wolfgang Iser and Robert Alter, should be

---

[74] A narrative analysis with and without such considerations will, in my opinion, arrive at different meanings regarding the interpretation of such elements. James L. Resseguie proves this point in an excellent way in his close reading of Vincent van Gogh's "The Good Samaritan" (Resseguie, *Narrative Criticism of the New Testament*, 26–30).

[75] Culpepper, *Anatomy of the Fourth Gospel*, 8–11.

[76] Ibid., 11.

[77] The idea of viewing construction of character as a continuous, accumulative, and cognitive activity "on the basis of a constant back-and-forth movement between specific textual data and general knowledge structures stored in the reader's long-term memory" (Uri Margolin, "Character," in *The Cambridge Companion to Narrative*, ed. David Herman [Cambridge: Cambridge University Press, 2007], 66–79, 78) is derived from studies on the cognitive dimensions of narrative, and seems to support the approach suggested by Bennema.

governed not by arbitrary whims on the part of the modern reader but by knowledge from the first-century world—the world of the text.[78] Thus, "knowledge of the social and cultural environment of the New Testament is essential for understanding the personality, motive, and behavior of ancient characters."[79] It is the nonfictional nature of New Testament narratives that merits the need to occasionally go beyond the text for the reconstruction of character. They are nonfictional because they refer to real events and people in history.[80] "This means we can fill the gaps in the narrative from our knowledge of the sociohistorical context of the first-century Mediterranean world (rather than our imagination.)"[81] Texts from this period will therefore be able to supplement the data from the text about the character. In nonfictional narratives there is continuity between reality and the narrative world. Since the narrative claims to refer to the real world, any reconstruction of character "shared" with this world in the narrative should be established on the grounds of textual evidence within the narrative with gaps filled in with relevant information from the real world referred to. To prevent some form of eisegetic reconstruction of character, Bennema suggests that when doing so "we must be careful that the character we reconstruct is in keeping with the particular perspective of the author."[82]

What extratextual material one should take into consideration depends on what kind of reader one assumes from the text: what kind of sources the author assumes for the intended audience. When a plausible explanation is given for the ancient sources assumed known to the implied reader, then the main enterprise of Bennema, the reconstruction of characters, may commence. The reconstruction of characters must primarily be based upon information found within the narrative itself. After this is done, one proceeds to fill in the remaining gaps with fitting material from the assumed

---

[78] Bennema, *A Theory of Character in New Testament Narrative*, 56; Robert Alter, *The Art of Biblical Narrative*, rev. ed. (New York: Basic Books, 2011), chapter 6; and Wolfgang Iser, "The Reading Process: A Phenomenological Approach," *New Literary History* 3, no. 2 (1972): 279–99, 284–5. The implications of these "whims" of the modern reader seem fittingly described by H. Porter Abbott when writing about how the world we live in, including history, plays a part in the made-up worlds of fiction: "But, uncorrected, we will nevertheless bring our understanding of history into the novel ... Our ideas may be correct or incorrect or just plain nuts; our feelings may be justified or unjustified; but they are, nonetheless, important features of our 'own experiential reality,' to use Ryan's phrase, and *they can flood the gaps of fictional narrative*" (H. Porter Abbott, *The Cambridge Introduction to Narrative* [Cambridge: Cambridge University Press, 2008], 152 [my italics]).

[79] Bennema, *A Theory of Character in New Testament Narrative*, 62.

[80] Even if we consider Jesus as only a literarily constructed character, as opposed to a historical figure, the principle remains valid because his character is a presupposed public point of reference and thereby assumed known to the implied reader. We witness the same phenomenon in motion when picking up a copy of a sequel of a known novel, say *Don Quixote Part 2* or *Harry Potter and the Chamber of Secrets*, or watching films in the James Bond movie franchise. A sequel points to a point of reference outside itself, usually to its predecessor, and is thereby free to omit a great deal of information on its characters. It is an elaboration on the universe of characters that is presumed known to its readers. In the scriptural tradition of the Bible, the authors theologically contribute to and elaborate on the salvific history of God. To the individual book of the Bible, this object of which they are elaborating is an extratextual reference assumed known to its reader. On the idea of carrying descriptions of literary figures over from one text to another, see Uri Margolin on the different approaches to this phenomenon in Margolin, "Character," 69–70.

[81] Bennema, *A Theory of Character in New Testament Narrative*, 63.

[82] Ibid., 65.

sources and/or the sociocultural climate of the first-century world. The result from this character reconstruction will be a character that fits realistically into the first-century world but is at the same time one viewed from a particular perspective—one who can be compared to other portrayals of the same character.[83] Bennema finds support in several important works of narrative criticism for such an abandonment of the idea of the narrative as an autonomous story world comprehensible to us when detached from its sociocultural context.[84] From these works and by the logic of his argument, he suggests we are witnessing an important shift in narrative criticism. As an alternative, he suggests we turn to "a form of *historical narrative criticism* that takes a text-centered approach but examines aspects of the world outside or 'behind' the text if the text invites us to do so."[85] With the terminology of Ferdinand de Saussure, one may say that in order to grasp the significance of the signifiers within a narrative, one must always strive to understand the system in which the signifiers take place—even if this occasionally takes us outside the text itself. The connotations between signifier and its significance can and must fully be addressed because language itself breeds a plethora of meaning. Even without the point origin of each word, we need to locate a destination in terms of possible meanings. As Roland Barthes wrote in his now famous essay "The Death of the Author," "it is language which speaks, not the author; to write is, through a prerequisite impersonality (not at all to be confused with the castrating objectivity of the realist novelist), to reach that point where only language acts, 'performs,' and not 'me.' "[86] This language is at our disposal in our hermeneutical enterprises, even if the author is not, and remains our object of scrutiny—to unravel its web of signified meaning.

This excursus has argued that the element of extratextual consideration is not entirely new within literary theory, and it has been regarded as a "given" by prominent scholars in works of narrative criticism, and can be seen at work throughout the evolving stages of this particular branch of literary theory. Still, the aversion to extratextual considerations within narrative criticism has proven to be a common and recurring misunderstanding among biblical scholars, especially among those not working themselves within this field of research. However, in the following, I will write and argue by applying narrative criticism open to extratextual considerations in the manner described in this chapter.

---

[83] Ibid., 72.
[84] Ibid., 62–7.
[85] Ibid., 67.
[86] Roland Barthes, "The Death of the Author," in *The Norton Anthology of Theory & Criticism*, ed. Vincent B. Leitch et al., 2nd ed. (New York: W. W. Norton, 2010), 1322–6, 1323.

3

Satan in the Messages to the Seven Congregations

3.1 Introduction

According to Craig Koester and Gregory K. Beale, the messages to the seven congregations function as a microcosm of the larger narrative of the book of Revelation.[1] The section on the congregations provides the reader with an earthly point of reference to the largely otherworldly visionary section of Revelation 4–22. This way they constitute the literary *Sitz im Leben*—the frame of reference of the visionary material of the rest of the book. The implications of such a hermeneutical premise can hardly be overstated, as by constituting a literary context for the visionary material, it is narrowing down the range of exegetical options. In short: what happens in the messages to the congregations relates directly to what happens in the macrocosm of Revelation 4–22, and what happens in the latter in turn elaborates the circumstances of the former. It is an argument of this reading that the semi-dualistic cosmology of chapters 4–22 is clearly meant to provide leverage to the parenesis of chapters 2–3.[2]

The argument for such a hermeneutical premise is in part derived from the focalization of the narrative, "the lens through which we see characters and events in the narrative."[3] Section 3.2 explores this argument as it consists of an analysis of how we come to know about the seven congregations through a multilayered mode of communication embedded in the literary frame of the letters.

The literary form and function of the seven messages and how they relate to the rest of the narrative is the object of examination in Section 3.3. This section will add further weight to the hermeneutical presupposition outlined above, as the problems, themes, and characters of the messages reappear several times in the book. Satan is one of these characters reappearing throughout the narrative, and the identification of him

---

[1] Beale, *The Book of Revelation*, 224; see also Koester, *Revelation*, 231.
[2] Even if the source-critical analyses of David E. Aune and Pierre Prigent diverge from the methodological premises of this reading, their line of argumentation for perceiving the messages to the congregations as later additions to the earlier written main body of the book (approximately Rev 4:1–22:5) emphasizes their close relation to the rest of the book precisely because of their purpose of providing the reader with a hermeneutical aid, altering the reading of the allegedly older components. See Aune, *Revelation 1–5*, cxx–cxxii, cxxxii–cxxxiv; Prigent, *Commentary on the Apocalypse of St. John*, 84–5, 149–51.
[3] Abbott, *The Cambridge Introduction to Narrative*, 73.

in this mirroring relation between the messages to the congregations and the visionary material is thus paramount.

Finally, in Section 3.4 I will analyze the seven messages in search of the narrative function of Satan by means of his relation to the plot, the way he is characterized, and how he is presented as perceived from the various points of view.

In the concluding remarks, I will sum up the findings of the analysis and try to define the narrative function of Satan in this hermeneutical microcosm. This will, in turn, be the context, the point of reference, in light of which the Satan of the rest of the book will be interpreted.

3.2 The Literary Frame of the Messages

When reading the messages to the seven congregations, one quickly observes that it is not part of a straightforward narrative. Someone is writing about someone telling someone to write something to someone. This structure reveals a rather complicated line of communication and the function of this process turns out to be of great importance to this reading since among the things being communicated we find the character of Satan.

As we will see, the different characters of Revelation interact across several levels of discourse.[4] I will map out this comprehensive scheme of focalization before analyzing the central part of this process, namely the messages to the seven congregations.

The narrative complexity of this section sets the messages to the seven congregations apart from the other texts of this reading in that they are not by definition directly driven by actions reported by a third-person narrator alone but also involve the main action being an action as discourse: it is at the center of what is narrated that we find the messages. It is a one-way line of communication consisting of a series of instructions advocating certain kinds of behavior among the members of the congregations, which in turn makes it a monologue of indirect speech act (commanding, exhorting, and warning, by proxy).[5] The whole scene takes the form of a dictate, while the rest of the book, including chapters 12-14 and 20-21, is formed as visions described by a first-person narrator. This point of view is stressed repeatedly throughout the book by the recurring formulaic expression καὶ εἶδον.[6]

Moreover, it is a narrative about a speech act within a speech act: John writes about Jesus instructing him to write to the seven congregations. Together with the prologue (1:1-8) and epilogue (22:6-21), the epistolary introduction (1:9-19) constitutes an

---

[4] I use the term "discourse" as defined by Daniel Marguerat and Yvan Bourquin: "Modern narratology arose out of this distinction between the 'what' of the narrative, what is called the *story*, and the way in which the story is told, which is called its *discourse* ... The discourse is the form given to the narrative by the narrator (narrativization), which in turn implies a choice of structure, style and disposition" (Marguerat and Bourquin, *How to Read Bible Stories*, 18).

[5] To use the nomenclature of speech acts theorist John Austin, these are illocutionary acts (the performance of the act in question), in turn constituting the overarching plot of the narrative with their embedded uncertainty of whether they will ever succeed in becoming perlocutionary acts (i.e., successful in light of their intent). See Chatman, *Story and Discourse*, 161-2.

[6] The phrase καὶ εἶδον is used about forty times in total throughout the book.

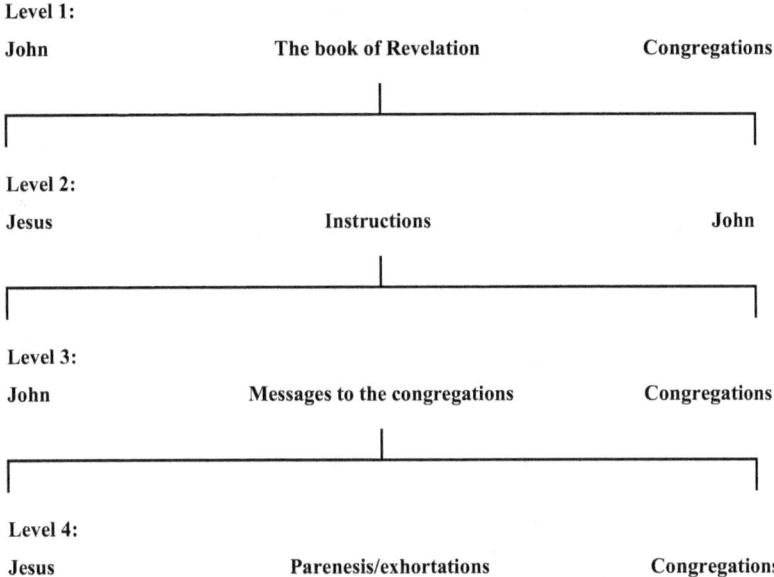

Figure 2 The diegetic levels of the messages to the seven congregations

inclusio that brackets the material in between. This enveloping structure describes a local world and how it relates to the universal one within by mixing the action bearers of both worlds. The literary function of this may be a way of framing the narrative to provide hermeneutical guidelines for the material in between.[7] It is a revelation, *from* Jesus (1:1; 22:16),[8] mediated *to* the seven congregations (1:4, 11, 20 as well as the messages themselves) *by* a human, John (1:1, 4, 9; 22:8). The whole book is backed up by a plethora of heavenly beings, the most important of whom is God (1:8; 21:16).

This epistolary framing of the visionary material involves several diegetic levels (see Figure 2).[9] Diegetic level 1, the book of Revelation in its entirety, involves narrator and his narratées, who due to the epistolary framework of the book are named and identified as John (1:1, 4, 9; 22:18) and the seven congregations (1:4, 11; 22:16). This is the level

---

[7] On framing narratives and examples of this in New Testament narratives, see Resseguie, *Narrative Criticism of the New Testament*, 54–6.
[8] On the translation of Ἀποκάλυψις Ἰησοῦ Χριστοῦ as subjective genitive rather than objective, see Beale, *The Book of Revelation*, 183; Koester, *Revelation*, 211; Aune, *Revelation 1–5*, 6; and Osborne, *Revelation*, 52. The narrative commentaries Resseguie, *The Revelation of John*, 62–3, and Barr, *Tales of the End*, 3–5, also side with such a reading, although they downplay the relevance of the distinction in that Christ is not only the medium of revelation but also plays a considerable role in what is being revealed.
[9] Plato distinguished between two ways of presenting a story. Diegesis refers to the telling of a story, whereas mimesis refers to acting/showing (Abbott, *The Cambridge Introduction to Narrative*, 75 and 231).

where the narration takes place, as distinguished from the story world, the visionary world, being narrated here.[10] This makes John the first-person narrator, and thus by his explicit identification an overt narrator—he is made known through the narrative and is thereby not hidden in the text.[11] Furthermore, the fact that John himself takes active part in what he is telling makes him what is called a homodiegetic narrator.[12] The seven congregations become his intrafictional addressee of the discourse—his narrated audience.[13] The story he writes to this narrated audience opens up a deeper, diegetic level of communication. This is what Mieke Bal refers to as the hypodiegetic level.[14] The transition in narration happens in 1:9, when the narrator begins to report what he saw and heard to his readers and listeners (1:3 tells us that the content of this book is to be read aloud). A part of this vision is the voice from one ὅμοιον υἱὸν ἀνθρώπου (one like the son of man, 1:13), who instructs John to write a message. The message itself can be considered as yet another hypodiegetic level—another story within the story. These levels actively relate to one another. The message in level 4 that stems from the voice of level 2 is obviously meant to communicate with the congregations of John of level 1 (1:4). In narratology, such an occurrence of multiple narrative levels such as this is referred to as multiple framing.[15]

Framing parenesis and hortatory material by ascribing it to the divine realm like this is a literary device well known from the commission narratives of the Hebrew Bible (cf. Exodus 3; Isaiah 6; Jeremiah 1) and a recurring element in other apocalyptic writings (cf. Daniel 7; 1 En. 60:1–6; Jub. 1:1–7; 4 Ezra 13:1–4; 14–25). Related to this is the constant interruption from the narrator in his own narrative. His first-person formulations in between the visionary material serve as a reminder to his narrated audience of the transcendental mode of revelation. This turns the framing narrative on diegetic level 2 into what is usually referred to as an interpolated frame.[16] This seems to be a recurring and organizing element of the narrative of Revelation. The element of interruption repeatedly appears throughout the book and adds gravity to the plot. It is an explication of the spatial point of view, the above–below element, which is by many regarded as a typical feature of apocalyptic literature.[17] This serves as a reminder of the origin of revelation, and it is an efficient rhetorical move, enforcing the parenesis of the message. This presentation of the book of Revelation

---

[10] For this distinction of the world of narration and story, see Abbott, *The Cambridge Introduction to Narrative*, 169–70. This level is by some referred to as the extradiegetic level (Fludernik, *An Introduction to Narratology*, 100).

[11] According to Monika Fludernik, "an *overt narrator* is one that can be clearly seen to be telling the story" (Fludernik, *An Introduction to Narratology*, 21). For the distinction between overt and covert narrators, see Chatman, *Story and Discourse*, 33, as well as chapter 5.

[12] The term "homodiegetic" was introduced by Gérard Genette to refer to narration coming from a character in the story world. See Abbott, *The Cambridge Introduction to Narrative*, 75.

[13] See Fludernik, *An Introduction to Narratology*, 23.

[14] "Hypodiegetic level" is Mieke Bal's term used to refer to the story told on the intradiegetic level of the narrative (Fludernik, *An Introduction to Narratology*, 100).

[15] Fludernik, *An Introduction to Narratology*, 28–9.

[16] On interpolated frames, see ibid.

[17] John J. Collins (*The Apocalyptic Imagination*, 6–7) and David Syme Russell (*Divine Disclosure*, 12) both agree with the SBL Genres Project (published in *Semeia* 14, 1979) and its definition of Apocalypse, which acknowledges the spatial element to be a defining feature of the genre.

as an authoritative, true, and trustworthy revelation of heavenly origins is part of what Adela Yarbro Collins describes as the most fundamental technique that underlies and reinforces all the other narrative techniques used to evoke emotional effect—in this case to gain trust and attention to the message by rhetorical invitation to imaginative participation in the plot of the text.[18] Why should the congregation in Smyrna, or any of the seven congregations, listen to this message? Because the source of revelation, one like a son of man, the first and the last, the living one, who was dead but is alive forever and ever (1:13, 17–18), Jesus (1:1; 22:16), instructed John to write *this* down to the congregations (1:11; 22:16). "This" refers to the individual message itself, and it is here we find the narrative landscape where Satan occurs as a character.

The following analysis of the focalization of the seven messages reveals several important issues for this reading, both to the analysis of the septet in itself, as well as to the book in its entirety:

Firstly, this mode of communication bears cosmological implications by characterizing God as the architect of history through the close relation between Christ and God (1:1, a relation that will be emphasized in Revelation 4–5; see Section 4.2.1 of this reading). God knows the current situation of the congregations, which in turn prompts the revelation by his son and prophet revealing what he is about to unleash upon the earth and accompanied by an elaborate description of how they should respond to this. Satan is one of the elements being unleashed and one that the congregations are to endure. Secondly, by revealing God as the origin of the messages, this establishes the evaluative point of view of the messages as his point of view, and thereby the preferred course of action for the narratées and implied reader. Thus, the way God views Satan is the way the congregation also should view him. Thirdly, if God is the guarantor of the rewards and punishments of the messages, this strengthens the rhetorical force of the narrative. Furthermore, this element also involves the point of view that as God is the one vouching for the rewards/punishments, he is also characterized as fully in control of their manner of impact. This includes Satan, as he is characterized in the messages as both punishment and intended obstacle on the path toward rewards in the messages. Fourthly, the casting of Christ as the messenger of God by the utilization of first-person perspective, the designation "revelation of Jesus Christ" (Rev 1:1), and Christ partaking in the knowledge, plans, and actions of God heighten the Christology of the book. When reading these elements in light of the worship of the Lamb (5:9–14), the role of Christ is elevated from mere divine agency to a more sovereign position in the cosmological hierarchy of the book. If Satan is characterized as a negative form of divine agency, which is the argument of this reading, then Christ is cast in a superior role to that. Fifthly, the focalization of the messages is also the introduction of the book in its entirety. Thus, the issues emphasized here will also be true of the other texts being analyzed in this reading.

---

[18] Adela Yarbro Collins, "The Power of Apocalyptic Rhetoric—Catharsis," in *The Revelation of St. John the Divine*, ed. Harold Bloom (New York: Chelsea House, 1988), 73–94, 77.

3.3 The Literary Form and Function of the Messages

According to David E. Aune, "There is now widespread agreement that the seven proclamations never existed independently of Revelation, but were designed specifically for their present literary setting by the author-editor at a final stage in the composition of the entire work."[19] This is a good observation relevant to my narrative endeavor, despite the significant differences in nature between the source-critical analysis of Aune and narrative critical readings, because several aspects of the literary form/structure of chapters 2–3 seem to indicate a deliberate function rather than arbitrariness. Revelation 2–3 cannot be treated separately, apart from the visionary body of the book, because they are too closely interwoven. The messages relate directly to the main body of the narrative as they introduce the reader to images and themes more fully developed and elaborated there.[20] A comparative analysis of the seven messages reveals a sandwiching of what appears to be individual prophetic oracles between a formulaic epistolary framework common for all of the seven messages:[21]

1. The *adscriptio*—to whom this is written.
2. The command to write.
3. The τάδε λέγει (this says) formula.
4. Christological predications.
5. The *narratio*—a description of each community, introduced by οἶδα (I know), which serves as the basis for the following *dispositio* (response). The *dispositio*—contains the central argument of the messages—the reason for which they were written.
6. The proclamation formula.
7. Promise of victory.

Much could and have been said about this pattern, but I will limit my comments to what I perceive as particularly relevant to this reading. The first four components, along with the seventh, provide the reader with the necessary point of view: here we can see the different levels of diegesis mentioned earlier at work. We get relevant information on who says what to whom: *Jesus* instructing *John* to write *this* to a certain *congregation*. The *narratio* describes the status of current affairs in the congregation and forms the basis for the parenetical *dispositio*. Perhaps the most important part of this aspect is the stressing that God/Christ is fully aware of what is going on, a point made clear by the οἶδα introductions. This is probably meant to comfort and motivate the congregations in the midst of their ordeals, yet turns out to be threatening for those in the process of lapsing into social conformity through religious compromise.

---

[19] David E. Aune, *Apocalypticism, Prophecy, and Magic in Early Christianity: Collected Essays* (Grand Rapids, MI: Baker Academic, 2006), 213.
[20] See Prigent, *Commentary on the Apocalypse of St. John*, 150.
[21] I follow David E. Aune and his categorization of the seven stereotypical features of the seven congregations here. See Aune, *Revelation 1–5*, 119–24, and *Apocalypticism, Prophecy, and Magic in Early Christianity*, 214–23.

Several aspects of the form and function of the messages to the seven congregations suggest a more general audience than just the ones named in the septet per se. Moreover, their form and function connect the messages to the rest of the book in a way that carries important hermeneutical implications for my thesis. In the following, I will explain why and how. The epistolary form of the book, both as a whole (1:4–6; 22:6–21) and the individual messages per se, is a distinctive formal aspect that provides a personal, and perhaps communal (in light of the remark in 1:3), setting for what is to be revealed. David E. Aune refers to the seven messages as parenetic salvation-judgment oracles, a subdivision under the label Christian prophetic speech, due to the fact that "all of them exhibit a strong emphasis on moral and behavioral exhortation" as well as the implications of the τάδε λέγει formula related to the prophetic books of the Hebrew Bible.[22] In a later article, Aune states that "most of the constituent features of this form must be regarded as *optional elements* rather than as fixed formal characteristics."[23] He finds a probable blueprint for this particular case of early Christian prophecy in the form of ancient royal or imperial edicts.[24] This last point lifts the messages out from the more introvert perspective of the apocalyptic, prophetic, and epistolary genres, as edicts are considered formal and public in nature. This adds a more general aspect to the individually addressed oracles. Thus, the very structure of the messages to the seven congregations indicates that what is true for the individual congregation also seems to be true for the church, and perhaps humankind, in general. The form of imperial edict also lends further rhetorical leverage to the messages in that it seems that, as Aune concludes, "John has consciously employed the form of the royal or imperial edict as part of his strategy to emphasize the fact that Christ is the true king in contrast to the Roman emperor who is both a clone and a tool of Satan."[25] For the implied author of Revelation, then, the sole royal authority to reckon with is thereby God/Christ, and not the emperor. Moreover, the concluding statements in each of the proclamation formulas are written to the congregations in plural: Ὁ ἔχων οὖς ἀκουσάτω τί τὸ πνεῦμα λέγει ταῖς ἐκκλησίαις (2:7, 11, 17, 29; 3:6, 13, 22)—"He who has an ear, let him hear what the Spirit says to the congregations." This indicates that they were written as a combined message to all of the seven. This general character of the messages is further backed up by the very number of congregations—seven. The number seven occurs fifty-four times in Revelation and forms something of a motif in the book.[26] According to Adela Yarbro Collins, the number seven was considered as

---

[22] David E. Aune, *Prophecy in Early Christianity and the Ancient Mediterranean World* (Grand Rapids, MI: Eerdmans, 1983), 326.
[23] Aune, *Apocalypticism, Prophecy, and Magic in Early Christianity*, 226.
[24] "The seven proclamations of Rev 2–3 are similar in form to ancient royal or imperial *edicts*, in that they exhibit formally and structurally similar *praescriptiones, narrationes, dispositiones* and *sanctiones*. In content, however, the *narrationes* and *dispositiones* exhibit the complex characteristics of the *paraenetic salvation-judgment oracles* widely used by Christian prophets" (Aune, *Apocalypticism, Prophecy, and Magic in Early Christianity*, 231; see also Koester, *Revelation*, 234–5; Beale, *The Book of Revelation*, 225–8).
[25] Aune, *Apocalypticism, Prophecy, and Magic in Early Christianity*, 232.
[26] A motif is a recurring, organizing element in a narrative, which in this case is symbolic. On the definition and function of motif, see Wilhelm Egger, *How to Read the New Testament: An Introduction to Linguistic and Historical-Critical Methodology*, trans. Peter Heinegg (Peabody, MA: Hendrickson, 1996), 115; Abbott, *The Cambridge Introduction to Narrative*, 237; and Resseguie, *Narrative Criticism of the New Testament*, 45–6.

having a major cosmic role in the Hellenistic world.[27] This cosmic role suggests that the congregations represent the church universal.[28] If so, this symbolical number would concur with the form of imperial/royal edict in hinting at a more general address of the messages.

Gregory K. Beale has pointed out yet another literary pattern found in the messages to the seven congregations that suggests a more general audience, in that they are presented in the literary form of a chiasm (a b c c c b a).[29] Ephesus and Laodicea (congregations "a") are in danger of losing their very identity as a Christian church. They are exhorted to repent. The Smyrna and Philadelphia (congregations "b") have proved themselves faithful even in the face of persecution. They are encouraged to continue in perseverance. The three central messages (congregations "c"), Pergamum, Thyatira, and Sardis, are facing the danger of compromise to a varying degree. At the center, according to Beale, we find the general statement καὶ γνώσονται πᾶσαι αἱ ἐκκλησίαι (and all the congregations will know, 2:23). This is the only reference to "all the congregations" besides the previously mentioned conclusions of the proclamation formulas. The chiastic form of the messages seems to point to this as the centerpiece, the point of reference that all the other oracles are pointing toward. This structure provides a claim for the universal relevance of the individual oracles with all their exhortations and parenesis.

This broader impact of the messages is further emphasized if one takes into consideration the relationship between the messages to the seven congregations to the rest of the book. If we compare the Christological predications of the messages to the prologue and the inaugural vision of the book, we find that they are closely connected. Similarly, the promises for those who conquer seem to resonate with the contents of the last three chapters of the book. Table 2 intends to draw attention to the parallel phrasing and themes that connect the septet to the first and last sections of the book.[30] In addition to these parallels, Leonard L. Thompson has pointed out that many of the elements that are developed throughout the visionary part of the book (chapters 4–22) are rooted precisely in the messages to the seven congregations. According to Thompson, the initial position of the messages makes them "the initial context—the bass line—for images, symbols, and motifs used later in the transcendent visions."[31] His main point is that the metaphoric language of the messages to the seven congregations links them with the rest of the book. W. Gordon Campbell argues along the same lines when he considers the septet of oracles as providing the outline for which the remaining septets of the book are worked out, and refers to this as a "splendid *orchestration* of leitmotifs

---

[27] Yarbro Collins, *Cosmology and Eschatology in Jewish and Christian Apocalypticism*, 127. In this chapter, Yarbro Collins reconsiders the traditional interpretation of the number seven in the book of Revelation as a number of completeness. She argues instead for a more contemporary Hellenistic interpretation of the usage of this number in the book of Revelation on pages 122–7 (see Section 4.4.2.1).

[28] Beale, *The Book of Revelation*, 59; and Resseguie, *The Revelation of John*, 83.

[29] Beale, *The Book of Revelation*, 226–7.

[30] See the survey of the various correlations between the messages and the final scenes of the book in Barr, *Tales of the End*, 91–4.

[31] Leonard L. Thompson, *The Book of Revelation: Apocalypse and Empire* (New York: Oxford University Press, 1990), 180.

Table 2 Cross-References to the First and Last Sections of the Book of Revelation in the Messages to the Seven Congregations

	Ephesus	Smyrna	Pergamum	Thyatira	Sardis	Philadelphia	Laodicea
Christological predication in the messages	The one who walks among the seven golden lampstands with seven stars in his right hand, 2:1	The first and the last, he who was dead and came to life, 2:8	He who has the sharp two-edged sword, 2:12	Eyes like a flame of fire and feet like burnished bronze, 2:18	The seven spirits of God and the seven stars, 3:1	Key of David, 3:7	The faithful and true witness, 3:14
Parallel in the inaugural vision of 1:9–20	1:12–13, 16	1:17b–18	1:16	1:14–15	1:4, 16, and 20	1:18	1:5
Promise to the victor in the messages	To eat from the tree of life, 2:7	Will not suffer the second death, 2:11	Receive a new name that no one knows except the one who receives it, 2:17	Authority over the nations; rule with iron rod and be given the Morningstar, 2:26–28	White robes, inclusion in the book of life; and have one's name confessed before God, 3:5	The name of God will be written on him, 3:12	Reign with Christ on his throne, 3:21
Parallel in the latter part of the book	22:2	20:14 and 21:8	22:4; and 19:12	19:15; 20:4–6; and 22:16	20:12, 15; and 21:27	22:4	20:4–6; and 22:5

introduced in the first septet."[32] The messages to the seven congregations provide an introduction as well as a frame of interpretation for the visionary material of the book.[33] This corresponds well with Gregory Beale's way of perceiving the messages as "the literary microcosm of the entire book's macrocosmic structure" and Craig Koester's hermeneutical deduction that "the messages to the congregations establish the context in which the rest of Revelation is to be understood."[34] The messages provide the reader with the necessary introduction to the language and imagery of the book. The understanding of Satan as he is presented in the messages to the seven congregations will therefore be of crucial importance for the interpretation of him in the other parts of the book.

We see from this that the literary form and function of the messages to the seven congregations are closely interwoven with the rest of the book, both structurally as well as semantically. This function is further emphasized by their initial location in the whole narrative. Thus, they provide us with a hermeneutical lens, a point of reference, to interpret the function of Satan in the rest of the book. This lens will be established from the results of a thorough analysis of the plot, point of view, and characterization of Satan in these messages, which is the goal and purpose of the following part of this chapter.

3.4 Analysis

In line with the methodological considerations of my chapter on method, I will analyze the primary texts first. These are the texts explicitly mentioning the Devil/Satan or other related names and epithets. After this, I will analyze the secondary texts in light of the findings from the analysis of the primary texts. Regarding the messages to the seven congregations this means that I will analyze the four messages directly mentioning Satan first (Smyrna, Pergamum, Thyatira, and Philadelphia) before I turn to the secondary texts, those not mentioning Satan by name or epithets (Ephesus, Sardis, and Laodicea), to see how they relate to the findings in the primary texts.

3.4.1 Smyrna

3.4.1.1 *Plot*

Defining the plot is crucial in order to grasp the characterization of Satan fully. His role as an agent provocateur to the congregations, the effective means to resolving the overarching plot of Revelation, must be taken into consideration when attempting to sort out the episodic plots of the messages to the seven congregations. I agree with W. Gordon Campbell in his description of the structure of the plot of Revelation as an

---

[32] Campbell, *Reading Revelation*, 104, n. 17; see also 76.
[33] See Martin M. Culy, *The Book of Revelation: The Rest of the Story* (Eugene, OR: Pickwick, 2017), 22–3, 261–2. Here, Culy explores an interpretation of Revelation 4–22 perceived as "the rest of the story" of Revelation 2–3.
[34] Beale, *The Book of Revelation*, 224, and Koester, *Revelation*, 231.

ascending, three-dimensional spiral against the U-shaped variant of James L. Resseguie, due to the implications of recapitulation in the book of Revelation (on recapitulation in Revelation, see Section 4.2.2).[35] The episodic plots of the messages relate directly to this overarching plot, overlap with it, and, with their prominent position in the narrative, contribute specifically in setting the stage for what is about to be revealed. The upper end of the spiral, the resolution of the overarching plot, therefore aligns with the resolution of the episodic plots of the seven messages. This resonates well with my baseline of interpretation—the messages being a microcosm of the macrocosmic structure of the book—as it is the same story told, yet through a different but closely related discourse.

As the diegetic analysis above made clear (Figure 2), there is more than one diegetic level of the narrative at play here. The very messages to the seven congregations are themselves the result of the transforming action of the plot on diegetic levels 2 and 3. The question of whether John would comply with the instruction to write or not have thus been resolved by the very existence of the letters.

On this hypodiegetic level, a new set of narrated plots unfold. In the message to Smyrna, the plot can be defined in the following manner with the use of the Quinary scheme:

The *initial situation* at Smyrna is a turbulent one. They are suffering affliction and poverty and being slandered (τὴν βλασφημίαν) by "the synagogue of Satan."

The *complication* for this congregation is that things are going to get even worse. The Devil is about to throw some of them into prison. This is only for a limited amount of time and is clearly described as a test of the congregation, by the formulation ἵνα πειρασθῆτε (so that you may be tested).

The *transforming action* will be one of endurance and perseverance. The test is to know whether they will remain faithful unto death or not.

If they succeed in their perseverance, they will receive the crown of life. Continued perseverance functions as the *denouement* of this plot—the symbol of resolution of the complication.

The *final situation* is described indirectly by the promise that conquerors will not be harmed by the second death. The meaning of conquest is unexplained along with the object to be conquered, but according to Richard Bauckham,

> the call to conquer, addressed to the Christians in each of the seven churches in chapters 2–3, is a call to engage in the eschatological battle described in the central chapters of the book, in order to reach the eschatological destiny described at the end of the book … While the book as a whole explains what the war is about and how it must be won, the message to each church alerts that church to what is specific about its section of the battlefield.[36]

---

[35] Campbell, *Reading Revelation*, 43. Part of his argument is based upon Elisabeth Schüssler Fiorenza and her argument in *The Book of Revelation: Justice and Judgment*, 5–6. This rejection of a linear or circular structure corresponds with David Barr and his arguments for a spiral structure of the book in David L. Barr, "Using Plot to Discern Structure in John's Apocalypse," *Proceedings of the Eastern Great Lakes and Mid-West Biblical Societies* 15 (1995): 23–33. For the U-shaped plot of Resseguie, see his *The Revelation of John*, 84–6.

[36] Bauckham, *The Theology of the Book of Revelation*, 14.

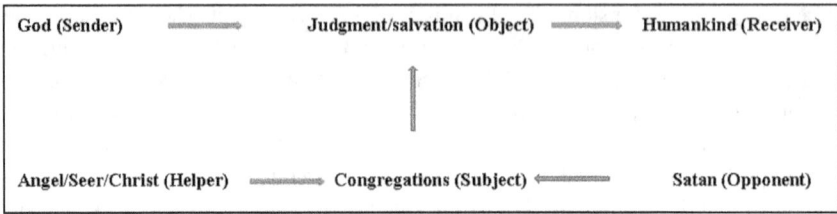

Figure 3 The actants of the message to Smyrna

It is a recurring feature of the narrative that the manner of conquest is both contingent on and modeled after the obedient and willingly suffering Christ on the cross (cf. Rev 3:14; 5:5–6; 12:11; 18:23–24; 19:2).

3.4.1.2 Characterization

The plot of the message to Smyrna is short and simple, yet serves its purpose well as an organizing design connecting the characters to its events. The congregation is about to face its last and final test. Eternity rests upon the outcome to which end the characterization of Satan depicts him as the agent provocateur.

The actantial scheme is centered on the object of desire aimed at by the subject. When applied to the message to Smyrna, we find the roles assigned to the characters in light of this as shown in Figure 3.

The precise identification of which actor belongs to which actantial role is a matter of interpretation. The premise for my identification here is to identify the primary pair of relations, that of subject–object, in light of the governing element of desire. Who desires what in this message? The main thrust of the letter seems fairly obvious: if the congregation (subject) complies with the instructions of the message, they will receive what they desire (object).[37] The object is specified as the crown of life and eternal life, which can be obtained through conquest unto death. The message is driven forth by this implicit desire of the congregation to be rewarded this way, and the objects serve to exemplify and point to the eschatological salvation described in the last section of the book. The other actantial roles follow from this key identification: John/Jesus helps the congregation in this search, while Satan and other opponents obstruct it. John is given the revelation, which is meant to help the members of the congregations to remain faithful through their afflictions. By him being obedient in his command to write down and send them this revelation, he functions as their helper on their

---

[37] The reference to the "angels" of the congregations in the *adscriptio* is another way of referring to the members of the congregation collectively. It is made clear in the messages themselves by the self-referential proclamation formula (2:7, 11, 17, 29; 3:6, 13, 22) that these messages are written to the congregations. According to Resseguie, these different ways of referring to the same object represent two perspectives on the congregations—the heavenly and earthly: "The angels of the churches most likely represent the heavenly reality, the spiritual condition of the church, the counterpart to its earthly reality" (Resseguie, *The Revelation of John*, 81). This is probably done in order to emphasize the often present clash of outward appearances with the inner reality, which is a recurring trait in Revelation (ibid.).

way. A great many things are opposing the members of the congregation in achieving their goal. They suffer affliction and poverty for reasons unknown. They are being slandered by some designating themselves as Jews. Finally, the Devil will imprison some of them in order to test their perseverance for ten days. All of these could be considered elements of opposition—obstacles on the congregation's way to becoming conquerors. The roles of sender and receiver are ambiguous within this text. The identification of God through Christ as sender relates to his role in the prologue as the one governing the quest: he governs the status of the congregation as a participant of the quest, thereby initiating its journey of conquest by establishing it as his congregation on his terms. The role of the receiver is humankind in general, as the offer of salvation/judgment goes out to all. The manner of how the subject responds to the opponents and helpers in the process of obtaining the object constitutes the foundation for whether to receive salvation or judgment: faithful through affliction or giving in to avoid further affliction. In light of the overarching plot, this process represents the eschatological ordeal as manifested to each congregation. In the end, God/Christ, the sender, can also be perceived as receiver—the final recipient of everything in the book of Revelation, including the fulfillment of his desire—the subject obtaining its object.

This is a rough identification of the main functions of the characters of the message to Smyrna. A more in-depth analysis in light of Revelation as a whole would reveal a more composite characterization of Christ in that he participates in more than one function of this scheme (sender, receiver, and helper), yet for an overview of the functions of characters in the message to Smyrna per se, this will suffice.

The Devil is, surprisingly, not cast as an opponent in this message. His main function is to oppose and obstruct the congregation from reaching its desired goal. Still, the book of Revelation contains several characters besides the Devil/Satan who function as opponents to the subject of the narrative. In the search for the more individualizing characteristics of Satan, a description of his function in the plot alone is not sufficient for my purpose here. By this, it seems that Seymour Chatman is right in claiming that there is more to be said about character than just describing its functions to the plot. He states that a viable theory of character "should argue that character is reconstructed by the audience from evidence announced or implicit in an original construction and communicated by the discourse."[38] This involves awareness of the traits connected to the characters, which will help us individualize characters in addition to their function to the plot. Furthermore, it is important to notice that the meaning of such traits is often culturally coded by the implied author's assumptions of his implied audience. I will argue for a probable contextual interpretation of the assumed meaning of several of these traits of Satan, even though they are "outside the text," as I believe these to be a decisive element of the characterization of him (cf. Section 2.5 above).

In the message to Smyrna, the Devil/Satan is mentioned twice. He is not described explicitly at any point (telling), so his characterization rests upon the description of his actions (showing) and on what the implied author assumes his audience knows and

---

[38] Chatman, *Story and Discourse*, 119.

thinks about him.³⁹ The latter function comes into play in 2:9, when his name is used to characterize a group of people and their slander or denunciation:

οἶδά σου τὴν θλῖψιν καὶ τὴν πτωχείαν, ἀλλὰ πλούσιος εἶ, καὶ τὴν βλασφημίαν ἐκ τῶν λεγόντων Ἰουδαίους εἶναι ἑαυτοὺς καὶ οὐκ εἰσὶν ἀλλὰ συναγωγὴ τοῦ σατανᾶ.

(I know of your affliction and poverty, even though you are rich, and the slander/denunciation of those who say they are Jews, though they are not, but [are] a synagogue of Satan.)

The context indicates that the activity of slandering is directed toward the congregation, first of all because it is sandwiched between two sentences explicitly concerned with the afflictions and poverty of the congregation (2:9–11) and, secondly, because its activity seems to lead to the soon-to-follow imprisonment of some of the congregation.⁴⁰ This could indicate use of τὴν βλασφημίαν as a reference to the act of denunciation of Christians before Greco-Roman authorities, and not necessarily blasphemy toward God.⁴¹ The combination of blasphemy and devastating consequences for the believing community is picked up again in 13:1, 5–6, 16–18, along with the interpretation of this vision in chapter 17. Moreover, unwarranted suffering unto death as a consequence of slandering and false accusation seems to be part of the characterization of Satan in 12:10–12, which eventually leads to his demise. The accusation of Christians leading to earthly afflictions seems by this to form a theme accompanying the characterization of Satan in the book of Revelation, a theme so obvious to the implied reader that this trait of Satan, in turn, can be used in a meaningful way to characterize the behavior of this neighboring synagogue in Smyrna as the συναγωγὴ τοῦ σατανᾶ—a synagogue of Satan. The slandering behavior of these may refer to a general hostility toward the Christian congregation, or be a by-product of its close integration into Roman culture (i.e., fallen prey to the sin of compromise). David L. Barr favors the latter but stresses that the text is too ambiguous for any certainty on the matter.⁴²

---

³⁹ On the differentiation of the two modes of exposition, showing and telling, see Marguerat and Bourquin, *How to Read Bible Stories*, 69; and Powell, *What Is Narrative Criticism?*, 52–3.

⁴⁰ On "sandwiching" as an expression of the rhetorical pattern of intercalation, see Resseguie, *Narrative Criticism of the New Testament*, 54–6. Elisabeth Schüssler Fiorenza seems to be referring to the same phenomenon, though deeming it "intercalation" when writing the following: "The author employs the method of intercalation in the following way: He narrates two formal units or two episodes (A and A') that essentially belong together. Between these two formal units or episodes he intercalates another form or scene (B) and thus requires the reader to see the combined text as a whole" (Fiorenza, *The Book of Revelation: Justice and Judgment*, 172).

⁴¹ For further arguments on the interpretation of τὴν βλασφημίαν as denunciation, slandering, or speaking abusively of Christians before Greco-Roman authorities, see Aune, *Revelation 1–5*, 162–3; Beale, *Revelation*, 240; Koester, *Revelation*, 274–5; Philip L. Mayo, *"Those Who Call Themselves Jews": The Church and Judaism in the Apocalypse of John*, PTMS 60 (Eugene, OR: Pickwick, 2006), 65–7; Paul B. Duff, *Who Rides the Beast? Prophetic Rivalry and the Rhetoric of Crisis in the Churches of the Apocalypse* (New York: Oxford University Press, 2001), 44–5; and Witherington, *Revelation*, 98–100.

⁴² David Barr lists four possible interpretations of the phrase "synagogue of Satan": a reference to specific hostile synagogues in the cities in question; a reference to Jews in general having lost their status as God's people; a reference to a rival Christian community who are claiming to be Jewish but are really Gentiles; and a reference to Jewish synagogues that are too closely integrated into

In 2:10b we read about the consequences of their slandering—imprisonment. This is credited to the Devil. The purpose of this is so that the members of the congregation could be tested (ἵνα πειρασθῆτε). The assumption that the afflictions of the congregation in Smyrna is linked to the slandering in the manner mentioned above (denunciation of Christians to authorities leading to poverty, afflictions, and future imprisonment) seems to be supported linguistically by the use of aorist subjunctive, as suggested by David E. Aune: "The aorist subjunctive πειρασθῆτε is used because the aorist summarizes the meaning that the Smyrnaean Christians will derive from the whole persecution experience, i.e., testing."[43] The whole experience of turmoil, then, is in the end the means to the process of testing. Whose tests are they, then? In light of the overarching plot as defined above as well as the monistic cosmology presumed in the narrative (see Section 4.2.1) I agree with Gregory Beale in concluding that "these are really 'divine tests' to distinguish genuine from false believers in the church (cf. 1 Cor. 11:19)."[44] In Rev 2:10 the activity is credited to the Devil, yet several elements in the context suggest a characterization of him more as an intermediary figure acting on behalf of the divine:[45]

Firstly, the limitation of the afflictions to "ten days" reveals the apocalyptic cosmology behind the book of Revelation.[46] The concept of time limitation on earthly matters established by the divine frequently appears in the book of Revelation (cf. 11:2; 12:6, 14; 13:5), is considered a feature of the apocalyptic genre, and serves to characterize God as the ultimate architect of history. If God is limiting this activity to "ten days," then he is also sanctioning it by being in complete control of the means of achieving it.

Secondly, the concept of testing is a recurring motif in the messages to the seven congregations. We encounter it in 2:2; 2:10; and twice in 3:10. In every instance, it involves testing of faith/loyalty in order to sift the members of the congregations. This dichotomy, the two potential outcomes of testing, constitutes the main plot of Revelation—the separation of those written in the book of life from those marked by the beast, the conquerors of the new heaven and earth or those inhabiting the lake of fire. The implied author might assume that the reader is familiar with related

---

Roman culture (Barr, *Tales of the End*, 86; see also Ian Boxall, *The Revelation of Saint John*, BNTC [London: A & C Black, 2006], 53–4).

[43] Aune, *Revelation 1–5*, 166.

[44] Beale, *The Book of Revelation*, 242; see also Fee, *Revelation*, 32.

[45] Martin M. Culy seems to be missing out on the meaning of this being a test in his otherwise interesting and comprehensive analysis of the book of Revelation in light of the messages of Revelation 2–3. Nowhere in his chapters on the message to Smyrna does he consider the cosmological implications of referring to the imminent suffering of the congregation as a test executed by the Devil and his liaisons. In light of his comments on the Devil not being able to do anything on his own without divine permission (Culy, *The Book of Revelation*, 68, 77–8, 98, 104), the question of the origin and purpose of such a test would in my opinion imply a need to modify Culy's characterization of the Devil as in "battle against God" (ibid., 78; see also 104). Moreover, a consideration of the relation between the testing of Smyrna and the test the congregation of Philadelphia is to be kept from (Rev 3:10, see ibid., 182–3) would further strengthen these otherwise intriguing chapters of Culy.

[46] See also Roloff: "This affliction serves to test the steadfastness of faith, and it stands indirectly under the permission of God (Job 1–2), which is also expressed in the announcement of its temporal limitation" (Jürgen Roloff, *The Revelation of John: A Continental Commentary*, trans. John E. Alsup [Minneapolis: Fortress, 1993], 48).

scriptural use of the term πειρασμός/πειράζω confirming this reading of the term. The apotropaic prayer directed to God, praying for him not to lead them into temptation (εἰς πειρασμόν, Matt 6:13), is one relevant text concurring with the cosmological premise for the reading above. This kind of prayer made sense in first-century Palestine precisely because they were familiar with the scriptural traditions attributing the origin of such acts of testing to God (cf. Gen 22:1 LXX; Deut 8:2 LXX; 1 Cor 10:13; Mark 1:12–13).[47] Moreover, Gregory Beale refers to several texts containing the act of divine testing combined with the number ten in the Hebrew Bible, which makes it a possibly known scriptural motif (Gen 24:55; 31:7, 41; Exod 7:14–12:36; Num 14:22; Job 19:2–3; Dan 1:12–14).[48] Among these, I find Job and the Exodus tradition especially relevant as they were eventually perceived to cast hostile intermediary figures (the adversary of Job and Mastema of the book of Jubilees) as mediators of divine trial.[49] In my opinion, the idea of celestial agents of divine trials such as these clearly lies behind much of the characterization of Satan in the New Testament—Revelation included.

Thirdly, the revelation of the transcendental reality behind the afflictions of the congregations in chapter 13 reveals this divine sanctioning by the fourfold repetition of the phrase καὶ ἐδόθη αὐτῷ (he was given) in 13:5–7.[50] As David E. Aune has pointed out, this use of the singular aorist passive means that "in each instance the passive voice of the verb can be construed as a passive of divine activity, i.e., as a circumlocution for the direct mention of God as the subject of the action of the verb."[51] The general cosmology behind the image of God in the book of Revelation points to the all-encompassing supremacy of God. Every intermediate figure, characterized as either good or bad from a human perspective, is being cast into their respective roles in the ordeal of sifting.[52]

---

[47] The tradition behind Jas 1:13 seems to contradict this idea and reveals in my opinion another contemporary tradition behind the term. It is important, though, to note that to the author of James, the testing comes about not from the Devil, mentioned in 4:7, but from our own desire (Jas 1:14–15). See Section 1.1 and the issue of tension in the New Testament traditions concerning these matters.

[48] Beale, *The Book of Revelation*, 243, n. 63.

[49] Mastema and his role in the Exodus plagues are somewhat complex, yet he is clearly subjected to the sovereignty of Yahweh. The plagues in their entirety are characterized as acts of Yahweh according to the wording of Jub. 48:5, yet the killing of the first-born sons is credited to Mastema in Jub. 49:2: "For on this night there was the beginning of the feast and there was the beginning of the joy. You continued eating the Passover in Egypt and all of the powers of Mastema were sent to kill all of the firstborn of Pharaoh to the firstborn of the captive maidservant who was at the millstone and to the cattle."

[50] This aspect of the Satan found in the book of Revelation bears clear resemblance to the scene where Mastema is given one-tenth of his spirits to continue with their intended activity of leading the children of men astray to reassure their evil ways (Jub. 10:7–14). The book of Jubilees, with its Midrash on Gen 6:1–4 and God's reluctant response to the prayer of Noah to completely destroy the spawn of the Watcher angels and the daughters of men, sheds light on the servant imagery of Satan in the book of Revelation as well as other similar parts of the New Testament.

[51] Aune, *Revelation 6–16*, 743. For comments on the concept of the divine passive, see Sections 4.2.2.2 and 4.4.2.3.1.

[52] W. Gordon Campbell stresses this element of divine supremacy to the malignant forces of Revelation several times in his reading of what he understands to be an antithetical characterization of God and the Lamb and their antagonists (Campbell, *Reading Revelation*, 71–111; in particular 73, 80, 87–9, 101). As mentioned above, such a reading creates narrative tension to a dualistic reading of the relation between Satan and God. This is because it renders God a self-harmer by proxy, and Satan his delusional opponent, obviously unaware of his inferiority, aiding and abetting to the divine governing of the earth, blinded by his own hubris to his incapability to usurp the throne of the sovereign God. It may seem that this is precisely the way Campbell perceives this relation in light

This point becomes particularly clear in the visionary sections on the seals, trumpets, and bowls of wrath (see Section 4.2.2). The point of origin of the calamities described there is the heavenly sphere, by the hand of the Lamb or the command of God. The presence of the many allusions to the Exodus tradition in these sections regarding the nature, function, and perspective of these "plagues" confirms such a reading.

The Devil/Satan of the message to the congregation of Smyrna is characterized primarily by his actions—his role and function in the testing of the congregation. The slandering or denunciation from members of the neighboring synagogue is described as part of his activity. They are therefore fittingly labeled a "synagogue of Satan," implying both the origin as well as the characterization of them by the satanic trait of testing.[53] This trait fits well with the overarching plot of the book of Revelation— the dividing of humankind. This brings me to the evaluative point of view, to which I now turn.

3.4.1.3 Point of View

In this section, I am concerned with what is sometimes referred to as the evaluative point of view.[54] The more technical aspect of the narrative, how and from which perspective we get to know Smyrna and their Devil by the focalization of the section, was explained in detail above (see Section 3.2). When looking for the point of view within a narrative, one is looking for what James L. Resseguie describes as "the ideological or theological position that the implied author wants the implied reader to adopt."[55] By adopting the point of view of the implied author, the reader is invited to feel sympathy, empathy, or antipathy toward the characters.[56] The position of the implied author of the message to Smyrna is to evoke sympathy for those afflicted in Smyrna, and antipathy toward the "synagogue of Satan" and the Devil behind the testing. The implied reader is directed toward perseverance in affliction, even unto death, and thus away from religious compromise. This is derived not from numerous imperatives in the text but from the characterization of characters conveying the evaluative point of view of the implied author. The reader is invited to share this evaluative point of view

---

of his characterizing nomenclature on the matter. He finds Satan a "bogus prosecutor" (ibid., 83), inspiring "bogus worship" (ibid., 103, 112, 115, 123, 134, 136–7, 154–5), partaking in a "hellish duo" (ibid., 91) with the beast from the sea, the "bogus risen one" (ibid., 174) as well as a "hellish trio" (ibid., 57) when including the beast from the earth, the "phoney paraclete" (ibid., 183), involved in a "silly alliance" (ibid., 97) with the kings of the earth. They are "bogus witnesses" to a "phoney proclamation" (ibid., 182), which renders the victims of his schemes (the earth-dwellers) "comical" (ibid., 88). This laden nomenclature corresponds well with his overall use of the term "monster" when referring to these agents.

[53] A similar occurrence of naming by function/characterization by action is the reference to Peter as Satan in Mark 8:33/Matt 16:33. Here, Peter unwittingly functions as a σκάνδαλον to the mission of Jesus and is subsequently named as the scriptural character epitomizing such acts—Satan.

[54] Powell, *What Is Narrative Criticism?*, 23–5 and 53–4; and Resseguie, *The Revelation of John*, 42–3, differentiate between the terms "point of view" and "evaluative point of view" instead of applying the narratological term "focalization," first introduced by Gérard Genette. On the term "focalization," see Marguerat and Bourquin, *How to Read Bible Stories*, 67–8; Abbott, *The Cambridge Introduction to Narrative*, 73–4; and Fludernik, *An Introduction to Narratology*, 36–8.

[55] Resseguie, *The Revelation of John*, 42.

[56] Powell, *What Is Narrative Criticism?*, 56–7.

because it is portrayed as God's own point of view—a rhetorical element brought forth by the enveloping structure of focalization (see Section 3.2). The concluding promise to the victor (2:11) is backed up by emphasizing the nature and origin of revelation, being Christ/God (2:8). This strengthens the exhortation to remain faithful unto the point of death in the dramatic ordeal of testing about to unfold in Smyrna. It is in this drama that Satan has been cast as opponent. He is therefore characterized in a way that evokes sympathy toward the congregation—the subject and protagonist of the narrative. Satan himself remains outside the center of attention and serves as an antithesis of the right course of action when his name and title is used to characterize a trait of the denunciating Jews.

Regarding the theological point of view, the characterization of Satan is completely in line with his function in the plot. This indicates that he is serving God's purposes by doing what he does. As a source of antipathy, he thus guides the reader toward sympathy for the afflicted. My remarks on testing as a characterizing trait of the Devil/Satan confirm that his function here is in line with the plot of the book in general, and hints toward an assumed traditional function of a tester in this text. To put it briefly, he is the antagonist, the opponent of the congregation, and he is bad news to those about to be imprisoned, but at this point, he is not characterized as an opponent of God.[57]

3.4.2 Pergamum

3.4.2.1 Plot

When applying the Quinary scheme on the plot of the message to the congregation of Pergamum, we find a divided congregation struggling with issues of religious compromise.

The *initial situation* is described by the presence of loyalty in a congregation having faced severe difficulties. Even in the days when Antipas was killed its perseverance did not waver. The emphasis on the faithfulness of Antipas, ὁ μάρτυς μου ὁ πιστός μου (my faithful witness, 2:13), suggests this as the probable cause of death.

The *complication* is introduced by the formulation ἀλλ' ἔχω κατὰ σοῦ ὀλίγα (but I have a few things against you, 2:14). These few things, however, are granted two-thirds the size of the body of the message and are thus given great priority by word count. It seems that although the members of the congregation have been successful in withstanding external pressure, they have fallen prey to internal compromise.[58] This compromise might also have been initiated by the death of Antipas, as suggested by Koester, in that "the condemnation of Antipas had the potential for making other

---

[57] G. B. Caird seems to be presuming some kind of involuntary service on the part of Satan in these verses, as he states on the matter: "But their ordeal will also be a divinely ordained **test** of their faith; for what Satan intends as a temptation, God uses as a **test** ... Satan can do nothing except by permission of God, who uses Satan's grimmest machinations to further his own bright designs" (G. B. Caird, *The Revelation of St. John the Divine*, 2nd ed., HNTC [London: A & C Black, 1984], 36). I find such a reading unlikely in light of the scriptural traditions behind the character of the Devil here, his function in the narrative as necessary opposition, as well as the apparent silence on any antagonism toward the divine plan on account of the Devil.

[58] Beale, *The Book of Revelation*, 248.

Christians abandon their faith in order to avoid a similar fate."[59] The main problem with the congregation of Pergamum, the complication, is that the members have among them those who hold to the teachings of Balaam and the Nicolaitans. This provokes an imminent coming of Christ in order to wage war on them with the sword of his mouth, which adds considerable weight to the complication.

Transforming action is here for those described as holding fast to the name of Christ, to persevere when facing external threats, and to no longer withstand (but to discipline and rebuke?) the compromisers. For the compromising party, the transforming action is found in the direct exhortation to repent in 2:16.

The resolution of the problem indicated will be stated by the preservation of the congregation. This is the *denouement* part of the plot.

The *final situation* is stated by the future reception of the hidden manna and the white stone with the new name inscribed on it. This initiates a new situation in which the complicating tension is no longer present.

3.4.2.2 Characterization

In light of this plot, the following actants can be discerned from the message to the congregation of Pergamum:

The subject is the angel/congregation, as is the case with all the messages. The object of desire is to obtain hidden manna and a white stone with a name written on it. This points to the eschatological salvation described in the final chapters of the narrative, thus making the object emblematic by reference and not exhaustive (i.e., not promised to the congregation of Pergamum alone). For those in need of repentance, another probable object would be to avoid Christ coming to wage war on them. For those not inclined toward compromise, it is important to root out this dividing element, to avoid spiritual contamination and maintain integrity. The sender is God/Christ as defined in Section 3.4.1.2—the voice behind the message and the architect of everything about to happen—the one who knows (οἶδα, 2:13). The receiver of eschatological salvation/judgment is humankind in general. The helper is primarily John as a mediator of what is revealed, but also encompasses Christ/God as both origin and, to some extent, content of the revelation (the congregations are clearly intended to gain motivational help from knowing what is about to happen). The opponent is found in the internal opponents of Pergamum—those who hold to the teaching of Balaam and the Nicolaitans. The external opponents are those responsible for the death of Antipas, and their presence is described metaphorically as the dominion and dwelling place of Satan (2:13).

We see from this short analysis that the subject, sender, receiver, and helper are the same as those found in the message to Smyrna. Their function as common denominators follows from their function in the formulaic structure of the seven messages as the variable actants (object and opponent) correspond to the individually shaped *narratio* and *dispositio*. These constitute the reason or motivation for the message and thus vary within the messages. These common and variable actants of the messages also relate to the focalizing elements of the messages. The mode of revelation—*who* reveals to

---

[59] Koester, *Revelation*, 292.

whom—corresponds to the actants of sender (revealer), helper (revealer, mediator), and subject (recipient of revelation/message). The receiver is also common to all of the messages as it is derived from the overarching plot of the narrative—the eschatological salvific outlook found in the last chapters of it. Since the focalization and the structural elements are common to all of the seven messages, we may expect both the unchanging and the variable actants of the other messages to be relating to each other in the same manner as in Smyrna and Pergamum.

Satan is not characterized as a self-sufficient actant in this message, but his name is used two times to characterize opponents in a manner similar to the one found in the term "synagogue of Satan" of Smyrna. In 2:13 we read οἶδα ποῦ κατοικεῖς, ὅπου ὁ θρόνος τοῦ σατανᾶ (I know where you live, where the throne of Satan is). This information is followed up by the acknowledgment of the endurance of the congregation, even when facing afflictions as grave as the death of Antipas. He is stated to have died among them, where Satan lives—ὅπου ὁ σατανᾶς κατοικεῖ. The *narratio* is thus being hermeneutically sandwiched between two characterizing remarks involving the name of Satan: the two formulations shed interpretational light on the text in the middle and vice versa. It follows from this that if the traits of Satan are used to describe a situation, then an understanding of that situation will shed light on what the implied author considers a trait of Satan.

The situation is that they are holding fast to the name of Jesus and did not deny their faith in him in the days of Antipas. It seems implied, by the formulations "holding fast" and "did not deny," followed by the death of Antipas, that they had good reason *not* to hold on to the name and to deny their faith, yet they did not do so. The fact that "throne" is articular may indicate a specific throne, one assumed known by the implied author and reader.[60] Laszlo Gallusz mentions four well-known but highly debatable candidates for this assumed known reference to the throne of Satan (political, religious, geographical, and center of Christian persecution). He concludes in the end with what is, in my opinion, the most important aspect of the reference: its antithetical function to the throne of Christ/God (3:21).[61] The throne of Satan is referred to by related formulations in 13:2 (τὸν θρόνον αὐτοῦ, "its throne") and 16:10 (τὸν θρόνον τοῦ θηρίου, "the throne of the beast").

In 13:2, the beast from the sea is given power, throne, and great authority from the dragon, earlier identified as Satan in 12:9. The context of chapter 13 is worship (13:4, 8, 12, and 15) under threat of death and other afflictions (13:15-16). The ἐδόθη αὐτῷ formulations here (13:5-7, 14, and 15) show that this transaction of power could be perceived as sanctioned by God.[62] The purpose of this is found in 13:14a: πλανᾷ τοὺς κατοικοῦντας ἐπὶ τῆς γῆς διὰ τὰ σημεῖα ἃ ἐδόθη αὐτῷ ποιῆσαι ἐνώπιον τοῦ θηρίου (It [the beast from the earth] deceives those who dwell on earth by the signs given it to do on behalf of the beast). This deception is what the call for endurance among the saints in 13:10b is directed toward. Endurance or giving in to deception divides the

---

[60] Aune, *Revelation 1-5*, 182.
[61] See Laszlo Gallusz, *The Throne Motif in the Book of Revelation: Profiles from the History of Interpretation*, LNTS 487 (London: T&T Clark, 2014), 206, 209.
[62] See Beale, *The Book of Revelation*, 695.

inhabitants of the world into two categories: those written in the book of life (13:8) and those marked by the beast (13:17).

In 16:10, the context is the seven bowls of wrath. When the fifth angel poured his bowl on the throne of the beast, it was followed by darkness and agony. It is specified in 16:9 that it is God who has authority over these plagues, yet those suffering from them continuously refuse to acknowledge him (16:9-10). These torments are poured out upon compromisers, those marked by the beast and its worshippers (16:2), and are justified by the blood of the saints and prophets (16:4-7). Of the three occurrences of the term "throne" related to Satan in the book of Revelation, all of them are found in contexts involving tribulation of the saints, calamities attributed to Satan or related epithets, and situations emphasizing the tension of choice between right and wrong course of action (hold fast to the name of Christ or not; worship the beast or not; repent or not). The last two occurrences (13:2; 16:10) explicitly describe the act of worship in connection to these tribulations. This may also be the case for the congregation of Pergamum. The identification of the dragon and the beasts with Babylon/Rome in chapter 17, along with the description of those coerced or deceived into worship, suggests imperial cult and Roman opposition toward Christians as a point of reference in chapters 13 and 16. Given that the situations described in chapters 2-3, 13, and 16 are the same but are seen from different points of view, this may also be the point of reference for Pergamum. This intratextual reading is in line with the readings of most commentaries on this text.[63] The "throne of Satan" in the message to Pergamum then refers to the enforced imperial worship backed up by Roman opposition toward Christians known from this area in this particular time. Within narrative criticism, this is referred to as the cultural point of view—what is assumed known by the implied author. The identification of hostile Roman presence is supported by the political implications by the very word θρόνος (throne), as a seat of rulers.[64] In the New Testament, the word always refers to a chair of state or seat of office (judge, king, God, Christ, and Satan).[65] In the book of Revelation, it also carries connotations of dominion. The term occurs forty-seven times here, and is part of the political imagery that is significant for one of the major plot conflicts: Who sits on the throne?[66] This in turn adds to the earlier mentioned inherent dichotomy of the book: What dominion do the characters belong to—the dragon/Satan/the beast or God/Christ?

These connotations associated with the term "throne" provide us with a probable explanation as to why Antipas had to die and why he is called ὁ μάρτυς μου ὁ πιστός μου (my witness, my faithful one): He would rather die than compromise his witness to Jesus. This makes him the ideal expression of the congregations' faith and conduct

---

[63] Aune lists eight more or less possible interpretations of the term, yet he seems to incline toward those regarding Roman oppression and imperial/pagan worship (Aune, *Revelation 1-5*, 182-4). For other interpretations along these lines: Colin J. Hemer, *The Letters to the Seven Churches of Asia in Their Local Setting* (Grand Rapids, MI: Eerdmans, 2001), 82-5; Beale, *The Book of Revelation*, 246-7; Koester, *Revelation*, 292-3; Mounce, *The Book of Revelation*, 96-7; Osborne, *Revelation*, 140-3; Martin Synnes, *7 profetiske budskap til menighetene: En gjennomgåelse av sendebrevene i Johannes' Åpenbaring* (Oslo: Verbum, 1996), 90-1; and Smalley, *The Revelation to John*, 68-9.
[64] Barr, *Tales of the End*, 97.
[65] Smalley, *The Revelation to John*, 68.
[66] Resseguie, *The Revelation of John*, 90.

of holding fast and not denying the name of Jesus. It is precisely his death that sets the congregation of Pergamum apart from the other congregations in that this is the only place in the septet that the death of a Christian is explicitly mentioned.[67] This qualifies the description as being at the center of Satan's presence—the throne of his dominion.

This survey, then, suggests that the connotations implied by the use of Satan to characterize traits of the opponents in Pergamum are probably (1) an opposing force on the congregation's path to spiritual conquest; (2) a manifest reason not to hold fast to the name of Jesus and to deny faith in him; or (3) an unpleasant object to endure. The term "Satan" is used in this way to characterize the perpetrators of afflictions—local Roman authorities—imposing cultic compromise on pain of death. As Robert H. Mounce points out, in light of the enveloping descriptions οἶδα ποῦ κατοικεῖς and ὅπου ὁ σατανᾶς κατοικεῖ: "both the believers and their ultimate adversary live in the same locality. Little wonder that martyrdom begins in Pergamum."[68]

The element of cultic compromise puts the external opponents of local authority in line with the internal opponents of the congregation—the followers of Balaam's teaching and the Nicolaitans. Due to the οὕτως (thus, so) coordinating the following phrase by referring to the previous one in 2:15, we learn that the teachings of the Nicolaitans are similar to that of Balaam, involving religious compromise in the eating of food sacrificed to idols and practice of (religious) fornication. This description makes it probable that Jezebel and her followers in Thyatira could be considered a faction of this group present in Pergamum.[69] The acceptance of these heresies is what the congregation is to repent from (2:16).

There is no explicit mentioning of Satan in the *dispositio*, yet we find a possible allusion to the origin of his office in the characterization of the internal ambassadors of compromise as followers of Balaam. The meaning of this allusive characterization is presumed known to the implied reader by its presence in the text. Balaam is given the blame for advising the Midianite women to instigate infidelity among the Israelites against Yahweh (Num 25:1-3; 31:16). In Rev 2:14, Balaam is also given credit for teaching Balak, the king of Moab, to be a stumbling block for Israel.[70] In the story of how Balaam was hired to curse Israel on behalf of Balak (Numbers 22-24), it is crucial for the narrator to state repeatedly that the sending of Balaam to Israel happens solely on Yahweh's terms (22:8, 12-13, 18-20, 35, 38; 23:3-5, 8, 12, 16-17, 19-20, 26; 24:1, 11, 13). It is on one of these occasions (22:22 and 32) that the angel of Yahweh is designated as לְשָׂטָן (as an adversary). The presence of the stumbling block of Israel, as Balaam is described in Rev 2:14, is in the book of Numbers explicitly governed by the presence

---

[67] Koester, *Revelation*, 292.
[68] Mounce, *The Book of Revelation*, 97.
[69] See Aune, *Revelation 1-5*, 148-9, for a thorough discussion on possible identifications of the Nicolaitans.
[70] The word σκάνδαλον is used in combination with the term "Satan" by Jesus in rebuking Peter and his attempt to urge Jesus to stray from his path toward his death in Jerusalem in Matt 16:23. According to Matt 18:7, the coming of such stumbling blocks is a matter of necessity (ἀνάγκη) and should probably be understood as part of the coming eschatological tribulations which also *must come* (δεῖ γὰρ γενέσθαι, Matt 24:6). In the end, they will be removed to purge the kingdom of the Son of Man (Matt 13:41).

of the Angel of Yahweh in the role of the antagonist.[71] Divinely sanctioned antagonists are, as we have seen, already present at Pergamum, which makes this allusion probable, if not compelling.

3.4.2.3 Point of View

Adela Yarbro Collins once wrote about Revelation as follows:

> The primary purpose of the book is not to impart information. It is rather to call for *commitment* to the actions, attitudes, and feelings uttered. It is thus primarily commissive language ... it provides a highly selective and perspectival view. Like a poem, it represents and interprets some aspect of reality, expresses a response to it, and invites the reader or hearer to share in the interpretation and the response.[72]

This evocative language of the book of Revelation is part of the narrative strategy of the implied author to evoke his reader to adopt his evaluative point of view. This is God's evaluative point of view, and should therefore be everyone's point of view. In the message to Pergamum, this language unfolds especially in the characterization of the external antagonists of Rome as representing the presence of Satan in their midst. The characterization of the imperial presence as the presence of Satan invites the implied reader to feel antipathy toward this path as an option. Like Job, Joshua the high priest, David, and Jesus, they are to resist, endure, and persist against whatever offer or threat is made by this party. The internal opposition is characterized by associating it with an archetype from Israel's history in Balaam.[73] This puts the implied reader in the position of Israel as described in Num 25:1-9; 31:16. The logic is simple: if you listen to these internal antagonists, you will be punished by God.[74] Antipathy is the feeling evoked by the characterization of these as well as the associated Nicolaitans.

The right course of action is evoked by the recurring element of divine revelation when Jesus gives the congregation credit for holding fast to and not denying his name (2:13). Like Antipas, the implied reader too should be faithful on pain of death, if necessary. The empathy is directed toward those holding fast and not denying, and the sympathy goes to Antipas and his likes. The promise of hidden manna and a white stone with a new name on it further enforces this evaluative point of view.

---

[71] In the Hebrew Bible, שָׂטָן is mainly used when referring to an adversarial role or function, not the name of a character—the most probable exception being 1 Chr 21:1 (see Pagels, *The Origin of Satan*, 39). The context of each use of the term displays a development from this first occurrence of the term being used on a heavenly being (Num 22:22 and 32), as a great number of scholars have given attention to. (See Russell, *The Devil*, 189-200; Forsyth, *The Old Enemy*, 111-23; Pagels, *The Origin of Satan*, 39-44; Almond, *The Devil*, 16-19; Messadié, *A History of the Devil*, 232-8; Kelly, *Satan: A Biography*, 13-31; and Maxwell-Stuart, *Satan: A Biography*, 19-23. Their thoughts on this development are not uniform, but they all agree on perceiving a development in the literary use of this character.)

[72] Yarbro Collins, "The Power of Apocalyptic Rhetoric—Catharsis," 76.

[73] See Greg Carey, "The Apocalypse and Its Ambiguous Ethos," in *Studies in the Book of Revelation*, ed. Steve Moyise (Edinburgh: T&T Clark, 2001), 178.

[74] See also Yarbro Collins, "The Power of Apocalyptic Rhetoric—Catharsis," 79.

As noted on the message to Smyrna, the characterization of Satan as representing the wrong course of action is completely in line with the function he is assigned in the plot, here as well as the book of Revelation in general. The results of this call to commitment divide the population of the world in two. It is the satanic traits of sifting and testing that we encounter in the message of Pergamum and not a rebel opponent of God.

3.4.3 Thyatira

3.4.3.1 *Plot*

When we turn to the message to Thyatira, we find a situation much like the one in Pergamum. An impending threat of religious compromise due to an acceptance of false teaching is present, yet at a larger scale. When identifying the different elements of the plot by using the Quinary scheme, the following structure emerges:

The *initial situation* is described with the good works of the congregation (2:19), which are defined by the following words: τὴν ἀγάπην καὶ τὴν πίστιν καὶ τὴν διακονίαν καὶ τὴν ὑπομονήν σου (your love, faith, service, and endurance). When these words appear elsewhere in the book of Revelation, they mostly refer to the persevering witness.[75] Furthermore, in contrast to the congregation of Ephesus, their last works are greater than their first.

Complication is presented as the tolerance of Jezebel and her teachings. She is leading the congregation astray, resulting in fornication (religiously; see Section 5.2.3) and eating of food sacrificed to idols. Because of her reluctance to repent from her behavior, Jesus will throw her on a bed, a Hebrew idiom meaning "to cast upon a bed of sickness."[76] This is probably done with the intention to discourage her followers from following in her footsteps. This rhetorical element is further emphasized with an accompanying threat to those committing adultery with her: they are to be cast into great tribulation and death if they do not turn from her behavior (2:22-23).

The *transforming action* for the adherents of Jezebel is to repent and turn from her teachings. The rest of the congregation is to hold fast to what they already have (2:26). We should probably understand the formulation ἀλλὰ ἔχω κατὰ σοῦ ὅτι ἀφεῖς τὴν γυναῖκα Ἰεζάβελ (but this I have against you that you tolerate the woman Jezebel), as an implicit call not to maintain this tolerance. The cessation of tolerance toward her and similar kinds of teaching could therefore also be considered part of the transforming action.

The *denouement* in Thyatira, as in Pergamum, is the preservation of the congregation. The sickness of Jezebel and, if repentant, the good health of her former followers will add to this resolution of the problem.

The *final situation* is stated by receiving authority over the nations and the Morningstar (2:27-28).

---

[75] ἔργον: 2:2, 5, 23 (probably), 26; 3:8; 14:13; ἀγάπη: 2:4 (antithetical); πίστις: 2:13; 13:10; 14:12; ὑπομονή: 1:9; 2:2, 3; 3:10; 13:10; 14:12 (see Beale, *The Book of Revelation*, 260).
[76] Aune, *Revelation 1-5*, 205.

3.4.3.2 Characterization

In line with what was noted on the message to Pergamum, the subject, sender, receiver, and helper seem to be identical in all of the seven messages. It is the object and the opponent that change within the septet. The actants of the plot of the message to Thyatira can thus be discerned in the following manner: the subject is the congregation; the sender is God/Christ; the receiver is humankind, and the helper is John.

The object, representing the salvation/judgment of the eschatological ordeal, is to obtain authority over the nations, to rule them with an iron rod, and to receive the Morningstar. For the followers of Jezebel, the object is to avoid great tribulation and death. For the congregation in general, salvation is achieved and judgment avoided by refusing religious compromise.

The opponent of the subject is Jezebel and her followers, in addition to possible external opposition. These works (love, faith, service, and endurance) are probably implying some sort of external opposition due to the fact that they seem acknowledged by the congregation as a single entity; furthermore, when such words of appraisal are found elsewhere in the book they mostly refer to the enduring witness (see above).

Whereas external opposition seems to be implied, the internal opposition is certainly explicit. In the message to Thyatira we find Satan absent as a self-sufficient character, but his name, and thereby related traits, are present in the description of the opposing party of Jezebel and her followers. More specifically, his name is used to denote her teachings by the formulation τὴν διδαχὴν ταύτην ... τὰ βαθέα τοῦ σατανᾶ ὡς λέγουσιν (this teaching ... they call the deep things of Satan). The question then arises: Who is referring to this teaching as "the deep things of Satan"? It could be attributed to the faithful ones of Thyatira. In that case, it could be a parody on the expression "the deep things of God" known from 1 Cor 2:10 and similar expressions as found in Rom 11:22; Dan 2:22; T. Job 37:6; and 2 Bar. 14:8. Another possibility is that John has substituted their self-proclaimed knowledge of the deep things of God with what he perceives it to be—the deep things of Satan.[77] This could be explained by the fact that Jezebel's teachings led to religious compromise in the congregation—a trait that is identified several times in the book in connection with Satan (2:9–10, 14–15; 13:12–14; cf. 14:11–12; 19:1–2, 20). A third option is that Jezebel and her followers themselves referred to this teaching as the deep things of Satan. This is in line with what some commentators have suggested that they might have fallen prey to the same spiritual hubris as the congregation in Corinth, as described by Paul.[78] The Corinthians were so confident in their spiritual growth and in the assertion that no other gods exist besides the Lord God that they could justify their attendance at cultic feasts. This pagan cultic infidelity is paralleled in the fate of the Israelites (Exod 32:6) and is tantamount to dining with demons according to Paul (1 Cor 10:19–22).[79] Whether or

---

[77] Beale, *The Book of Revelation*, 265–6; and Hemer, *The Letters to the Seven Churches of Asia*, 122; see also Aune, *Revelation 1–5*, 207.
[78] Koester, *Revelation*, 301; and Beale, *The Book of Revelation*, 265–6.
[79] Craig Koester lists this as an optional interpretation, though he does not favor it (Koester, *Revelation*, 301).

not the tradition of Paul is implied, it is important to state that the possibility of this interpretation is present within the text.

Even though we cannot determine with any certainty which one of these possible interpretations lie behind the designation "the deep things of Satan," it is sufficient here to point to the fact that all of them define religious compromise as something to be avoided at all costs. Furthermore, they all connect this infidelity to Satan, thereby confirming what we found in the message to Pergamum: that deception into religious compromise is a characteristic trait of Satan in the book of Revelation.

This is further supported by the description of the prophetess as leading the servants of Jesus astray (πλανᾷ τοὺς ἐμοὺς δούλους). As James L. Resseguie has pointed out, the act of leading astray is a trait only found in evil characters in the book of Revelation: Satan is leading the whole world (12:9; 20:3, 8, 10) astray, the beast from the sea leads the dwellers of the earth (13:14; 19:20) astray, and the whore of Babylon leads the nations (18:23) astray.[80] This verbal thread is one of the motifs connecting the seven messages to the rest of the book and affirms the methodological choice of reading them as earthly aspects of the more vertical and visionary part of the book. Her activity of leading astray is probably the main reason for her allusive characterization as Jezebel, Queen of Phoenicia, responsible for leading King Ahab of Israel astray and for compromising worship of Yahweh with Baal (1 Kgs 18–22; 2 Kgs 9:22). The designation of the self-proclaimed prophetess of Thyatira in association with the archetype of Jezebel of tradition functions in the same manner as the allusion to Balaam in the message to Pergamum.[81] Just as the actions of the Jezebel of Ahab lead to religious compromise followed by disaster, the actions of Jezebel of Thyatira will also lead to disaster for her followers, and thereby possibly destroy the congregation from within.[82] The Jezebel of the Deuteronomistic history is described as the cause of the downfall of King Ahab. Interestingly, Ahab dies in the battle at Ramoth Gilead after having been advised by his court prophets, which the context connects to the worship of Baal and Asherah. In 1 Kgs 22:19–23 the favorable prophecies of these prophets are described as originating from a רוּחַ שֶׁקֶר בְּפִי כָּל־נְבִיאָיךְ (a deceiving spirit in the mouth of all your prophets) sent by Yahweh to cause the death of Ahab. This kind of deceptive activity on behalf of Yahweh is a task that scriptural tradition later attributes to Satan (see the development from 2 Sam 24:1 to 1 Chr 21:1).

We cannot conclude with any certainty whether or not this association with the "deep things of Satan" of Jezebel of Thyatira with the lying Spirit of Yahweh of Ahab and her Jezebel is assumed known by the implied author, and is thereby being part of the cultural point of view embedded in the text. It is, however, in line with the assumed competence of the implied reader of this reading. If one assumes that the reader is well acquainted with the Hebrew Bible, then these stories most likely form a considerable

---

[80] Resseguie, *The Revelation of John*, 93.
[81] Adela Yarbro Collins refers to this allegorical technique of inviting one's readers "to see analogies between classic situations in Israel's past and their own situations" as *typology*—the use of archetypes to give meaning to a present event. Unlike this reading, she finds the ancient combat myth to be "the most powerful use of this technique" in Revelation (Yarbro Collins, *Crisis and Catharsis*, 147).
[82] See David A. deSilva, *Seeing Things John's Way: The Rhetoric of the Book of Revelation* (Louisville: Westminster John Knox, 2009), 139.

Table 3 Parallels in the Jezebel Stories of 1 Kings and the Book of Revelation

Jezebel of 1 Kings	Jezebel of the Book of Revelation
Leading astray resulting in cultic fornication	Leading astray resulting in cultic fornication
Jezebel as cause of the downfall of herself and Ahab	Jezebel as cause of the downfall of herself, her followers, and possibly the congregation
False prophets as medium of the lying spirit from Yahweh	Pagan prophetess as medium of "the deep things of Satan"
Truth revealed by the Prophet of Yahweh, Micaiah son of Imlah	Truth revealed by the prophet of Christ, John

part of the implied characterization of Jezebel of Thyatira.[83] The reading is also probable due to the themes, motifs, and plot present within the message of Thyatira, and thus they form a powerful rhetorical characterization by association (see Table 3).[84]

3.4.3.3 Point of View

By utilizing the principle of characterization by association, the implied reader is guided toward the emotional response of antipathy toward Jezebel of Thyatira and her teachings. The large amount of text dedicated by the Deuteronomistic editors in characterizing the Jezebel of 1 Kings as the archetypal pagan, the seducing and idolatrous Phoenician Queen responsible for the fall of the king, makes the probable presence of this allusion in Revelation a powerful rhetorical hyperbole. The function of this is to make sure none of the faithful of Thyatira chooses to follow in the compromising ways of her teaching. To enhance impact, the repelling characterization is further backed up by threats of impending sickness and death to those unwilling to exclude themselves from her fornication and repent from committing adultery with her (2:21–22).[85] Finally, these teachings are referred to as the deep things of Satan, to make sure the nature and function of her prophetic office are fully grasped for what they really are—a way of deception. If antipathy is evoked by the characterization of Jezebel of Thyatira, then sympathy is the proper response to those exhibiting honorable deeds of love, faith, service, and endurance (2:19). The works of Christ could be referring to the words of 1:5 in which Christ's works are described to include love, faithfulness, and witness to the truth, yet the addition of ἄχρι τέλους (unto the end) could indicate Christ and his loyalty unto death as the intended works to exhibit. Another possibility

---

[83] Cf. Section 2.5, "Excursus: On the Use of Extratextual References in Narrative Criticism."

[84] This is in line with the rhetorical analysis of David A. deSilva on the matter: "One blatant strategy for undermining the more threatening rivals (i.e., those that have gained a foothold among the congregations) involves naming them not by their proper names, but by strategically chosen pseudonyms associating them with unflattering characters of the Jewish Scriptures, names that reveal their 'true' character ... John's rivals are associated with notorious false prophets, associations that will adversely color the churches' perception of them" (deSilva, *Seeing Things John's Way*, 138; see also Culy, *The Book of Revelation*, 90).

[85] The sexually laden metaphors of leading astray enhance the intertextual link between the Jezebel of 1 Kings and that of Revelation as well as connecting her and her party thematically to Babylon the Great in Revelation 17–19. See Duff, *Who Rides the Beast?*, 56–7, 89–91.

is to interpret the ἄχρι τέλους temporally—to do Christ's works until their own end.[86] In any case, there is no doubt that this is the right course of action according to the evaluative point of view in the message to Thyatira because the rewards are promised to those doing such deeds.

The rewards themselves elevate the evaluative point of view in the text. In the same manner as Christ (ὡς κἀγώ, 2:28), the Son of God (2:18), received his authority from his father (2:28), everyone who conquers will receive authority and partake in his messianic rule (2:26b–27 alluding to Ps 2:8–9). This is probably also the meaning behind the promise of being given τὸν ἀστέρα τὸν πρωϊνόν (the Morningstar). The Morningstar could allude to the prophecy of Balaam (Num 24:14–20) and its connection to Ps 2:8–9, especially considering that both Psalm 2 and Balaam is being alluded to in the context of this verse. Moreover, the Morningstar was commonly identified as Venus in the ancient world, a symbol of sovereignty. It was an important symbol in a Roman context in that Roman emperors claimed to be descendants from Venus and Roman legions carried her sign on their standards.[87] If the promised reward to the faithful of Thyatira carries such implied cultural connotations, then it serves as a means to establish and elevate the view that the real sovereign ruler of the world is not the Roman Empire but Christ. Jewish sources interpreted the star of Num 24:17 to refer to a messianic, royal figure (T. Levi 18:3; T. Jud. 24:1; 4Q175 I, 12; cf. CD VII:18–20 and 1QM XI, 6).[88] It seems as though the use of this epithet in Revelation combines these two motives in its application of it to Christ (here in Rev 2:28 and as a Christological predicate in 22:16). In Isa 14:4–21 the fall of a tyrant, the king of Babel, is celebrated. In the LXX translation of 14:12, he is referred to as ὁ ἑωσφόρος ὁ πρωὶ ἀνατέλλων (Morningstar the one rising at dawn). If this connection is intended, implied culturally by the use of the expression in a Judeo-Christian context, then Christ is characterized as the successful ruler, unfallen and sovereign to the end.[89] The reference to Satan as Lucifer, a Latin rendering of "Morningstar," is a later development and is therefore not found in Revelation or any other New Testament text.[90]

The identification of the speaker as the Son of God and the Messiah, displaying sovereign authority granted to him by his father, strengthens the recommended course of action by aligning it with God's preferred course of action. From this point of view, Satan is associated with the wrong course of action. The path of severe punishment is contrasted with the rewards promised to the victor. An interesting result of the sickness of Jezebel and imminent death of her followers is that the congregations *will know* by inference that Christ is the one searching their minds and hearts in order to reward each one in accordance with his works (2:23). The punishment of Jezebel and her followers in Thyatira is thus considered a revelation in itself and serves as a warning

---

[86] Beale, *The Book of Revelation*, 267.
[87] Beale, *The Book of Revelation*, 269.
[88] Koester, *Revelation*, 302.
[89] See Aune, *Revelation 1–5*, 212–13, for further discussion on the cultural meaning behind the expression.
[90] Forsyth, *The Old Enemy*, 136; Russell, *The Devil*, 229, 256–7; and Kelly, *Satan: A Biography*, 164–7, 172. For the use of the traditions of Isaiah 14 and Ezekiel 28 in explaining the fall of the Devil in early Christian literature, see Bell, *Deliver Us from Evil*, 13; and Forsyth, *The Satanic Epic*, 43–5.

for others considering following their teachings. This lesson taught in Thyatira is a lesson served for all the congregations: a collective recognition of this wretched fate as the justified wages of their heretic teachings acknowledged and executed by Christ.[91] From this perspective, the Jezebel incident functions in the same manner as the lying spirit of Yahweh and the angel of death of Exodus, later to be identified with Mastema. The Deuteronomist redactors are careful to stress that the fates of Jezebel and Ahab, along with his house, have been effectuated according to the word of Yahweh (1 Kgs 21:19–24, 29; 22:23, 38; 2 Kgs 9:25–26; 10:10, 17, 30). The logic implied is, in this way, similar to that of the message to Thyatira and the book of Revelation: the word of Yahweh is reliable and trustworthy, for the entire world to know (cf. 2 Kgs 10:10).[92]

The parallels in the messages to the congregations of Pergamum and Smyrna justify the suggestion of viewing Satan in line with the function assigned to the lying spirit: as a sanctioning and indirectly executing element of divine chastisement and retribution. This element works well with the overarching plot of sifting in Revelation by functioning as a rod to measure and justify divine judgment. Pagan prophets or prophetesses are not to be consulted. Finding the voice of a lying spirit of Yahweh or the deep things of Satan within it only confirms the error made in the first place. The severe punishment is thereby justified.

3.4.4 Philadelphia

3.4.4.1 Plot

The last explicit reference to Satan in the messages to the seven congregations is found in the words written to Philadelphia. The *initial situation* at Philadelphia is much like the one found at Smyrna—dire, but spiritually healthy. They have works paving the way to an open door leading to God because they have kept the word of Christ and not denied his name (3:8). The contrast to the message to Laodicea is striking in that they form directly opposed situations (on the verge of relief/judgment).

The *complication* is probably implicit in the reference to them not denying the name of Christ, suggesting that they have reasons to do so. Perhaps related to this is the more explicit complication referred to as those ἐκ τῆς συναγωγῆς τοῦ σατανᾶ τῶν λεγόντων ἑαυτοὺς Ἰουδαίους εἶναι, καὶ οὐκ εἰσὶν ἀλλὰ ψεύδονται ([those] out of the synagogue of Satan, calling themselves Jews and are not but are lying). Further complication is referred to as the hour of trial that is coming to the whole world, yet due to their endurance, they will be kept from it (3:10).

The *transforming action* in the message to Philadelphia is to maintain their good works by holding fast to what they already have been doing (3:11).

The *denouement* is the eventual preservation of the congregation after the hour of trial has swept through the earth, and no one has seized their crown (3:11).

---

[91] The Christological implications of attributing this allusion to Jer 17:10—speaking of Yahweh as the one searching mind and heart—to Christ make sense in light of the high Christology of the book of Revelation, and confirm that the evaluative point of view in question is in line with God's own.

[92] The same logic can be discerned in the purpose of the plagues of Yahweh and the hardening of Pharaoh ("So that you may know that I am Yahweh," Exod 10:1–2).

The *final situation*, the resolving of complicating tension, is stated by the promise of rewards to the conqueror: being made a pillar in the temple of God with the name of God, the city of God, and the name of Christ written on it.

3.4.4.2 Characterization

The actants of the plot can be discerned in the following manner:

The congregation is the subject, striving to achieve the object—eschatological judgment/salvation—here exemplified as being made a pillar in the temple of God with the name of God, the city of God, and the name of Christ engraved on it. The sender is God/Christ, the voice behind the message, and the receiver is humankind in general. The helper is primarily John, the mediator of what is revealed, but also God/Christ as this is the force behind the promise to be spared from the coming ordeal as well as the humbling of their opponents.

The opponent is the synagogue of Satan, those calling themselves Jews and are not, but are lying. Implied opponents are possibly the reasons to deny the name of Christ (3:8) and those liable to try to seize the crown of the congregation (3:11).

As at Smyrna, we find a characterization of the opponent of the congregation by association to Satan. The immediate mention of those of the synagogue of Satan after commending the congregation for its refusal to deny the name of Jesus suggests a connection. Do we see an internal or external conflict here? Despite several recent contributions suggesting a reference to internal opposition, Paul B. Duff suggests another option better able to explain the hostile imagery along with the positive outcome hinted at in 2:9.[93] He argues that the synagogue of Satan must refer to an external threat and not an internal one based on the following arguments: (1) The lack of a call to repent in the messages to Smyrna and Philadelphia suggests different underlying circumstances than the congregations troubled with internal conflicts. (2) The eschatological fate of this opposition is different from Jezebel and the Nicolaitans, describing salvation through humbling, not death. And (3) the generally positive attitude toward Jews in Revelation tips the scales against perceiving any kind of demonization in these two instances. In his conclusion, he suggests a scenario where John has to clarify the boundaries between the neighboring synagogues and the Christian congregations so that they do not become attractive as a more viable and steadier alternative in light of the ongoing conflict between John and the compromising party of Jezebel and the Nicolaitans. I find his arguments convincing and helpful regarding the understanding of the relation between the congregation and this external opposition. Utilizing Satan to define and highlight the boundaries between heterodox and orthodox faith is a typical trait of Satan in Revelation, and provides the congregation with a greater sense of distinctive identity.[94] The context of the use of the expression here is similar to the one found in Smyrna despite the absence of any specific

---

[93] For a thorough discussion on the matter, see Paul B. Duff, "'The Synagogue of Satan': Crisis Mongering and the Apocalypse of John," in *The Reality of Apocalypse: Rhetoric and Politics in the Book of Revelation*, ed. David L. Barr, SBLSymS 39 (Atlanta, GA: Society of Biblical Literature, 2006), 147–68, 151–68.

[94] This corresponds with the definition and function of vilification in the book of Revelation in Adela Yarbro Collins, "Vilification and Self-Definition in the Book of Revelation," *HTR* 79 (1986): 308–20, 314.

mentioning of "slandering" activity (cf. 2:9). In Smyrna the adversaries represent a catalyst of affliction, making it harder for the congregation to remain faithful. In Philadelphia, they represent a peaceful alternative to the tense situation in the congregation. They are both referring to themselves as Jews, yet they express the traits of Satan rather than the virtues of Moses. The designation "synagogue of Satan" is therefore a denunciation of any claim on their behalf to be a "synagogue of the Lord" (Num 16:3) and thereby efficiently denies the opponent any allegiance to God.[95] By opposing the congregation of Christ, the Son of God, they stand in opposition to God as well. These opponents are clearly characterized as the enemies of the congregation by the fate awaiting them: they will be made to come and bow down before the feet of the congregation. Through this, they will know/come to learn (γνῶσιν) that Christ has loved his congregation. How this is going to happen is not explained, but the event will convince some from the synagogue of Satan that to prostrate themselves in front of the congregation is the proper thing to do. This purpose-driven action may be revealing something similar to what would be done to Jezebel of Thyatira, in that divine intervention is meant to remind its objects of its divine origin. The humbling of the opponents of the congregation is sandwiched between two commendations of them for keeping to the word of Christ (3:8, 10) and suggests a causal connection. If this is an assumed familiar allusion to the implied reader of the promise of a future reversal of fate as found in Isa 60:14 and 49:23, it introduces the element of vindication of the saints, and possibly retribution.[96] Vindication of the saints is a key motif in the book of Revelation and is meant to motivate conquest by endurance unto death.[97] This is also the purpose of the last part of the verbal thread of the verb τηρέω (to keep, preserve): because they have kept the word of Christ (3:8, 10a), they in turn will be kept from the coming hour of trial (3:10b).[98]

They will be spared from this final period of sifting of the inhabitants of the earth. They have already proven themselves loyal. There are no critical remarks in the message to Philadelphia, only an exhortation to stay the course to the end.

3.4.4.3 *Point of View*

As with the congregation of Smyrna, the characterization of the opponents of Philadelphia evokes the emotional response of antipathy by way of their connotations

---

[95] Steven J. Friesen, "Sarcasm in Revelation 2–3: Churches, Christians, True Jews, and Satanic Synagogues," in *The Reality of Apocalypse: Rhetoric and Politics in the Book of Revelation*, ed. David L. Barr, SBLSymS 39 (Atlanta, GA: Society of Biblical Literature, 2006), 127–46, 138.

[96] This motif is also found at Qumran in 1QM XII, 14–15; XIX, 6; see Aune, *Revelation 1–5*, 237.

[97] Besides the presence of vindication found in the message to Philadelphia, it is probably also an intended aspect of the partaking of Thyatira in the messianic rule of Christ by exercising authority over the nations (2:26–27) and the promise to Laodicea to sit on the throne of Christ (3:21). The saints under the altar in heaven, revealed by the opening of the fifth seal, are told to wait a little longer for their sacrifice to be vindicated/avenged (6:10–11). The promise is considered fulfilled when the whore of Babylon has received her judgment (19:2). The conquest and expulsion of Satan on the grounds of the blood of the Lamb and the testimony of the saints unto death is another element of vindication of the faithful victims of the text (12:10–11). The reign of a thousand years is probably the most powerful symbol of vindication for those suffering pain and death for their testimony to Jesus (20:4). The element of retribution is most clearly evoked by the vision of the torments by fire and sulfur of those who worship the beast and its image in the presence of the Lamb and the holy angels (14:10–11) (see Section 5.2.2).

[98] Resseguie, *The Revelation of John*, 98.

to Satan and promise of imminent humbling. They are characterized as contrasting the values of the ideal point of view. The proper response when finding oneself in such a position to God is to humble oneself by admitting defeat. The characterization of the congregation itself, portrayed as exhibiting the ideal virtues of patient endurance and keeping the word of Christ, evokes empathy. This is the proper course of action when facing the coming hour of trial. John thus leaves nothing to chance in his writing to the congregations. The evaluative point of view is in the end further emphasized by the promise of rewards to the victor (3:12).

The formulation κἀγώ σε τηρήσω ἐκ τῆς ὥρας τοῦ πειρασμοῦ τῆς μελλούσης ἔρχεσθαι ἐπὶ τῆς οἰκουμένης ὅλης πειράσαι τοὺς κατοικοῦντας ἐπὶ τῆς γῆς (and I will keep you from the hour of temptation which is about to come upon the whole world, in order to test the inhabitants of the earth) reintroduces the concept of πειρασμόν, known from the messages to Smyrna (2:10) and Ephesus (2:2). In the message to Philadelphia, Satan is not given any explicit part in the process of temptation and sifting, as we saw in the message to Smyrna. Still, the description found here is highly relevant to this reading as it confirms both the origin and the function of the final hour of trial being unleashed upon humankind throughout Revelation. Satan, as well as numerous other heavenly agents, is assigned several different roles and functions in this process of sifting the loyal from the disloyal—those willing to confess to the name of Christ on pain of death, from those not.[99] The concept of πειρασμόν, as described in 2:10 and 3:10, epitomizes the main plot of the book of Revelation and thus provides us with a hermeneutical background to the various functions of Satan there. This is an explication of the evaluative point of view of the message and the characterization of the opponents of the congregation that fits well with the main plot by way of the embedded connotations of traditional satanic activity: the tempting and inflicting of affliction in order to test and sift the population of the earth.[100] This is further supported by the phrase τῆς οἰκουμένης ὅλης, which implies the global impact of the hour of trial that is coming. This phrase connects the hour of trial with the deceitful activities of the dragon (12:9) and gathering of the kings of the earth for war by the demonic spirits (16:14) by their common reference of impact.[101] The hour of trial that is coming upon the whole earth is therefore both under the supervision of Christ/God, as he will spare the congregation of Philadelphia from its afflictions, and at the same time executed by agents often associated with Satan and his coworkers. Here we see the contours of a monistic cosmology that will be presented in full scale later on in the throne vision of Revelation 4–5.

I now turn to the three messages not mentioning Satan explicitly, namely Ephesus, Sardis, and Laodicea. Here I will be searching for a plausible correspondence in theme, function, and purpose, as well as their function as a relevant context for the characterization of Satan in the primary texts.

---

[99] See also Boxall, *The Revelation of Saint John*, 73.
[100] The use of πειρασμόν, in light of its use in Rev 2:2, 10, suggests a test of character of both the faithful and unfaithful, and not the judgment of an unbelieving world (see Koester, *Revelation*, 326).
[101] Trafton, *Reading Revelation*, 119.

3.4.5 Ephesus

3.4.5.1 *Plot*

The *initial situation* of the congregation of Ephesus seems promising. They are given credit for keeping in line with the most prominent virtue of Revelation: endurance in faith when facing tribulation. Moreover, they have tested and exposed false apostles. Finally, they cannot bear the presence of evildoers. An additional phrase is added in verse 6, expressing a similar attitude: they hate the Nicolaitans, also mentioned in the message to Pergamum (2:15), just as Christ does.

The *complication* of this plot is the danger of Christ coming to remove the lampstand. The reason for this is that the congregation of Ephesus has abandoned its first or most important love.[102] The message is not clear on how this has happened, though the severity of this fall seems to outweigh all of the virtues above. This might indicate a decline in priority due to the eagerness to test (ἐπείρασας) and to second-guess anyone who attempts to proclaim the truth in Ephesus. Perhaps even the message of Christ failed the eager testing of the Ephesian congregation? If so, this would explain how the congregation could be so right and wrong at the same time.

The *transforming action* is to remember, repent, and do the works they did at first.

By returning to the works they did at first, they obtain the resolution of the problem indicated, thereby constituting the *denouement*. This is how the congregation will prevail.

The *final situation* is stated when the lampstand remains with the angel of Ephesus. This corresponds with the initial state, yet a new element is added by the element of eating from the tree of life, which then will be at hand (2:7).

3.4.5.2 *Characterization*

The actants of this plot could be mapped out as was done with the preceding messages, whereas the opponent is represented by evildoers, pseudo-apostles, Nicolaitans, and possibly external opponents responsible for the need for patient endurance.

In the characterization of this opposition, we find two elements associated with Satan in the messages in which he is explicitly mentioned. The first is the element of testing. In 2:2 we read that Jesus knows about their good works, toil, and patient endurance, ὅτι οὐ δύνῃ βαστάσαι κακούς, καὶ ἐπείρασας τοὺς λέγοντας ἑαυτοὺς ἀποστόλους καὶ οὐκ εἰσὶν καὶ εὗρες αὐτοὺς ψευδεῖς (because you cannot stand evil, and you have tested those calling themselves apostles but are not, and have found them to be false/lying). The congregation is commended for keeping up the virtue of patient endurance and resisting the pitfalls of heresy because they have tested so-called apostles and found them wanting. The characterization in 2:2 is similar in structure to that of 2:9; 3:9; and perhaps 2:20: *those who say* that they are apostles/Jews/prophets, and *are not, but are* a synagogue of Satan/found to be lying/misleading Jesus's servants.[103] They have endurance, elsewhere defined as keeping the commandments as well as holding

---

[102] As David L. Barr points out, the Greek is ambiguous at this point and may refer to either temporal priority or priority of status (Barr, *Tales of the End*, 95).
[103] Aune, *Revelation 1–5*, 145–7.

fast to the name of Jesus (14:12), and have endured much for the sake of this name. Yet they have not grown weary up to this point (perfect tense). By exposing the false apostles and their hostile attitudes toward the Nicolaitans, the congregation of Ephesus have succeeded in the test of falsehood and truth, both in the past (false apostles) as well as in the present (Nicolaitans), and are thus successful in the trial failed by the dwellers of the earth in their encounter with the beast (13:14). They have succeeded where Pergamum and Thyatira have failed in exposing false doctrine. Also, they have succeeded where Smyrna and Philadelphia did, regarding endurance. Yet, they seem to have a blind spot in their self-perception akin to the situations found at Sardis and Laodicea. They have left their first love. This cannot be referring to the love for Christ, of which they already have been commended for (2:3). It is probably more in line with the context that they have become increasingly suspicious of everyone around them. A general hermeneutics of suspicion has replaced their love for each other. Their repentance, then, is to do the works they did at first, acts of service to each other. As Ben Witherington suggests, "perhaps, in their zeal for orthodoxy or orthopraxy, they have lost their ability to distinguish between hating the sin and loving the sinner … without love the church loses its status as the church."[104] Their lampstand carries no light, or is deemed incapable of doing so, and will therefore be removed from its place.

The characterization is interesting in that it casts the congregation of Ephesus in the role of victor in terms of discerning falsehood, endurance in struggle, and overbearing for the sake of the name of Christ, yet at the same time their status as victor has in turn become a stumbling block, the reason for their fall. Maybe they became obsessed with suspicion? Maybe they lost sight of the truth in their search for falsehood? This way of reading the pros and cons of the congregation of Ephesus follows the line of logic seemingly displayed by the Satan of the book of Revelation. He is given to test, to sift and to deceive humankind, but will in the end suffer the lake of fire, possibly for doing so. Something happened on the way toward the end. Perhaps the adversary became too eager, lost sight of the cause, and went rogue? We will consider this option in the analysis of chapters 12–14 and 20, but for now, it will suffice to point to these possible parallels between the characterization and downfall of the congregation of Ephesus and Satan.

3.4.5.3 Point of View

The text invites the reader to take part in the discernment of falsehood and endurance for the sake of the name of Christ. One is to empathize with the virtues of the congregation of Ephesus. The antipathy is to be evoked toward lying apostles and compromising Nicolaitans. This element is enforced by the mentioning of Christ being of a similar attitude (2:6). Finally, the mistakes of the congregation are to be avoided. The love and intensity for the name of Christ must be brought out to those around, in order to fully function as a lampstand—and not to be proven dysfunctional and

---

[104] Witherington, *Revelation*, 96. For a similar approach to the interpretation of the loss of love in Ephesus, see Koester, *Revelation*, 269; Resseguie, *The Revelation of John*, 87; Synnes, *7 profetiske budskap til menighetene*, 72–3; and Smalley, *The Revelation to John*, 61.

subsequently removed. The congregation has been tested and found wanting on the part of inner motivation and Christ-like attitude toward one another.

There is no Satan mentioned in the message to the congregation of Ephesus. The function of opposition, elsewhere assigned to Satan, is here given to lying apostles and compromising Nicolaitans. The role as tester is given to the congregation itself, which, along with their destined fate unless repentant, also aligns with the one of Satan in Revelation. It seems to follow from this that the role assigned to Satan in the messages to the seven congregations is not definite, but interchangeable. It is the function to the plot that is essential—a function that is not dependent on the agent fulfilling it. The evaluative point of view is thus the same in the message to the congregation of Ephesus as in the previous messages, even without Satan explicitly mentioned.

The plot is the same as the other congregations. The same goes for the controlling element: It is Christ who has the seven stars in his hand; Christ is the one who knows the conditions of the congregations; it is Christ who will come and discipline the congregation if they do not repent. Yet if they repent, Christ will grant them access to the tree of life. The disciplining side of Christ is a feature also very much present in the message to Sardis, to which I now turn.

3.4.6 Sardis

3.4.6.1 Plot

The *initial situation* at Sardis is critical. The congregation is characterized as (spiritually) dead, despite them having a reputation for being the opposite (3:2). Still, there are some members left that are considered alive, those who have not soiled their clothes (3:3–4).

The *complication* is that the remaining part of the congregation is also about to spiritually wither and die (3:2). This will in turn lead to Christ coming like a thief in the night.

The *transforming action* is to strengthen those who remain to do works in obedience and repentance that correspond with what they received and heard.

The problem indicated by the complication will be resolved when the remnant repent in obedience, causing Jesus not to come like a thief in the night. The *denouement* is, in other words, the preservation of the congregation.

The *final situation* is the preservation of the congregation, realized by the future fulfillment of the eschatological promise of being clothed in white robes, to remain written in the book of life, and to get one's name confessed before the Father and his angels.

3.4.6.2 Characterization

The actants of the plot can be discerned in the same way as the previous messages, whereas the object (eschatological judgment/salvation) is exemplified by receiving white robes and having one's name written in the book of life and confessed before the Father and his angels—in other words, the preservation of the congregation.

The opponent in Sardis is above all ignorance. The source of this ignorance is not stated, but their works have been tested and found wanting in the sight of God.

Furthermore, the source of ignorance is still at work, causing the remnant to be dying as well. The consequence, displaying a more threatening coming of Christ, is similar to the fate of Ephesus and Pergamum (2:5, 16). The structure of the message is probably more akin to the message to Ephesus than Pergamum by way of the call for a return to former greatness (2:5; 3:3), the threat of the imminent coming of Jesus (2:5; 3:3), and the interpolated exhortation after the warning (2:6; 3:4). Both Ephesus and Pergamum have problems with heresy and intruding ambassadors of compromise, though their respective response to this threat differs—suspicion versus acceptance. This could suggest that the opposition of the congregation of Sardis is the same as found in Ephesus and Pergamum and that their wanting works (3:2) could be categorized with either of them and still warrant the threatening coming of Christ.

If there is a Satan in Sardis opposing the congregation, he is narrated not by telling but by showing, indirectly, through the fruits of his labors. Yet, we cannot conclude on this matter due to the brevity of the text. A possible reason for the absence of Satan in Sardis is the complex characteristics of Christ coming to show there. Christ refers to his own coming disciplining by the words ἥξω ὡς κλέπτης, καὶ οὐ μὴ γνῷς ποίαν ὥραν ἥξω ἐπὶ σέ (I will come like a thief, and you will not know at what hour I come upon you, 3:3). The formulation carries at least two possible allusions to knowledge presumed known to the implied reader. Firstly, this language, also used in Rev 16:15, is known from several other eschatological texts from the Christian tradition (Matt 25:42-43; Luke 12:39-40; 1 Thess 5:2; 2 Pet 3:10; Gos. Thom. 21; 103). These texts are all used in parenetical contexts to promote the preferred behavior, which will exempt them from falling prey to the abruptness of the thief coming at night. To be alert, stay awake, and exhibit works proper to a life in repentance, then, fits the purpose of the message to Sardis perfectly. Secondly, Sardis was famed in its time for its failure to stay awake and be alert in times of danger. Herodotus writes that Cyrus's armies managed to seize and plunder Sardis by entering the side of the citadel where no guard had been positioned because they had no fear that it would ever be taken from that side. They were so confident that this part of the wall was unassailable and precipitous that the king did not even carry their protective lion there.[105] If this knowledge is presumed known and alluded to in the text, it fortifies the irony of the initial statement of the city having a reputation for being awake, as well as strengthens the call for awareness and strengthening of their defenses. These two possible allusions mold the characterization of Christ from mere antagonism to a round protagonist character. In light of these, the imminent coming of Christ becomes a sharpening motivator. The parenetical motivational pattern at play here (if *you* do/do not do *this*, then *this one* will come and with him *something negative* will follow) is found many times in the book of Revelation, with a variety of divine agents cast in the wielding function. In chapter 13, Satan is given this function through the office of his triune manifestation.[106]

---

[105] Herodotus, *Histories*, 1:84. Antiochus III is reported having repeated the deed in 214 BC, in Polybius, *Histories*, 7:15-18 (see Koester, *Revelation*, 313; and Barr, *Tales of the End*, 100).

[106] The beast and its prophet are given to seduce and deceive the inhabitants of the earth, those whose names are not written in the book of life (13:7-8, 14-16; see Section 4.2.2.3), thus constituting a

If Satan were present as a character in the message to Sardis, we would expect him to be cast in one of his traditional functions to the plot—tester, deceiver, accuser, or punisher/rehabilitator. Yet, in Sardis, the tester/deceiver that made them fall into spiritual sleep, leading to their works being found wanting before God, remains unknown. However, the accuser, punisher, and rehabilitator is Christ himself.

3.4.6.3 *Point of View*

The scenario found in Sardis is a sad one. There are no commendations except for the mention of a small remnant that has not yet fallen to sleep. From the point of view from below, the congregation has a reputation for being alive, yet from the point of view from above, it is dead.[107] Spiritually, the congregation is dying and is in dire need of repentance. Antipathy is evoked and directed toward those asleep, and sympathy to those about to/struggling not to. The characterization of Christ evokes antipathy at first, but this evolves into empathy when the purpose and rewards are revealed. The threat is presented as cathartic and necessary.

The theological perspective follows the pattern found in the other messages. God has found their works wanting, and Christ speaks and threatens to motivate the congregation. There is no presence or need for a Satan in this message, though he may be the implied reason for spiritual sleep.

3.4.7 Laodicea

3.4.7.1 *Plot*

The message to Laodicea is very much akin to that of Sardis. The difference is that in Laodicea there is no mention of a remnant, and thereby no grounds for commendations.

The *initial situation* at Laodicea is a congregation believing that everything is fine.

The *complication* is that the reality is completely different from what they believe it to be. They think of themselves as in need of nothing, but in reality, it is the other way around. They think their spiritual health is good, but in reality, they are spiritually wretched, pitiable, poor, blind, and naked (3:17).

The *transforming action* is to be earnest and repent from this status (3:20). It is to open the door for Christ standing on the outside.

If they hear the voice of Christ and let him in, the resolution to the problem will be stated. This is the *denouement*: Christ will come in and eat with anyone listening to his voice and opening the door.

The *final situation* is stated by the eschatological promise of sharing the messianic throne with Christ.

---

powerful parenetical incitement to those considering switching allegiance. In the New Testament tradition outside Revelation, the function of Satan as wielder of parenetic punishment is found in 1 Cor 5:5; 2 Cor 12:7; and 1 Tim 1:20.

[107] Resseguie, *The Revelation of John*, 95.

3.4.7.2 Characterization

The actants of the plot can be discerned in the same way as the previous messages, whereas the object (eschatological judgment/salvation) is exemplified by a promise to eat with Christ and share a place on the throne with him. As was the case with Sardis, the main opponent in Laodicea is the congregation's own ignorance. The reason for this is unknown.

The problem at Laodicea is that they see themselves as rich, prosperous, and in need of nothing. Yet, from the perspective of Christ, they are wretched, pitiable, poor, blind, and naked (3:17). Christ states that the remedy for this is for them to buy from him the things they do not know they are in need of (3:18). A parenetic threat is then made in order to motivate their repentance and to be zealous (3:19). This is perhaps the hermeneutical key to interpreting the rather odd formulation of 3:15–16: οἶδά σου τὰ ἔργα ὅτι οὔτε ψυχρὸς εἶ οὔτε ζεστός. ὄφελον ψυχρὸς ἦς ἢ ζεστός. οὕτως ὅτι χλιαρὸς εἶ καὶ οὔτε ζεστὸς οὔτε ψυχρός, μέλλω σε ἐμέσαι ἐκ τοῦ στόματός μου (I know your works that you were neither cold nor hot. I wish you were either cold or hot. Because you are tepid, and not cold nor hot, I am about to vomit you out from my mouth). The hermeneutical challenge is to explain why tepid is stated to be worse than both cold and hot. This could be referring to the need for repentance from a state of being not zealous. Perhaps it is to be interpreted as ineffectiveness as witness in contrast to the faithful and true witnesses of Christ (3:14).[108] Several commentators prefer this interpretation by pointing to the possibility of tepid being a metaphor referring to the drinking water conditions of the city—allegedly tepid and distasteful.[109] Yet this reading has been contested and refuted, and has been shown to be superfluous in explaining why tepid is worse than cold/hot.[110] Craig Koester suggests that we should rather understand cold/hot as superior to tepid in the context of a banquet.[111] Tepid water was used to make dishonest slaves vomit and thereby prove alleged stealing from their master's food. Furthermore, the spitting out of wine was a strong indicator of the guest finding the beverage distasteful, and thereby ineffective in meeting its intended purpose. On the other hand, the serving of cold or hot drinks was considered refreshing because of their differing from the surrounding temperature. I find this reading probable in that it makes sense from the perspective of the overall plot of the book of Revelation as well as the seven messages. The purpose of the envisioned calamities of the book is to rattle the cage in order to divide the population of the earth into saints or dwellers of the earth. Tepid is neither cold nor hot, and could in light of the plot of Revelation be deemed unresolved, and thereby unacceptable. The message to Laodicea pushes toward the resolution of this question by way of threats to discipline and reprove. The theme of polarized decision-making is known from the synoptic tradition (Mark 9:40;

---

[108] Beale, *The Book of Revelation*, 303.
[109] Aune, *Revelation 1–5*, 257–8; Beale, *The Book of Revelation*, 303; Barr, *Tales of the End*, 102; Resseguie, *The Revelation of John*, 100–1; Witherington, *Revelation*, 107; and Mounce, *The Book of Revelation*, 109–10.
[110] Koester, *Revelation*, 337.
[111] Ibid., 344–6. The argument of Koester is probable, if not compelling, since the context contains a meal reference in Christ eating with those who open the door for him (3:20).

Matt 6:24; 12:30; Luke 11:23; 16:13), yet we have no sure textual indicators of this being presumed knowledge as an intended allusion by the implied author here.

In the context of the seven messages, the theme of blending in with its surroundings, not being able to tell apart the loyal from the disloyal—the heretic from the believer—is criticized several times. Smyrna, Pergamum, Thyatira, Sardis, and Laodicea are all characterized as facing the problem of religious compromise. Philadelphia succeeded in taking a stand against it, whereas Ephesus became too eager and seems to have lost itself in the process. Laodicea can be perceived as the apex expression, the ultimate manifestation of failure, of this common denominator among the dangers facing the seven congregations. This fits well with its position in the septet as the seventh message, being the climax. James L. Resseguie comments that "it is the representative city, summing up the dangers within the churches as well as the rewards that await the faithful."[112] Despite the fragile conditions of the congregations, the main purpose of the messages is to initiate repentance. Even for Laodicea, it is possible to hear the voice of Christ and open the door, and thus gain access to his throne.

As with Sardis, Satan is not present in this message. The test is done, and the congregation has fallen prey to its own ignorance, being assimilated into the general population of Laodicea. Christ is about to spit them out of his mouth, and the message can be seen as a last effort to discipline and motivate the congregation into action.

3.4.7.3 Point of View

The point of view is the same as the one found in Sardis. From the above-below perspective, they seem at best ignorant, perhaps in denial or, even worse, self-righteous. The characterization of the congregation evokes both sympathy and antipathy in that they are the perfect example of what doctrinal and cultic compromise may cause. The description of them being wretched, pitiable, poor, blind, and naked in a message intended for others to read supports these two emotional responses, as well as heightens the sense of shame and thereby the need for change.[113] The threatening image of a disciplining Christ is carefully balanced out by the image of him standing on the outside, knocking and calling. He wants to come in, but the congregation is in danger of not hearing and thereby not responding by opening the door.

To this reading, however, the most interesting part of the message is found in 3:19: ἐγὼ ὅσους ἐὰν φιλῶ ἐλέγχω καὶ παιδεύω (Those I love, I reprove and discipline). This is probably a loose allusion to Prov 3:11–12b, and takes up the motif of educative discipline motivated by love.[114] Christ is characterized through this as a father disciplining his congregational children. According to David E. Aune, "the theme of educative discipline was applied to the relationship between God and his people, at least in part, to explain the deeper significance of the experience of suffering and

---

[112] Resseguie, *The Revelation of John*, 100.
[113] Koester, *Revelation*, 347.
[114] This image is used on the relationship between God and his people several times in the biblical tradition. See the substantial lists of attestations on this in Aune, *Revelation 1–5*, 260; and Koester, *Revelation*, 339.

deprivation."[115] We have already seen this disciplining perspective at play in Thyatira (3:23), yet it can also be seen as part of the perspective behind much of the suffering in the other cycles of seven (9:20–21; 16:9, 11).[116] Since a host of other divine agents besides Christ, among them Satan, are being utilized by God in this process, this implies a theological point of view in the characterization of Satan that is highly relevant for the topic of this reading.[117]

3.5 Concluding Remarks

The analysis of the literary frame of the messages showed that it heightens the God of the book of Revelation as the architect of history, an element that governs the contents and premises of the visionary material of the rest of the book. The role assigned to Christ in the narrative is closely related to that of God and reveals a considerably high Christology as well as a characterization of him as both messenger and part of the message mediated.

From the analysis of the literary form and function of the messages, I found that they provide an introduction to as well as a frame of interpretation for the visionary material of the book. The messages provide the reader with the necessary introduction to the language and imagery of the visions following them. They are the context in light of which the rest of the book is to be interpreted. Moreover, due to the formulaic structure of the septet, as well as their literary function to the rest of the book, I found that all seven messages, by representing different perspectives on the same plot, could be seen as relevant in understanding the characterization of Satan. Finally, the form of the messages as Christian prophecy in form of imperial or royal edicts, the

---

[115] Aune, *Revelation 1–5*, 260.
[116] Koester, *Revelation*, 468; Smalley, *The Revelation to John*, 242; and Osborne, *Revelation*, 384–6, find in the plagues of Revelation a genuine call for repentance. Aune, *Revelation 6–16*, 541 and 889, does not follow this line of interpretation and instead interprets them in light of the Exodus tradition, using the hardening of hearts as a demonstration of God's power. Beale, *The Book of Revelation*, 517, offers a middle road that allows for a genuine call to repent for the remnant of compromisers within the congregations as well as those of the idolaters eventually have been sealed beforehand, but not for the others.
[117] Leonard L. Thompson (*The Book of Revelation: Apocalypse and Empire*, 91) identifies in these blurred cosmological lines a vision of what he calls an "unbroken world" in Revelation. According to him, metaphysical dualism is antithetical to John and his vision due to the sovereign rule of God. "Transformations and changes permeate every boundary and break down every distinction because there is an underlying dynamic system into and out of which all distinctions fold and unfold." Moreover, because God's power sustains all of creation, "this monistic flow of divinely ordered being can never quite be compartmentalized into creature and creator, God and Satan, this age and the age to come, or heaven and earth." In this idea of an unbroken world in Revelation, Thompson finds that "the logic of the vision does not progress from oppositions to their resolution. Rather, in all its aspects the language speaks from unbroken wholeness to unbroken wholeness." I will in this reading challenge this "holistic" reading of the conflicts of Revelation by offering some form of middle ground in the appreciation of the rhetorical meaning behind the life/death axis of Revelation 20. In light of it, the conflict of Revelation between those faithful or repentant versus those that are not is resolved not merely by subjugation to the sovereign God but also by way of death encompassing a second way of resolving the conflict (see Chapter 5, and Section 5.4.2.4 in particular).

number seven, the chiasmic structure of the septet, the metaphorical language and its relation to the rest of the book, the general addressee of the proclamation formula—all indicate a broader audience than what the individual names of the introductory formula suggest. The form reveals a universal, combined with the local, truth behind the imperial presence described in the book.

The analysis of the narrative function of Satan in the messages to the seven congregations revealed the following regarding his character and relation to the plot. Firstly, he is portrayed as testing the congregations on behalf of God. This activity is sometimes carried out by himself, at other times by using humans as agents. In this way he serves as a necessary function to a plot revolving around the division of humankind. Secondly, his traits seem to be well known by the congregations and in some cases serve to characterize other opponents of the congregations by association. Thirdly, he is part of an evocative language that makes use of archetypes from the history of Israel to promote a certain course of action by employing characterization by association. Fourthly, the testing of the earth mentioned above will eventually lead to the vindication of the saints. Those who fall prey to his snares will eventually be subjected to the mercy, judgment, and rule of God, and possibly of the saints. In this way, his function is described as important on both sides of the outcome of the trial of testing. Fifthly, from the messages not mentioning Satan, it may be inferred that the role and function of Satan is possibly being assigned to other characters of the narrative. It seems to follow from this that the actantial function within a plot does not depend on the fulfilling of it by any specific agent. This suggests that the general plot, with its functions and purposes in the messages, is the governing principle in the seven messages. This plot revolves around the division of humankind, of which the actants of the plot are subordinate and interchangeable. Sixthly, a recurring element in the characterization of Satan in the messages is deception into religious compromise. Finally, the characterization of Satan as opponent is directed toward the subject of the plot—the congregations. In the messages to the seven congregations he is not cast as the enemy of God (sender) but in his traditional role as adversary, tester, and tormentor of humankind. Moreover, this opponent in the messages constitutes an important part of the ordeal (containing the object) sent by God to humankind (receiver).

Due to the high Christology and the strong monistic cosmology of Revelation, the functions of Satan and Christ occasionally seem to overlap concerning the negative functions in the plot of the messages. When Satan or his traits are accentuated, it seems to be in order to stress the function of the opponent in its purpose to test and sift the congregations. The fate of those who fail to perform the transforming action is described as objects of Christ's more negative traits. He will remove their lampstand (Ephesus), he will make war against them with the sword of his mouth (Pergamum), he will give to each whatever his works deserve (Thyatira). Philadelphia is admonished to hold fast to what they have because there are those out there who may want to steal their crown. In Sardis, it is Christ himself who is coming like a thief at an unexpected hour unless they wake up. Christ is, as the "I" of the narrative, indirectly causing, or in control of, the function of opposition in several messages. The testing activity of the Devil of Smyrna will last for ten days. Christ will spare the congregation of Philadelphia from this test because they have already proved their loyalty. Thyatira has already experienced the reproving and disciplinarian function of Christ, while Laodicea may expect to if they do not engage in transforming action. The role assigned to the opponent displays the characteristics typical of biblical characters, often referred to as the nonautonomy of characters. God is the architect of history, in constant control over earthly matters. In the messages to the seven congregations, the distinction between Christ and God is blurred by the exalted Christ wielding the authority and powers reserved elsewhere in the biblical tradition for Yahweh of Hosts. In the characterization of Satan this is important as it makes the Devil and his testing of the congregation of Smyrna into a test sanctioned and supervised not only by God, as was the case with Job, Joshua the high priest, possibly David, and later Paul, but also by Christ—the first-person dictator of what is written. This characterizes Satan not as the enemy of God and Christ but as a tool in the testing of the congregations. He is thus not the antagonist of Christ, but of the congregations—a heavenly sanctioned adversary of man.

The characterization of Satan in the seven messages is governed by his assigned function in the plot, which is a call for commitment to the transforming action instigated by Christ. The authority and elevation of Christ is in turn sanctioned by God in the prologue to the book (1:7–8). In short, the Satan present within this particular septet is mainly a traditional one, subjected to God and the plot of the narrative—an opposing character among several, serving as obstacles in the quest of the subjects. He serves the purpose of his assigned function. He is a necessary evil, so to speak.

4

Satan in the Story of the Woman, the Dragon, and the Beasts

4.1 Introduction

One of the main purposes of this chapter is to highlight the intrinsic continuity of the plot, the function of heavenly agents, and theological point of view *from* the messages to the seven congregations *to* that of the story of the woman, the dragon, and the beasts. I find this approach to be the most promising in light of the scope of this book as the textual evidence seems to suggest that the characterization of Satan in Revelation is a dynamic one, not static (heavenly accuser → earthly, angry, deceiver → lake of fire). It is thus important to pay attention to any trace of development in his assigned function to the plot and the characterization of him in the three text units in which he is mentioned.[1] It is my opinion that several of the narratological elements present in the messages to the seven congregations reoccur throughout the narrative, though perceived and told from a gradually more vertical point of view. If this is so, we might expect a Satan characterized and cast in a correspondingly oppositional role in the plot of Revelation 12–13 compared to the one in Revelation 2–3. Furthermore, we may also expect further light to be shed on the evaluative point of view of Satan, due to the gradually elevated vertical perspective. What is stated about Satan and his relation to God in Revelation 12–13 will have to be compared and added to what was concluded on the matter in the messages to the congregations.[2]

---

[1] According to James L. Resseguie, utilizing the terms and definitions of Thomas R. Arp, "a dynamic character undergoes radical change throughout the course of a narrative, displaying new behaviours and changed outlooks … A *static* character, however, does not develop or change; he or she remains stable in outlook and disposition throughout the story" (Resseguie, *Narrative Criticism of the New Testament*, 125).

[2] Note that this is the direct opposite hermeneutical approach to how Sigve Tonstad considers the storyline of the book of Revelation in the revised version of his doctoral dissertation in New Testament studies, *Saving God's Reputation: The Theological Function of Pistis Iesou in the Cosmic Narratives of Revelation*. He begins his enterprise by reading it in light of its "peculiar ending" in Revelation 20. This interpretational move, along with the interpretation of the term ὁ ὄφις ὁ ἀρχαῖος (Rev 20:2) as a reference to the serpent of Genesis 3, allows for him to establish the central conflict within the narrative as one between God/Christ and Satan (Tonstad, *Saving God's Reputation*, 14–15, 41–3). My reading diverges from such an approach by interpreting the ending in light of its beginning rather than the other way around, and perceives the seven congregations as a microcosm in light of which to interpret the remaining parts of the book. I also disagree on the identification of an Eden serpent

As argued for in the previous chapter, I believe that a thorough consideration of the context of a text is important in order to grasp the scope and intention of it fully. In the case of Revelation 12–13 this context is rather substantial. After the throne vision in chapter 4–5, we find the narrative of Revelation 12–13 embedded between the second and third of three succeeding septets (seals [5–6], trumpets [8–11], and bowls [15–16]), in the manner shown in Table 5 later on in this chapter. Satan is not present as a self-sufficient character in the throne vision or the septets per se. Still, I find these adjoining texts (Revelation 4–5; 6–11; 14–16) important to the scope of my reading because they convey valuable information on the general cosmology presupposed in the book of Revelation. In the first part of this chapter (Section 4.2, "The Literary Context of Revelation 12–13") I will emphasize how this cosmology is present within the text and how one's understanding of it determines how one perceives the function, characterization, and point of view regarding Satan in Revelation 12–13. The argument will be derived from an eclectic analysis of the throne vision of Revelation 4–5 (Section 4.2.1) and the septets of 6–16 (Section 4.2.2). A delimiting premise of this preliminary analysis will be to incorporate only elements relevant to my understanding of the narrative function of Satan in the main object of analysis, Revelation 12–13 (Section 4.4, "Analysis").

4.2 The Literary Context of Revelation 12–13

4.2.1 The Throne Vision

According to Craig Koester, Revelation 4–5 forms the heart of the book of Revelation: "For here its essential revelation is to be found. Through the images of the throne and the Lamb, readers learn how God's will is done through the crucified and risen Christ."[3] Here at the heart of the book, Koester finds the presence of worship indicating the prominence of worship above visions of disaster. One day God will universally be recognized and worshipped.[4] I concur with Koester in that the throne vision seems to form the center of Revelation, from the initial placing of the text, the scriptural traditions alluded to within it, but first and foremost from its contents as it describes the origins and proves the validity of the rest of the book. It is in essence an elaboration of the general point of view of the book—God's own point of view—first presented to us in the prologue. Any role and function of Satan in a revealed fate of the world must be reckoned with the contents of this particular section of the book because it is here we get to know the origins of revelation. The God of Revelation

---

present in Revelation (see Section 4.4.2.1). Besides such hermeneutical contingencies, I agree with Tonstad in his understanding of Revelation as a "loosely conceived theodicy" (Tonstad, *Saving God's Reputation*, 15), and that certain elements of the narrative (for instance, the binding and release of Satan in Revelation 20) emphasize Satan as "an important character in the narrative and allots to him a central role in the plot of the story on literary and narrative terms alone" (ibid., 48). I will return to Tonstad's analysis of Revelation 20 in my own analysis of this text in Chapter 5.
[3] Craig R. Koester, *Revelation and the End of All Things* (Grand Rapids, MI: Eerdmans, 2001), 72.
[4] Ibid., 71–2.

4–5 is both the source of revelation as well as the architect of the history revealed. Whenever we encounter an aorist passive within the narrative or read of the finger of God explicitly at play (cf. Rev 17:17), it is the God of the throne vision that is its point of reference. This makes this textual unit a key text to the narrative.

In 4:1 we find a shift in the spatial point of view, from earth to heaven, starting with the phrase μετὰ ταῦτα (after these [things]).[5] This indicates that a major shift in scenery is about to take place. If the messages to the seven congregations serve as a presentation of the earthly perspective of the visions revealed, then the throne vision (Revelation 4–5) serves as a presentation and proclamation of the heavenly one. Three elements of the throne vision are of particular importance for my reading here: the ethos ascribed to John, the characterization of God, and the Christological implications of the characterization of the Lamb.

4.2.1.1 The Ethos of John

The ethos of John is fortified by associating him with several great men and prophets of the Hebrew Bible. In keeping with the assumed knowledge of the implied reader, the gemlike throne, the crystal sea, the rainbow, and the four heavenly creatures are probable allusions to Ezekiel 1–2. The stressing of the six wings of the creatures, the fact that Revelation 4–5 reflects the scene of a throne room in a heavenly temple, and the wording καὶ ἀνάπαυσιν οὐκ ἔχουσιν ἡμέρας καὶ νυκτὸς λέγοντες· ἅγιος ἅγιος ἅγιος κύριος ὁ θεὸς ὁ παντοκράτωρ, ὁ ἦν καὶ ὁ ὢν καὶ ὁ ἐρχόμενος (day and night without ceasing they are saying: Holy, Holy, Holy is the Lord our God almighty, the one who was, who is and who is coming, Rev 4:8) are reminiscent of the visions of Isaiah 6. The presence of a throne in heaven with God appearing as sitting upon it, the presence of other thrones around the throne of God, fire in front of the throne, and books before the throne are all probable allusions to Daniel 7. Furthermore, the language of worship itself recalls several themes from Israel's worship, in particular, the element of grounding the worship in God's acts of creation (4:11).[6]

With these textual elements, John's visions seem to relate directly to similar visions from Scripture, and by doing so ensure that his message is interpreted *in light of* this tradition, as much as it is to be considered *part of* this tradition.[7] The logic seems obvious: the authority of the messages of Isaiah, Ezekiel, and Daniel should, through their common source of origin, apply and add considerable weight to the message of John. The vision of Revelation 4–5 thus forms a powerful reaffirmation of John's commission to prophesize by means of a careful construction of ethos. Revelation 4:1 picks up the theme of revelation and the call to prophesize from the prologue (1:9–10, 19), via the invitation to enter the heavenly sphere in order to receive revelation.

---

[5] The phrase is used in Revelation only for major breaks in sequence: 1:19; 4:1; 7:9; 9:12; 15:5; 18:1; 19:1; 20:3. See Aune, *Revelation 1–5*, 276.
[6] See Koester, *Revelation*, 367, for the main point of this argument. Gregory Beale finds no less than fourteen elements from Daniel 7 in Revelation 4–5. He finds it probable that the whole throne vision section of Revelation reflects the dominant framework of Daniel 7, hinting at a Danielic pattern present here (see Beale, *The Book of Revelation*, 313–16).
[7] See Yarbro Collins, *Crisis and Catharsis*, 145–7.

The language is that of a visionary journey and differs in its very nature from the spatial context of Patmos, as was the case with the prologue.[8] Through this vision, the throne of God is portrayed as the origin of the visions and the commission of John.[9] It validates both him and his message.[10] The commission language of the prologue and the epilogue, the throne vision, the elaborate use of the phrases εἶδον and ἤκουσα (I saw and I heard), as well as the repeated exhortation to write throughout the book all continue to add strength to the ethos of John and align him with former heroes known from the scriptural tradition of the Hebrew Bible.[11] Chapters 4–5 serve as a precise identification of the God of Scriptures and the Christ event, and reveal their relation to both the origin and scope of the book. Furthermore, the embedding of chapters 4–5 between the septet of chapters 2–3 and the septets of chapters 6–16 seems to provide an interpretative key to the septets by presenting the image of a symmetrically designed order of creation and its creator, with his host wedged in between them. This is consistent with James L. Resseguie's suggestion that "Revelation 4–5 forms a liturgical diptych that provides the interpretative key to understanding the Apocalypse" in that it presents the ideal symmetry of the created order.[12] Where the first septet (Revelation 2–3) describes a dire and perilous situation for the congregations, the throne vision serves as a comforting and awe-inspiring adjustment to this perspective. The succeeding septets (Revelation 6–16) present an eschatological and apocalyptic view of the situation of the first septet (Revelation 2–3) in light of this corrective perspective (Revelation 4–5). If this is so, determining the characterization of God upon the throne, his host and the Lamb, and their relation to the ordeals dealt upon the earth and the vessels of calamities and destruction will be important to the scope of this reading.

4.2.1.2 God upon the Throne and His Assembly

As mentioned earlier (Section 3.4.2), the use of the term "throne" in the book of Revelation involves the idea of dominion. According to James L. Resseguie, it also represents one of the major plot conflicts of the book: Who sits upon the throne?[13] Who has dominion over earth? Who is the ruler of this world? Elisabeth Schüssler Fiorenza suggests that "the book's central theological symbol is therefore the *throne*, signifying either divine and liberating or demonic and death-dealing power."[14] Thus, the theme of

---

[8] For similar texts witnessing visionary journeys, see 1 En. 14:8–9; T. Levi 2:6–5:7; 4Q213a 1 II, 18; Mart. Ascen. Isa. 7:2–6. See Koester, *Revelation*, 359.

[9] According to Greg Carey, John struggles for validation of his vision among a host of competing voices. Thus, through emphasis on John's status as eyewitness (I saw and heard), the pastoral closeness to his audience, the heavenly origins of his revelations, as well as his elaborate efforts in disclaiming his opponents, "he constructs an unstable ethos. John's ethos is at once egalitarian and authoritarian, inviting and exclusivist. John reaches out to the audience, yet locates himself as sole mediator of truth; he calls his opponents to repentance, yet depicts them in the most abject terms" (Carey, "The Apocalypse and Its Ambiguous Ethos," 163–80, 180).

[10] See also Yarbro Collins, *Crisis and Catharsis*, 145.

[11] deSilva, *Seeing Things John's Way*, 119–20, 131.

[12] Resseguie, *The Revelation of John*, 105.

[13] Ibid., 90.

[14] Elisabeth Shüssler Fiorenza, *Revelation: Vision of a Just World* (Minneapolis: Augsburg Fortress, 1991), 120; Fiorenza, *The Book of Revelation: Justice and Judgment*, 24; see also Witherington,

Revelation 4–5 is power—God's power. The seventeen references to the term "throne" in Revelation 4–5, a text mainly concerned with the power and worthiness of God and the Lamb, suggests the sovereignty of God as the central theme of this section of the book.[15] Whoever is in charge of things is the only relevant court of appeal for the suffering saints (Rev 6:10–11) because whoever is in control is also capable of relieving and in the end removing the afflictions. These afflictions are in turn the very objects of their perseverance. From an evaluative point of view, the power structures revealed in chapters 4–5 are highly important for answering who Satan might be, and how he functions in relation to God as well as to Christ in the book of Revelation. The God of the throne vision, the one who sits on the throne (4:9), is the κύριος ὁ θεὸς ὁ παντοκράτωρ, ὁ ἦν καὶ ὁ ὢν καὶ ὁ ἐρχόμενος (the Lord Almighty, the one who was and who is and who is coming, 4:8) and he is worthy to receive worship, glory, and power from his host because of his acts of creation (4:11). As the creator of everything, he is set apart from his creation, that is, he is sovereign, and thus worthy of worship. The praise of the twenty-four elders accompanies the Trisagion of the creatures in affirming the holiness of God being grounded in or at least related to his acts of creation. The seven occurrences of the full title κύριος ὁ θεός ὁ παντοκράτωρ in Revelation, which is a standard translation of the divine name Yahweh Elohim Sebaoth, is present here to further underscore this element of sovereignty.[16] As the throne vision is predominantly concerned with presenting God as the one upon the throne, worthy to rule, and worthy of receiving worship, the occurrence of a divine title literally stressing his almighty sovereignty comes as no surprise—especially not if one considers the general character of the book of Revelation as something close to "a loosely conceived theodicy," as one of the main concerns of the narrative is to explain the origins, means, and end of the suffering of the saints.[17] According to Richard Bauckham, the title "is very common in the Old Testament prophets because it indicates Yahweh's unrivaled power over

---

Revelation, 113. Laszlo Gallusz concludes that the throne motif "constitutes the major, though not the only, interpretative key to the complex structure and theology of the book" (Gallusz, *The Throne Motif in the Book of Revelation*, 330). Gallusz concludes his section on Revelation 4 by stating that it functions by its location in the book as the axis mundi of the universe, and that it is "conveying a message not only about the structure of the universe, but also about the function of God within it and about the dynamics of human history" (ibid., 140). I agree with him in this and therefore find it strange that Gallusz consistently insists that Satan is characterized in the two sections his throne is mentioned (Rev 13:1–18; 16:1–21) as the opponent/antagonist/adversary/enemy of God (ibid., 210, 214, 334–5). He admits that the last septet (Revelation 15–16) is modeled on the Egyptian plague narrative (ibid., 215, 220–1) yet does not in my view consider the possible cosmological implications of this. Similarly, he elaborates on the implications of the triple authorization formula of Rev 13:1–2 and the giving of authority from the dragon to the beast, yet when stating that "the repeated divine passive ἐδόθη in ch. 13 implies the underlying assumption of divine sovereignty and stresses that the ultimate power, throne and authority is derived *from God*" (ibid., 215, my italics), any possible implications of this again go unnoticed.

[15] Beale, *The Book of Revelation*, 172.
[16] Rev 1:8; 4:8; 11:17; 15:3; 16:7; 19:6; 21:22.
[17] The description "loosely conceived theodicy" is derived from Sigve Tonstad's work, *Saving God's Reputation*, 15. It should be noted that Tonstad concludes his view of Revelation as theodicy by writing, "There can be no doubt that the author of Revelation sees God as the solution to, and not as the cause of, the perplexing reality of evil" (ibid., 15), whereas I will argue that we find in Revelation a cosmology more akin to the one found in Isa 45:7. The building block, the point of reference, of this cosmology is the sovereign God of the throne vision.

all things and therefore his supremacy over the course of historical events. Its use in Revelation testifies to John's desire to continue the prophetic faith in God."[18] This imagery derived from the Hebrew Bible is further enhanced by the presence of several beings in the proximity of the throne (the twenty-four elders on their thrones, the seven spirits of God, and the four creatures), evoking associations of the scriptural tradition of the heavenly assembly—the very host of the Yahweh of Hosts, so to speak.[19]

The understanding of the divine assembly and of how the adversarial character of Satan gradually emerges from it has proved to be contingent to one's understanding of how celestial adversarial characters/Satan function within the monotheistic framework of the Hebrew Bible.[20] As the notion of the divine assembly is clearly presupposed in Revelation 4–5, one's understanding of it will in turn automatically reflect upon the understanding of the sovereign God of the throne vision per se, and in the book of Revelation in general. In his studies on the development of the Israelite religion, from polytheism to monotheism, Mark S. Smith argues for the presence of a redefinition of the old gods and divine creatures within the transition of the old pantheon, toward a subjugation of them under the supreme God within the Godhead and the idea of the heavenly assembly.[21] The old gods of the nations turned into the angels of the nations subjugated under the dominion of the supreme God.[22] This left the head of the divine assembly, as expressed in Deutero-Isaiah, in charge of not only the benevolent activities of the divine but also the malevolent activities of the malignant (cf. Isa 45:5–8). In the apocalyptic period, this monistic perspective saw a need for a reintroduction of the more malignant forces, outsourcing the more shady business of the Godhead.[23] In his

---

[18] Bauckham, *The Theology of the Book of Revelation*, 30.

[19] Texts reflecting the tradition of the heavenly assembly abound in the Hebrew Bible, yet due to the imagery, the prophetic language, and purpose of the throne vision, the following texts seem for me to be the most probable candidates to any intended association assumed known to the implied reader: Isaiah 6; Ezekiel 1; 1 Kgs 22:19–23; Daniel 7; Job 1–2; Deut 32:8–9; and Zechariah 3.

[20] I have included this rather large section on Satan and his relation to the divine assembly here because it constitutes one of the major differences between this study and Steven Grabiner's work, *Revelation's Hymns: Commentary on the Cosmic Conflict*. These differences lead to two diametrically opposing understandings of how celestially adversarial characters function within the monotheistic framework of the Hebrew Bible, which in turn reflects upon the understanding of the sovereign God of the throne vision per se, and in the book of Revelation in general. For the differences between Steven Grabiner's work and this reading, see Section 1.7 in this book.

[21] See his section on anti-polytheistic alteration of Deut 32:8–9 in the Masoretic Text from the probably more original texts as attested in the traditions of the Septuagint and the Dead Sea Scrolls, which displays a discomfort in the earlier polytheistic theology of Israel. This example may serve as a good entrance to the main thrust of the argument of his book. See Mark S. Smith, *The Origins of Biblical Monotheism: Israel's Polytheistic Background and the Ugaritic Texts* (New York: Oxford University Press, 2001), 48–53; see also Smith, *The Memoirs of God: History, Memory, and the Experience of the Divine in Ancient Israel* (Minneapolis: Fortress, 2004), 107–10.

[22] Smith locates the reason or trigger for such an evolution of theology in the rise of the Neo-Assyrian empire in the eighth century BC and onwards: "Only after this alteration of the world scene did Israel require a different 'world theology' that not only advanced Yahweh to the top but eventually eliminated the second tier [of the pantheon of gods] altogether insofar as it treated all other gods as either nonentities or expressions of Yahweh's power" (Smith, *The Origins of Biblical Monotheism*, 49).

[23] Note the transition from 2 Sam 24:1 to 1 Chr 21:1, as well as the targumic rendering of the latter. As Ryan E. Stokes has rightly pointed out, this is not a way of relieving Yahweh of any charge of wrongdoing: "Any distance between Yhwh and David's sin created by this substitution is very slight" (Stokes, "The Devil Made David Do It," 99–100). Perhaps this text too could be a trace of what Mark Smith refers to as the bureaucratic model (a term he derives from L. K. Handy's book *Among the*

concluding remarks on the transition of Satan from a general adversary principle in the Hebrew Bible into "the personified cosmic principle of opposition to the divine will and human life," Smith stresses the basic premise of the biblical tradition of Satan: "this *satan* depends ultimately on the good reality sustained by God. Take God out of the system, and the figure of *satan*, however powerful he may seem, has no meaning or reality."[24] I concur with Smith in his main argumentation here (though I question the idea of Satan representing a "principle of opposition to the divine will" due to the lack of textual evidence to support this), because it is an elaboration on the monistic features of biblical theology, of which the result of any alleged Persian influence in this could only become semi-dualistic at best, and never radically dualistic (see Section 1.1.4).[25] It is therefore a working hypothesis of mine that it is from this background that we find the preservation of the servant imagery of Satan later found in the book of Revelation.

The παντοκράτωρ of the throne vision, the almighty Lord of Hosts, is the sovereign ruler responsible for what the scroll of chapter 5 will reveal in the following three septets. That is why the vision of Revelation 4–5 is wedged between the first and the succeeding three septets. It is a powerful display of the sovereignty of God. It reveals the evaluative point of view—God's own point of view—as the supreme one. This supports the idea of the throne vision functioning as an adjustment of perspective, aligning what is being revealed and what must take place after this with the evaluative point of view of God.

In short, we may deduce from the display of power, divine titles, the attribution of glory, honor and power, the proclamation of worthiness, and the act of worship in this vision, in connection to the formulation δείξω σοι ἃ δεῖ γενέσθαι (I will show you what must take place), that it is the God of the throne vision who is the architect and instigator of what must soon follow. This implies divine determinism (Beale) as it serves to underscore that everything is happening and will happen according to God's will or plan without eliminating the possibility of human response effecting the outcome (Koester).[26] In any case, the revelation of history as orchestrated by divine will as a pre-text to the succeeding septets (Revelation 6–16) adds considerable leverage to an understanding of this section of the book, with its numerous vessels of mayhem as divine agents and not self-sufficient enemies of God acting on their own accord.[27] This interpretational perspective will in turn be applied in the analysis of the narrative function of Satan in Revelation 12–13. The throne vision thus functions as a necessary hermeneutical lens, not just for strengthening the ethos of John, but also to properly understand and justify the calamities unleashed upon the earth in the

---

Host of Heaven, and his application of Max Weber's category of bureaucracy to the pantheon), as it is a possible individuation of a divine being within the divine household. As a means to distinguish between the head of office (God), intermediary functionary (Satan), and employee (David), I find the term rather fitting (see Smith, *The Origins of Biblical Monotheism*, 52–3).

[24] Smith, *The Memoirs of God*, 119.
[25] On the issue of possible influence of Persian dualistic ideas on Jewish apocalyptic, see Bell, *Deliver Us from Evil*, 14–15.
[26] Beale, *The Book of Revelation*, 317; Koester, *Revelation*, 222.
[27] See also Peter-Ben Smit, "Sadomasochism and the Apocalypse of John: Exegesis, Sensemaking and Pain," *BibInt* 26 (2018): 90–112, 105–7.

soon-to-be-revealed septets. This is important information to anyone questioning the authority or sovereignty of God in such perilous times as those described in Revelation. He is the creator of everything, he is the architect of history, and he is in total control of his dominion.[28]

4.2.1.3 The Lamb

Revelation 5 reintroduces the Christological component of the narrative already touched upon in the prologue and the messages to the seven congregations: The revelation of Christ is the revelation of God, given to John (1:1). It is the revelation given *from* God *by* Christ and *to* John and his readers. God as the supreme source of revelation is mentioned again in 1:8 before the next narrative level is introduced (1:9). In Revelation 4–5 this mode of focalization is repeated. God is characterized as the ultimate source of everything by merit of creation, and it is from his hand the scroll of revelation is derived. Still, to John and everyone else, the contents of the scroll remain hidden and unknown. Only the Lamb is worthy of opening and revealing its contents to John and his readers by means of its sacrificial death (5:9–10). Thus, as a means of revelation, God and the Lamb/Christ are characterized as entities that are both overlapping and separate. From the analysis of the messages to the seven congregations, I concluded that the distinction between Christ and God is blurred by the exalted Christ wielding the authority and powers reserved elsewhere in the biblical tradition for Yahweh of Hosts. This impression is further enhanced by the obvious parallel presentations of God and the Lamb in Revelation 4–5. As can be seen in Table 4 from the analysis of Charles H. Talbert, there is a clear case of parallelism between Revelation 4 and 5.

In addition to these parallel elements, the theme of worthiness (ἄξιος, Rev 4:11; 5:2, 9, 12–13) and the subsequent act of worship (5:13–14) seem to further bind the venerations of God and the Lamb together. God is worthy of glory, honor, power, and worship due to his acts of creation, and the Lamb is worthy of opening the scroll as well as of taking a share in the praise of God due to his acts of conquest (5:5, 9–10, 12–13). The question of who conquers is, as I have shown in Section 2.3, part of the main plot of Revelation, whereas the Christ event serves as model, means, and goal in this ordeal for the saints. Important here is the separation of the Lamb/Christ from the other members of the heavenly assembly as well as the heavenly agents of the following three septets—benevolent or malignant. Christ is set apart from the others by being elevated as an object of worship beside God (Rev 5:13–14). The creatures and elders who bowed before the throne of God now bow before the Lamb (4:10; 5:8). The harps that were traditionally used to praise God (Ps 150:3) now sound praises to the Lamb (Rev 5:8). The bowls of incense that signified prayer to God (Ps 141:2) are now placed

---

[28] See also Yarbro Collins, *Crisis and Catharsis*, 152. I therefore find her combat myth paradigm problematic in light of such statements. The idea of God causing and controlling the very events that inflict suffering upon the saints ("they [the events] are God's and God is in control") seems incompatible with the idea of "The forces of chaos are dominant now, but their defeat is certain" (ibid.). It is unclear how Collins reconciles the idea of God both instigating, endorsing, and/or allowing these forces while at the same time fighting them.

Table 4 Parallels in the Presentations of God and the Lamb in Revelation 4 and 5

Revelation 4—God	Revelation 5—The Lamb
God's glory (4:2b–8a)	The Lamb's glory (5:5–7)
Worship of God (8b–11)	Worship of the Lamb (8–12)
First Hymn (8b)	First Hymn (9–10)
Narrative (9–10)	Narrative (11–12a)
Second Hymn (11)	Second Hymn (12b)

Source: Charles H. Talbert, *The Apocalypse: A Reading of the Revelation of John* (Louisville, KY: Westminster John Knox, 1994), 26–7; cf. Witherington, *Revelation*, 113–15.

before the Lamb (Rev 5:8). In the same way a "new song" celebrated God's rule over the earth (Ps 96:1), a "new song" is now sung to proclaim the Lamb's power and might (5:9). And the heavenly chorus that proclaimed God "worthy" (Rev 4:11), now does the same for Christ (5:9). And as the four creatures instigate the worship of God (4:9–10), they also include the Lamb (5:14). In short, the Lamb is honored and worshipped alongside God, in the same manner in which God is honored and worshipped (4:11; 7:12 = 5:12–14).[29] The language of the hymn of Rev 5:9–12 suggests that the Lamb/Christ partakes in the deity rather than being a mere agent working on behalf of it.[30] The formulation of Gregory K. Beale therefore seems warranted when he states, "The clear deduction from chs. 4 and 5 is that the Lamb is in the same divine position as God."[31] This confirms the presence of what many scholars refer to as the "high" Christology of the book of Revelation. A high Christology such as this, combined with the presence of monistic cosmology, may challenge the usual perception of an overtly polarized relation between Christ and Satan in Revelation.

The vision of Revelation 4–5 functions as an introduction to the visions of 6:1–22:5 much in the same manner as 1:1–20 did for the messages to the seven congregations. Furthermore, it is an elaboration on the information given in 1:1. It is the revelation *of* Jesus Christ *from* God *to* John, who in turn writes down all these things that he is shown must take place (4:1; 5:1, 9). We see the diegetic levels 1–3 at play here, while the hypodiegetic level—that is, the communication of what is seen and heard to a third party (the congregations)—is not mentioned again until 22:16, though the commission to write implies this level throughout the book (Rev 10:4; 14:13; 19:9; 21:5). The latter part of the book follows from the contents and premises of the throne vision. This is particularly important for this reading, namely that the premises of this section serve as theological contingencies for the visions of the book. As Gregory K. Beale puts it, "God and Christ are in ultimate control of all the woes of both believers and unbelievers."[32] This follows from the sovereign perspective of the throne vision itself, the monistic cosmology of the book of Revelation in general, and the formative passages from the Hebrew Bible behind the three septets of Revelation 6–16[33] (an argument for the

---

[29] See Koester, *Revelation*, 388, 390–1.
[30] Beale, *The Book of Revelation*, 358.
[31] Ibid., 172; see also Witherington, *Revelation*, 122.
[32] Beale, *The Book of Revelation*, 172.
[33] Ibid., 172–3.

latter will be presented below). This monistic cosmology, implying a God in control of everything and everyone, often finds its ultimate expression in the divine governing of things[34]—another common feature within the genre of apocalyptic literature.[35] This determinism, derived from the sovereign position of God in the book of Revelation, is in turn the very thing that makes revelation possible. In the throne vision, this sovereignty is deduced from his status as creator. The scroll comes from the hand of God, and even the Lamb must prove itself worthy in order to open it and subsequently reveal its contents. This element separates the Lamb/Christ from God.

Thus, from the throne vision, I find the resonance of—as well as strong support for—my findings in Revelation 2-3 regarding the image and role assigned to God, Christ, and other heavenly agents. Moreover, if I am correct in my understanding of Revelation 4-5 being an introductory vision to the three septets of Revelation 6-16, we may expect its cosmological premises to govern the plot, characterization, and point of view of this particular section of the book as well as the book in general.

4.2.2 The Septets of Revelation 6-16

The main purpose of this section of the chapter is to understand the relation between the three septets, to argue for a close literary connection between the septets and Revelation 4-5, and to stress the presence of subjugation of heavenly agents under the divine will in this section of the book. Together the data from this and the previous section (4.2.1) will provide the literary and theological context and thus the premises for the concluding section of this chapter—the narrative analysis of the first part of the interlude of Revelation 12-15. It is my view that this is necessary in order to grasp the relation between the Satan of the seven messages and the one of Revelation 12-13.

---

[34] If the term "determinism" is to be used on this matter in Revelation, it must be with a meaning allowing for human response to effectuate the outcome of the divine governing of things. Without this aspect, the admonitions to the saints (as well as the evaluative point of view of the implied reader) to persevere and stay faithful to their testimony in Christ becomes devoid of meaning. Consequently, the use of this term in this reading is done with this scope of meaning in mind.

[35] David Syme Russell writes in his *Divine Disclosure* on this recurring feature within "apocalyptic books" that they by their divisions of history are "underlining still further both the unity of history and the complete control of God over its movements, who has determined from the beginning not only the course of its events but their climax as well ... the apocalyptists build up a schematized pattern of history which, given the fiction of 'prediction' here adopted, proves irrefutably that history both in whole and its several parts has been predetermined by the sovereign will of God" (Russell, *Divine Disclosure*, 89-90). The motivation for this, Russell suggests from a swift reference to Daniel 7 and 11; 1 Enoch 1-36; 4 Ezra 14; 2 Baruch 53; and more general references to similar divisions of history in the book of Jubilees, the Assumption of Moses, and the Enoch Apocalypse of Weeks, is to be able to identify themselves as authors very near to the culmination of the historical process in order to project a powerful rhetorical message to their readers: "Nothing that the most powerful ruler could do could in any way alter the fact that God had determined all things from the beginning and would bring them to their successful conclusion" (Russell, *Divine Disclosure*, 90-1). Mladen Popović adds considerably to our understanding of this element, by underlining the fact that determinism is by no means restricted to the apocalyptic genre of its time. Still, the purpose seems to be the same wherever this feature is found in literature from this period: to adduce and reinforce a particular view of history as governed by God. See Mladen Popović, "Apocalyptic Determinism," in *The Oxford Handbook of Apocalyptic Literature*, ed. John J. Collins (New York: Oxford University Press, 2014), 255-70.

4.2.2.1 *The Literary Structure of Revelation 6–16 and Its Relation to Revelation 4–5*

The throne vision paves the way to the revelation of what must take place after this (ἃ δεῖ γενέσθαι μετὰ ταῦτα, 4:1). The point of reference here is probably the content of the scroll mentioned in chapter 5, which is gradually revealed through the succeeding three septets and their respective interludes. The use of δεῖ (it is necessary, must) expresses divine determination, picking up the idea already touched upon in 1:1 and 19, and serves to underscore the sovereign role of God in what is to be revealed through the scroll.

A closer look at the compositional structure of the septets reveals complex interrelations between the three. This structure indicates several areas of overlaps and expansions regarding structure and meaning, which become apparent when seen side by side in a synoptic diagram (Table 5).

From Table 5, we can perceive the various degrees of overlapping and repeating themes and motifs, indicating some form of alteration in the otherwise linear shape of the narrative. The three septets share a common structure of progression. Firstly, they all conclude with some form of the end of the world. Secondly, they all include an intercalation between the sixth and seventh object. Thirdly, they all use the sixth event to finish the action, whereas the seventh functions as a form of consolidation of the septet in its entirety, perhaps modeled after the seven days of creation of Gen 1:1–2:4a. Fourthly, the events of the first four trumpets/bowls indicate escalation and intensification, as the areas of impact are the same. And fifthly, the three septets are succeeded by an interlude expressing the severity of the overarching plot of Revelation through vindication and retribution.

The events connected to the stars and other heavenly bodies in the three septets may serve as an illustrative example of how these septets cannot be interpreted along a linear timeline, but rather a progressively repeating one. When the sixth seal is opened, we read that the stars of heaven fell to the earth (οἱ ἀστέρες τοῦ οὐρανοῦ ἔπεσαν εἰς τὴν γῆν, Rev 6:13). We may infer from this that this goes for all of the stars of heaven because heaven itself is said to be split apart and rolled up in the following verse (6:14), removing the natural habitat of stars and other heavenly bodies.

When we turn to the septet of trumpets, we notice from the sounding of the third and fourth trumpet that the stars have returned, as has heaven itself.[36] In Rev 8:10 we read that a great star fell down from heaven (ἔπεσεν ἐκ τοῦ οὐρανοῦ ἀστὴρ μέγας) and in Rev 8:12 that one-third of the light of the stars was darkened, both verses suggesting the presence as well as the radiance of stars. In the story of the woman and the dragon, we are told that one-third of the stars of heaven are swept down to the earth (Rev 12:4). Regarding the bowls of wrath, no stars are mentioned there, but the sun receives attention when the fourth angel pours out his bowl of wrath upon it, thus allowing it to scorch people with fire (Rev 16:8–9). Now the sun has gone through a lot in the

---

[36] Abaddon, another star fallen from heaven, is a possible third attestation of the returning presence of stars upon the heaven (Rev 9:1–2, 11). However, the perfect participle (πεπτωκότα) says nothing about when he fell. It merely states that he is presently in the status of having fallen down.

Table 5 Synopsis on the Seals, Trumpets, and Bowls of Revelation 6–16

Septet	Seals	Trumpets	Bowls
1	White horse: Given the means to conquer (6:2)	Hail and fire mixed with blood are thrown down on the earth, burning up ⅓ of the earth (8:7)	Sores come upon those who worshipped the beast and its image (16:2)
2	Red horse: Given to take peace away and a great sword (6:3–4)	A mountain is thrown down into the sea, turning ⅓ of the sea into blood, and destroying ⅓ of the creatures and ships there (8:8–9)	The sea turns into blood and everything in it dies (16:3)
3	Black horse: Given limitations of famine (6:5–6)	⅓ of the waters is made bitter by the falling of a star (Wormwood) on ⅓ of the rivers and springs of waters (8:10–11)	The rivers and springs of water turn to blood. Note on justification of retribution (16:3–7)
4	Pale horse: Death and Hades are given to kill ¼ of the earth (6:7–8)	⅓ of the sun, the moon, and the stars is smitten in order to darken ⅓ of the day and the night (8:12)	The sun is given to scorch people with fire. Statement of lack of repentance. God is identified as having authority over the plagues (16:8–9)
5	The cries of the martyrs under the altar of heaven (6:9–11)	A fallen star from heaven is given to open the bottomless pit. From the pit the locusts of Abaddon are given authority and permission to torture, but not to kill, those without the seal of God on their forehead (9:1–11)	The kingdom of the beast is darkened, resulting in pain and sores for its inhabitants. They blaspheme God for this and their refusal to repent is stated once more (16:10–11)
6	The end of creation (6:12–17)	Four angels bound at the Euphrates are released to kill ⅓ of humankind. Statement of lack of repentance (8:13–9:21)	Drying up the river Euphrates to prepare the way for the kings of the east (16:12)
Interlude	The sealing of the 144,000 and the great multitude of martyrs (7:1–17)	Renewed commission to prophecy, and the vision of the two witnesses (10:1–11:14)	The malignant trinity prepare for the battle of Armageddon. Admonition to stay awake (16:13–16)
7 Consolidation	Silence in heaven for half an hour (8:1)	The giving of worship to and proclamation of God as sovereign ruler (11:15–19)	Theophany supporting the proclamation "it is done" followed by painful hail dropped upon the people of Babylon (16:17–21)
Interlude of vindication and/or retribution	The prayers of the saints are added to the incense of the heavenly altar. This fire is then subsequently thrown upon the earth (8:2–5)	An above-below perspective on the enemies of the saints, and their envisioned judgment (12–15)	Elaboration on the judgment of Babylon as vindication and retribution of the saints (17–18)

Note: This table is an elaboration of a diagram presented by Dr. Reidar Salvesen in a lecture on Revelation delivered at Ansgar University College.

septets at this point of the narrative: it has been blackened by the opening of the sixth seal (6:12), a third of its light has been darkened by the sounding of the fourth trumpet (8:12), and it was darkened once again by the smoke pouring out from the bottomless pit at the sounding of the fifth trumpet (9:1-3). My point is that the darkened sun without a heaven (6:13) reappears several times in the septets of trumpets and bowls, fully equipped with radiance to be darkened and a heaven to shine from.[37] The bottom line is that there are not enough stars, heavens, radiant suns, and moons to go around to be able to maintain a strictly linear narrative of the three septets of Revelation 6-16. Instead, there is a sense of repetition at play here that is further enhanced by the fact that each septet has its own closure. At the end of the seventh seal, trumpet, and bowl there is some form of consolidation, followed by an interlude of vindication and probably retribution. As Robert H. Mounce has pointed out, the visions unfold progressively, each new vision intensifying the realization of the coming judgment. The three numbered septets reveal this intensification: "The seals allow the scroll to be opened and in the process anticipate its contents. The trumpets announce that divine retribution has arrived. The bowls are the pouring out of God's wrath."[38] This anticipation is close to what is commonly referred to as recapitulation.[39] Recapitulation is a way of describing the linear progression of a plot by going back over and over again by adding to the story by changing the angle, going deeper, farther up, but never just simply repeating—constantly adding new color or light to the big picture.[40] Thus, it reveals a plot development in the shape of a spiral rather than a straight line.[41] The three septets of Revelation 6-16 tell the same story three times over, but each time more intensively than the last. I am not going to elaborate on the ongoing debate between adherents of recapitulation and adherents of progression, simply because they both seem to be at least partially correct in matters relevant to this reading. Richard Bauckham argues convincingly in his book *The Climax of Prophecy: Studies on the Book of Revelation* that the three septets conclude with the same final judgment, as well as pointing out the close linkage between chapters 6-16 and the throne vision of Revelation 4-5.[42] The three septets reveal both progression as well as intensification

---

[37] Further argument could be made from the reference of the woman clothed with the sun in 12:1. If the woman's brightness "connotes the heavenly identity and heavenly protection of the people of God" (Beale, *The Book of Revelation*, 627) and is intended as a symbol of divine grandeur or majesty (Koester, *Revelation*, 543-4), the imagery of radiance must be said to be misleading if the sun still was blackened, darkened, and scorched people with fire. The same point could be made regarding the angel standing in the sun (19:17).

[38] Mounce, *The Book of Revelation*, 46-7.

[39] For a fairly brief and informative introduction to the adherents of recapitulation, see Yarbro Collins, *The Combat Myth in the Book of Revelation*, 8-13. She herself explains the apparent overlapping in this section of the book by a theory of interlocking (ibid., 16-18). Her somewhat complex scheme of interlocking elements corresponds in essence to the exegetical premises of this reading: that the three septets of Revelation 6-16 refer to the same incidents in that they partly overlap, yet each septet also adds information and increased severity, and thus progresses by adding information to the preceding septet.

[40] It is worth noting the implications of recapitulation to the element of time within the narrative, as the same event is told several times but from different angles. See Trafton, *Reading Revelation*, 13.

[41] See Campbell, *Reading Revelation*, 43, n. 46; and Fiorenza, *The Book of Revelation: Justice and Judgment*, 5-6.

[42] Richard Bauckham, *The Climax of Prophecy: Studies on the Book of Revelation* (Edinburgh: T&T Clark, 1993), 1-37, especially the pages 8-9, 14; Bauckham, "Judgment in the Book of Revelation,"

by telling the same story but through a slightly altered discourse, each one shedding further light upon the things that must come to pass.

An important element in the argument of Bauckham for the close relationship between Revelation 4–5 and 6–16 is the use of an allusion to the Sinai theophany to express that "the End has been reached, though not yet exhaustively described."[43] The septets are linked to each other as well as to the God of the throne vision by the literary device of a repeating formula occurring at the seventh item of each septet, which is progressively expanded in the following manner:[44]

4:5: ἀστραπαὶ καὶ φωναὶ καὶ βρονταί [lightning, rumbling, and thunder]
8:5: βρονταὶ καὶ φωναὶ καὶ ἀστραπαὶ καὶ σεισμός [thunder, rumbling, lightning, and earthquake]
11:19: ἀστραπαὶ καὶ φωναὶ καὶ βρονταὶ καὶ σεισμὸς καὶ χάλαζα μεγάλη [lightning, rumbling, thunder, earthquake, and heavy hail]
16:18–21: ἀστραπαὶ καὶ φωναὶ καὶ βρονταὶ καὶ σεισμὸς μέγας … καὶ χάλαζα μεγάλη [lightning, rumbling, thunder, large earthquake, and heavy hail]

According to Bauckham, the main purpose of this formula is to "anchor the divine judgments of chapter 6–16 in the initial vision of God's rule in heaven in chapter 4."[45] This corresponds well with the main point of my conclusion of Section 4.2.1 above, perceiving the throne vision as an introductory vision, a corrective point of view, to the visions of Revelation 6–16. Furthermore, it indicates that it is the same final judgment that is reached through the seventh element of each of the three series; it binds the three septets together and the element of expansion corresponds to the intensification of each septet. We see from this that not only does Revelation 4–5 function as an introduction to the three septets, but the septets contain elements pointing back to Revelation 4–5 as well, further emphasizing the interwoven relation by pointing back to the source of origin of the septets.[46] As the image of God presented in the throne vision functions as an introduction to the elaborate revelation of his imminent plans with his creation, the scope of this reading suggests a consideration of the cosmological function of the heavenly agents operating within the septets. If the throne vision serves as a reassurance that the God of creation is in control and that the implied reader is to

---

in *The Book of Revelation: Currents in British Research on the Apocalypse*, ed. Garrick V. Allen, Ian Paul, and Simon P. Woodman, WUNT II/411 (Tübingen: Mohr Siebeck, 2015), 55–80, 59; see also Witherington, *Revelation*, 18–22.

[43] Bauckham, *The Climax of Prophecy*, 204.
[44] Ibid., 7–8.
[45] Ibid., 8.
[46] As Stephen Finamore has pointed out in his reading of the plagues of Revelation from the philosophical perspective of René Girard, it flows from the visions of Revelation 4–5 that it is God who is casting chaos upon the world (Stephen Finamore, *God, Order and Chaos: René Girard and the Apocalypse* [Milton Keynes: Paternoster, 2009], ccvi, 56). However, Finamore has not yet encountered an explanation of the plagues of the three septets that sufficiently explains *why* "God, who elsewhere in the biblical tradition acts in the world to bring order out of chaos, should here be the source of disorder" (ibid., 56). Finamore finds his answer in that the violence of Revelation is a means to unmask, through chaos and uncreation, the violence that lies at the base of all human culture.

recognize that what follows is due to the Lamb's initiative, which in turn falls within the scope of God's will,[47] how is this point of view reflected in the role and function assigned to intermediary agents in the septets of Revelation 6–16?

4.2.2.2 Intermediary Agents in the Three Septets of Revelation 6–16

As an introduction to my analysis on the narrative function of Satan in the story of the woman, the dragon, and the beasts of Revelation 12–13, it seems relevant to figure out how the agents of the three septets are subordinated to the governing sovereign image of God, since they are clearly intermediary, and thereby not self-sufficient, agents as indicated by the analysis of the introductory throne vision. As this is not the main analysis of my reading, I will limit myself to a brief presentation of seven mechanisms present in the text that express a subordination of the agents promoting the events of the septets under the will of God. The identification of these is important here, if rather obvious, in that they express the inherent monistic cosmology of the book, which in turn governs the characterization of Satan in the story of the woman, the dragon, and the beasts.

Firstly, the general chain of command expressed in the throne vision, as a pre-text to the septets, clearly reveals God as the architect of the events unfolding. God provides the scroll (5:1) containing the events of the septets. Moreover, the link between the God of the throne vision and the agents of the septets is explicitly close, thus making it clear that "they emerge from God's heavenly throne room or temple … The judgments issue from God's presence":[48] It is the four creatures from the throne vision that summon the four horsemen (6:1, 3, 5, 7). The seven trumpets are blown by the seven angels standing in God's presence (8:2, 6). And the angels who are to pour out the final wrath of God (15:1) are given the bowls from one of the four creatures (15:7). Finally, the Lamb is proven worthy of receiving and opening it (5:7). After this, each seal broken by the Lamb initiates anticipation of the contents of the scroll. The logic of this hierarchy seems obvious: without a scroll derived from the hand of God as well as the Lamb's subsequent opening, nothing of its contents would be revealed and/or effectuated.[49]

Secondly, the scroll contains what *must* come to pass—a formulation implying divine determination. Δεῖ is used seven times in the book of Revelation, of which 1:1; 22:6; 17:10; and 20:3 parallel the usage found in 4:1 expressing divine determination. In 11:5, δεῖ expresses in a similar manner to what Grant R. Osborne refers to as divine necessity. "God has sovereignly decreed that they 'must be killed.' The judgment does not just come from the two witnesses but from God himself."[50] In 10:11, in the reaffirmed commission to John to write, we find δεῖ expressing divine will rather than divine determination. The main point here is that in all of the seven occurrences of δεῖ, the element of divine will or determination is present—God is initiating the action

---

[47] Talbert, *The Apocalypse*, 30.
[48] Bauckham, "Judgment in the Book of Revelation," 59.
[49] See also Ian Boxall: "As the Lamb begins to open the seals which will enable the scroll's contents to be read, and thereby put into effect … From this chapter onwards, the Lamb's role in enabling the fulfillment of God's salvific plan will be evident" (Boxall, *The Revelation of Saint John*, 103).
[50] Osborne, *Revelation*, 423.

or ordeal by divine will. This is the reason why it *must* come to pass. The element of necessity as an expression of divine will is also reflected in the response to the cry for vengeance from the martyred saints in 6:10-11. There exist a fixed number of martyrs determined to be killed within a limited period. As I have pointed out above, time limitations are a typical feature in apocalyptic literature expressing divine control of the course of history. The presence of divinely ordained time limitations in close proximity to other strong indicators of divine determination such as δεῖ and the monistic throne vision strongly suggests that the septets and its contents are divinely ordained.[51]

Thirdly, of the twenty-one occurrences of the so-called divine passive ἐδόθη (it/he was given/permitted) in the book of Revelation, nineteen are found within Revelation 6–16.[52] As mentioned above, this use of the singular aorist passive means that "in each instance the passive voice of the verb can be construed as a passive of divine activity, i.e., as a circumlocution for the direct mention of God as subject of the action of the verb."[53] By utilizing this grammatical clue, God is implied as what James L. Resseguie refers to as the "'hidden actor' in this drama."[54] In the septets this formulation is used several times to express the divine will controlling and enabling intermediary agents (horsemen, 6:2, 4, 8; angels, 7:1–2; 8:2–3; 16:8; the fallen star, 9:1; the locusts from the abyss, 9:3, 5; and the beasts, 13:5, 7, 14, 15). In a similar mode with a closely related purpose, we read that John is given a measuring rod (11:1). The context of this scene implies that what he measures is spared from at least some of the coming tribulations.

---

[51] In line with this reading, Gregory K. Beale argues for an understanding of Rev 6:1–8 as an expression of Christ exercising his messianic kingship. Christ has begun his rule and this affects, among other things, the situations of suffering that many Christians find themselves in. This in turn connects the contents of the letters to the seven congregations to the contents of the septets. See Beale, *The Book of Revelation*, 370-1.

[52] 6:2, 4 (×2), 8, 11; 7:2; 8:3; 9:1, 3, 5; 11:1, 2; 13:5 (×2), 7 (×2), 14, 15; and 16:8. The last two occurrences are found in 19:8 and 20:4.

[53] Aune, *Revelation 6–16*, 743. For a comprehensive critical recension of the concept of the so-called *Passivum Divinum*, see Peter-Ben Smit and Toon Renssen, "The *Passivum divinum*: The Rise and Future Fall of an Imaginary Linguistic Phenomenon," *Filología Neotestamentaria* 17 (2014): 3–24. Here they stress the invalidity of approaching these aorist passives as a theologically informed grammatical construction to avoid using the divine name and argue for a broader understanding of the aorist passives of the New Testament. Relevant to my reading here is their suggested interpretation of it to emphasize the action to that of the actor in question, and to reduce embarrassment of directly associating acts that have an adverse effect on the community of the faithful to the deity, often by reasons of theodicy (ibid., 23–4). I would add to this that the only valid way to identify an implied agent of a Greek passive form of the verb is to deduce from its intratextual context. In this reading I therefore argue for God as the hidden subject in the passive forms in question, not as a default subject in every passive as some notions of the concept of a *Passivum Divinum* seem to suggest, but because their context in Revelation invites its readers to do so.

[54] Resseguie, *The Revelation of John*, 142. Regarding the use of this literary device, Richard Bauckham writes, "The meaning is that these evils do not happen without the knowledge and authority of God. They are in some sense authorized by him—but again there is the distancing use of the passive" (Bauckham, "Judgment in the Book of Revelation," 62). Bauckham seems to be opting for a "both … and" solution to this "distancing" when he states, "The Book of Revelation has its own way of treading the very fine line between making God the direct cause of such vast human misery and denying that the world has got out of God's control" (ibid.). If it is the distance created by the aorist passive that is the intended point of reference of this "very fine line," then it is a distance of (direct) association, and not one that alters the cosmological hierarchy (as is the case with the alteration of 2 Sam 24:1 to 1 Chr 21:1, and the possible similar transition from Ezek 38:3–4 to Rev 20:8–9; see discussion in Section 5.4.2.3 below).

The court outside the temple is thereby not to be measured because it is given over to the nations to be trampled upon in forty-two months (11:2).[55] In addition to the singular aorist passive, we also have the plural aorist passive functioning in the same manner in 8:2 and 12:14. The former is especially important in this context because it reveals that the trumpets causing the events of the second septet are given to the angels standing *before* God (ἐνώπιον τοῦ θεοῦ), thus expressing at the very least God's approval.

Fourthly, we have the different statements uttered by God and/or by agents/messengers of the heavenly assembly, expressing the actions ordered as divinely ordained. In 16:1 where the seven angels are ordered by a voice from the temple to pour out their bowls of wrath upon the earth, it is probably God himself who is speaking. The basis for this assertion is the probable presence of an allusion to Isa 66:6, as well as God being mentioned in connection with the temple in the preceding verses of 15:5–8. In 15:1, 7 and 16:1 the bowls are referred to as containing the τοῦ θυμοῦ τοῦ θεοῦ (the wrath of God), also suggesting the pouring out of wrath as originating in the divine will. In 9:13 we read of a voice from the altar before God (ἐνώπιον τοῦ θεοῦ) instructing the sixth angel to release the four angels of destruction. Again, the phrase "before God" suggests that their voice speaks on behalf of God and/or his assembly, or at least that his silence indicates his approval of what is being said. In 10:6–7 the angel standing on sea and land refers to the fulfillment of the seven trumpets as the fulfillment of God's mystery (ἐτελέσθη τὸ μυστήριον τοῦ θεοῦ). In 8:13 the last three trumpets are proclaimed by an eagle flying in mid-heaven, declaring them as woes to the dwellers of the earth. The limitation of their effect to the unsealed (9:4) and those living in sin (9:20–21) suggests that these are woes of judgment. This is referring to God's judgment if we consider the hymn of the twenty-four elders where the fulfillment of the trumpets and/or woes are described as such: as judgment and wrath from God over those who destroy the earth, and as a reward for the saints and prophets (11:17–18).

Fifthly, the septets abound with various limitations, expressing God's control on the course of history in general and the events linked to the septets in particular—implying that the events of the septets are representative of his will. For instance, the limitation of the two witnesses to prophesy for 1,260 days (Rev 11:3) correspond temporally to the forty-two months the beast from the sea is given to exercise authority (13:5) and to the time of nourishment of the woman in the desert (Rev 12:6, 14). In the book of Revelation the spirit of prophecy, as well as authority and shelter from adversarial affliction, is derived from and contingent upon God. Limitations on the impact of the seals, trumpets, and bowls are found in 6:6; 7:4–8; 9:4–5, 15, 18; 11:2. Several of these also function to express the embedded intensification from trumpets to bowls. Limitations regarding time occur in 6:11; 7:3; 11:2–3, 9, and 11.

Sixthly, as many scholars have pointed out, the Exodus tradition clearly serves as a model for the three septets, and in particular for the trumpets and the bowls. Table 6

---

[55] Taking measures is here a sign of preservation, probably alluding to Zech 2:1–9 and Ezekiel 40–43, and it is reminiscent of the sealing of the 144,000 in Rev 7:4–8. The temple in 11:1 is probably an image for the community of believers and their relationship to God (see Resseguie, *The Revelation of John*, 160; Barr, *Tales of the End*, 164).

Table 6 Bowls and Trumpets Compared to the Plagues of Exodus

S. No.	Trumpet	Related Exodus Plague	Bowl	
1	On the earth causing hail and fire	Seventh	Sixth	On the earth causing sores
2	Sea turns to blood	First	First	Sea turns to blood
3	Rivers and springs turn bitter	Not a plague, but see Exod 15:22–25	First	Rivers and springs turn to blood
4	Sky: Loss of ⅓ light	Ninth	Ninth	Sky: Sun scorches
5	Abyss: Locusts	Eight	Ninth	Realm of the beast: Darkness
6	Euphrates: Army of horses	Not a plague	Second	Euphrates: Frog-demons
7	Kingdom of God announced with thunder and hail	Seventh, alluded	Seventh	Great city: Thunder, quake, and hail

Source: Derived from David L. Barr, *Tales of the End: A Narrative Commentary on the Book of Revelation*, 2nd ed. (Salem, OR: Polebridge, 2012), 211.

shows how the septets of trumpets and bowls are built upon the plague traditions of Exodus (Exodus 7–11). The apparent allusions to the plagues of Exodus are probably knowledge assumed known to the implied reader, and their presence within the text seems highly relevant to the understanding of the septets of Revelation 6–16. The Exodus plagues served as an opportunity for God to present his power, might, and omnipotence to the Israelites as well as to the Egyptians (Exod 7:3, 5, 17; 8:10, 22; 9:16, 29; 10:1–2). In the process of doing so we find the twofold hardening of Pharaoh: hardening as a result of his own merit (Exod 3:19; 5:2; 7:22; 8:15, 32) and hardening caused by God (Exod 4:21; 7:3; 9:12; 10:1; 10:27; 11:10). The main purpose of the plagues is to make God's capability known to his people and at the same time to signify God's glory (Exod 14:4, 8, 17).

Furthermore, the plagues are functioning as warnings to promote possible repentance. These warnings, in the end, turn out to function as validation of judgment due to the lack of repentance from most of the Egyptians in general and Pharaoh in particular. The presence of a joining crowd (Exod 12:38) and the biblical tradition supporting the perception of the presence of repentant Egyptians as a result of the plagues (Josephus, *Ant.* 2.14.1; Philo, *Mos.* 1.95; 1.147) is important to this reading, as I believe this also to be the case with the septets.[56] It sheds light on a possible function of the eschatological ordeal ushered through the septets besides the obvious pouring out of wrath and validating judgment. It opens up for human response to the calamities—an element constituting the main rhetorical thrust of the messages to the congregations.[57]

---

[56] See Beale, *The Book of Revelation*, 465–7, and his excursus "The Old Testament Background of the Trumpet Judgments," from which I have derived much of the content of this section.

[57] According to David A. deSilva, repentance stands as a goal behind God's punitive actions and the response of the congregations to continue to walk in line with their own repentance is to be motivated from the lack of repentance of the general population—the targets of God's punitive

From this and the presence of the Exodus tradition within the septets, we may infer that the limitations in judgment of Rev 8:7–9:21 are there to encourage repentance, yet the results seem to be severely lacking (9:20–21). Gregory K. Beale argues that the Exodus tradition is not only a literary model for the septets but also a theological one.[58] If this is the purpose of the presence of the tradition within the septets, then we may assume that the God of the Exodus tradition is present by association in the characterization of God in the three septets of the book of Revelation. This could explain the meager results from the call to repentance as well as the thematic convergence of purpose in the two traditions: (1) the sovereignty and incomparability of God is presented in Revelation 4–5; (2) the fairness of his judgments are secured by the repeated mention of lack of repentance in Rev 9:20–21; 16:9, 11; and (3) the judgments as a means to glorify God are found in Rev 11:13, 15–16; 15:4; 19:1–7. In the same manner as the Exodus plagues were meant to promote fear in God (Exod 14:31) and to motivate their obligations in the covenant (Exod 20:2), the revelation of the events of the three septets seems to be intended to have a similar effect upon the congregations of Revelation 2–3.

The afflictions of the septets are probably also intended as a direct answer to the cry for vengeance in Rev 6:10–11, and thus serve as comfort and vindication to the suffering community. Yet, the explicit call for endurance in Rev 14:12 and the elaborate interlude of Revelation 12–13 indicate that the saints too will experience this eschatological trial. As we will see later in this chapter, the thematic relation between Rev 6:10–11, 12:10–12, and the related effects of this relation to the events of chapter 13 indicate that the septets describe present time as well as eschatological future for the congregations. If so, the admonition to hold fast to their faith in Christ in endurance (14:12) reveals a real possibility for apostasy in the believing community. Seen from this perspective, the pedagogical and/or parenetic purposes of the Exodus tradition also seem to be very much present in the three septets. The main point here is that the modeling of the septets after the Exodus tradition seems—both literarily and theologically—to characterize (by association) God as the sovereign controlling figure behind the plagues and septets.[59] Furthermore, the plagues and the septets serve to glorify God, to display his incomparability, to justify his judgments, and to warn and motivate both believers and nonbelievers to subject to him.

Seventhly, the presence of an allusion to the Exodus tradition in the septets characterizes and emphasizes the sovereignty of God in a way that reads well with the main plot of the book of Revelation as defined in my chapter on method. God is doing these things in order to sift the population of the earth—separating the unrepentant from enduring believers. The septets serve as an effective means to this overall plot, especially since the contents of the septets anticipate the final judgment as vivid warnings of what lies ahead if one fails to endure or repent. From the perspective of this reading, 16:15 constitutes an intriguing element of fortifying such an evaluative point of view. Here the first-person pronoun referring to Christ is wedged in between the gathering of people and nations

actions. This way their testimony will support God's general call to repentance, as the narrative repeatedly emphasizes the ineffectiveness of the latter in achieving repentance on its own (deSilva, *Seeing Things John's Way*, 290–2).
[58] Beale, *The Book of Revelation*, 467.
[59] See ibid., 811.

at the battle of Armageddon on the great day of the Lord. This associates Christ with the events in question, possibly in the same manner as we saw at play in Section 3.5 regarding the overlap of functions between Christ and Satan (the activities of deception and gathering are equal to the thieving activity of Christ, indicating that success on either part reflects a state of unpreparedness, which in the case of Sardis is implied antithetically to a state of salvation, cf. 3:2–5). There is no reason to perceive the exhortation and beatitude of 16:15 as a later interpolation, "unrelated to what precedes or follows," as belonging to an alleged second edition of Revelation.[60] Instead, this combination of two of the messages to the seven congregations (3:6, 22) functions as a parenetical exhortation to the believers, representing the word of Christ in order to encourage and motivate them in light of his imminent Parousia.[61] As similar exhortations were found in 13:9–10 and 14:12–13,[62] "the interjection of a warning in the midst of a prophecy of final conflict is entirely appropriate. When all the forces of the beast are gathered for the last battle, the believer will enter a period of supreme crisis."[63] In the emblematic reference of 16:12–16, we have no less than five celestial agents facilitating the final battle of Armageddon on the great day of the Lord. Moreover, as has been the case throughout the three septets, here at the very end there is no anti-divine/pro-divine dichotomy at work, but rather an emblematic expression of the total subjugation of the events of history to the eschatological plan of the sovereign God.

The main thrust of the argument here is that the plot of Revelation in general, and the purpose of the septets in particular, does not make sense if God is not the instigator and architect of their events, because every part of the book seems to point in this direction.[64]

The seven arguments above indicate that the events and functions of the septets of Revelation 6–16 are expressed as the will and intention of God and that intermediary

---

[60] Aune, *Revelation 6–16*, 896.
[61] See also Beale, *The Book of Revelation*, 836–7.
[62] Koester, *Revelation*, 659; Beale, *The Book of Revelation*, 836.
[63] Mounce, *The Book of Revelation*, 300.
[64] Ian Boxall (*The Revelation of Saint John*, 103–4) includes several of the elements from the list of seven arguments here in his exposition of this passage (εδοθη, the divine limitation and control of the events, the recognition of the presence of the Exodus tradition, and the Lamb having a key role in unleashing these calamities). However, after having recognized the hermeneutical dichotomy of opting either for interpreting God as the instigator of the malice, and thus posing a question of his righteousness, or considering these agents forces opposed to God, and thereby reducing God's omnipotence, Boxall concludes in the case of the four horsemen: "This means that all four horsemen are to be understood as demonic rather than angelic figures, the agents of chaos and destruction who are not simply behind the human activity of warfare and disaster throughout history, but also play a key role in that time of intense tribulation prior to the End, which affects even God's people" (ibid., 107). The reason he concludes in this manner is because he finds in the likeness of the first rider to Christ a satanic parody—false Christs, even Antichrist. Moreover, he considers the whiteness of his horse a demonic parody. After having pointed out the fact that God is giving the rider to do these things, he comments that "it is one of the paradoxes of the Christian gospel that even the forces of Satan can be used for divine purposes" (ibid., 108). I find this conclusion unwarranted by the text, as the only thing making this rider a parody and the whole enterprise paradoxical is the a priori assumption that these agents are anti-divine. Without this assumption, the element of parody vanishes, and one is left with malevolent servants of the divine—a conclusion that fits well with the cosmology of the text from the Hebrew Bible, which Boxall initially identifies as the primary antecedent of the four horsemen—Zech 1:7–17; 6:1–8 (Boxall, *The Revelation of Saint John*, 104–5).

agents present in the septets act according to his will and purposes.[65] This fits well with the conclusion of Section 4.2.1 on Revelation 4–5, and will therefore serve as a hermeneutical premise for reading the story of the woman, the dragon, and the beasts.

4.2.3 Preliminary Conclusion on the Literary Context of Revelation 12–13

Revelation 4–5 functions as a key of interpretation to the book of Revelation in general, and the succeeding septets of Revelation 6–16 in particular. The two chapters fortify the point of view of the whole narrative and function as an adjustment of perspective from which to perceive the reports of the ordeals of humankind that both precede and succeed it. Furthermore, they form a natural center of the book and draw an image of a supreme and monistic God. The section is a theological elaboration of the contingencies of the events of Revelation. The way the Lamb is characterized in this section aligns with the findings in the messages to the seven congregations: the God and Lamb/Christ of Revelation overlap in terms of divine position.

The septets of Revelation 6–16 are interwoven with Revelation 4–5 both thematically and literarily. It follows from this connection, as well as from the contents of the septets, that all intermediary agents, good or bad in relation to humankind, are subjected to the will of the sovereign monistic God as presented in Revelation 4–5. This subordination seems to dominate this section of the narrative, and its implications for the resolving of the plot of the narrative seem highly relevant to my efforts to decipher the role and function of Satan in the embedded section of Revelation 12–13.

4.3 The Literary Form and Function of Revelation 12–13

As can be seen from Table 5 above, each of the septets in Revelation 6–16 ends with an intermezzo of vindication and/or retribution. The interlude of Revelation 12–15 is sandwiched between the seven trumpets and the seven bowls and forms the centerpiece regarding the septets as well as the book in general. The demarcation of this section as a self-contained textual unit is further enhanced by the presence of the two sentences enveloping it: καὶ σημεῖον μέγα ὤφθη ἐν τῷ οὐρανῷ (and a great sign appeared in heaven, Rev 12:1) and καὶ εἶδον ἄλλο σημεῖον ἐν τῷ οὐρανῷ μέγα καὶ θαυμαστόν (and I saw another great and marvelous sign in heaven, 15:1). This invites the reader to read Revelation 15 as a separate sign and unit, apart from the first sign in Revelation 12–14.[66] The first half of the sign of Revelation 12–14 seems to follow a chiastic pattern, an ABA pattern.[67] The story of the woman and the dragon is divided into two

---

[65] See also Peter-Ben Smit, who comments, "In general, in this last book of the New Testament, devils, beasts and the like appear in the end more as divine(ly sanctioned and temporary) instruments of testing rather than of actors of their own right in control of what is taking place on earth (which, in fact, is a major part of the literary strategy of the work as such)" (Smit, "Sadomasochism and the Apocalypse of John," 105).

[66] See Georg S. Adamsen, *Johannes Åpenbaring: En Indledning og Fortolkning*, Credo Kommentaren 23 (Fredericia: Lohse, 2010), 97–8 and 275.

[67] Resseguie, *The Revelation of John*, 169.

by the intercalation of the story of the war in heaven. This element of intercalation will prove to be important for the evaluative point of view in the analysis below, due to the spatial and temporal implications at play. The structure of this interpolation (ABA) shows that the events described from a horizontal perspective in the story of the woman and the dragon have a transcendental counterpart in the vertical perspective of the story of the war in heaven.[68] We have here another hermeneutical sandwich present in the text, inviting us through literary structure to interpret the two textual units in light of each other. The outcome of these events is the concern of the latter part of the narrative (chapters 13-14) and bears considerable consequences for the characterization of Satan. Revelation 12-14 is further subdivided by the formulaic line καὶ εἶδον (13:1 and 11). The same words mark the end of the narrative unit concerning Satan by their occurrence in 14:1. This introduces the latter part of the intercalation where Satan is not present, only being referred to indirectly (14:8-9, 11; 15:2). This last section contains several elements emphasizing the gravity of the situation, elevates the importance of the outcome of the call for endurance (14:12), and will subsequently be conferred with in the discussion of the point of view.

These subdivisions of the interlude of Revelation 12-15 allow me to treat Revelation 12-13 as a separate textual unit in the analysis below without losing any important data concerning the function of Satan in this section. The literary structure of the intermezzo could thus be organized as follows:

A The dragon and the woman, 12:1-6
B Intercalation: the war in heaven, 12:7-12
A The dragon and the woman continued, 12:13-18
C The beasts from the sea and the earth, 13:1-18
D Call for endurance backed up by the rhetoric of vindication/retribution—
    presented to enhance the preferred outcome of the tribulations reported in A-C, Revelation 14-15]

The different parts of Revelation 12-13 contain two verbal threads of satanic epithets connecting the different parts together: the repeated references to δράκων (dragon, 12:3, 4, 7, 9, 13, 16, 17; 13:2, 4, 11) and θηρίον (13:1, 2, 3, 4, 11, 12, 14, 15, 17, 18; 14:9, 11). The presence of these satanic epithets thus bind the narrative units together in a way that effectuates the scope of the first part (ABA) to both differ from and relate to the latter (C): they are both elaborations on the crisis of the seven congregations (cf. 13:9, which clearly echoes the concluding statement to each of the proclamation formulas in 2:7, 11, 17, 29; 3:6, 13, 22, and effectively reminding the reader of the perspective of the narrative presented initially), of which Revelation 12 develops the external conflict, and Revelation 13 the inner conflict of decision.[69] In contrast to the mostly secondary and sometimes merely implied role Satan is assigned in the letters to the seven congregations, here Satan is both directly and indirectly cast in one of

---

[68] See ibid., 172; Trafton, *Reading Revelation*, 124.
[69] Resseguie, *Narrative Criticism of the New Testament*, 221 and 230; see also Beale, *The Book of Revelation*, 623.

the main roles of the plot. The centerpiece of the narrative seen from the perspective of this reading is found precisely in this section of the book, in the hymnic passage of Rev 12:10–12.[70] This cluster of satanic names and epithets, along with the elaborations on his activities and purposes in Revelation 12–13, indicates that in Revelation, Satan is a complex literary construct, carefully designed for its narrative purposes—a patchwork character, so to speak.[71] Moreover, it is from this hymnic passage that we find the semantic connection being established between the dragon and Satan, in turn justifying an analysis of the beasts of Revelation 13 as aspects of satanic activity. In addition to the dragon connotation, we find explicit mention of several other satanic epithets tying together many of the textual traditions behind the characterization of Satan in the New Testament. Neil Forsyth is therefore probably right in insisting that "it is chapter 12, however, that is most important for the role of Revelation in the mythology of Satan."[72] The main object in this book is the narrative function of Satan in the book of Revelation, and from that perspective, Revelation 12–13 seems to provide the most elaborate data on the matter.

4.4 Analysis

4.4.1 Plot

The plot of Revelation 12–13 consists of several parts (ABAC) joined in a causal relationship within the discourse. By sandwiching them together in this particular sequence, the narrative indicates to its reader how they relate to each other. This causal relation is what defines the plot: parts A and B narrate the premises for part C. We saw earlier that the satanic epithets appearing throughout the various parts tie them together thematically. We may therefore expect the events concerning Satan, as a recurring character in all three parts, to define the plot of the section to some extent. The plot of Revelation 12–13 can thus be defined in the manner suggested in Table 7 with the use of the Quinary scheme. In this scheme, we can perceive how the narrative consists of and moves through three linked plot strands.

The development of the plot strands seems to be related through their respective transforming actions (the Christ event ushering in the age of eschatological salvation → triggering the ousting of Satan → which sets of the intensified eschatological ordeal of sifting before the end comes with its judgment). Strands A and C seem to overlap to some extent in that the end of the former functions as the beginning of the latter (note

---

[70] It is also the centerpiece of the entire book as communication to the seven congregations (see Fiorenza, *The Book of Revelation: Justice and Judgment*, 175–6).
[71] See Labahn, "The Dangerous Loser," 156–7.
[72] Forsyth, *The Old Enemy*, 252. To Forsyth, this is an important text due to the nature of his combat myth enterprise, yet others too have noticed the importance of this text in their research on Satan. To Henry Ansgar Kelly, Rev 12:10–12 "is the most important Biblical text in the whole history of Satan" because, according to him, it refutes the unbiblical idea of a primeval Luciferian fall (Kelly, *Satan: A Biography*, 153). To Darren Oldridge, Rev 12:7–9 is an important text because it came to be the "standard account for the Devil's origin" (Oldridge, *The Devil: A Very Short Introduction*, 22–3; see also Maxwell-Stuart, *Satan*, 24–5).

Table 7 A Survey of Plot Strands in Revelation 12–13

	Plot A: Woman and the Dragon (Rev 12:1–6,13–17)	Plot B: War in Heaven (Rev 12:7–12)	Interpretational Hymn (Rev 12:10–11)	Plot C: Beasts from the Earth and the Sea (Rev 13:1–18)
Initial situation	A woman in birth pangs giving birth to a boy	[implied] Peace in heaven	Brethren being accused by the accuser before God	Dragon standing at the shores of the sea
Complication	A dragon appears, ready to devour her child	Michael and his angels wage war on the dragon and his angels	[implied] The lamb appears and is slaughtered	Two beasts appear; one arises from the sea and the other from the earth
Transforming action	God snatches the boy up to heaven while the woman flees into the desert, where she is protected from further attacks from the dragon	The dragon and his angels fight back but are defeated	The brethren fight back by the blood of the lamb and their testimony unto death	The beasts are given authority and power to lead astray humankind, and to wage war on the saints and win
Denouement	The dragon is angry and walks away to wage war on the rest of her children	The dragon and his angels are thrown down to the earth	The accuser is thrown down from heaven	The beasts lead astray the dwellers of the earth and kill those who don't submit
Final situation and rhetorical purpose of the narrative	[implied] The woman prevails and the boy resides in heaven. The fate of the rest of her children is left unspecified since this is the pedagogical point of the story	Heaven rejoices for the outcome, whereas the dragon (now the Devil) is left on the earth with great wrath	The salvation, power, and the kingdom of God have come, and so has the authority of the Messiah	Admonition to endure the afflictions (cf. 14:9–13). The outcome here is not stated; since the rhetorical purpose of the narrative is to promote preferred course of action by telling this story

the transition from chapters 12 to 13 in 12:17–13:2). The story of the war in heaven is inserted, wedged in, between the two parts of the story of the woman and the dragon, clearly implying that they should be interpreted in light of each other.[73]

The interwoven state of these three plot strands suggests that the overall plot of Revelation 12–13 seems to consist of three smaller stories with their own distinct plot, all revolving around the actions of the dragon—thereby constituting an overarching plot. As mentioned earlier, the central character in this plot is the dragon. He is the common denominator of all of the different parts of Revelation 12–13. If the plots are interwoven, and if the section 6–16 is in turn an elaboration of the situation of the seven congregations (as suggested in chapter 2), then the identity and fate of the seven congregations could be found among the objects (victims) of his actions. These objects of the actions of the dragon constitute another common denominator of the different parts of the narrative: In 12:1–6 it is the woman and her son; in 12:7–12 it is the accused of the accuser; in 12:13–17 it is the woman and the others of her offspring; and in chapter 13 it is those persistent in resisting their henchmen (13:10, 15, 17). The woman (12:13–16), the rest of her kind (12:17), and the persecuted victims of Revelation 12–13 thus represent the role and function of the congregations of Revelation 2–3, whereas the fate of the boy (Christ/Messiah) is to be shared both in suffering as well as in vindication.[74]

---

[73] The literary effect of interlocking two stories is found in several places in the New Testament. According to Daniel Marguerat and Yvan Bourquin, "the procedure of insertion is the instrument of a narrative strategy of which the reader is the target; the integration of one episode within a wider story is aimed at allowing a migration of information from the inserted story to the story into which it is inserted. Here it is the story into which another is inserted which requires the implantation of this narrative graft to be understood" (Marguerat and Bourquin, *How to Read Bible Stories*, 54). New Testament critics refer to this practice using a variety of different terms such as framing narratives, intercalation, and sandwiching; see Resseguie, *Narrative Criticism of the New Testament*, 54–5.

[74] The symbolism of the woman of Revelation 12 and her child is, in my opinion, best understood as the scriptural people of God perceived as the cradle of messianic expectations, with their fulfilment through the birth of Jesus as the Messiah. The events of Rev 12:13–16 separate the woman herself from τῶν λοιπῶν τοῦ σπέρματος αὐτῆς (the rest of her children, 12:17), those keeping to their testimony of Christ. The information of 12:17 thus presupposes a distinction between the two (see also Trafton, *Reading Revelation*, 117–18). The distinction and concurrent close relation (mother and her children) is probably meant to underscore the relationship between the scriptural people of God and the followers of Christ. Commentators differ on how to interpret this distinction, but a consensus seems to have surfaced regarding the interpretation of the woman as the people of God. See Beale, *The Book of Revelation*, 625–32; Osborne, *Revelation*, 456–9, 485; Mounce, *The Book of Revelation*, 236; Resseguie, *The Revelation of John*, 171; Smalley, *The Revelation to John*, 313–16; John Sweet, *Revelation*, TPINTC (London: SCM, 1990), 195, 201, 205; Witherington, *Revelation*, 167–8, 172; Adamsen, *Johannes' Åpenbaring*, 292; Koester, *Revelation*, 542–3. Yarbro Collins, *The Combat Myth in the Book of Revelation*, 106–7; 134–5 does a similar interpretation of the symbolism, though her presupposing different redactional levels within the narrative complicates her interpretation somewhat. The same goes for Aune, *Revelation 6–16*, 682, 708, 712–13. Robert H. Charles perceives the woman as the church in its entirety but subdivides the symbolism further by perceiving the woman of 12:13–16 as referring to Jewish Christians, and in 12:17 as Gentile Christians (Robert H. Charles, *A Critical and Exegetical Commentary on the Revelation of St. John. Vol.1*, ICC [Edinburgh: T&T Clark, 1920], 299). Pierre Prigent argues at considerable length for an understanding of the woman *and* her children as the church (Prigent, *Commentary on the Apocalypse of St. John*, 377–9, 395–6). His arguments seem persuasive per se, but cannot in my opinion escape the fact that such a reading makes the very image of mother/children superfluous. The parental/genealogy metaphor becomes void with no point of reference.

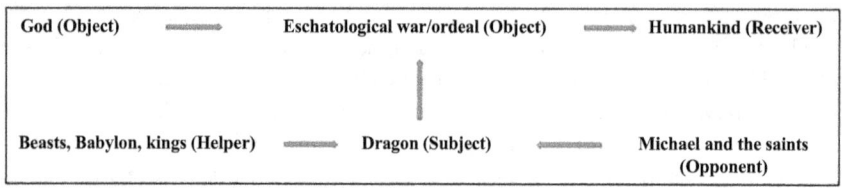

Figure 4 The actants of the story of the woman, the dragon, and the beasts

The hymnic passage in Rev 12:10–12 serves as an interpretational key to Revelation 12–13 and the three plot strands. It is here we get to know why and how the saints must conquer by suffering. This intercalated hymn also involves an element of time, indicating when the events of the three plots are taking place. From this we learn that the suffering of the saints is both effectuating the ejection of Satan from heaven as well as resulting in his amplified presence on earth. Since these verses are probably functioning as a hermeneutical intersection of the three plot strands of Revelation 12–13, they will be of great importance to the analysis of the characterization of Satan as well as in determining the evaluative and theological points of view.

4.4.2 Characterization

As Elisabeth Schüssler Fiorenza has pointed out, Revelation 12–13 is part of a section of the book of Revelation that represents a shift in actantial levels compared to that of the rest of the book.[75] In this particular section of the book, the actantial positions are structured and govern the action of the narrative in the manner shown in Figure 4.

These are the overarching actantial levels of this part of the book. As the centerpiece of a revelation from Christ to the seer and the congregations, this sudden reversal of actantial roles represents a powerful rhetorical element. The congregations are now to perceive their situation from a vertical, and perhaps somewhat misanthropic, perspective. As the actantial scheme is centered on the object of desire aimed at by the subject, the act of desire here has shifted from being one of the congregations to the one of the dragon. The dragon, characterized and identified as Satan in Rev 12:9 and 20:2, is cast as subject and thereby the central actant of this section of the book. In this setting, he is therefore not the antagonist, but the protagonist.[76] It is only when perceived from

---

[75] Fiorenza, *The Book of Revelation: Justice and Judgment*, 174–5. I agree with her structural analysis of the distribution of actants here, but not on the length of the structural unit. There is no need to accept her inclusion of chapters 10–11 to this section, as they clearly belong to another section of the inherent structure of the book; see Table 5.

[76] Joseph L. Trafton makes a good observation when concluding on the identity and function of the woman: "what is important is that the woman serves as a foil for the dragon" (Trafton, *Reading Revelation*, 118). A clear-cut identification of the allegorical point of reference behind the symbolism of the woman may be unavailable to us, but her literary function seems to be clear. She is the victim and object of the dragon. Yes, she is the foil character of the dragon making his malevolence come to the fore, yet there is more to say on her function as a secondary character. Her secondary function in Revelation 12–13 constitutes a literary device emphasizing the severity of the coming eschatological ordeal to that of the saints. True, there is a temporary reversal of focus that elsewhere

The Woman, the Dragon, and the Beasts 123

the perspective of the overarching plot of the book that his antagonistic features come to show. As the central character, he steps out from the scenery, so to speak, and is characterized more fully than was the case with the messages to the congregations. In Revelation 20 he will once again be cast as the opponent and thus characterized in light of his role and function to the subject. The sudden change in characterization and plot that Revelation 12–13 represents makes this text particularly valuable in deciphering the narrative function of Satan in the book of Revelation. Here we have a narrative unit with Satan as the main character. And as such he is still subordinated to the grand eschatological plan of God—still a pawn played to measure the believers of the earth (cf. Rev 13:10, 15; 14:9; 17:17). In light of the concluding remarks of Section 3.5, the Satan of this section of the book represents both an elaboration and an intensification of the function assigned to him in the messages to the seven congregations. This prominent role given to the dragon in the eschatological ordeal of God resists the often polarized and anti-divine identification of him, in favor of a more nuanced understanding of his assigned part in the divinely sanctioned plan.[77]

In Rev 12:9 the dragon is identified as Satan. This is the first reference to him as such in the book of Revelation, which is fitting considering the progressively more vertical and visionary nature of this part of the narrative. It is this explicit identification that connects the idea and persona of Satan with the actions of the dragon and the beasts of Revelation 12–13, 16, and 20, which in turn justifies perceiving the actions of the beasts as part of the characterization of him. In the following, I will therefore consider the characterization of Satan as part of his assigned function in each of the plot strands identified above.

4.4.2.1 *The Satan of Plot A—The Story of the Woman and the Dragon (12:1-6, 13-17)*

In Plot A (see Table 7), Satan is characterized visually as a δράκων μέγας πυρρὸς ἔχων κεφαλὰς ἑπτὰ καὶ κέρατα δέκα καὶ ἐπὶ τὰς κεφαλὰς αὐτοῦ ἑπτὰ διαδήματα (a great red dragon with seven heads and ten horns, and on its heads [it had] seven diadems, Rev 12:3). The word "dragon" appears thirteen times in Revelation (12:3, 4, 7 (×2), 9, 13, 16, 17; 13:2, 4, 11; 16:13; 20:2) and always represents the wrong course of action for the dwellers of earth. The dragon is described as πυρρός (red), as was also the second horse of Rev 6:14. These are the only two instances in Revelation where πυρρός is mentioned. Both the dragon and the second horseman function as vehicles of death and suffering, and as such represent the trials, obstacles, or ordeals to be overcome in order to prevail toward the end of time.[78] If we perceive κόκκινον (scarlet) as chromatically related to

---

in the narrative remains centered on the saints—but as such, it functions as a rhetorical message to the saints (congregations), which in the end elevates them toward the center of attention even in Revelation 12–13.

[77] I find this to be the main objection to Michael Labahn and his otherwise well-written article on the function of the Devil in the book of Revelation. Considering the amount of space he spends on Revelation 12–13, it is surprising to find this element lacking. Moreover, it would render his persistent use of the term "anti-divine" and related language of enmity to Satan throughout the chapter unwarranted (see Labahn, "The Dangerous Loser," 156–7, 160, 165, 170, 176, and 177–8).

[78] See Koester, *Revelation*, 544–5.

πυρρός (the color of both the beast and the woman of Revelation 17–18), this adds suppression and hubris to the palette of meaningful semantic references, as well as the explicit mention of the (red) blood of the saints.[79] In my opinion, the explicit causal relationship of the dragon and the beasts (Rev 13:2, 4) and the subsequent likeness between the beast/dragon and the scarlet beast and its woman (17:16–18) make a good argument for perceiving a semantic connection between the two colors.[80]

Why the dragon imagery was thought to be a meaningful characterization of Satan is not stated in the text itself, and thus represents something implied or "given" to the implied reader. Yet its function as a grotesque visualization of the Roman Empire can be seen from the elaborate explanation in Rev 17:1–17. This way of portraying one's adversaries by "demonization" is a common feature of the apocalyptic genre, which in turn inherited the habit from the Hebrew scriptural tradition. In line with my defined reader, one may assume the reader to be acquainted with the Scriptures of the Hebrew Bible, where dragons occur frequently. In order to fully appreciate the associations embedded with the use of this imagery in the characterization of Satan, I will take an intertextual detour here. Within the book of Revelation, the characterization of Satan as a dragon carries little meaning other than appealing to antipathy as the proper response to its grotesque visualization (see the Section 4.4.3 on point of view below). It is a dreadful and repellent creature in the process of devouring a newborn child. As such, it is merely a beast, with no other meaning within the narrative than antagonist to the protagonists (the congregations). Yet, as argued in my chapter on method,

---

[79] See also Beale, *The Book of Revelation*, 634; Boxall, *The Revelation of Saint John*, 179; Resseguie, *The Revelation of John*, 171–2; Smalley, *The Revelation to John*, 318. Aune, on the other hand, emphasizes that 17:3 reads scarlet and not red, and therefore turns to contemporary literature in his search for points of reference (Aune, *Revelation 6–16*, 683; see also Koester, *Revelation*, 544–5; Osborne, *Revelation*, 459; Witherington, *Revelation*, 165–6).

[80] Paul B. Duff utilizes the example of colors as an organizing principle in Revelation to explain the rhetorical concept of "homology"—a device used to tie together characters of either side of the narrative dichotomy of Revelation. According to Duff, "homology consists of a literary relationship between or among various phenomena in the narrative" (Duff, *Who Rides the Beast?*, 76; see also Greg Carey, "A Man's Choice: Wealth Imagery and the Two Cities of the Book of Revelation," in *A Feminist Companion to the Apocalypse of John*, ed. Amy-Jill Levine and Maria Mayo Robbins [London: T&T Clark International, 2009], 147–58, 147–8, 154, on how color is part of the rhetography of Revelation—how the rhetoric of the senses is used to dramatize the difference between factions). This rhetorical device allows the narrative to connect characters across the different realms of the universe. However, Duff stops short of agreeing with Leonard L. Thompson (from whom he derives the idea of homology, see *The Book of Revelation: Apocalypse and Empire*, 78–9) and the possible consequences of this organizing principle: "Partly on the basis of his understanding of the seer's use of homology, and especially the surprising homologies linking all three realms (the divine, the earthly, and the demonic), Thompson argues that the Book of Revelation presents a vision of an unbroken world" in that John "employs homologies to blur those boundaries normally considered hard and fast, including the fundamental boundaries separating the opposing forces of God and Satan" (Duff, *Who Rides the Beast?*, 78). Duff finds Thompson's conclusions on the matter unconvincing and explains this blurring of sides as an attempt to compare and contrast characters rather than link them together in a vision of an unbroken world. My own contribution on the matter through this reading will be a middle road: John is envisioning an unbroken world in a monistic sense, by organizing oppositions under the reign and distribution of God. The comparing and contrasting of characters are relevant for John's narratées, which sees the path of fidelity somewhat blurred. For a survey on how Revelation uses colors to organize its characters, see Lourdes García Ureña, "The Book of Revelation: A Chromatic Story," in *New Perspectives on The Book of Revelation*, ed. Adela Yarbro Collins (Leuven: Peeters, 2017), 393–419, and in particular 406, 418–19.

narratives of the New Testament writings presuppose knowledge of the Scriptures of the Hebrew Bible and related pseudepigrapha.[81] In the scriptural tradition of the Bible, the authors theologically contribute to and elaborate on a presupposed known salvific history of God present in texts written prior to their own work. The many allusions to this tradition within the narrative of the book of Revelation suggest a similar literary approach in the characterization of Satan by association to these writings. To the implied author this is probably assumed known to its reader, and thus part of the intertextual meaning connected to the narrative. In the chapter on the messages to the seven churches, we saw this literary mechanism at play in the Balaam reference of Rev 2:14. Without taking into consideration the element of characterization by association there, one might mistake it to be a reference to an individual by that name within the congregation, which in my opinion is clearly not the case. Such references to the traditions of the Hebrew Bible are even more clear in Revelation 12–13, among which the close to verbatim allusions to the book of Daniel may serve as an excellent point (see below in the characterization of Satan in Plot C for this). The presence of such scriptural references, as well as those less verbatim, suggests that the narrative of the book of Revelation invites a close reading in light of and as an elaboration on the scriptural tradition of the Hebrew Bible. I concur with Sigve K. Tonstad when he states that Revelation is

> soaked in, and suffused by, the language and narratives of the Old Testament … and it suggests a profound and organic relationship between Revelation and the narrative and prophetic themes of the Old Testament … Undoubtedly, whatever model is invoked to facilitate understanding of the book, it must be acknowledged that the author of Revelation uses the Old Testament as the substrate of his own message and looks to the Old Testament to bring its own unveiling of God's ways to light.[82]

Though, as pointed out in the chapter on method, since narrative criticism is my main hermeneutical tool, this should only be done when the text invites us to do so and subsequently makes the analysis contingent upon it (i.e., names/places, allusion, close to verbatim quotations, and so forth). As most scholars performing narrative readings of the book of Revelation have seen it necessary to incorporate intertextual references to a larger degree than similar works done on more linear and less symbolically laden narratives, this phenomenon is probably in part due to the nature of apocalyptic literature, as its rich symbolism assumes a point of reference outside the text known to its implied reader.[83] In the analysis of the characterization of Satan in Revelation 12–13, the scope of intertextual elements seems to increase. I will therefore in the following argue rather substantially for their presence (as assumed known references

---

[81] See Section 2.5 for references.
[82] Tonstad, *Saving God's Reputation*, 27–8.
[83] Resseguie, *The Revelation of John*, 18, 170–8; Barr, *Tales of the End*, 186–93, 215–19; Grabiner, *Revelation's Hymns*, 14–17, 40–67; Tonstad, *Saving God's Reputation*, 5–7, 15, 26–9; and Labahn, "The Dangerous Loser," 168, 174–5, 178.

to the implied reader) as well as elaborate on the possible theological impact of their presence.[84]

The dragons of the Hebrew Bible serve mainly one function: to display the sovereign greatness of God by comparing him to the dreaded monsters of its time. Δράκων is used four times in the LXX tradition to translate the Hebrew term לִוְיָתָן (Leviathan, Job 40:25; Pss 73:14; 103:26; Isa 27:1) and fifteen times for תַּנִּין (Tannin, sea serpent/monster, cf. Exod 7:9–12; Job 7:12; Ps 73:13; Isa 27:1).[85] These were dreaded sea monsters representing "chaotic forces that needed divine control" known from Canaanite religion.[86] In these texts the sovereignty and control of God form a central theme. The dragon/serpent imagery serves as an object of comparison to illustrate the sovereignty of the God of Israel compared to that of the force/authority in question (cf. Exod 7:9–12; Job 7:12; 26:13; 41:1–34; Ps 73:13; Isa 27:1; Ezek 32:2).[87] Another related function of such characters in the Hebrew Bible is to symbolize/characterize, and thus demonize, the enemy nations of Israel by the process of "Historicization of the Divine Conflict with the Dragon and the Sea."[88] This is done in order to denote a particular conflict with a nation or nations: Egypt is referred to as לִוְיָתָן, (Leviathan) and תַּנִּין (Tannin) in Isa 27:1 and as רַהַב (Rahab) in Isa 30:7 and in Ps 87:4; Babylon is referred to as תַּנִּין (Tannin) in Jer 51:34 and as הַנָּחָשׁ (sea-serpent) in Amos 9:3; and Rome is referred to as δράκων in Pss. Sol. 2:25–26.

As the prophetic tradition gradually gives birth to the apocalyptic genre we find this imagery evolving to a more complex level, often including combinations of symbolic numbers (of heads, horns, wings, feet), animistic features as well as other symbolic artifacts (cf. Daniel 7; 4 Ezra 11; and 2 Baruch 36–39). Furthermore, dragon imagery is used in early Judaism to designate Satan in 3 Bar. 4:3–5, though the late provenance of this text probably indicates influence from Revelation 12–13 and not the other way around. Still, the inherent eschatological expectation of God to vindicate his people by overthrowing and punishing these nations is already present in Isa 27:1. This text relates thematically to the envisioned eschatological future without the presence of

---

[84] Extensive argumentation on implied references to the traditions of the Hebrew Bible becomes even more important if one takes into consideration that it is the interpretation of precisely these elements that separates this reading from its counterparts (i.e., Grabiner, *Revelation's Hymns*; and Tonstad, *Saving God's Reputation*; see the excursus in Section 4.4.2.1.1).

[85] Aune, *Revelation 6–16*, 683.

[86] Koester, *Revelation*, 544. For parallels in Canaanite religion, see Smith, *The Origins of Biblical Monotheism*, 33–40; and John Day, *Yahweh and the Gods and Goddesses of Canaan* (London: Sheffield Academic, 2000), 98–107. Both Smith and Day find the origins of the divine conflict with a dragon and the sea as echoing Canaanite mythology rather than Babylonian.

[87] According to Göran Eidevall in his analysis on the function of the enemies of Yahweh in the book of Isaiah and Psalms, the idea that the supplicant and Yahweh share common enemies (cf. Ps 139:21–22) underlines the sovereignty of their god by reference to his earlier victories with chaos monsters. Moreover, the idea that this sovereign god is currently combating enemies shared by themselves contributes to their handling the question of theodicy. Finally, the raising and externalizing of enemies detach the god from being responsible for suffering to constituting its solution. See Göran Eidevall, "The Role of the Enemies of YHWH in the Book of Isaiah and in the Psalms," in *L'Adversaire de Dieu—Der Widersacher Gottes*, ed. Michael Tilly, Matthias Morgenstern, and Volker Henning Drecoll, WUNT 364 (Tübingen: Mohr Siebeck, 2016), 27–40, 30, 37–8.

[88] Day, *Yahweh and the Gods and Goddesses of Canaan*, 103, see 103–5.

Satan, Azazel, or Semyaza found in the traditions of the book of Jubilees and 1 Enoch, by envisioning an eschatological future without the dreaded sea serpent.[89]

By utilizing dragon imagery known from the Hebrew Scriptures/LXX, which was in turn derived from Canaanite mythology, in order to characterize Satan, the following three connotations may be considered implied known and thus intended associations to the implied readers of Revelation 12:

Firstly, the dragon of Rev 12:1–6 represents a grotesque visualization of hostile forces opposing the people of God. Egypt represented a lethal threat to the people of God in the Exodus narrative and is later depicted as the dragon Rahab and Tannin in Isa 51:9 (cf. Pss. Sol. 87:4; 89:8–10). In the same manner, the Roman Empire is depicted here as the lethal enemy of the people of God, which is the woman clothed with the sun, with the moon under her feet and a crown of twelve stars on her head. Her offspring, the ones who hold fast to the testimony of Jesus, will later on be cast as prey to the dragon (Rev 12:17), clearly a reference to the suffering congregation of believers frequently mentioned throughout the book and among which the narrator counts himself (1:2, 9; 6:9; 19:10; 20:4; and probably implied in 2:13 and 14:12).

Secondly, one of the main functions of such imagery is traditionally to reveal the sovereignty of God. We may therefore expect this element to be at play here as well. The dragon is subjected to the divine plot, as could be seen from the plot analysis above (this implicit element is later made explicit in Plot C). In Plot A, this element is further enhanced by the imposed time limitations upon the dragon postponing its impact upon the woman (12:6, 14), as well as the series of miraculous aids she is given: shelter prepared by God in the desert (12:6), wings of the eagle (12:14, the aorist passive indicating God as hidden subject of the action), and the earth itself coming to her aid by neutralizing the attack of the dragon (12:16).[90] This last element picks up on the Exodus tradition again, as the earth is described as swallowing both Pharaoh and his hordes (Exod 15:12), as well as Korah, Dathan, and Abiram (Num 16:32–34). Both of these texts state the actions of the personified earth as acts of Yahweh. The overall context of Plot A indicates that this is also the case for Rev 12:16. As the adversarial structure of Plot A is not God versus the dragon, but rather the dragon versus the

---

[89] 1En. 10:4–7; 11–19; and Jub. 23:29.

[90] Brigitte Kahl ("Gaia, Polis, and Ekklēsia at the Miletus Market Gate: An Eco-Critical Reimagination of Revelation 12:16," in *The First Urban Churches 1: Methodological Foundations*, ed. James R. Harrison and Larry L. Welborn, WGRWSup 7 [Atlanta, GA: SBL Press, 2015], 111–50) has brought attention to the autonomous characterization of the earth in the scene of Rev 12:16, which is often overlooked by scholars. According to Kahl, Rev 12:16 is best seen as part of a religiopolitical critique of Rome in casting earth as autonomous opponent to the dragon. Here John's vision presents the reader with an "apocalyptic counterimagination" to the more common visualization of Rome's supremacy to the conquered nations and Gaia, as can be seen in the two statues of Hadrian at the Miletus market gate and the Zeus altar at Pergamum. Although Kahl is probably right in her claim that "images may provide an indispensable *intertextual* dimension for reading the text critically in its interaction with a given context" (ibid., 115), with regard to Rev 12:16 it provides a visual backdrop to what is already present in the narrative: the adversarial function of earth in Rev 12:16; her function as opponent of the dragon in a God-driven plot. The latter, along with the probable allusion to Numbers 16 in the event, suggests that the earth in the end is ultimately subdued to the divine order of events.

woman/child, it leaves God as the sovereign puppeteer, present by implication from his actions. He is the one in control, and he is the one delimiting the actants of the plot.

Thirdly, the dragons of the Hebrew Bible tend to suffer eradication in the end. This is also the case with the dragon of the book of Revelation (20:2 and 10). Having served their purpose, their presence is no longer necessary. In this context, the dragon of Plot A is close to the notion of "objects of divine domestication" in the vein of the dragon adversaries of the book of Job (Job 7:12; 38:8–11; 40:29) and perhaps the divine subjugation of one's earthly enemies (Ps 74:12–17; Isa 27:1).[91]

As the dragon imagery and the color red find their natural explanations within the book of Revelation and the Hebrew scriptural tradition, this also seems to be the case with the dragon's seven heads and diadems, and its ten horns. The dragon and the beasts of Revelation 12–13, along with their interpretational counterpart in 17:7–18, all have seven heads and ten horns. The number seven was considered to have a major cosmic role in the cultural encyclopedia assumed familiar to its implied reader.[92] As mentioned in the analysis of the messages to the seven congregations, the number seven occurs fifty-five times in Revelation and forms something of an organizing motif in the book. It is often used as a literary organizing principle (as with the septets) and with possible allusions to intertextual traditions such as the Jewish tradition of sabbatical eschatology, reference to the seven planets, the general idea of seven having a major cosmic role in the Hellenistic world, and various ancient Near Eastern mythical motives.[93] A brief survey of the intratextual use of the number seven reveals that it is used to characterize celestial beings and/or their artifacts: stars—1:16; 2:1; 3:1; angels—1:20; 8:2; spirits of God—3:1; 5:6; burning torches—4:5; seals—5.1, 5; 6:1; the horns and eyes of the Lamb—5:6; angels with trumpets and bowls—7:2, 6; 15:1, 6, 7, 8; 16:1; 17:1; 21:9; thunders—10:3–4; congregations—1:4, 11; 2–3; lampstands as congregations—1:12, 20; and satanic forces as earthly Rome—12–13; 17.[94] From this survey it could be argued that the objects in question all seem to represent a symbolic reference to cosmic totality (i.e., the congregations representing the totality of believers, the heads/kings the totality of oppression/deception, the three septets of Revelation 6–16 each representing God's eschatological endgame in its completeness and the celestial beings representing the totality of God and its impact upon his cosmos). Any reference to the number seven as a cosmic principle in the book of Revelation is thus related to the image of God as a cosmic ruler.[95] Seen from this perspective, the seven

---

[91] Smith, *The Origins of Biblical Monotheism*, 36–7.
[92] On the term *encyclopedia* as encompassing "the conventionalized knowledge of a given society" that needs to be conferred with in the act of interpretation of signs, see Stefan Alkier, "New Testament Studies on the Basis of Categorical Semiotics," in *Reading the Bible Intertextually*, ed. Richard B. Hays, Stefan Alkier, and Leroy A. Huizenga (Waco, TX: Baylor University Press, 2009), 223–48, 233, see also 233–7.
[93] Yarbro Collins, *Cosmology and Eschatology in Jewish and Christian Apocalypticism*, 122–3, 127.
[94] The seven thousand casualties of 11:13 complete the second woe on a cosmic scale, using imagery of theophany to imply the elevated status of the witnesses by the presence of God and his favor.
[95] According to James L. Resseguie, seven "is a number associated with completeness, plenitude, or perfection" (Resseguie, *The Revelation of John*, 29; see also Barr, *Tales of the End*, 12). Adela Yarbro Collins argues for the number seven symbolizing the governing principles of the cosmos but finds the arguments for it symbolizing completeness wanting. See Yarbro Collins, *Cosmology and Eschatology in Jewish and Christian Apocalypticism*, 124–7.

heads and diadems of the dragon could be seen as God's way of organizing cosmic opposition, rather than imitating the divine.[96] This would certainly fit the point of view established by the throne vision (Revelation 4–5) and aligns with the overarching plot as defined in Section 2.3. Regarding the dragon and his associates, the symbolic number of seven encompasses the totality of opposition as seen from the perspective of the saints.

The number ten occurs less frequently in the book of Revelation (nine times), and with the exception of the ten days of affliction in Rev 2:10, it always refers to the ten horns/kings (12:3; 13:1; 17:3, 7, 12, 16). This number is usually taken as a reference to totality but is also used to amplify and intensify other symbolic numbers (e.g., two thousand years, 144,000 sealed, and twelve thousand stadia). It is possible to see an earthly inclination attached to the idea of totality related to the number ten, with its possible reference to ten fingers and toes (Resseguie) and the perception of time as something orderly fixed within a society ordering time in decades (Yarbro Collins).[97]

Seen from an intertextual perspective, in line with my defined implied reader, the seven heads and diadems and the ten horns constitute a clear allusion to the apocalyptic vision of Dan 7:2–8 where the four beasts have a total of seven heads, and the fourth beast has ten horns. In keeping with the dragon imagery of the Hebrew Bible, Leviathan is described with multiple heads in Ps 74:14 ("You crushed the *heads* of Leviathan and fed him as food to the wild animals"). The plural heads of Psalm 74 might in turn be a reference to the seven heads of Leviathan as mentioned in *KTU* 5.I.1–3.[98] John Day has thus suggested that the seven heads of Revelation 12 carry connotations to the seven heads of Leviathan, yet only by allusion primarily to Daniel 7 and possibly Psalm 74.[99] Horns refer in Dan 7:24 to kings, which could also be the case here (cf. Rev 17:12 and 16). Diadems refer here and elsewhere in the book of Revelation to authority and power (13:1; 19:12), which is fitting for a symbol of royalty of cosmic proportions. I will elaborate further on these possible intertextual traditions implied known in Revelation 12–13 in my analysis of Plot strand C (Section 4.4.2.3), as the dragon only shares the visual appearance of the beasts of Daniel.

Before considering the actions of the dragon in determining his role and function in Plot A, the reference to him as ὁ ὄφις (Rev 12:14–15; 12:9; 20:2) needs to be examined. The epithet is not mentioned elsewhere in the book of Revelation, and any narrative critical interpretation of it therefore largely relies upon any potentially implied known extratextual references.[100] I will in the following argue for an

---

[96] Resseguie, *The Revelation of John*, 30.
[97] Resseguie, *The Revelation of John*, 31–2; see also Barr, *Tales of the End*, 12–13; Yarbro Collins, *Cosmology and Eschatology in Jewish and Christian Apocalypticism*, 80–3.
[98] "When you smite [Lôtan, the] fleeing [serpent], finish off [the twisting serpent], the close-coiling one [with seven heads]" (William W. Hallo and K. Lawson Younger, eds., *The Context of Scripture* Vol 1. (Leiden: Brill, 1997), 265; see also Aune, *Revelation 6–16*, 684–5).
[99] Day, *Yahweh and the Gods and Goddesses of Canaan*, 107.
[100] See Resseguie, *The Revelation of John*, 173, 176; Barr, *Tales of the End*, 188; Grabiner, *Revelation's Hymns*, 147–8, 155 n. 204, 156–7, and 164. In his analysis of the narrative and rhetorical function of the Devil in the book of Revelation, Michael Labahn does not consider this epithet, as he limits his analysis to unambiguous terminologies such as the Devil, Satan, and the Dragon (Labahn, "The Dangerous Loser").

understanding of the characterization of Satan as ὁ ὄφις in light of the related dragon imagery as presented above, and why it probably does not constitute a reference to the Eden serpent.[101] With the presence of dragon imagery derived from the Hebrew scriptural traditions concerning ancient dreaded sea serpents, it is not surprising to find this epithet here. In these traditions, Leviathan is described as the fleeing and twisting serpent (ἐπὶ τὸν δράκοντα ὄφιν φεύγοντα ἐπὶ τὸν δράκοντα ὄφιν σκολιόν, LXX Isa 27:1), an object for a fishhook (Job 41:1), and as a dragon living in the waters (Ps 74:13–14). These references display the fact that serpents and dragons were considered interchangeable entities at this point in history.[102] A dragon was simply a large serpent.[103]

The possibility here of having an early identification of the Eden serpent as Satan is a popular notion, yet highly improbable for several reasons.[104] Firstly, there is no reference to the narrative of the fall of Genesis 3 in the biblical tradition[105] outside the Pauline corpus (and when Paul refers to this textual tradition, it is never with any reference to Satan as the serpent).[106] A probable reason for this lack of references to the Eden fall is that the narrative of Gen 6:1–4 proved to be more popular when it came to explaining the origins of sin and/or suffering in the period when apocalyptic

---

[101] The length of this extratextual argument serves, in addition to providing a plausible interpretation of the use of ὁ ὄφις in the narrative, to underscore again the level of divergence between this reading and that of Steven Grabiner. His interpretation of Revelation 12 in light of Genesis 3 is contingent on a primeval fall of Satan present or implied in the Hebrew Bible (cf. my comments on this matter in Sections 4.2.1 and 4.4.2.1.1).

[102] As Jürgen U. Kalms has pointed out (*Der Sturz des Gottesfeindes: Traditionsgeschichtliche Studien zu Apokalypse 12*, WMANT 93 [Göttingen: Vandenhoeck & Ruprecht / Neukirchener Verlag, 2001], 137–8), in Job 26:13 and Isa 27:1, נָחָשׁ בָּרִחַ (fleeing serpent) is used as synonym for Leviathan. This reveals the close connection between the serpent and dragon imagery in these texts of the Hebrew Bible. Nevertheless, he sees in the designation ἀρχαῖος (old) an obvious reference to the Eden serpent: "Dabei wird durch den ausdrücklichen Verweis auf die *Alte* Schlange explizit an die Paradiesgeschichte angeknüpft. Damit wird an die Schlange als Verführerin gegen Gott erinnert" (ibid., 138). How he arrives at the conclusion that the deception of Adam and Eve equals deception against God is not emphasized or explained in his argument, but it aligns with his consistent use of the term "Gottesfeind" on the dragon of Revelation 12.

[103] Daniel Ogden, *Drakon: Dragon Myth and Serpent Cult in the Greek and Roman Worlds* (Oxford: Oxford University Press, 2013), 2–4; Kelly, *Satan: A Biography*, 148–53; Kelly, *The Devil, Demonology, and Witchcraft*, 18; Kelly, *Satan in the Bible: God's Minister of Justice*, 122–3.

[104] Due to the open-ended use of metaphors and allusions in Revelation (see Section 2.2.2), it is not possible to determine with certainty the full range of possible semantic references to the implied extratextual references. The reference to ὁ ὄφις in Revelation 12 and 20 is no exception, and it is therefore an argument of probability, the most probable reading, and not certainty that I explore here. That being said, it is both possible and not far-fetched to imagine an implied reader with the implied literary competence of a first-century Christian reader with access to LXX (see Section 2.5) associating on some level the serpent of Eden when encountering the term ὁ ὄφις in the narrative.

[105] The possible allusion to the fall of Eve in Sir 25:24 remains as a possible exception to this, yet does not mention any external deceiver causing it.

[106] Neil Forsyth states that "Paul nowhere explains how the adversary was linked with Adam's sin at the beginning," and "the passages in which Paul links Adam and Christ lack any reference to the angel, or to the serpent. This absence would pose serious problems and allow interpretive latitude to later commentators" (Forsyth, *The Old Enemy*, 277–9). A similar argument, yet more extensive, can be found in Kelly, *Satan: A Biography*, 32–3, 63–4, 152–3. Regarding Rom 16:20, Derek Brown argues convincingly for this being an allusion to Ps 8:7 and 110:1 here, rather than the Genesis narrative. See Brown, *The God of This Age*, 102–7, 173.

literature was written (250 BC–AD 250).¹⁰⁷ It is this tendency we are witnessing in texts where allusions to Gen 6:1–6 abound at the cost of the Eden narrative.¹⁰⁸ Secondly, the numerous allusions in Revelation 12 and its context to the dragon imagery of the Hebrew Bible suggest Leviathan and his kind, rather than the Eden serpent, as the primary point of reference. Thirdly, the lack of any overlap between the activities of the serpent of Revelation 12 and Genesis 3 further widens the distance between the two characters. The Eden serpent is primarily verbal and not stated to act through any other means, whereas the serpent of Revelation 12 is the complete opposite: no words, only action.¹⁰⁹ He is sentenced to crawl on his belly and eat dust for the rest of his life.¹¹⁰ This is not even close to the kind of behavior that is described in Revelation

---

¹⁰⁷ According to John J. Collins, the renowned definition of apocalyptic literature in the SBL Genres Project (published in *Semeia* 14 [1979]) "was based primarily on Jewish and Christian writings from the period 250 BCE to 250 CE" (John J. Collins, "What Is Apocalyptic Literature?, in *The Oxford Handbook of Apocalyptic Literature*, ed. John J. Collins [New York: Oxford University Press, 2014], 1–18, 2).

¹⁰⁸ The Midrash of the book of Jubilees on Genesis exemplifies this tendency as it includes the character of Mastema/Satan as an ambivalent figure, hostile to humankind but subjugated to God's will and intentions. In its retelling of the Eden narrative, it does so by following the Genesis narrative and not by inserting Mastema/Satan (Jub. 3:17–25). To the author of Jubilees, "supra-human evil enters into the world through the disobedient action of the Watchers, mating with the daughters of men (4.22; 5.1–2; 7.21, 27)" (Jason M. Zurawski, "Separating the Devil from the *Diabolos*: A Fresh Reading of Wisdom of Solomon 2.24," *JSP*, 21 [2012]: 266–399, 380).

¹⁰⁹ Gregory Beale suggests that the river spewing from the serpent's mouth symbolizes "attempts to deceive the latter-day woman with a flood of words" (Beale, *The Book of Revelation*, 673). This could be the case, as it connects well with the activities of Satan as a tempter and sifter in the messages to the seven congregations as well as his epithet of ὁ πλανῶν τὴν οἰκουμένην ὅλην (the deceiver of the whole world, 12:9). Yet, the argument of Beale is based upon an a priori assumption of a reference to the Eden serpent by the term ὄφις, and not the other way around. The common denominator of the two traditions is found in the lust of the Watchers and Eve (see 1 En. 69:6, where the angel Gadreel has replaced Asael in inventing war and teaching metallurgy and is referred to as seducing Eve; see Forsyth, *The Old Enemy*, 223). By the time of Augustine, the Eden narrative has replaced the Watcher myth as the definite narrative describing the start of redemption theology. It is in the Eden narrative that he finds the traces of the origins of sin and suffering in relation to the serpent, now firmly identified as Satan/the Devil (Forsyth, *The Old Enemy*, 421–8)—not the Watcher myth. Perhaps the gnostic affinity toward the Eden narrative known from several of the Nag Hammadi writings contributed to this shift of focus from Genesis 6 to Genesis 3. According to Elaine Pagels (*Adam, Eve and the Serpent* [New York: Random House, 1988]), it was particularly in the period of Christianity's transition from persecuted minority to world imperial religion that led to renewed interest in Genesis 1–3—especially in light of the doctrinal challenges of so-called Gnosticism. "What Christians see, or claim to see, in Genesis 1–3 changed as the church itself changed from a dissident Jewish sect to a popular movement persecuted by the Roman government, and changed further as this movement increasingly gained members throughout Roman society, until finally even the Roman emperor himself converted to the new faith and Christianity became the official religion of the Roman Empire" (ibid., xxi). Through her book, she shows how this text turned into something of a key passage promoting celibacy and proved to be an efficient tool in demonizing doctrinal opponents (i.e., heresy).

¹¹⁰ In Gen 3:14–19 one of the etiological consequences of the Eden incident is found in the words given to the serpent (*sic!*) regarding the enmity between the seed of the woman and the seed of the serpent (3:15). Reading the events of Revelation 12 as an eschatological fulfilment of the moment in time when the seed of the woman finally crushes the head of the serpent (הוּא יְשׁוּפְךָ רֹאשׁ) clearly misses the function of the verb and the generic nature of the sentence. The verb שׁוּף (bruise, cover, strike; LXX: τηρέω) is used there to describe the acts of *both* the serpent and the seed of the woman, clearly implying mutual hostility, and not referring to a specific eschatological incident. Moreover, if the verb refers to mortal impact (crushing), then it must be generic as the seed of the woman is "hit" first.

12, of which the least compatible element of characterization to this tradition is his function as a *heavenly* accuser *before God* (Rev 12:10). The Eden serpent of Genesis 3 functions in the similar vein to animistic pedagogic characters found in the donkey of Balaam (Num 22:28–30) or the fables of Aesop—a character of opposition furthering the pedagogical plot. This characterization is further developed with a mythical language conveying elements of etiology, which frequently appear throughout Genesis 1–11 (i.e., we get to know why the serpent crawls on his belly and why there exists a constrained relationship between humans and serpents).[111] Fourthly, the first known explicit link and identification between the Eden serpent and Satan/Devil is found in the Adam books (*Vita* 33.2; Apoc. Mos. 16:1–5; 17:1–18:6),[112] and seems to represent the end of an ongoing merging of the traditions of the Watchers and the Eden fall. The provenance of the literary sources for the Greek and Latin recensions of the Adam books is disputed, but according to M. D. Johnson, "the most natural span for the original composition would be between 100 B.C. and A.D. 200, more probably toward the end of the first Christian century."[113] This is a rather late identification of the two,

---

This does not mean that the implied author of Revelation could have made a connection between Gen 3:15 and Revelation 12, regardless of the rather obvious etiological and thereby generic intent of Gen 3:15. Yet it adds to the list of arguments above suggesting otherwise. It constitutes another incentive warning us not to perceive the ejection of the dragon from heaven in Revelation 12 as related to the Eden incident.

[111] See also Annette Yoshiko Reed:

The notion that the sins of Adam and Eve caused the 'Fall of Man' and the equation of the serpent with Satan have now gained a normative aura due to their dominance in the Christian tradition. Yet, this reading of Gen 2–3 is hardly inherent to the biblical passage, which only purports to explain how humankind came to know good and evil [טוֹב וָרָע], why clothing was invented, how agricultural labor became a hardship, why childbirth is painful, why wives are subordinate to husbands, and why serpents and women dislike one another. (Reed, *Fallen Angels and the History of Judaism and Christianity*, 52)

[112] According to Jan Dochhorn (*Schriftgelehrte Prophetie*, 6): "Generell sollte man beachten, daß—abgesehen vielleicht von der Teufelsfallsgeschichte in der Vita Adae et Evae und im 2. Henoch—keine der protologischen Teufelsfallserzählungen früher zu datieren ist als die Apokalypse des Johannes (vgl. § VI,1)." Hence, if Revelation is not making this identification, then these are the first writings that do so.

Regarding Wis 2:24, a text often referred to as the earliest known identification of the serpent of Eden with the Devil (cf. Mark S. Smith, *The Genesis of Good and Evil: The Fall(out) and Original Sin in the Bible* [Louisville, KY: Westminster John Knox, 2019], 27), Jason M. Zurawski has made an excellent argument challenging the majority view on this verse (Zurawski, "Separating the Devil from the *Diabolos*: A Fresh Reading of Wisdom of Solomon 2.24," 366–99). By analyzing the Greek text of the verse in light of both the overall worldview of the book and the range of meanings related to the various contemporary uses of the term, he concludes that the διάβολος of Wis 2:24 "does not refer to any sort of supra-human, anti-divine force, but to the ungodly described in the previous section of the text, those who kill their own souls" (ibid., 390). Moreover, in light of the worldview of the book he comments, "Wisdom has no room for an evil, anti-divine, force which seeks to prevent humankind from finding wisdom. Therefore, despite the eschatological nuances of the text, the worldview of our author is much more in line with the sapiential than the apocalyptic" (ibid., 383). His analysis results in a different translation than what the majority of scholars have settled for so far: "But through an adversary's envy death enters the world, and those who belong to death's party put humanity to the test" (ibid., 398). Henry Ansgar Kelly argues for an interpretation of this adversary as Cain in light of Rom 5:12–14 and 1 Clement 3–4 (Kelly, *Satan: A Biography*, 70–9; see also Kelly, *Satan in the Bible: God's Minister of Justice*, 28–30).

[113] M. D. Johnson, "Life of Adam and Eve," in Charlesworth, ed., *The Old Testament Pseudepigrapha Vol. 2*, 249–95, 252.

and it seems more in line with a more autonomous devil—akin to the murderer and liar of John 8:44 and the sinner of 1 John 3:8—rather than the subordinated Satan of Revelation.[114] Fifth and finally, for many it is the deception of the Eden serpent that suggests that this is the same serpent as mentioned in Revelation since he, too, is described as deceiving/testing and leading astray. However, a closer look at the text of LXX Gen 3:13 reveals a diverging use of verbs between the two texts regarding the serpent's acts of deception: εἶπεν ἡ γυνή ὁ ὄφις ἠπάτησέν με καὶ ἔφαγον (The woman said, "the serpent tricked me and I ate"). The verb ἀπατάω (trick/deceive) is not used to refer to the Devil/Satan anywhere else in the Bible. It is only used with reference to human deception with the exceptions of 1 Tim 2:13, which is an allusion to Gen 3:13, and the lying spirit of 2 Kgs 22:20-22 / 2 Chr 18:19-21.[115] Instead it is the verbs πειράζω and πλανάω that are primarily used to refer to the deceptive activities of Satan in the New Testament—including Revelation (Rev 2:10; cf. 3:10 and 12:9; 20:3, 8, 10; cf. 13:14; 19:20). If deception is the key to identify the serpent imagery of Revelation 12 as an allusion to the serpent of Genesis 3, it is curious that the term itself differs from the LXX version of it. In the end, even if the narrative of Revelation translates its own allusion to the expression הַנָּחָשׁ הִשִּׁיאַנִי (the serpent tricked me), any reading finding a reference to the gentle and smooth talker of Genesis 3 in the violent imagery of Revelation carries, in light of all of the arguments above, a heavy burden of proof.[116] The reference to ὁ ὄφις is therefore, in my opinion, best interpreted as an implied known allusion to the beasts of Daniel 7 and the dragons/sea serpents of the Hebrew

---

[114] According to Apoc. Mos. 16:1–5, the serpent himself is tricked by Satan into being his vessel (see 3 Bar. 9:7, where Samael takes on the serpent as a garment to deceive Adam). This reveals that even at this point the identification of Satan and the Eden serpent was seen as problematic. Moreover, this text allows for both the deceptive nature of Satan known from the New Testament and the mythological symbolism behind the Eden serpent to play their part.

[115] The monistic cosmology present in 2 Kgs 22:20–22 / 2 Chr 18:19–21 and the Pauline Satan, also part of the literary competence of the implied reader, reveals that an eventual identification of an allusion to the Eden serpent in Revelation 12 does not make him the enemy of God on grounds of his deception. Instead, as judged deceiver (Gen 3:14–15), he would fit the characteristics of the all too eager Satan of Job 1–2 and Zech 3:1–2, both of which are proven wrong, yet at the same time their satanic office is not liquidated because of it. His "sentence," it could be argued, only affirms the prior state of enmity that caused the act of deception in the first place. Still, the main pedagogical point of the Eden narrative is the guilt and punishment of Adam and Eve, not the serpent. This in turn is reminiscent of the plot of Revelation, where adversarial agents serve to test and divide humankind before the eschatological age of salvation arrives. In both narratives, the serpent serves as tool of deception subjected to the focus on the humans of the narrative.

[116] Steve Moyise emphasizes the difficulties of both a primordial fall of Satan (Osborne) and a fall caused by the Christ event (Caird) in stating, "If the primordial view is correct, then what is Satan (identified as the ancient serpent) doing in the heavenly council in Job 1–2? On the other hand, if the Christological view is correct, what is the serpent doing in the Garden of Eden when he is only thrown down to earth as a result of the cross?" (Steve Moyise, "Genesis in Revelation," in *Genesis in the New Testament*, ed. Maarten J. J. Menken and Steve Moyise [London: T&T Clark, 2012], 166–80, 174). In spite of these objections and apparent knowledge of the possible Leviathan references to Ps 74:14 and Isa 27:1 in the epithet (see ibid., 173), he ends his section on the serpent by insisting, "What is certain is that John's identification of the serpent with the fallen dragon aims to bring the rebellion begun in Genesis 3 to a close" (ibid., 174). It is the view of this reading that these challenges of chronological and spatial inconsistency stem exclusively from a faulty preconceived identification of the Eden serpent with the ancient serpent of Revelation 12. The liquidation of the satanic office in Revelation 12 should probably be seen to mark the end of the age characterized by the consequences of the Eden fall rather than a reappearance of the serpent itself.

Bible, constituting powerful and violent imagery in explaining the dire situation of the believers. This grotesque/violent mythical imagery provides a vertical perspective on the earthly ordeals described in Revelation 2–3 (see Section 4.4.3 below).

If we turn from the descriptions of the visual traits of the dragon to its actions, further light is shed on the violent nature of his appearances. The first act of the dragon is mentioned in 12:4: καὶ ἡ οὐρὰ αὐτοῦ σύρει τὸ τρίτον τῶν ἀστέρων τοῦ οὐρανοῦ καὶ ἔβαλεν αὐτοὺς εἰς τὴν γῆν (And his tail swept a third of the stars of heaven, and threw them down to the earth). Most commentators recognize this to be an allusion to Dan 8:10 ("And it grew up to the host of heaven and caused some of the host and some of the stars to fall to the earth, and trampled them down").[117] If this is the case, my concern here is what this allusion signifies within the narrative of Plot A. In its own context Dan 8:10 is, according to Stephen S. Smalley, "a reference to the 'angels' (people, as in Dan. 10.20–21; 12.1) and 'saints' (stars, as in Dan. 12.3; cf. Gen. 15.5; Matt. 13.43) of Israel being persecuted, but eventually delivered from captivity; cf. Dan. 8.22–25; 12.1–3; 2 Macc. 7.1–42."[118] Gregory Beale has also argued convincingly for the interpretation of stars as representing people and saints, and not only angels, by pointing to the earliest interpretation of Dan 8:10, found in Dan 8:11 Theod. and LXX, and understanding it to be a representation of the captivity of Israel.[119] The common interpretation of Dan 8:10–11 as referring to the Seleucid ruler Antiochus IV Epiphanes and his violent conduct toward Israel fits well with the allusion to Dan 8:10 in 1 En. 46:7–8, a text that also contains an identification of the saints dwelling on earth as angels described as stars of heaven (1 En. 43:1–4).[120] If Rev 12:4 is an allusion to Dan 8:10, and the latter is a symbolic description of an earthly king suppressing and persecuting the people of God, then we should probably expect this meaning to be reenacted somehow in the context of Plot A. However, what we do *not* have here is a reference to a primordial fall of Satan or any of his angels.[121] This follows not only from the allusion to Dan 8:10 in Rev 12:4 but also from the chronological implication of Plot B as discussed in Section 4.4.2.2.[122] As the conduct of the congregations reflects upon their respective angels and vice versa (Rev 1:16, 20), we may open up for the stars of Rev 12:4 to be able to encompass both entities as well. The dragon casts down one-third of the stars, the same measure found in the indication of the level of destruction from the septet of trumpets

---

[117] Aune, *Revelation 6–16*, 685–6; Beale, *The Book of Revelation*, 635–7; Koester, *Revelation*, 545–6; Mounce, *The Book of Revelation*, 238; Osborne, *Revelation*, 460–1; Smalley, *Revelation to John*, 318–19; Sweet, *Revelation*, 196.

[118] Smalley, *The Revelation to John*, 318; see also Beale, *The Book of Revelation*, 635–7.

[119] Beale, *The Book of Revelation*, 636.

[120] Ibid.

[121] I follow here the line of argumentation of Mounce, *The Book of Revelation*, 238; Beale, *The Book of Revelation*, 635–7; and Smalley, *The Revelation to John*, 318, although Smalley here opens up for the scene of Rev 12:4 to "echo the narrative of the descendants of Satan and his angels in the traditional saga of the Watchers in *1 Enoch 6–11*." Where David E. Aune opens up for the possibility of the text containing an allusion to the Watcher myth (Aune, *Revelation 6–16*, 686), Grant R. Osborne, on the other hand, rejects any other reading, as "in the Apocalypse, whenever ἀστέρες (*asteres*, stars) refers to beings, they are always angels" (Osborne, *Revelation*, 461).

[122] According to Joseph L. Trafton, "the reference to one third is probably intended as an indication of the constraints within which the dragon acts (cf. 8:7, 9, 11, 12, 15, 18). Any suggestion that John is speaking of fallen angels misses the clear allusion to Dan 8:10" (Trafton, *Reading Revelation*, 119).

(Rev 8:7–12; 9:15, 18). As the septet of trumpets proved to be a powerful sifting strategy in the analysis above, the events of Revelation 12–13 seem to serve the same purpose (Rev 14:12–13; note the means and effect of conquest in 12:11). In the septet of trumpets, we saw that stars falling down to the earth is generally not considered good news to humankind (Rev 8:10; 9:1), yet they are a necessary means to an end—and more important, initiated by God. Furthermore, the effect of the tail of the dragon in this context is reminiscent of the malignant effect of the tails of the locusts of Rev 9:10. The septet of trumpets and Plot A seem to have several motifs in common: falling stars, tails suppressing humankind, and the limited effect in both to one third. The latter limitation could, together with the allusion to Dan 8:10 and the parallels to the septet of trumpets, signify divine supervision and/or control.[123] It would fit the overall cosmology of the book of Revelation, the governing perspective of the throne vision, and the servant/tester side of the character of Satan as seen in the messages to the seven congregations. If this is the case, we have here another argument for not reading the Watcher myth present in Plot A, as their demise is generally considered *not* to be intended by God—at least not the version found in 1 Enoch 6–10.

After having swept down one-third of the stars of heaven, the dragon positions himself in front of the woman, now giving birth to the boy Messiah, in order to devour him as soon as he is born (ἵνα ὅταν τέκῃ τὸ τέκνον αὐτῆς καταφάγῃ). However, when the child is born, he is snatched up to the throne of God before the dragon manages to devour him. As we saw earlier, the dragon represents the presence and conduct of the Roman Empire toward the believing community (cf. Rev 17:7–18, and the function of Satan in Pergamum, 2:13). An attempt to devour the boy at birth must therefore probably refer to the events reported in the infancy traditions known from the Gospel of Matthew (Matt 2:1–18), yet at the same time also the event of crucifixion, as the resurrection/ascension (the snatching away of the boy to God and his throne) is also the event that, in the end, prevents the dragon from devouring the child.[124] In

---

[123] I will try to be careful not to read too much into the text at this point as I am aware of the fact that parallel motifs do not necessarily indicate parallel meaning in every aspect of the text, but only possible parallel motion and purpose. Where the dragon and Antiochus Epiphanes IV both represent earthly kingdoms and/or leaders struck with hubris causing the people (of God) to suffer afflictions and possibly apostasy, we cannot deduce from this parallel and the general silence in the text that the falling stars of the septets of trumpets too were victims of oppression or that the stars of Dan 8:10 eventually turned out to be sadistic monsters themselves. Still, the "Jews that are not Jews" and "the synagogue of Satan" (2:9; 3:9), and the possible reference to King Herod the Great in 12:4, could all be possible candidates for such characteristics.

[124] See also Fee, *Revelation*, 166. According to Joseph L. Trafton (*Reading Revelation*, 119), the birth of the boy is not a reference to the birth of Jesus for several reasons: Firstly, the woman is not Mary. Secondly, the "birth" is immediately, and oddly, followed by the "ascension." And thirdly, John shows no interest in the birth of Jesus elsewhere in Revelation, but rather on his death. In my opinion, only the third argument can carry some weight in this context, yet as an argument from silence, it is not compelling. However, it is possible to argue for the death and resurrection/ascension of Christ as the most probable point of reference in the birth and ascension of the boy, as it is these events that constituted the essence of Christian preaching, the kerygma, of the Jesus movement in first century AD, and not his birth (cf. 1 Cor 15:3–11; the lack of interest of the infancy of Christ in the Gospel of Mark, the recurring elements of the speeches of Acts, and the partly legendary character of the infancy narratives of Luke and Matthew). This latter point concurs with the argument of Raymond E. Brown that the infancy narratives are incorporated relatively late into the Gospel tradition: "The oldest Christian preaching about Jesus concerned his death and resurrection, as may be seen

both instances, it is the Roman authority that makes the attempt to devour possible, through King Herod the great and Pontius Pilate. The scarcity of the text regarding the motivations of the dragon to eat the child leaves us with an open-ended range of interpretational possibilities. The attempt to devour could also be said to refer to the historical calamities surrounding the birth and death of Christ. The central meaning of this incident within the narrative makes it possible to offer some explanation as to how things came to be, how salvation is gained through faithfulness in tribulation and suffering. Such a reading is in line with the conquest paradigm of the book, where the death of the Lamb is put forth as an exemplary model to the envisioned immanent fate of the saints. This reading would fit even better if the child was in fact eaten, though it does not exclude such a reading, as the envisioned ordeals of the saints are not exclusively centered on dying but also encompass other forms of obstacle.[125] However, the child escapes the efforts of the dragon.[126] The subsequent elevation to heaven and God's throne (Rev 12:5) associates the ascension to his act of ruling and authority (cf. 12:10). As Christ is the exemplary model for the saints' own conquest, the very means to defeat their adversary (Rev 12:11), this also suggests the possibility of a reference to the various temptations of Christ in the attempt to devour the boy.[127] In other words, as Christ was sent into the desert by the spirit in order to be tested (ὑπὸ τοῦ πνεύματος πειρασθῆναι ὑπὸ τοῦ διαβόλου, Matt 4:1), the saints must also expect to be tested. As we saw in Section 3.4, this element is made explicit in the messages to the congregations of Smyrna (πειρασθῆτε, Rev 2:10) and Philadelphia (πειράσαι, Rev 3:10). In this way, in order to resist being devoured by the dragon/Satan, the saints must

---

in the formulas of Acts 2:23, 32; 3:14–15; 4:10; 10:39–40; and 1 Cor 15:3–4. Not only did these events constitute the clearest instance of God's salvific action in Jesus, but also it was through them that the disciples came to a more adequate understanding of who Jesus really was. The preaching was eventually shaped into an account of the passion which constituted the oldest consecutive narrative about Jesus" (Raymond E. Brown, *The Birth of the Messiah: A Commentary on the Infancy Narratives in the Gospels of Matthew and Luke*, ABRL [New York: Doubleday, 1993], 26). Perhaps we could side with G. B. Caird in that the emphasis in the imagery of the earthly fate of the boy is on the crucifixion and ascension as primary points of reference, but at the same time acknowledge the possibility of encompassing at least the earthly trials and tribulations of Christ as well (Caird, *The Revelation of St John the Divine*, 149–50).

[125] See the passage in Section 4.4.2.2 regarding the emblematic martyr language of Revelation encompassing more than just those dying for the sake of their testimony in Christ.

[126] Robert W. Canoy argues that the dragon is successful in its attempt to devour the child and that this can be deduced from the woman fleeing into the wilderness to save her life, unlike the child who forfeited his life. Although this reading is possible due to the ambiguous nature of the narrative, I find it unpersuasive as her flight into the desert is approved and endorsed by God through divine intervention. If this was a flight to save her life rather than an attempt to escape and avoid the cunning snares of the Devil, metaphorically speaking, this runs counter to the central idea of conquest unto death in the manner of Christ. See Robert W. Canoy, "Time and Space, Satan (Devil, Ancient Serpent, Deceiver, and Accuser), and Michael in Revelation," *RevExp* 114 (2017): 254–65, 255, 259.

[127] G. B. Caird excludes any possibility for perceiving a reference to the nativity of Jesus in the birth of the boy. This is because Caird interprets this scene as continuing the exposition of Psalm 2 in the vision of the seventh trumpet, and the fact that a king's enthronement marks his reign, not his birth (Caird, *The Revelation of Saint John the Divine*, 149–50). However, the attempt to devour the boy seems to inflict his exegesis on the matter: "The dragon's attempt **to devour** the child may include the temptations and dangers of Jesus' earthly life, but its primary reference is certainly to the crucifixion" (ibid., 150). I concur with this softening of his otherwise stern focus on the crucifixion as hermeneutical premise for this passage.

endure and overcome the various temptations and deceptions of the world. This would be in line with the deceiving nature of the dragon, just as the boy prevailing would concur with the gospel traditions on the matter[128] (cf. 1 Pet 5:8, where we have a similar combination of διάβολος and the desire to devour [καταπιεῖν] as a reference to leading believers astray). Both of these optional readings (attempted killing and temptation) fit well with the general context of the narrative as they are both central elements of the story (the birth/death of Christ and deceptive nature of Satan) and they correspond well with the implied known Jesus traditions that the narrative possibly elaborates on.[129] Perhaps more importantly, by taking into consideration the deceiving nature of Satan in this imagery, one broadens the meaning behind the attempt to devour the boy from a simple threat of killing to that of the deceiving and corrupting purpose of violence in the book elsewhere: to test one's allegiance. Perceived this way, the dragon is not able to devour the child even though Christ was in fact crucified—meaning he did not falter, but stayed faithful to his mission unto death, and serves in these regards as an exemplary model for the saints. It is not death or violence they should fear, but what the fear of it may impinge on their loyalty. Death is in the end inevitable, but its outcome is determined in the loyalty of the one dying (cf. 13:10; 14:9–13).[130]

This reading corresponds well to the heavenly perspective of Plot B (see the next section) as the triumph of Christ deems the prosecuting activities of Satan unnecessary, and thus triggers the liquidation of the satanic office. However, a third reading is also possible. In the intention to eat the boy, there may be a reference to the element of hubris— of Satan overstepping his divinely set boundaries.[131] Perhaps this is why Michael and his angels attack the dragon in the vision of the heavenly perspective of things, in Plot B. This would introduce a new element to the narrative in that it implies an autonomous interest on behalf of Satan. This could explain several things that otherwise create narrative tension: the timing of the liquidation of the heavenly prosecuting office of the accuser (Rev 12:8–9), the subsequent anger (12:12), and the harsh fate of this once celestial being

---

[128] This concurs with the comments of Craig Koester that although this might seem like a miraculous deliverance of the child, the literary context reveals that "the Messiah escaped death not by avoiding it, but by dying and being raised to life again—and the same will be true for the Messiah's followers" (Koester, *Revelation*, 562).

[129] It is possible to perceive the baptism and testing of Jesus at the beginning of his public ministry, and the end of it through crucifixion and ascension as a twofold birth of the Messiah, in that both events are crucial turning points in the ongoing disclosure of the nature of the Messiah in the Gospels. Moreover, both "births" are associated with Satan in these traditions (Mark 1:12–13 with par; Matt 16:23; John 13:27). This adds further strength to a reading of the attempt of the dragon to devour the child as encompassing these traditions. The divine governing of the events of these traditions supports an interpretation of the acts of the dragon of Revelation 12 as subjected to the will and purpose of the divine will.

[130] As W. Gordon Campbell aptly puts it: "So the decisive thing is not at all the war waged on the saints by the monster (13.7), but their own endurance and faith (13.10), since the victory of the Lamb whom they follow everywhere proves to be an irrevocable triumph for them, too" (Campbell, *Reading Revelation*, 89).

[131] Joseph L. Trafton's original suggestion that the dragon is "eagerly hoping to devour the dead Lamb so as to retain his role as accuser" clearly belongs to this category of readings (Trafton, *Reading Revelation*, 124). Another creative interpretation is found in Ian Boxall's identification of an ironic contrast here in "John, who ate up the scroll in order to absorb God's word and pass it on (10:10); the dragon's desire is to eat up the word of God (19:13) in order that he may be destroyed" (Boxall, *The Revelation of Saint John*, 180).

(20:10). This would make Revelation 12 the decisive turning point in the history of the Devil—the exact moment in time where his status changes from a divinely sanctioned accuser to something of a tolerated and utilized antagonist. As the text of Plot A is too scant for certain conclusions on the matter, I will entertain the possibility of this third optional reading in addition to the other two, until the analysis of the whole section is complete.

After having failed to devour the child, the dragon goes on to pursue the woman (Rev 12:13b) and subsequently to wage war on the rest of her children, those keeping the commandments of God and holding the testimony of Jesus (Rev 12:17). It is in his effort to do this that the dragon is interchangeably referred to as a dragon (12:13, 16–17) and a serpent (12:14–15). The conclusion of Plot B introduces the pursuit of the woman of Plot A (Rev 12:13a and b). The intention to wage war on the rest of her children introduces Plot C, where this war is carried out in effect (12:17–18).

4.4.2.1.1 Excursus on the Combat Myth and Revelation 12

Many commentators have pointed out the possible presence or echo of the ancient Near Eastern combat myth, or alternate versions of it, in Revelation 12.[132] The main thesis of Adela Yarbro Collins and Neil Forsyth in this respect is to show that the basic motifs and pattern of the Near Eastern combat myths play a dominant role in the portrait of Satan in the Bible in general (Forsyth) and in the book of Revelation in particular (Yarbro Collins). According to Forsyth, "the separate devil-tales were all seen as cases of one basic opposition, that of Christ and Satan, and that opposition was conceived throughout the whole of the early Christian period in the terms provided by one of the most widespread of Near Eastern narrative patterns, the combat myth."[133] From this perspective, the Christian variant of the plot is something like this:[134]

- A rebel god challenges the power of Yahweh, takes over the whole earth as an extension of his empire, and rules it through the power of sin and death.
- This dark tyrant is eventually thwarted by the Son of God (or man) in the crucifixion, which combines both defeat and victory.
- The function of Christ is to be the potential liberator of humankind from this tyranny, while the function of Satan is to be the adversary in this Christian variant of the ancient Near Eastern combat narrative.

If the narrative in Revelation 12 is read from the perspective of such combat myths, with a cosmic fight between a giant serpent/dragon and a godlike protagonist at the center, then a comparison seems inevitable. Narratives of such showdowns were

---

[132] Aune, *Revelation 6–16*, 667–74; Barr, *Tales of the End*, 27–8; 187–8; Bauckham, *Climax of Prophecy*, 186–98; Beale, *The Book of Revelation*, 624–5; Koester, *Revelation*, 554–60; Mounce, *The Book of Revelation*, 237–8; Osborne, *Revelation*, 454–5; Smalley, *The Revelation to John*, 312–13; Sweet, *Revelation*, 194; Witherington, *Revelation*, 164–6.
[133] Forsyth, *The Old Enemy*, 6.
[134] Ibid., 6–7.

probably familiar to any Christian reader as part of the mythical cultural heritage at the time when the book of Revelation was written, though it is found in many versions: the Babylonian conflict between Tiamat and Marduk; the Canaanite conflicts between Baal and Yamm and Lotan; the Egyptian conflict between Osiris and Set (or Typhon); and the Greek versions of Zeus versus Typhon or Apollo versus Python.[135] The strength of such comparative studies is that they provide valuable information on possible sources to the violent imagery that the general adversarial figures in the book of Revelation consist of, and perhaps the dragon imagery in particular. This could in turn contribute to our understanding of any possible "hostile-to-God" features of Satan in the abundant war imagery, as well as the other malignant creatures and mediums of wrath and affliction. Yet, as we saw in the analysis above, the dragon imagery of Revelation 12 is first and foremost derived from the scriptural traditions of the Hebrew Bible. If traces of Near Eastern combat myths have found its way into the book of Revelation, it is by proxy through the version it is found in the Hebrew Bible. Furthermore, it has been significantly molded to fit the strict, monistic cosmology of the book. This is, in my opinion, the main weakness of the enterprise of Yarbro Collins and Forsyth—they both fail to address the distinct Hebrew features of the figure of Satan. Their lens of interpretation is not able to help us comprehend why it comes naturally to the book of Revelation to combine two such seemingly contradictory features (enemy/servant) in a single concept as Satan/the Devil. Forsyth's combat myth in its allegedly Christian version above does not resemble the plot structure of Revelation 12 as outlined above. The dragon is not explicitly stated to challenge God at this point. He is not thwarted by the Son of God per se, but the crucifixion/resurrection provides the means for the saints to do so (Rev 12:11), thus indicating a more complex combat pattern. Moreover, Christ is not present as the opponent of the dragon, but Michael is (the overlapping functions of God and Christ as perceived in the messages to the seven congregations and the throne vision serve to underscore this point further). David E. Aune has pointed out several flaws in Yarbro Collins's analysis of Revelation 12 and concludes that "the author has not used a coherent pagan myth; rather he has created a pastiche of mythological motifs."[136] This fits well with the "open-ended" use of Scripture in the book of Revelation. Scriptural traditions are molded to fit an already carefully defined plot structure, and not the other way around. The monistic features of the God of the book of Revelation are derived from the seed of the apocalyptic genre: the prophetic tradition of the Hebrew Bible. This background disrupts the combat myth pattern and subdues satanic activity to God's eschatological wrath, sifting, and judgment of humankind. This aspect of Satan cannot, as I see it, be explained through the narrow lens of Near Eastern combat myths. To put it short: it is not just the features of *Satan* in the book of Revelation that challenge the combat myth as modeling pattern, but the image and functions of the *God* presented there. The war imagery becomes complicated when one of the participants is in complete control of the situation. The presumption of Yarbro Collins that "the author of the Book of Revelation is working within a dualistic

---

[135] For an exhaustive list of possible parallels, see Yarbro Collins, *The Combat Myth in the Book of Revelation*, 61–85.
[136] Aune, *Revelation 6–16*, 672.

framework" along the God–Satan parameter fits neither the plot structure of the book in general nor that of Revelation 12 in particular.[137] It is my distinct impression that the relation between Satan as antagonist and God as sovereign cannot be adequately explained through only applying the combat myth as a means of interpretation. It follows from this that I do not concur with the thesis of Yarbro Collins that "its major images and narrative patterns are best understood in the framework of the ancient myths of combat."[138] Neil Forsyth comes very close to my objections when he states,

> Cosmological dualism, which is to say some variant of the combat myth, was influencing the mythology of Israel more and more, and hence the problem of evil became more difficult to resolve. Job may ultimately have come to see that what humans experience as evil is the darker aspect of God, but in the combat myth God and his adversary are radically distinct. The idea of an adversary of man who works somehow with God's permission, obvious enough in Job, becomes less conceivable when the adversary becomes a rebel against God himself.[139]

I intend to argue that the latter point is not the case, based upon the grounds of the former: the book of Revelation contains several elements indicating that God is in control of the adversary; hence, the idea of Satan as the archenemy of God becomes "less conceivable."

Still, we may assume that the implied reader of the book of Revelation is familiar with the Hebrew Bible and pseudepigrapha, and the use of monstrous imagery used to visualize the enemies of Israel, and is thus capable of and expected to decipher the meaning behind the dragon and beast imagery of Revelation 12-13 in the same manner. In light of the reworking of ancient Near Eastern sources in the Hebrew Bible and in keeping with my defined reader, I will therefore not consider the ancient Near Eastern combat myth as something implied within the text other than by proxy through the Hebrew Bible.[140]

In the thesis of Steven Grabiner, *Revelation's Hymns: Commentary on the Cosmic Conflict*, we find an approach to the book of Revelation similar to that of Yarbro Collins and Forsyth. The main premise for his analysis is that a cosmic conflict between God and the Devil is the main drive of the narrative. He understands Revelation 12

---

[137] Yarbro Collins, *The Combat Myth in the Book of Revelation*, 231. Her view on the dualistic nature of the book of Revelation is presented on pages 158–61, where she states that "the sectarian dualism expressed in the book is primarily shaped by the combat myth. It must be seen in the context of the idea that the present time is characterized by a universal struggle between the allies of God and the forces of Satan" (ibid., 160).

[138] Yarbro Collins, *The Combat Myth in the Book of Revelation*, 2.

[139] Forsyth, *The Old Enemy*, 191.

[140] For similar conclusions and further arguments, see Osborne, *Revelation*, 459–60; and Smalley, *The Revelation to John*, 312–13, and in particular 317. Richard Bauckham argues for the unique creative work of John behind the reworking of material derived from the Hebrew Bible and mythological knowledge into the dragon imagery of Revelation 12 (see Bauckham, *Climax of Prophecy*, 193–8). Gregory K. Beale, on the other hand, states that "it is absurd to think that John is 'a copyist of ill-digested pagan myths,' since it is clear that the thrust of his whole book is a polemic against tolerance of idolatry and compromise with pagan institutions," and he argues that the Hebrew Bible is the primary source for the dragon imagery (Beale, *The Book of Revelation*, 634).

to attest to such a conflict, and he interprets it as describing a primeval rebellion of Satan and his minions. Grabiner's work is not specifically about Satan but on the hymns of Revelation interpreted in light of this cosmic conflict. He locates the origins of the hymns of Revelation in the heavenly throne room, and as accompanying and commenting on all the major events in Revelation.[141] There are several overlapping elements between Grabiner's dissertation and this reading: the choice of narrative criticism as the main tool of analysis; the acknowledgment of the hymns of Revelation as hermeneutical elaborations on the central events of the narrative; the recognition of the central function of Satan to the overarching plot;[142] the recognition of the pivotal role that Revelation 12 plays in the storyline, thus "holding a central key for a proper interpretation of the book";[143] understanding the element of theodicy as central to the understanding of the narrative;[144] and the recognition of the importance of taking the implied references to the traditions of the Hebrew Bible and pseudepigrapha in the text into consideration in a work based largely upon narrative criticism. This last point is important in establishing his hermeneutical premise—a primeval fall of Satan. This element also introduces the main differences between this work and his. Grabiner bases his understanding of the beginning of the cosmic conflict upon what Henry Ansgar Kelly would deem a "retrofitted understanding" of Satan in the Hebrew Scriptures:[145] He argues for a Satan in opposition to God in the manner of Revelation 12, not only in the New Testament but also in the Hebrew Bible—even when not mentioned (see his understanding of Satan in Ezekiel 28).[146] By assuming a reference to a primeval fall in Revelation 12, and assuming that the background of this can be found in texts from the scriptural traditions of the Hebrew Bible, he establishes the idea of an ever-present cosmic conflict where there is no explicit mention of it. This hermeneutics of assumption can also be found in his reading of the hymns of the book of Revelation.[147] In addition to being derived from what could be referred to as dubious

---

[141] Grabiner, *Revelation's Hymns*, 3–4.
[142] Ibid., 40–6.
[143] Ibid., 37. Grabiner builds much of this part of his thesis on the work of Sigve K. Tonstad, *Saving God's Reputation*.
[144] Grabiner, *Revelation's Hymns*, 60–7.
[145] See Kelly, *Satan: A Biography*, 2.
[146] Even though the work of Grabiner includes formulations such as "another OT passage that informs John's development of Satan's character in Revelation's storyline ... is Ezek. 28.12-19" (Grabiner, *Revelation's Hymns*, 55) and "from the vantage point of Revelation" (ibid., 56), the main argument of the section is that these texts from the Hebrew Bible shed further information on the Satan found in Revelation 12, and serves to establish the impression that the allegedly primeval fall can be discerned in these texts. A phrase such as "Elements within Ezekiel's dirge contribute to a further understanding of Satan's position within the divine council" (ibid., 56) underscore the impression that his reading is "retrofitted," as Satan (obviously) is not mentioned in the book of Ezekiel. In short, Grabiner finds Satan as the scheming and plotting enemy of God throughout the Hebrew Bible, primarily by means of his reading of Revelation 12. Grabiner spends over twenty pages of his fourth chapter in establishing his understanding of this conflict element by appealing to the Hebrew Scriptures: it is an understanding that is contingent upon a reading of Satan based on elements found in the narrative of the book of Revelation (ibid., 40–6) read in light of an interpretation of his alleged role in the divine council (ibid., 46–60).
[147] In his analysis of Rev 4:8–11; 5:9–14, he states that "God's sovereignty is clearly in view, but it needs to be remembered that it is a sovereignty contested by the attempts of Satan to undermine God's authority. While there is no explicit mention of his rebellion in this passage, there are thematic hints that connect the hymns to the larger theme" (Grabiner, *Revelation's Hymns*, 70–1).

hermeneutical grounds of retrofitted assumptions, the main weakness of Grabiner's work is its failure to respond to challenges from the text of Revelation itself. Firstly, it fails to convincingly explain why Satan is given opportunity and additional time in Rev 12:12 to continue his work after having lost the cosmic conflict, and why he *must* be released after his imprisonment in Rev 20:3.[148] Secondly, it reduces the role of the martyrs of Rev 12:11[149] and its relation to 6:9–11,[150] despite their active role as (the only) subjects in the act of conquering Satan in 12:11. Thirdly, it fails to argue convincingly for his original reading of the aorist passives of the book.[151] And fourthly, as his idea of the inherent cosmic conflict is derived from Adela Yarbro Collins's work,[152] it fails to convincingly explain the presence of a dualistic antagonism between the Devil and God within a narrative with a thoroughly monistic cosmology.[153] For these reasons, I find the thesis of Steven Grabiner suffering from what I perceive as unconvincing hermeneutical premises.[154] I have defined my hermeneutical premises differently, and the results from the narrative analysis on the function of Satan within the book of Revelation will therefore differ considerably from his. The differences reveal the extent of the interpretational consequences that follow from how one defines the overarching plot of Revelation. Grabiner reads the hymns of Revelation in light of his definition of a cosmic conflict, while I interpret the texts concerning Satan in light of the sovereign God's sifting of humankind. This might be a good example of what David Barr has in mind when he discusses whether or not all readings are valid. Are some readings better

---

[148] Grabiner suggests that this must happen in order to highlight Satan's importance to the narrative as a whole, to demonstrate Satan's uniqueness in the unfolding drama by presenting him alone in the final stage of it, and to connect his deceptive traits as deceiver (Rev 20:10) to the Genesis narrative and the serpent's actions there (Gen 3:13). I find this unconvincing for several reasons. Firstly, I agree that Satan is released partly to serve literary means of separation not mainly to single himself out, but rather primarily to separate the earthly vindication of the saints (reigning for a thousand years with Christ) from the ushering in of the universal age of salvation (see Section 5.4.2). Secondly, the arguments of Grabiner are based upon an assumed primeval individual rebellion of Satan, and without this assumption, the necessity of his singularity disappears. Thirdly, his last argument rests on both the assumption of a primeval rebellion present in Revelation 12 as well as the identification of Satan in the Eden narrative. Both of these assumptions are contested and refuted in this reading. See Grabiner, *Revelation's Hymns*, 41–3, 171–2.

[149] See Grabiner, *Revelation's Hymns*, 168–9.

[150] Ibid., 62–4.

[151] Grabiner and his highly original reading of the aorist passives as satanic passives is grounded on these pages: "a closer reading suggests that this is part of the texture of John's development of the role of Satan. Instead of indicating a divine passive, the usage of εδοθη here signals Satan's role in giving the sea-beast and the land-beast their role in the controversy" (Grabiner, *Revelation's Hymns*, 46).

[152] Ibid., 141, 157–8.

[153] In his reading of the hymnic pericope of the throne vision, he argues that even though the more traditional readings here find an anchoring of the events of the septets in the sovereignty of God, it is important to remember that this sovereignty is contested by Satan's attempts to undermine God's authority. Grabiner admits that Satan is not explicitly mentioned in this section of the narrative, but argues for the presence of thematic hints in the text connecting it to what he identifies as the larger theme (of cosmic conflict) (Grabiner, *Revelation's Hymns*, 70–1). See my critical comments on the hermeneutical premises of Grabiner in Sections 1.2.2 and 4.4.2.1.1.

[154] Grabiner reveals a considerable degree of influence from Sigve K. Tonstad and his *Saving God's Reputation* regarding these matters. This is particularly visible in his chapter on his understanding of the conflict of the narrative, "Conflict and Theodicy" (Grabiner, *Revelation's Hymns*, 35–67). Refer to Section 1.2.2 for my view on Tonstad's arguments for this way of perceiving the conflict.

than others? Why do different readers give different interpretations?[155] The answer he suggests is that the different readings of Revelation depend on the different initial choices one makes.[156]

The works of Yarbro Collins, Forsyth, Grabiner, and Tonstad have shown that an initial choice to read the book of Revelation from the perspective of a combat myth or cosmic conflict bears considerable impact on one's understanding of the function of Satan there. My own contribution here represents a different reading based upon different initial choices, thus answering the same questions with different answers. It is an argument for a different Satan present in the text: a Satan, whether credited with autonomous aspirations or not, who is part of the divine distribution of the forces at hand.

4.4.2.2 The Satan of Plot B—The War in Heaven

The reoccurrence of the dragon imagery of Plot A in Plot B provides us with a link to perceive the two sections as interconnected. There was a war in heaven, and Michael and his angels waged war/had to wage war against the dragon, and the dragon and his angels fought back (12:7). The translation of ὁ Μιχαὴλ καὶ οἱ ἄγγελοι αὐτοῦ τοῦ πολεμῆσαι μετὰ τοῦ δράκοντος is debated, because of the unusual combination of the nominative case (Michael and his angels) instead of the accusative in combination with the articular infinitive (τοῦ πολεμῆσαι). Several possible options for the translation have been proposed, with the majority of them revolving around the occurrence of a war in heaven as either instigated or followed by Michael's involvement. In any case, it is the subsequent involvement of the dragon, described as a reaction to the action preceding it, that is most important to this reading.[157] The dragon is cast as the object

---

[155] David L. Barr, "Choosing between Readings: Questions and Criteria," in *Reading the Book of Revelation: A Resource for Students*, ed. David L. Barr (Atlanta, GA: Society of Biblical Literature, 2003), 163–72, 163.

[156] See ibid., 167. Both Grabiner's readings and my own could be said to meet the four criteria of Barr's to discern between multiple valid readings of Revelation (ibid., 171), thus suggesting both works as valid yet incompatible readings of the same narrative. For a more open attitude to the plethora of possible readings of Revelation, see Carey, "The Apocalypse and Its Ambiguous Ethos," 170.

[157] According to Robert H. Charles (*A Critical and Exegetical Commentary Vol.1*, 321–2), the unusual formulation with the nouns in nominative preceding the articular infinitive is a construction "found *several times* in the LXX, and found as a *literal reproduction of a pure Hebraism*." He mentions the examples of Hos 9:13; Ps 24:14; 1 Chr 9:25; Eccl 3:15 to support his translation of Rev 12:7, which according to him expresses an element of necessity: "Michael and his angels had to fight with the Dragon." Since several leading scholars on Revelation have followed Charles's interpretation, often without much argument besides a recitation of Charles's own argument, I will here stress that the argument is too scant to allow for certainty, yet should be considered a possible reading among others (see also Aune, *Revelation 6–16*, 654; Beale, *The Book of Revelation*, 653–4; Smalley, *The Revelation to John*, 322–3; cf. David L. Mathewson, *Revelation: A Handbook on the Greek Text* [Waco, TX: Baylor University Press, 2016], 161). Koester (*Revelation*, 548) perceives both purpose and result clauses as possible translations, whereas Osborne (*Revelation*, 468), Trafton (*Reading Revelation*, 121), and Mounce (*The Book of Revelation*, 241) favor the idea of Michael instigating the waging of war. From the examples of Charles, Hos 9:13 and 1 Chr 9:25 seem most promising to prove his case, as Ps 24:14 and Eccl 3:15 seem to fall outside the range of a translation in the vein of "necessity." This is partly due to God being the acting subject in both instances, and partly because they rather express causality/divine order. There is little in the context of these texts hinting

of aggression in Plot B and is characterized as the weaker part of the warring parties. The reason for this sudden aggression is not stated explicitly, but I will in the following argue along the lines of eschatological necessity.[158] The outcome of the war in heaven is described like this: οὐδὲ τόπος εὑρέθη αὐτῶν ἔτι ἐν τῷ οὐρανῷ (There was no longer any place for them in heaven, Rev 12:8b; cf. 1 En. 14:5). This implies that up until this point, there was a place for them in heaven, but now (ἔτι) there is not. The subsequent result of this is the casting out of heaven of the dragon and his angels.[159] The aorist passive (ἐβλήθη) is probably to be taken as a divine passive, which frequently occurs throughout Revelation 12-13.[160] However, the reference could imply Michael as the

---

at necessity in the manner that Charles suggests for Rev 12:7. This would suggest that God *had* to make his covenant known to those who fear him (Ps 24:14) and that all things that *had* to be (created by God) already have been made (Eccl 3:15)—both translations obviously awkward to their respective contexts. My point here is that Charles seems to be right in detecting a reproduction of an idiom from the LXX in this unusual combination of nominatives preceding the infinitive in Rev 12:7, but his own examples show that this idiom is not always used to express necessity. Similarly, the syntactical possibilities behind an infinitive construct in Hebrew with the preposition ל (which Charles suggests lies behind the construction of Rev 12:7) is not limited to only expressing result (i.e., "There was a war ... Michael and his angels had to"). It can also express purpose (i.e., "There was a war ... because Michael and his angels went to wage war") or time (i.e., "There was a war in heaven; Michael and his angels waged war," as Osborne [*Revelation*, 468] suggests; see Bruce K. Waltke and Michael Patrick O'Connor, *An Introduction to Biblical Hebrew Syntax* [Winona Lake, IN: Eisenbrauns, 1990], 605-11). In light of this, Sigve K. Tonstad (*Saving God's Reputation*, 68-9) seems to overstate the evidence at hand when he concludes that this formulation "assigns blame to one of the parties, laying the responsibility squarely on Satan"; moreover, "the notion that 'war burst forth' as well as the necessity of the action taken in the heavenly realm oblige temporal primacy for this verse"; and finally, that "the primordial and heavenly origin of the conflict is grounded in the suggestive wording of this text" (ibid., 69). Tonstad uses this formulation as part of an elaborate argument as to why the events of Rev 12:7-12 must be seen as a primordial event, a move that allows him to read several texts from the Hebrew Bible as supporting such a reading (see Section 1.2.2). I will argue below for an interpretation of Rev 12:7-12 as imminent future in the process of unfolding, thus making the possible necessity of Michael waging war in heaven an eschatological necessity initiated by God, and therefore not necessarily due to satanic hubris. This fits well with the advent of Michael and the envisioned salvation devoid of any Satan, several times expressed as future eschatological events in the Hebrew Bible and pseudepigrapha (cf. Dan 12:1; 1 En. 24:4-5; T. Dan 6:1-5; Jub. 23:29).

[158] Forsyth suggests interestingly that it is the rescue of the child that "triggers the War in Heaven, in which Michael, now the Champion of the church, does battle with and defeats Satan (each with a host of angels in support)" (Forsyth, *The Satanic Epic*, 39).

[159] It is this (involuntary?) ejection from heaven that separates the angelic fall of the Watcher myth from the fall of Satan in Revelation 12. According to Loren T. Stuckenbruck and Mark D. Mathews, "since in the Enoch tradition it is emphasized that the angels' descent occurred by their own volition (1 En. 6:6; 12:4; 15:3; 19:1; apparently also in 86:1, 3), its texts offer an unlikely background against which to interpret Rev 12:7-9" (Loren T. Stuckenbruck and Mark D. Mathews, "The Apocalypse of John, 1 Enoch, and the Question of Influence," in *Die Johannesapokalypse: Kontexte—Konzepte—Rezeption*, ed. Jörg Frey, James A. Kelhoffer, and Franz Tóth, WUNT 287 [Tübingen: Mohr Siebeck, 2012], 191-234, 212). They also write that it is unlikely "that the downthrow of 'the Devil and Satan' (Rev 12:9) was influenced by the Enochic fallen angels tradition" (ibid., 215). Instead, they suggest that "the mythic *hubris* is more conditioned by the tradition of Isaiah 14:12-21 than by the Enochic fallen angels tradition" (ibid., 212). The separation of the fall of Satan from the primordial fall of the Watchers seems to confirm that the Satan of Revelation is closer to the Mastema/Satan of the book of Jubilees than the Watchers of the Enoch traditions (see Sections 1.1 and 3.4.1.2), as the former is reported to have an active part in the divine ordering of things due to the great evil of men (Jub. 10:8-11), whereas the latter is incarcerated until the day of judgment (1 En. 10).

[160] See also Osborne, *Revelation*, 471; Aune, *Revelation 6-16*, 695.

hidden subject of the action, due to the context of him carrying out the acts of war. Yet, with the battlefield of heaven, the courtyard of God, and the strong Danielic overtones of this section of the book, God is in the end the supervising actant of this scene and thus the most probable subject of the passive.[161]

Preceding the hymnic interpretation of the events in Rev 12:10–12, a series of satanic names and epithets are clustered together as if to make abundantly clear the implications of what has just happened: ὁ δράκων ὁ μέγας, ὁ ὄφις ὁ ἀρχαῖος, ὁ καλούμενος Διάβολος καὶ ὁ Σατανᾶς, ὁ πλανῶν τὴν οἰκουμένην ὅλην (The great dragon, the serpent of old, the one called the Devil and Satan, the one leading astray the whole world, Rev 12:9)—it is *he* who has been thrown down from heaven. The intertextual meaning and to some extent the intratextual meaning of these names and epithets have been explained above, and their occurrence here connects the dragon and the events described semantically with these occurrences elsewhere in the book. Σατανᾶς is mentioned in the message to Smyrna (2:9, 13), to Pergamum (2:13), and to Thyatira (3:24); as well as in connection with the thousand-year reign of Christ (20:2, 7). Διάβολος is mentioned in the message to Smyrna (2:10) and in connection with the thousand-year reign of Christ (20:2, 10). ὁ πλανῶν τὴν οἰκουμένην ὅλην is connected to the deceiving acts of Jezebel of Thyatira (2:20); the beast from the earth (13:14; 19:20); the whore of Babylon (18:34); and serves as a description of the main activities of Satan (20:3, 8, 10). In addition to these intratextual references, we have the intertextual references implied known to the reader, reenacting the eschatological hope of the final removal of the satanic office, which was expected to bring about the end of oppression and inaugurate the vindication of God's people. The texts of Jub. 23:29 and T. Mos. 10:1 envision the removal of Satan as initiating an era of eschatological salvation. Similarly, the advent of Michael, the eschatological prince of Israel, also ushers in the fulfillment of similar eschatological expectations (Dan 12:1; cf. 1 En. 54:6; 1QM XVII, 5–9). The envisioned ejection of the dragon from heaven thus initiates the final removal of him through this spatial decline in status of the heavenly adversary of the saints. With his ejection, the future cessation of the transcendental common denominator of the saints' immanent afflictions is at hand. From this perspective, the war in heaven is eschatologically necessary. Furthermore, the expectations explain why Michael and his angels *had* to go to war. If salvation is characterized as cessation of afflictions (cf. Rev 21:3–4), it is only logical that its main source must be removed before its completion.

The act of war encompasses the functions of *complication* and *transforming action* in Plot B, and thus parallels the attempt to devour the child and the subsequent ascension of the Messiah in Plot A according to the plot analysis above (see Table 7). As the two plots are describing approximately the same scenario yet from different aspects of reality (transcendent/immanent), their parallel functions could indicate a causal relation between the two events. Perhaps the idea conveyed by this binary relation is that the Christ event on earth rendered the satanic office as heavenly accuser no longer necessary, and thereby superfluous in the heavenly sphere (see Section

---

[161] Michael waging war on hostile enemies as God's commander is probably an allusion to Dan 12:1; see parallel wording in Dan Theod. 10:20 and 7:21 to Rev 12:7–8 (Beale, *The Book of Revelation*, 652).

4.4.3.3). By perceiving the war as an eschatological event initiating the coming age of salvation, such a reading could make sense: the whole plot is initiated by the advent of a renowned warrior in the character of Michael ushering in the expected riddance of the adversarial forces in heaven/on earth, an event which in turn initiates a new era of peace and prosperity. Still, even if the parallel events of Plots A and B are in this way perceived as interrelated events (initiating the age of eschatological salvation), they are clearly separated by the perspective of time at play in the narrative. The Christ event (birth, death, and resurrection) constitutes an obvious part of Plot A and can be considered recent past for the implied reader, but when in time is the ejection of Satan from heaven envisioned as taking place?

The answer to this question, I believe, is found at the heart of the explanatory intercalation of Rev 12:10-12. It is a poetic celebration of the arrival of a series of elements following the ejection of the dragon: the salvation (ἡ σωτηρία), the power (ἡ δύναμις), and the kingdom (ἡ βασιλεία) of our God (τοῦ θεοῦ ἡμῶν) as well as the authority of his Messiah (καὶ ἡ ἐξουσία τοῦ χριστοῦ αὐτοῦ). Salvation as envisioned in Revelation 20-22 is already at hand within the heavenly sphere at this point, and it is initiated by the removal of the satanic office—anticipating what soon will be an earthly reality as well. Here the dragon is characterized by yet another epithet: ὁ κατήγωρ τῶν ἀδελφῶν ἡμῶν, ὁ κατηγορῶν αὐτοὺς ἐνώπιον τοῦ θεοῦ ἡμῶν ἡμέρας καὶ νυκτός (the accuser of our brethren who accuses them before our God day and night, Rev 12:10). This is the only place in the New Testament where Satan is referred to as ὁ κατήγωρ, though it is a literal translation of the Hebrew שָׂטָן (Satan). It is most likely a reference to his office as heavenly accuser in the Hebrew tradition (Job 1:6, 7, 9, 12; 2:1-7; Zech 3:1; cf. T. Job 8:1-3; 16:2-4; 20:1-3; 1 En. 40:7-8; Apoc. Zeph. 3:8-9; 6:17; 3 En. 26:12; m. Avot 4:11; Tg. Exod 32:19.)[162] The verb κατηγορέω is elsewhere in the LXX and the New Testament used to describe acts of testing/accusing as a means to reveal one's inner character (Matt 12:10; Mark 3:2; Luke 6:7; Rom 2:15) and mere legal accusations (before God: Luke 23:2, 10, 14; John 5:45; before humans: Dan 6:5; 1 Macc 7:6, 25; 2 Macc 4:47; 10:13, 21; Matt 27:12; Mark 15:3-4; Acts 22:30; 24:2, 8, 13, 19; 25:5, 11; 16; 28:19). By this the reference to the dragon as ὁ κατήγωρ could, in addition to the apparent judicial connotations of the title, also encompass the acts of testing as a means to reveal the inner character of the brethren of Rev 12:10. As already pointed out in the analysis of Revelation 2-3, such activities frequently appear as a prominent part of Satan's adversarial repertoire.

The time when Satan will be ousted from heaven is indicated in 12:11: καὶ αὐτοὶ ἐνίκησαν αὐτὸν διὰ τὸ αἷμα τοῦ ἀρνίου καὶ διὰ τὸν λόγον τῆς μαρτυρίας αὐτῶν καὶ οὐκ ἠγάπησαν τὴν ψυχὴν αὐτῶν ἄχρι θανάτου (And they conquered him by the blood of the Lamb, and by the blood of their witness, [as] they did not love their lives unto

---

[162] I am indebted to David E. Aune for several of these attestations (Aune, *Revelation 6-16*, 701). According to Elaine Pagels, the term "Satan" in the Hebrew Bible "describes an adversarial role. It is not the name of a particular character" (Pagels, *The Origin of Satan*, 39). The individualization of such a celestial character was irrelevant as its function was subordinated to the heavenly assembly and its supreme God. It is this divinely sanctioned adversarial role of the Hebrew Bible that is implied in the reference to Satan as ὁ κατήγωρ in Rev 12:10.

[the point of] death).¹⁶³ These are the events that prompted a war in heaven, the advent of Michael, and the dissolving of the satanic office: the conquering of the dragon by the blood of the Lamb and the blood of their own witness. Blood refers in this context to death, as it is juxtaposed with the blood of the Lamb referring to the Lamb having been slaughtered (5:9–10), which in turn is an obvious reference to the Christ event at the cross. The third-person plural endings of the verbs are referring back to the τῶν ἀδελφῶν ἡμῶν in Rev 12:10. Note that this is a two-step process, the Christ incident and the blood of the saints. By faithfully witnessing unto death, the Lamb conquered (5:5–6), and when a fixed amount of martyrs have been reached in the same manner, then the moment of salvation, vindication, and retribution will come (6:9–11; the implied element of retribution is made explicit in texts like 14:9–12 and 18:4–6). Satan is thus both the object and means of conquest. Persevering with the satanic ordeals is for the believing community the very means of salvation, as it was for Christ to provide it.¹⁶⁴ This is the point of reference of the exhortation to conquer present in the messages to the seven congregations (2:7, 11, 17, 26; 3:5, 12, 21). Here we have the explicit answer to whom or what the congregations are to conquer: "*The conqueror conquers the accuser.*"¹⁶⁵ Both Koester and Beale argue for a reading of the martyr language of this passage to be emblematic.¹⁶⁶ This seems reasonable in light of the general language of the context of Rev 12:11, where the sovereign God has more subjects than those dying for the cause and the accusing activity of Satan strikes in more ways than death. Also, this is supported by a similar use of language (perseverance and conquest) found in the messages to the congregations where it includes all of the believers, and not only Antipas the sole martyr (2:13). Finally, we have the inclusion of John, who counts himself among those suffering and patiently enduring, though he is not dying (1:9). The main point is to persevere in faith through any affliction unto the point of death, as this perseverance will be their means of salvation through the blood of the Lamb.¹⁶⁷ The nature of these afflictions is presented in the second half of Plot A when the dragon is unleashing his fury upon the woman and the rest of her children (12:13–17). Plot C is an extensive elaboration on these afflictions (13:1–18; cf. 14:12–13).

The demise of Satan in Revelation is presented in three stages: heaven to earth (12:7–12), earth to the abyss (20:1), and in the end into the lake of fire (20:10). Most important at this point is to underscore that the expulsion of Satan from heaven is

---

¹⁶³ For the translation of ἄχρι denoting extent and not time, see Beale, *The Book of Revelation*, 665, and for intertextual parallels to the meaning of this expression, see Aune, *Revelation 6–16*, 703.

¹⁶⁴ On the testimony of the saints as an instrument in defeating Satan, Gregory K. Beale states, "The notion that their testimony is not only the basis but also the instrument by which their 'overcoming' is accomplished may be implied, since διά with the accusative to indicate the basis of something is very close to the idea of means, as in 13:14" (Beale, *The Book of Revelation*, 663–4).

¹⁶⁵ Trafton, *Reading Revelation*, 122.

¹⁶⁶ Beale, *The Book of Revelation*, 665–6; Koester, *Revelation*, 552; cf. Bauckham, *Theology of the Book of Revelation*, 93; Trafton, *Reading Revelation*, 190–1.

¹⁶⁷ This concurs with the argument of Peter-Ben Smit in that one prominent aspect given to the function of the suffering of the saints in Revelation is a highly sophisticated way of dealing with pain, exclusion from society, and denial of all humanity. According to him, "highly cultured writing about pain, as the Apocalypse of John contains, is a (literally [re]creative) way of dealing with pain, both in terms of coping and in terms of (subversively) regaining agency" (Smit, "Sadomasochism and the Apocalypse of John," 104).

not presented as a primordial event, but as something about to happen through the faithfulness of the believing community.[168] Joseph L. Trafton states fittingly on the matter, "The notion that this passage describes the primeval fall of Satan—a story that, contrary to what many people assume, is not found in the Old Testament and, moreover, is of no interest to John elsewhere in the book—*misses the point completely*" (my italics).[169] Their faithfulness unto death will bring about Satan's downfall and usher in the eschatological age of salvation.[170] Against this background, his subsequent increased activity (12:12) presents us with a circular narrative. This will be further discussed below in Section 4.4.3 on point of view.

The precise wording of 12:12 is important as it concludes the hymnic interpolation of 12:10–12 with an interesting choice of words: διὰ τοῦτο εὐφραίνεσθε, [οἱ] οὐρανοὶ καὶ οἱ ἐν αὐτοῖς σκηνοῦντες. οὐαὶ τὴν γῆν καὶ τὴν θάλασσαν, ὅτι κατέβη ὁ διάβολος πρὸς ὑμᾶς ἔχων θυμὸν μέγαν, εἰδὼς ὅτι ὀλίγον καιρὸν ἔχει (Because of this, rejoice heavens and you who dwell in them. Woe to the earth and the sea, because the devil has come down to you with great wrath, because he knows he has little time). Firstly, the word καταβαίνω (go down) is preferred to βάλλω (cast [out]), which is used elsewhere in this plot strand. The former suggests, in light of how it is used elsewhere in Revelation, a controlled and deliberate coming down on behalf of the heavenly agent (cf. 10:1; 18:1; 20:1), or driven/guided by purpose when used with inanimate objects (cf. 3:12; 13:13; 16:21; 20:9; 21:2, 10). In each instance, the outcome of the "coming down [from heaven]" is driven by divine initiative, not by the will of the agent. Secondly, the word οὐαί (woe) forms a word thread in the book of Revelation and is elsewhere always used with reference to the wrath of God (8:13; 9:12; 11:14; 18:10, 16, 19). In my view, the context invites us to perceive the woe of 12:12 to have the same reference here as

---

[168] See also Beale, *The Book of Revelation*, 654–60; Koester, *Revelation*, 550–1; Kelly, *Satan: A Biography*, 153–6; Mounce, *The Book of Revelation*, 240; Witherington, *Revelation*, 170; Aune, *Revelation 6–16*, 695–6; Charles, *A Critical and Exegetical Commentary Vol.1*, 323–4; Yarbro Collins, *The Combat Myth in the Book of Revelation*, 108; Smalley, *The Revelation to John*, 323–4; Derek Brown, *God of This Age*, 27; Resseguie, *The Revelation of John*, 174; Barr, *Tales of the End*, 217–18; Dochhorn, *Schriftgelehrte Prophetie*, 395–6, 399. For opposing arguments perceiving Rev 12:7–12 as referring to a primordial event, see Tonstad, *Saving God's Reputation*, 66–7. Grant R. Osborne (*Revelation*, 468–71), followed by Stephen Grabiner (*Revelation's Hymns*, 164–5), opts for a reading encapsulating "all three bindings of Satan" (primordial, at the Christ event, and at the eschaton) present in Revelation 12, whereas Neil Forsyth (*The Old Enemy*, 254–5) explains how the text, with its "visionary present," could later be understood as referring to both primordial past and eschatological future.

[169] Trafton, *Reading Revelation*, 121–2; see also Caird, *The Revelation of St John the Divine*, 153.

[170] Edmondo F. Lupieri has found another interpretational way to encompass a primordial sin of Satan and his angels, an identification of Satan as present in the temptation at Eden as well as keeping up his mandate as heavenly accuser, and at the same time retaining all his celestial powers at the time of his attempt to devour the child in Rev 12:4. According to Lupieri, "these events are independent of what will take place in history, when there is such a thing as history. John does not see the vision of the woman and the dragon as a description of the order of events, but rather as an understandable explanation that God prepared for him of heavenly events before or outside of the created world" (Edmondo F. Lupieri, *A Commentary on the Apocalypse of John* [Grand Rapids, MI: Eerdmans, 1999], 194; see also 197–8). This way of relativizing temporal indicators and elements of the narrative in light of a concept of "God's eternal present" may work within a theologically motivated reading of Revelation. However, I suspect that such a reading may ignore or undermine the function and reasons for differentiating between past, present, and future tense within the narrative.

well.¹⁷¹ Thirdly, the word θυμόν (wrath) itself always refers to the wrath of God as the means of his judgment and/or retribution (14:8, 10, 19; 15:1, 7; 16:1, 19; 18:3; 19:5).¹⁷² Hence these arguments may be taken as indicators that the "great wrath" of Rev 12:12 is actually referring to Satan functioning as a vessel of God's wrath, and not so much a personal vendetta on the grounds of his previous exclusion from heaven.¹⁷³ Interpreted as a vessel of God's purpose, the reading is more in line with the context of Revelation 6–16 in general, and Revelation 12–13 in particular, than a "Satan gone rogue" reading¹⁷⁴ (see Section 4.4.3 on point of view in this chapter). These three elements found in the final verse of a hymnic passage, functioning both as an intersection of three overlapping plot strands and as interpretational aid for the reader, suggest that the coming of Satan on earth is explained as part of the divine initiative and purpose. This is supported by the occurrence of an indicated time limitation (12:12), which in Revelation always serves as a reminder of divine control and/or supervision on the matters at hand.¹⁷⁵ Seen from this perspective, the reason for him being described as coming with the great wrath (of God) is to explain the intensification of his earthly activities. This is probably due to the expected increase in tribulation and deception as the imminent eschatological end approaches. This phenomenon could be an implied reference to the widely attested expectation of such activities within the New Testament (cf. Matt 24; Mark 13; Luke 21; 1 Tim 4:1-3; 2 Tim 3:1-5). It is also possible that Satan is aware that the final day of judgment is approaching, and "the little time" is best spent doing as much deception as possible.¹⁷⁶ An increase in antagonistic activities is

---

[171] The use of the word in the New Testament may also be conveying, according to David E. Aune (*Revelation 6-16*, 704), "a prophetic gravity that calls to mind the great prophetic speeches of denunciation in the OT, particularly in Isaiah and Jeremiah." I agree that this *could* be a possible implication of the use of the word, and if this is the case, it would support the reading here of "woe" as an object of God by the cosmology inherent within these two prophetic books.

[172] The use of θυμὸν in 14:8 and 18:3 is in both instances used in the phrase ἐκ τοῦ οἴνου τοῦ θυμοῦ τῆς πορνείας αὐτῆς (of the wine of the wrath of her fornication). According to James L. Resseguie, the appearance of wrath in this string of genitives suggests that "Babylon's influence is not only intoxicating but wrathful, causing destruction and dissolution of the self-absorbed way of life it has created" (Resseguie, *The Revelation of John*, 199; and Osborne, *Revelation*, 538-9).

[173] The situation seen from this perspective is reminiscent of the scene found in Jub. 10:1–11, where Mastema finds himself deprived of all his minions after having been defeated by the angel of the presence and his coworkers. The "us" and "we" of 10:7 and 11 is probably referring to the angel of the presence, since no other mediator agent has been presented in the text since the mention of him in 1:27. In 18:10 he is identified as the Angel of the Lord, cf. Exod 22:11. Even when facing defeat his one concern is to carry out his mission, because the wickedness of men is great. He is left with one-tenth of the spawn of the Watchers to do his job. The parallels to Revelation 12 are obvious: battle, Michael, defeat, maintained activity of the antagonist but with divinely ordained limitation. If nothing else, this parallel serves as precedence to the reading of Rev 12:12, thus suggesting that the cosmological implications of such a reading would neither be novel nor be seen as contradictory to a reader assumed familiar with the scriptural traditions of the Hebrew Bible.

[174] Koester, *Revelation*, 565.

[175] ὀλίγον καιρὸν is possibly referring to the same timespan as χρόνον μικρόν in Rev 6:11, and ὀλίγον used as an adverb in Rev 17:10. Gregory Beale (*The Book of Revelation*, 668, 986-7) interprets the μικρὸν χρόνον of Rev 20:3 as referring to the same timespan as ὀλίγον καιρὸν. However, this seems forced since the period preceding the two events, the coming down of Satan in Rev 12:12 and the release of Satan in Rev 20:3, seems incompatible (war vs. incarceration). I will comment further on the function of this term in Rev 20:3 in Chapter 5.

[176] See Beale, *The Book of Revelation*, 667.

thus to be expected as the end approaches. This equals satanic activity in the book of Revelation. It is a woe to the earth and the sea, but as with every other woe in this book, it is a woe initiated by God to serve his purpose.

4.4.2.3 *The Satan of Plot C—The Beasts of the Sea and the Earth*

The implications of the dragon going away to wage war on the rest of the children of the woman (Rev 12:17) are described in detail in Plot C. The dragon is characterized as pulling the strings of the events as he summons the two beasts from the sea and the earth, and gives the first beast his power (τὴν δύναμιν αὐτοῦ), his throne (τὸν θρόνον αὐτοῦ), and great authority (ἐξουσίαν μεγάλην). The second beast wields the authority of the first beast to deceive the dwellers of the earth into worshipping the first beast (13:12–13). In this manner, they appear codependent, which in turn suggests that we probably should perceive the three as various aspects of the activities of Satan rather than three separate entities acting on their own accord. Their joint activities and fates in Rev 16:13; 20:2 and 10, further support such a reading. This means that the characterization of the two beasts, both in nature and in action, reflects the function of Satan in Revelation.

4.4.2.3.1 *The Beast from the Sea*

The visual appearance of the two beasts, like the dragon, conforms well to the genre of apocalyptic literature with their symbolical number of heads, horns, and diadems.

The beasts of Revelation 13 are both described as coming *up from* (ἀναβαῖνον) the sea/earth. Otherworldly agents surfacing, passing the borders of the world below to the world of humankind, is always bad news in the book of Revelation (9:1–20; 11:7; 17:8; 20:7–8). In the world below we also find ἡ ἄβυσσος (netherworld, abyss, 9:1–2; 11:7; 17:8; 20:1, 3) and τὴν λίμνην τοῦ πυρός (the lake of fire, 19:20; 20:8, 10, 10, 14–15, and probably implied in 14:10). In addition to these, we have the mention of Hades (ὁ ἅδης) along with the sea (ἡ θάλασσα) in Rev 20:3, which probably also suggests a location below.[177] The reference to the beast in 11:7 and 17:8 ascending from the abyss may suggest overlapping points of reference in some of these locations, possibly the sea (13:1), the earth (13:11), the many waters (17:1), and the abyss (11:7; 17:8). That is if all beasts in question are taken to refer in some way to the same binary relation

---

[177] ᾅδης (Hades) is the Greek word that is usually used to translate the Hebrew שְׁאוֹל (Sheol) in the LXX (Prigent, *Commentary on the Apocalypse of St. John*, 142). Although the references in Rev 1:18; 6:8; 20:13–14 are not sufficient to determine the exact location of Hades as below the inhabited world on mere intratextual evidence, the intertextual evidence is overwhelming, and I therefore assume this to be part of the implied known knowledge of the implied reader (cf. going down into Hades, Isa 5:14; Job 7:8–9; 17:16; Tob 13:2). Texts like this from the Hebrew Bible reflect a tripartite universe (heaven, earth, and underworld) known from various ancient Near Eastern texts. See Jaime Clark-Soles, *Death and the Afterlife in the New Testament* (New York: T&T Clark, 2006), 20–2; Bernstein, *The Formation of Hell*, 34; John Casey, *After Lives: A Guide to Heaven, Hell and Purgatory* (New York: Oxford University Press, 2009), 43–64.

(Rome-Satan) or at least to the beast from the sea.[178] Both the abyss and the lake of fire are places of incarceration or punishment, and will later on be hosting Satan and his minions (20:1-3; 20:10), whereas Hades and the sea seem to imply storage/confinement. Perhaps the movement itself from below and upward is more important than the precise location of such places. The beasts of Revelation 13 are summoned from the world below to do service to a dragon having descended from the world above. The world below could then, in Revelation, function as a place of imprisonment, punishment, and incarceration—a storage room for creatures intentionally kept from the world above it. The exact opposite could in turn be stated about the world above the earth—the heavenly sphere.[179] As seen earlier in the three septets, whether the intermediary agent comes from the abyss below or the heaven above, it generally involves bad implications for the inhabitants of the earth. For the unbelievers and unrepentant, this is stated to be just (9:20-21; 15:3; 16:5-7; 18:7; 19:2), and for the saints they function as trials of faith (6:10-11; 7:14; 11:18; 14:13). The movement from beneath to the surface sets the stage for new scenes in the overarching plot of Revelation, implying new ordeals for the inhabitants of the earth to either overcome or succumb to.

The visual appearance of the beast from the sea is clearly derived from a reworking of the four beasts of Dan 7:1-7. The blasphemous names on its heads associate it with the fourth beast of Dan 7:8-28, the one representing the acts of hubris of Antiochus Epiphanes IV, as well as the scarlet beast of Rev 17:3. The parallels with the antagonist of Daniel 7 is substantial and close to verbatim in the description in Revelation 13: it blasphemes against God (13:5a and 6 = Dan Theod. 7:25 and the loud speech of verses 8 and 20); it wages war on the saints with success (Rev 13:7 = Dan Theod. 7:21); and it is given authority over the people of the earth for a limited amount of time equalling three and a half years (Rev 13:5b, 7b = Dan Theod. 7:25b). The beasts of Daniel and Revelation are characterized in a similar manner, and the parallels are considerable, yet they are not identical. The submissive language used in describing the beast of Rev 13:1-10 is more substantial than is the case with the fourth beast of Daniel 7. The fourfold use of the aorist passive in 13:5-7 (ἐδόθη αὐτῷ, it was given) serves

---

[178] Resseguie, *The Revelation of John*, 179-80; Beale, *The Book of Revelation*, 684; Koester, *Revelation*, 569; Aune, *Revelation 6-16*, 732.

[179] Perhaps an argument could be made here regarding the trespassing of boundaries between the divine and mundane realms. As Neil Forsyth has pointed out, the error of the Watchers as it is found in 1 En. 6-9 is reflecting the Yahwistic idea of error through transgression as conspiracy: "Lust causes the transgression of the boundary between divine and human; this results in humans learning forbidden mysteries, and this in turns leads to the corruption of the earth" (Forsyth, *The Old Enemy*, 174). The problem in Gen 6:1-4, then, is not so much the sexual lust itself, but the transgression of the divine order. The blurring of boundaries between gods and humans is touched upon several times in Gen 1-11: obtaining prohibited knowledge in Genesis 3 leads to geographical demarcation of the sphere of humankind; delimitation of human age (Gen 6:3) demarcating mortality; the transgression of boundaries at the tower of Babel in 11:4 with subsequent resolution in 11:7, as well as the transgression of the sons of God in Gen 6:1-4 resulting in the need for global cleansing in Gen 6:5. Bearing in mind the close affinity of apocalyptic literature to the various myths of creation, any hint or reminder of the dire consequences for humans due to the crossing of boundaries between the celestial and divine realm to the mundane is rather fitting. See Stuckenbruck, *The Myth of Rebellious Angels*, 14-15, 82, 154.

to underscore the subdued status of the beast to a larger extent than in the book of Daniel. Still, an important common denominator of the two texts is the emphasis on the element of hubris by presenting oneself as the object of worship. This element is further enhanced and subsequently founded in the imitation of the resurrection of the Lamb. The sentence μίαν ἐκ τῶν κεφαλῶν αὐτοῦ ὡς ἐσφαγμένην εἰς θάνατον (one of the heads of the beast [was] like it had been slain to death, Rev 13:3) likens the beast with the Lamb. It is clear from 13:14 that it is the beast and not just one of the seven heads that was like it that had been slain to death. Both the Lamb and the beast are stated to have been slain (13:3, 8; 5:6, 9, 12), and it is described as the very reason for receiving worship. The whole world follows the beast in amazement and is stated to worship the dragon and the beast as a direct consequence of this, thus mirroring the throne vision and the worship of the Lamb and God as a response to the appearance of the Lamb that had been slaughtered (5:13-14). The act of worship probably functions as the key concept of Plot C. It is the element by which every part of the plot is connected. Revelation 13:4 states that the inhabitants of the earth worship the beast in amazement, awestruck by the power displayed. This is the very power it received from the dragon—and ultimately from God. Worship constitutes the rod of measure for the sifting of the earth (13:4, 8, 12, 15; 14:9, 11; 16:2; 19:20; 20:4) and efficiently separates those worshipping the beast and receiving its mark from those faithful to the name of Christ. In such a context, the mark of the beast (13:18) is best understood as an indicator of cultic belonging/property. Such an understanding seems to fit well with the corresponding functions, between carrying the mark of the beast (13:16-18; 14:9-11; 16:2; 19:20; 20:4) and the sealing of the servants of God (7:3-4; 9:4) with his name (14:1 and 22:4).[180] A similar point could be made of the reference to being written in the book of life (13:8; 17:8; 21:27), which is antithetical to worshipping the beast. According to David E. Aune, the beasts of Revelation 13 and the book of Daniel reflect the presence of a traditional character often referred to as "the eschatological antagonist" through the pursuit of being worshipped: "One of the characteristic motifs that make up the image of the eschatological antagonist is the claim to be divine. The historical Antiochus IV Epiphanes was remembered as claiming divinity (Dan 11:36-37), and that claim became integral to the Jewish myth of the eschatological antagonist."[181] This claim to be divine and subsequently worshipped evokes the notion

---

[180] See Resseguie, *The Revelation of John*, 191: "The number of the Beast is identical with its name, and to receive a name is to take on the characteristics represented by that name. Those who are stamped with the name of the beast exhibit the character traits of humanity striving to be like God, while those who are stamped with Christ's name renounce self-deifying traits and, instead, give allegiance to the one true deity" (see also Section 4.4.2.3.2 in this reading).

[181] Aune, *Revelation 6–16*, 755. This tradition is under continuous development in this period and incorporates historical elements of actual rulers and opponents with mythical imagery, themes, and motifs. The evolution of this tradition can be traced back to traditions before the depiction of Antiochus IV in the book of Daniel and onward, beyond the beasts of the book of Revelation, and is thus sufficiently attested to assume that the implied reader of Revelation is familiar with the presence of such a tradition behind the characterization of the beasts. David E. Aune argues that the emphasis on the wisdom and general depiction of Antiochus in Dan 8:23-2 and 11:29-39 reveals the incorporation of earlier typologies such as the one found in Ezek 28:3. This indicates that the tradition did not originate with the characterization of Antiochus in the book of Daniel but erupts from traditions considerably older than that. The presence of the Gog and Magog

of hubris clearly present in Dan 8:23-26 and later explicated in 1 Macc 6:10-17 (for the presence of hubris in the eschatological antagonist myth elsewhere, see 2 Thess 2:4; Sib. Or. 5:33-34; Ascen. Isa. 4.6; 2 En. 29:4). Apart from the obvious parallels to the book of Daniel, with its vivid depiction of Antiochus's hubris, we find further trace of hubris in the characterization of the fall of Rome in 18:1-24.[182] The wording of 18:7-9 is particularly interesting as it connects the hubris (of Rome) with its downfall: In her heart she says, "I sit as a queen and no widow I am, and no grief I will see." Because of this, in one day her torments will come—death, mourning, and famine—and she will be burned in fire, because strong is the Lord and God who judges her.[183]

Hubris connected to possible downfall is also present in the message to Laodicea (3:17, 19), the city representative of how wrong things can possibly go in this direction.[184] The hubris of Babylon and Laodicea along with the presence of the eschatological antagonist myth connects this element by association to Satan. This is further emphasized in the characterization of the beast from the sea along the same lines. Satan is thus clearly connected to the element of hubris in Revelation, and perhaps this element can shed light on why the heavenly prosecutor is in the end thrown into the lake of fire. This possibility will be considered in the analysis of Revelation 20 below. In any case, Satan instigating Roman imperial worship as a means of deception or testing does not clarify whether he himself has an autonomous agenda in these matters or is just serving a divine purpose.[185] Hence, a possible implied reference to an autonomous agenda on the part of Satan here is literarily subtle, peripheral, and thus clearly does not constitute the main message or purpose of the text.

The beast from the sea resembles not only the beasts of the book of Daniel but also the appearance of the dragon, with its seven heads and ten horns, though its diadems are worn on its horns and not its heads (13:1; cf. 13:2). The latter detail could function as an indicator of the superiority of the dragon to the beast.[186] On its heads, blasphemous names

---

traditions of Ezekiel 38-39 in Rev 20:8 and 3 En. 45:5 similarly suggests that we find in Daniel the incorporation of an already existing tradition rather than its point of origin. In the Johannine and patristic literature, we find the eschatological antagonist myth present in the Antichrist tradition (1 John 2:18, 22; 4:3; 2 John 7; Pol. Phil. 7:1), where it is often used to designate human figures who represent Satan (Justin, Dial. 32.4; 35.3; Eusebius, Hist. eccl. 4.22.6; Apos. Con. 6.9.6; Did. apost. 11.5.6; Sib. Or. 3:63-74; Ascen. Isa. 4:1-7). See Aune, Revelation 6-16, 753-5; David E. Aune, The Westminster Dictionary of New Testament and Early Christian Literature and Rhetoric (Louisville, KY: Westminster John Knox, 2003), 49.

[182] John Sweet argues for a rendering of the rare στρῆνους (sensuality/luxury, Rev 18:3) and στρηνιάω as hubris, precisely due to the context of Revelation 13 as well as the use of the term in 2 Kgs 19:28 concerning the Assyrian king. See Sweet, Revelation, 268.

[183] Imputed speech such as this, as well as in the critique of Laodicea (3:17), is found in other implied familiar soliloquies known from the Hebrew Bible (Isa 14:13-15; Jer 5:12-17; Ezek 28:2-10). The explicit connection between hubris and downfall makes these texts possible implied allusions in the characterization of Satan of Revelation 13 through its connection to the characterization of Rome in Revelation 18; see Koester, Revelation, 700-1.

[184] See Section 3.4.7.

[185] See other scriptural references about acts of testing where the distinction of those conducting the testing and the divine purpose behind it is blurred: 1 Kgs 22:19-23; Job 1-2; Matt 4:1; 6:13; Luke 4:2; 22:31-32; 1 Cor 10:13; 2 Cor 12:7-10.

[186] According to James L. Resseguie, "'Head' is a well-known metonym for ruling authority (cf. Judg. 10:18) and horns are symbolic of power (cf. Deut. 33:17; 1 Kgs 22:11; Ps. 89:17; Rev 5:6; 1 En.

are written (13:1). The term ὀνόμα (name) refers elsewhere in the book of Revelation to (1) the name of Christ as the reason and motive for enduring afflictions (2:3, 13; 3:8, 12; 11:18; 13:6); (2) in the sense of belonging/allegiance (2:17; 3:5; 13:8; 14:1, 11; 17:8; 22:4); and (3) as indicating/defining character/person (3:1, 4; 6:8; 8:11; 9:11; 11:13; 13:17; 15:2, 4; 16:9; 17:5; 19:13, 16).[187] Revelation 17:3 and 19:12 probably reflect the same use of ὀνόμα as in 13:2. In 13:2 the modifying genitive βλασφημίας associates the names with the slandering activities of the synagogue of Satan in Smyrna (2:9) and the names written on the scarlet beast of Babylon the Great (17:3, 6). This suggests that the use of ὀνόμα in 13:2 indicates allegiance and belonging to the negative sphere of cosmology, thus promoting the wrong course of action for John and the saints. It is also possible to argue that the names reflect the character and conduct of the beast in terms of anticipating what blasphemous impact to expect from its appearance. The same reciprocal relation between names and action could be seen between the acts of Babylon the Great (17:1–18) and the names on her scarlet beast (17:3) and on her forehead (17:5); and the victorious acts of the rider (19:11–16) and the many names he carries (19:11–13, 16).

The act of blasphemy occurs again in 13:5: Καὶ ἐδόθη αὐτῷ στόμα λαλοῦν μεγάλα καὶ βλασφημίας καὶ ἐδόθη αὐτῷ ἐξουσία ποιῆσαι μῆνας τεσσεράκοντα [καὶ] δύο (It was given a mouth uttering great [words] of blasphemy, and it was given authority to do [this] in forty-two months). The act of blasphemy reported in 13:6 follows from this and could be interpreted as a process of devaluating possible alternate objects of worship (God, his name, and those who dwell in heaven), which further emphasizes the presence of hubris in its characterization.[188] The use of the aorist passive (ἐδόθη) to identify God as the hidden actor of the drama in these verses is a phenomenon that has been recognized by several scholars on the subject.[189] Here the beast is given

---

90.6–16). The crowns on the dragon's heads suggest that it is the ruling authority, the puppeteer behind the beast" (Resseguie, *The Revelation of John*, 180; see also Smalley, *The Revelation to John*, 336).

[187] In addition, the use of the term in Rev 21:12 and 14 constitutes a fourth category as it refers to the naming of things/objects, but is irrelevant to the meaning of the ὀνόμα in 13:2.

[188] On the blaspheming of those who dwell in heaven, Paul Henry Yeates makes a probable argument for finding here at least a partial reference to the act of blasphemy offending not only God but also those whom God chose to elevate to heaven to be his dwelling—the martyred saints. Such a reading corresponds well with the abovementioned theory of Revelation 12–13 representing a gradually more vertical perspective than that of Revelation 2–3. In light of the slanderous acts that the congregation of Smyrna are reported to experience in Rev 2:9 and the blasphemous nature of the Roman Empire reflected in the names written on Babylon in Rev 17:3, the word thread of βλασφημία in Revelation seems both to encompass offense against God as well as to have severe social impact on the saints on earth. See Paul Henry Yeates, "Blaspheming Heaven: Revelation 13:4–8 and the Competition for Heaven in Roman Imperial Ideology and the Visions of John," *NovT* 59 (2017): 31–51, 35–9.

[189] Aune, *Revelation 6–16*, 743; Beale, *The Book of Revelation*, 377; Boxall, *The Revelation of Saint John*, 190; Caird, *The Revelation of St John the Divine*, 167; Campbell, *Reading Revelation*, 80; Koester, *Revelation*, 572; Mounce, *The Book of Revelation*, 254; Osborne, *Revelation*, 498; Resseguie, *The Revelation of John*, 184; Smalley, *The Revelation to John*, 340; Witherington, *Revelation*, 182. Pierre Prigent represents a modifying voice as he interprets the passive voice as God allowing or permitting the act by authorizing it (Prigent, *Commentary on the Apocalypse of St. John*, 407, 527; see also Fee, *Revelation*, 181–2). Peter J. Leithart refrains from commenting on the aorist passives of this passage, even though he is obviously familiar with this literary device (Peter J. Leithart, *Revelation 12–22*, International Theological Commentary [London: T&T Clark, 2018], 326).

a mouth continuously (note the aspect of the present participle) speaking great words of blasphemy, yet does not open the mouth to speak until verse 6. Perhaps this grammatical tension is best resolved by reading the expression as an idiom in the vein of "giving mouth to utterance" as attested in Luke 21:15; Ezek 29:21; and Eccl 5:5.[190] This reading would certainly fit the context as it highlights the sovereignty of God in a manner similar to the source text of this allusion, Dan 7:8, 20 (see below).[191] This reading suggests that interpreting the string of aorist passives as *allowing, permitting, authorizing* becomes too weak to express the active role of God in the reported action.[192] The element of sovereignty is further enhanced by the explicit time limit of forty-two months restricting the executive power, impact, and reign of the beast. The length corresponds to the 1,260 days of Rev 11:3; 12:6; and the phrase καιρὸν καὶ καιροὺς καὶ ἥμισυ καιροῦ (time, times and half a time, 12:14)—both referring to the length of the persecution of the church. The persecution and afflictions of the church are also the main issue in verses 7–8. The beast is once again given several elements— to wage war on the saints, conquer them, as well as assume authority over every tribe, people, tongue, and nation.[193] The result of this is the global worship of the beast by

---

Due to the pastoral nature of his commentary, it is hard to avoid the sense of an effort to avoid scriptural inconsistency here. Concerning, for example, the blaspheming acts of the beast from the sea and its delimited war against the saints, he states, "God opposes blasphemy against his saints, treating it as if it were blasphemy against himself. Because it is. ... Both time periods are half-times, broken sevens, because God will not allow the night of the beast to last forever" (ibid., 60–1). Such statements do not resonate well with the idea of God giving the beast a mouth to blaspheme with, and to wage war against the saints and to conquer them (Rev 13:5–7).

[190] See the related combination of διδωμι and στομα as an expression of the ability to speak the words of God, Isa 59:21; Jer 1:9; 5:14; Mic 3:5; Sir 22:27, and the general reference to speaking at the mercy of God in Exod 4:11. According to David E. Aune, "διδοναι στομα is an idiom meaning 'to help someone to say something' or 'to give someone something to say,'" hence his translation "it was given haughty and blasphemous things to say" (Aune, *Revelation 6–16*, 717, 742).

[191] The use of στόμα (mouth) in Revelation is varied and may deserve a study on its own in another context. The many things stated to come out of mouths in the narrative suggest the mouth having an important role in indicating power and vigor: the sword coming out of Christ's mouth (1:16; 2:16; 19:15, 21); the power of the horses is in their mouths, which is from where fire, smoke, and sulfur comes out (9:17–19); fire comes out of the mouths of the two witnesses (11:5); the water comes out of the mouth of the serpent/dragon in order to sweep away the woman (12:15–16); the foul spirits gathering the kings of the earth to war come out of the mouths of the dragon and the two beasts (16:13). Similarly, the mouth given to the beast from the sea speaking words of blasphemy (13:2, 5, 6) is closely related to the other things it has been given (authority, waging war, and conquering the saints). In other words, it is given the means to afflict the inhabitants of the earth, including the saints, to constitute the opposite choice of conduct. The mouth of the earth swallowing the water from the serpent/dragon (12:16) is also part of this power-language, though the power lies in the ability to devour threat rather than something coming out of the mouth. Besides the use of "mouth" with power connotations, we have the threat of being spat out to the congregation of Laodicea (3:16), which indicates in/out of salvation; the absence of lies in the mouths of the 144,000 reflecting their purity (14:5); and the eating of the scroll as a means of absorbing/internalizing the prophetic message (10:9–10).

[192] See Prigent, *Commentary on the Apocalypse of St. John*, 407–8.

[193] That the hidden subject behind the aorist passives here is God, and not the dragon, which also gives its power to the beast in Rev 13:2, can be argued from the objects that are being given. The beast is given to blaspheme God and his abode without suffering any consequences, but more importantly, it is given to wage war against the saints, *and* to conquer them (Rev 13:5–7). Both acts are associated with a detailed time limitation for the activities in question: forty-two months. In the book of Revelation, only God can give anyone power over his elect and detain repercussions of

anyone not written in the book of life (13:8). The rhetorical element, and thus the purpose of the section, is then found in 13:9–10. The events reported here are divinely ordained in the sense that they must come to pass. The right course of action for the saints is to succumb to the consequences, that is, to die if it comes to that because Ὧδέ ἐστιν ἡ ὑπομονὴ καὶ ἡ πίστις τῶν ἁγίων (here is [or perhaps, *herein lies*] the endurance and faith of the saints). The latter point suggests that even if the names of the saints are written in the book of life from the foundation of the world (13:8), there is some uncertainty as to whether they will remain so to the end of the world (cf. 2:10).[194] God is characterized as the architect of history in the book of Revelation by controlling the persecution and oppression of believers through his establishment of quantitative (6:9–11 in particular) as well as durational limits for activities of oppression (2:10; 3:10; 11:2; 12:14; 13:5; 20:1–3).[195] The very nature of the revelation revealed implies God as completely aware of the things unfolding in the visions of John, as he is described as the origin of the revelation of Christ (1:1). In order to reveal the revealed, he must know what will come. In short, the repeated use of the aorist passive, along with the cosmological implications of the divinely ordained time limit of forty-two months, supports the conclusion of David E. Aune when he states, "This makes it clear that John does not see the conflict between God and Satan (historically manifested in the conflict between Christians and the state) in terms of a cosmic dualism; rather he emphasizes the ultimate sovereignty and control of God over events that occur in the world."[196] I suggest we add the following considerations to the words of Aune in light of the results found in this section of the text so far. God enables adversarial forces in their activities throughout the narrative.[197] He is stated to delimit the impact

---

severe blasphemy on this scale. Moreover, the imposing of time limitations is a typical trait of the divine ordering of things in Revelation and adds to the characterization of him as the architect of history. The complexity of God's orchestration of evil according to his purposes in these chapters are clearly reflected in the acts of the kings of the earth and the beast toward Babylon in Rev 17:16–17 and 18:9.

[194] In light of the same phrase being used in Rev 17:8, yet without the element of the slaughtering of the Lamb, it is probably the names that are the point of reference of the expression ἀπὸ καταβολῆς κόσμου (from the creation of the world). See also Beale, *The Book of Revelation*, 702–3; Koester, *Revelation*, 575.

[195] The phrase ἀπὸ καταβολῆς κόσμου (from the creation of the world, 13:8; 17:8) suggests that the scenario unfolding in the book of Revelation transcends the local and finite events it envisions. They are rather to be seen as part of a much broader cosmological struggle for the earthly souls.

[196] Aune, *Revelation 6–16*, 743; Boxall, *The Revelation of Saint John*, 190.

[197] Klaus Wengst recognizes the implications of the divine endorsing the enemies of the saints and the limitations imposed on their activity as a revelation of power—an expression of God as the true sovereign (Klaus Wengst, "The Devil in the Revelation of St John," in *The Problem of Evil and Its Symbols in Jewish and Christian Tradition*, ed. Henning Graf Reventlow and Yair Hoffman, LHBOTS 366 [London: T&T Clark International, 2004], 68–74, 72–3). However, after having laid out the problematic implications of God endorsing the enemies of believers, he concludes as follows: "The logical contradiction is nothing else but the consequence of the fact that God himself participates in a contradictory reality, suffers from it and contradicts, and thus lets the contradiction exist. This way of speaking seems to be dualistic and contradictory but makes us realize at the same time that God has not achieved his goal yet" (ibid., 72). In other words, Wengst seems to be interpreting the tension in Revelation with some version of the "irresoluble" argument (Russell, *The Devil*, 242–3; see also Sections 1.2.1 and 5.1 in this reading). Yet, according to Wengst, John is revealed this seemingly contradictory side of God as an aspect of the dynamic monotheism of the Bible: his oneness is yet to be recognized by the world in its entirety. As long as God is on

of suffering actively throughout the book repeatedly. He sends, gives, releases, and enables a plethora of heavenly agents in the three septets of Revelation 6–16 by the means of sifting and punishing the inhabitants of the earth. Furthermore, he is occasionally taking the sifting, disciplining, and testing matters into his own/Christ's hands (2:21–24; 3:3, 9–10, 19). Thus, it follows from the function assigned to God in the narrative that the combat is not so much combat but a rhetorical display of power, perhaps to comfort and invigorate faith among the suffering Christians of Revelation 2–3. This would leave the conflict not as one between God and Satan, but rather one of loyalty/disloyalty and faithfulness/faithlessness in the veins of the book of Job, the book of Isaiah, and particularly the book of Daniel.

4.4.2.3.2 The Beast from the Earth

The beast from the earth is described as having two horns like a lamb and speaking like a dragon (13:11). The resemblance of a lamb could be a parody of the messianic Lamb of Rev 5:6, but the two horns (13:11) instead of seven (5:6) could be an instance of characterization by association to the evil ruler of Dan 8:3 depicted as a ram with two horns.[198] Another, perhaps more plausible reading compares its modest appearances to its grotesque and deceiving function.[199] This would make more sense, since lambs do not have horns, but rams do, thus indicating that something is wrong with its appearance. That it speaks like a dragon further enhances this impression. Its modest number of horns creates a perception of harmlessness and perhaps innocence, yet its actions indicate otherwise.[200] It promotes the worship of the beast from the sea on pain of death (13:15). Promoting or enforcing apostasy instead of orthodoxy is a religious act that is probably the reason for its reference elsewhere as ὁ ψευδοπροφήτης (the false prophet, 16:13; 19:20; 20:10). The designation of prophet, along with heterodox teaching, groups its function within the narrative of the book of Revelation with the Nicolaitans (2:6, 15), Balaamites (2:14), and Jezebel of Thyatira (2:20)—the self-designated prophetess promoting a heterodox teaching labeled as the deep things of Satan (2:24). Jezebel is clearly not a prophetess, despite her own self-designation, because genuine prophecy derives from truth vouched by the very God it points to and venerates (22:6–7). The same principle probably suggests that the designation false *prophet* is a sarcastic one. As suggested in the conclusion of the previous chapter, Section 3.5, Revelation 2–3 functions as a microcosm of the rest of the book. From

---

his way to being the only one, the reality is experienced as contradictory—i.e., evil. The strength in Wengst's argument is that it takes the divine endorsement of evil forces at face value, and perceives it as emphasizing the sovereignty of God. The weakness is that the ultimate sovereignty of God is pushed forward in time as a future event. Moreover, the presence of evil does not warrant the divine endorsement of it. In other words, Wengst's contradiction paradigm cannot explain why God fuels the very engines maintaining the idolatry that stands in the way of his "becoming."

[198] Aune, *Revelation 6–16*, 757; Beale, *The Book of Revelation*, 707.
[199] Koester, *Revelation*, 590, 602.
[200] Horns are often used to symbolize power and honor (Deut 33:17; 1 Kgs 22:11; Pss 89:17, 24; 92:10; 112:9; 1 Sam 2:1; 1 En. 90:6–16; 1QM I, 4) and are often used as an image for kingship in the Bible (1 Sam 2:10; Ps 132:17; Ezek 29:21; Sir 47:11; Luke 1:69). See Koester, *Revelation*, 377; Resseguie, *The Revelation of John*, 180.

this point of view, the activities of the false prophet and the problems of apostasy and religious syncretism of the congregations of Asia Minor are probably one and the same. However, they are perceived from different angles—moving from a horizontal (Revelation 2–3) to a more vertical (Revelation 13) point of view.

The beast from the earth is also stated to exercise the authority of the first beast on behalf of it (13:12), thus exposing an internal link/relation between the three antagonists: dragon → beast from the sea (13:4) → beast from the earth (13:12). This element of interrelatedness could be indicating what Grant R. Osborne refers to as the great parody of the Godhead.[201] In terms of where believers are to put their fidelity, the dragon functions as the antithesis to God/Christ, as well as manifests an earthly counterpart to express and effectuate its intentions; the beast from the sea is antithetical to Christ, resembling him with its apparent death and resurrection, its claim to be worshipped, and its overlapping traits with the dragon;[202] the false prophet can be seen as functioning antithetical to the spirit of prophecy by its acts of promoting acts of worship, wielding great signs, and deriving the capacity for this as well as its voice from its "supervisors."[203] As with God, Christ, and the spirit of prophecy, the characteristics of the three antagonists overlap in regard to the course of action: they encourage the desired acts of conduct and fidelity.[204] The function of this resemblance of the antagonistic trio to the Godhead points to the saints as the intended target for blurring the distinction between heterodox and orthodox worship. The congregations of Ephesus, Pergamum, Thyatira, Sardis, and Laodicea all have in common a lack of sufficiently spiritual self-insight. They believe the state of matters to be good, whereas the revelation of Christ indicates otherwise. An imitation of the God/Christ/spirit of prophecy could hardly make sense to anyone other than those already akin to this God. As part of an elaboration of the messages directed to the seven congregations, this would make sense.

The beast from the earth is given (ἐδόθη) to perform signs on behalf of the beast from the sea in order to promote worship (13:13–14), and to give breath to the image of the beast so that (ἵνα) the image of the beast can speak, and that those not worshipping the image would be killed (13:15). This element efficiently prohibits the fallacy of assuming some sort of dualistic opposition between the dragon and its beasts to God/

---

[201] Osborne, *Revelation*, 511; see also Mounce, *The Book of Revelation*, 255.

[202] These overlapping traits followed by their converging acts and fate indicate the three, the dragon and the two beasts, as reflecting a unified principle. They represent three sides of the same principle, the wrong course of action, manifest on earth as the Roman Empire and its officials. The latter is made explicit in Revelation 17, and it is here we find the antithetical designation ἦν καὶ οὐκ ἔστιν καὶ μέλλει ἀναβαίνειν ([the beast who] was, and is not, and is about to ascend, 17:8) as mirroring the divine title ὁ ὢν καὶ ὁ ἦν καὶ ὁ ἐρχόμενος (he who is and who was and who is coming, 1:4, 8; 4:8).

[203] To speak of any kind of antithetical *trinity* in these matters would, of course, be anachronistic. According to Charles H. Talbert, in Revelation "the pervasive view of the Holy Spirit is that of the prophetic spirit … In Revelation the ultimate sources of the prophetic word are God (22:6) and Christ (1:1; 19:10). The prophetic Spirit's message consists of words of the risen Christ (cf. 2:1 with 2:7; 3:1 with 3:11, etc.)" (Talbert, *The Apocalypse*, 14). In other words, the activities of the prophetic spirit function in the same manner as those of the false prophet, yet with the diametrical antithetical outcome.

[204] See also Campbell, *Reading Revelation*, 92.

Christ and the spirit of prophecy. The general use of the aorist passives in Revelation supports such an interpretation of the occurrences in Rev 13:13-14: in chapter 6 the second horseman is *given* a great sword and power to take peace from earth (6:4); the fourth horseman is *given* authority over a fourth of the earth, and to kill with sword, famine, pestilence, and animals (6:8); the four angels are *given* to harm the earth and the sea (7:2); the locusts following the fifth trumpet are *given* power, instructions, and a prohibition to kill (9:3-5); the court outside the temple is stated to have been *given* to the nations (11:1-2); the beast from the sea is *given* a blaspheming mouth, to exercise authority for forty-two months over the people of the earth and to wage war on and conquer the saints (13:6-7); the sun is *given* to scorch mankind (16:8); the bride is *given* to dress in the righteous acts of the saints (19:4); and those sitting on the thrones are *given* judgment (20:4). In the same manner, the twofold repetition of the aorist passive in Rev 13:13-14 serves to emphasize the subordination of the beast, both to the beast from the sea and to the dragon, but ultimately, to the sovereign God as described in Revelation 4-5. This element aligns with the overarching plot of the book of Revelation and the perspective of the throne vision, and functions as an elaboration on the critical situation of the seven congregations: celestial intermediary figures are given these warrants in order to divide and sift the inhabitants of the earth (cf. 14:12-13).

As the section on the beast from the sea is concluded with a rhetorical closure, ending with an exhortation to remain faithful in endurance (13:9-10), the section on the beast from the earth concludes similarly. It concludes with an admonition to the ones having understanding to ψηφισάτω τὸν ἀριθμὸν τοῦ θηρίου (calculate the number of the beast). This is important because this number and its name refer to the mark (χάραγμα) of the beast (13:16-17), which functions as the antithesis of the seal of the Lamb/God (7:2-3; 9:4; 14:1; 22:4).[205] In both cases, the sign (mark and seal) represents belonging, loyalty, and inner commitment,[206] and functions thus as an expression of the resolving of the overarching plot of the book of Revelation: the sifting of the inhabitants of the earth.

The number ἑξακόσιοι ἑξήκοντα ἕξ (666) remains enigmatic and ambiguous, despite the numerous efforts in resolving its meaning. Perhaps its meaning can never fully be disclosed,[207] yet I will in the following argue for an interpretation of its function in light of the overarching plot of Revelation—delineating allegiance in the dichotomy of the narrative.[208] The number itself probably refers to the beast from the sea, as both 15:2 and 20:4 make it clear that the mark refers to the beast, which has an image made representing it (cf. 13:14-15).[209] In 13:18 we read that ἀριθμὸς γὰρ ἀνθρώπου ἐστίν (for it is a human number). James L. Resseguie argues convincingly for interpreting

---

[205] The terms σφραγῖδα (seal, Rev 7:2; 9:4) and σφραγίζω (to seal, 7:3, 4, 5, 8; 20:3) are reserved as indicators of those belonging to God/the Lamb, whereas χάραγμα is referring only to those belonging to the dragon/beasts (13:16, 17; 14:9, 11; 16:2, 19:20; 20:4).

[206] See Craig R. Koester, "The Image of the Beast from the Land (Rev 13, 11-18): A Study in Incongruity," in *New Perspectives on the Book of Revelation*, ed. Adela Yarbro Collins (Leuven: Peeters, 2017), 333-52, 344-5.

[207] Campbell, *Reading Revelation*, 56-7.

[208] See also ibid., 206-7.

[209] Beale, *The Book of Revelation*, 718.

this as a generic reference rather than a specific one (i.e., referring to an individual).²¹⁰ Firstly, the traditional reading of it as a transliteration of the usual suspects (Caesar Nero; the abbreviation of Domitian found on coins from the period, A.KAI.ΔOMET. ΣEB.ΓE.; or Lateinos, as a synonym for the Roman Empire) into Hebrew numerical values seems unintended since John ordinarily alerts the reader to symbolic names in Hebrew or Greek (Rev 9:11; 16:16).²¹¹ Furthermore, even the most popular candidate of a reading of the mark in terms of gematria, נרון קסר (Nrwn Qsr), seems forced due to the deficient transliteration with an added final nun.²¹² Secondly, the idea that this particular number should refer to a historical person while the other numbers in the book of Revelation are symbolic seems rather odd.²¹³ Thirdly, the parallel expression in 21:17 μέτρον ἀνθρώπου (a human measure) obviously warrants a generic reading and should not be taken to refer to a certain individual, that is, the measurement of person X.²¹⁴ Perhaps the humanness of the number points to what David L. Barr refers to as "humanity claiming more for itself than warranted."²¹⁵ Humans were created on the sixth day according to Gen 1:27–31, whereas the seventh day is the focal point of Gen 1–2:2a—the day of the creator and the day of fulfillment. The throne vision links the worship of God to his acts of creation. A human striving to be worshipped (Rev 13:4, 8, 12, 15) could then be perceived as a 6 (human) pretending or aspiring to be a 7 (God).²¹⁶ This fits the general perspective of Revelation 12–13, where human antagonists of the congregations of Revelation 2–3 (horizontal perspective) are revealed as a means of satanic testing (vertical perspective). Rome is thus revealed as the human face of a satanic agenda—hence the humanness of its expression. Several commentators have suggested that the number six could represent an imperfect or pretend seven, the number of completeness.²¹⁷ Even though such a reading could be implied, one has to consider the fact that the number seven is used several times in relation to satanic characters (dragon: 12:3; beast: 13:1; 17:3, 7, 9), as well as that the creatures of the throne room are reported to have six wings each (4:8).²¹⁸ In the analysis of the three septets, the sixth seal/trumpet/bowl all seem to anticipate the end, yet the end itself is not signaled until the seventh. According to James L. Resseguie, the sixth seal, trumpet, and seal "are all penultimate events, anticipating the end but failing to signal the end until the seventh bowl. They represent an incomplete series in this book with the seventh bringing the series to completion."²¹⁹ This form of interpreting the number six as incompleteness could thus be stated to be attested within the book

---

210   Resseguie, *The Revelation of John*, 189–90.
211   Beale, *The Book of Revelation*, 721; Resseguie, *The Revelation of John*, 189; Koester, *Revelation*, 597.
212   See Koester, *Revelation*, 597; and Beale, *The Book of Revelation*, 718–20, for a brief introduction on the issue.
213   Beale, *The Book of Revelation*, 721; Resseguie, *The Revelation of John*, 189; Smalley, *The Revelation to John*, 352.
214   Resseguie, *The Revelation of John*, 190.
215   Barr, *Tales of the End*, 190.
216   See Barr, *Tales of the End*, 190–1.
217   Beale, *The Book of Revelation*, 722; Mounce, *The Book of Revelation*, 265; Osborne, *Revelation*, 521; Resseguie, *The Revelation of John*, 190; Smalley, *The Revelation to John*, 352.
218   Yarbro Collins, *Cosmology and Eschatology in Jewish and Christian Apocalypticism*, 115–18; Koester, *Revelation*, 598.
219   Resseguie, *The Revelation of John*, 190.

of Revelation. As such it could be a reference to the godlike self-designated position with regard to the worship of the beast. Moreover, the element of anticipation could be seen as underscoring an element of subordination under God of the antagonists (see the ἐδόθη argument above) also to be reflected in the χάραγμα. Fourth and finally, the threefold repetition of the number could be a reference to their "three-in-one hegemony" resulting from their interrelations of dependence as well as their converging activities of promoting and enforcing apostasy.[220] Thus, the triune number of the beast reflects the three aspects of God mentioned above: the sovereign God, the Lamb, and the spirit of prophecy. The frequent association with each of the three to the number seven within the narrative supports the notion of an intended corresponding structure between the two "trios."[221] God is associated with his seven septets of sifting and wrath (Revelation 6–16), using seven seals on prophetic books (5:1, 5), with seven angels by his throne (8:2), and is the possible originator of the seven thunders (10:3, 4; cf. 4:5; 8:5; 11:19; 16:18). The spirit of prophecy is referred to seven times as the voice of the message to the congregations, and possibly connected to the seven spirits of God standing in front of God (1:4; 3:1; 4:5; 5:6). And the Christ/Lamb with his seven stars in his hand (1:19), walking among the seven lampstands (Rev 1:12–13), and having seven horns and eyes, as well as managing the seven spirits of God (5:6).[222] Grant Osborne's suggestion that the triune sixes reflect (as a threefold counterpart) the "holy, holy, holy" of Rev 4:8 could fit well with this if such an "aspiring trio hypothesis" could be stated as implied within the text.[223]

Intertextual considerations in line with my defined reader indicate that the characterization of Satan in Plot C depicts him as fulfilling several expected events that must take place before full inauguration of the eschatological age of salvation according to the scriptural traditions of the Hebrew Bible. The advent of the beasts of Revelation 13 clearly reflects the eschatological expectation of the arrival of Leviathan and Behemoth (1 En. 60:7–11, 24; 4 Ezra 6:49–52; 2 Bar. 29:4; B. Bat. 74b–75a) and motifs from the eschatological antagonist myth (see above). According to David E. Aune, the latter is found in two variants, both reflected in the characterization of the two beasts of Revelation 13: "One of which was based on the tradition of the godless tyrannical ruler (largely dependent on the depiction of Antiochus IV in Daniel) and the other of which was based on the figure of the false and seductive prophet."[224] The beast from the sea corresponds to Leviathan, the mythical sea serpent, and the beast

---

[220] See Campbell, *Reading Revelation*, 92.
[221] It is possible to perceive ἑξακόσιοι ἑξήκοντα ἕξ as a triune number of sixes—even if the koine Greek rendering of the number does not render it with three identical numbers/letters side by side, as with Arabic numerals (666). A similar Greek rendering of the number (χξς) is not found in the text. Attention is therefore drawn to the three sixes of the text (600—60—6). There is a possibility that the three levels of sixes could refer to the hierarchical levels of the dragon, the beast, and the prophet, but that is probably pushing the evidence at hand.
[222] Several commentators have noted this parodic parallel: Campbell, *Reading Revelation*, 92; Beale, *The Book of Revelation*, 722; Mounce, *The Book of Revelation*, 265; Resseguie, *The Revelation of John*, 190–1; Prigent, *Commentary on the Apocalypse of St. John*, 428; Smalley, *The Revelation to John*, 352.
[223] See Osborne, *Revelation*, 521.
[224] David E. Aune, "Apocalypse Renewed: An Intertextual Reading of the Apocalypse of John," in *The Reality of Apocalypse: Rhetoric and Politics in the Book of Revelation*, ed. David L. Barr, SBLSymS 39 (Atlanta, GA: Society of Biblical Literature, 2006), 43–70, 58–9.

from land to Behemoth as tradition associates him with the land/desert. The wording of 1 En. 60:24–25 is particularly interesting as a possible parallel to the necessity of a war in heaven (Plot B), as it states,

> And the angel of Peace who was with me said, "These two monsters, prepared according to the greatness of the Lord, will provide food for <the chosen and righteous>} . . . . . so that the punishment of the Lord of Spirits rests upon them, in order that the punishment of the Lord of Spirits does not go forth in vain. And the children will be killed with their mothers, and the children with their fathers. When the punishment of the Lord of Spirits rests upon them, afterwards will be the judgment according to his mercy and his longsuffering."[225]

The precise function of Behemoth and Leviathan on the Day of Judgment cannot be determined as the passage concerning their status either as food for the righteous or to devour the wicked is defective.[226] Nevertheless, according to this textual tradition they are expected to have a necessary and specified function in the eschatological plan of the Lord of Spirits—not as self-sufficient antagonists, but as a means to see to it that the judgment of the Lord does not go forth in vain. Their advent, like Michael in Plot B, indicates eschatological judgment and salvation through dividing the just from the judged. Another interesting aspect of this tradition is that their advent and subsequent punishment is necessary as part of the punishment of the Lord of Spirits upon humankind. They are a means to God's cosmological wrath. They have been prepared for the day of the Lord in this specific task. Their own merit goes unnoticed. It is not their deeds or actions that demand their harsh treatment but their function in the outpouring of punishment. The presence of such a tradition in direct association with the deceiving activities of Satan may be helpful in understanding why Satan and his associates suffer a fate in the lake of fire in the end (Rev 20:10).

4.4.3 Point of View

4.4.3.1 God's Point of View

The focalization of Revelation 12–13, that is, how the narrative is told, is the same as was found in the chapter on the messages to the seven congregations: we see what John is seeing. He is the means of internal focalization of the narrative—we see what Christ/God reveals to John as seen from his point of view. It is from his perspective that we perceive a great sign appearing in heaven (12:1) and the beasts ascending from the sea and the earth (13:1, 11). It is still the revelation of Christ to John on behalf of God, revealing what must soon take place (ἃ δεῖ γενέσθαι ἐν τάχει, Rev 1:1). This point of view indicates a hierarchical structure behind the contents of the vision, which is

---

[225] George W. E. Nickelsburg and James C. VanderKam, *1. Enoch: The Hermeneia Translation* (Minneapolis: Fortress, 2012), 76–77.
[226] See Michael A. Knibb, *Essays on the Book of Enoch and Other Early Jewish Texts and Traditions*, SVTP 22 (Leiden: Brill, 2009), 136–7.

later enhanced by several elements in the text: the corrective perspective of the throne vision of Revelation 4–5; the presence of characteristics derived from the prophetic books of the Hebrew Bible suggesting John as being in line with, as well as one like, the prophets (see Section 4.2.1.1); the high frequency of revelatory language ("I saw," "I heard," and the repeated commissions to write in 1:11, 19; 2:1, 8, 12, 17–18; 3:1, 7, 12, 14; 10:4; 14:13; 19:9; 21:5); and 22:16, 18–20, where Christ explicitly vouches for the content of the revelation. The implications from these elements suggest God as the central narrator of the things revealed and thus constitute the theological point of view: the revelation revealed is God's own point of view. This adds considerable rhetorical leverage to the narrative and the desired implications on the implied reader.

4.4.3.2 *Sympathy, Antipathy, and the Evaluative Point of View*

Regarding the evaluative point of view, the search for "the ideological or theological position that the implied author wants the implied reader to adopt," the primary focus is to discern how the text invites the reader to feel sympathy, empathy, or antipathy toward the characters in general and Satan in particular.[227] The evaluative point of view will be deduced from the previous analysis of plot and characterization and subsequently compared to the overarching plot as defined in the chapter on method.

In plot strand A, our antipathy is drawn toward the dragon. It is characterized grotesquely by association to the primeval monsters of the scriptural traditions of the Hebrew Bible, thus making it abundantly clear who the villain of the scene is. According to Craig Koester,

> Readers would have been sympathetic toward a woman giving birth and repelled by a dragon so terrible that it seeks to devour a newborn child. This attraction and repulsion, which occurs even before readers learn the identities of the woman and dragon, is rhetorically powerful since it fosters a sense of loyalty to those whom the woman represents and readiness to resist what the dragon symbolizes.[228]

Our sympathy is thus drawn toward the mother in labor and the child—both seemingly about to fall prey to the dragon's desire to devour.

The same scenario is told in plot strand B, yet from a different perspective. This time the sympathy is initially drawn toward the dragon, which is attacked by Michael and his angels, seemingly for no good reason. The dragon and his angels are characterized as the weaker party of the two and are thrown down to earth.

Plot C is presented as the consequences of A and B, yet it describes the elements that make the events of Plot B and possibly A conceivable. Here the antipathy is directed toward the two beasts by means of characterization by association with the eschatological antagonist myth and the Leviathan and Behemoth myth, both derived from the traditions of the Hebrew Bible. The dragon and the two beasts are characterized as an antithesis to the Godhead by their appearances resembling the

---

[227] Resseguie, *The Revelation of John*, 42; Powell, *What Is Narrative Criticism?*, 56–7.
[228] Koester, *Revelation*, 558.

various visual traits of God, Christ, and the spirit of prophecy, yet their actions display their devious and suppressing nature. This antithetical characterization is probably meant to underscore the vertical reality behind the admonition to persevere (13:10; 14:12) and to be alert to any attempt at deception (13:14, 18). As was the case with the seven congregations, rewards and punishment contribute toward fortifying the evaluative point of view. The rewards of perseverance and loyalty unto death are described as future rest from one's toil and work (14:13). Another motivational aspect of the pericope is that the perseverance of the saints is in itself a means to an end of the adversarial office of Satan in heaven (12:11). The punishment for not persevering is equal to being marked with the mark of the beast and qualifies as the punishment described most vividly in Rev 14:10-11. The moral is thus to sympathize with and do as the woman and the suffering saints do by persevering with the affliction unto death, and to feel antipathy toward and to refuse the agents of Satan, and their admonition to worship the beast, and to be marked by its name.

4.4.3.3 *The Horizontal/Vertical Point of View*

Plot B functions as a hermeneutical intercalation that interrupts the flow of plot strand A, and serves as an elaboration on the narrative of Plot A. The vertical narrative of Plot A is meant to shed light on the horizontal events of Plot B.

In Rev 12:7 there is a spatial change in the narrative, from the earth to heaven. The interpolation of 12:7-12 serves as an embedded narrative unit, disrupting the flow of the story of the dragon and the woman (12:1-6, 13-17), that provides the reader with a perspective from above of the events taking place below on earth.[229] A war breaks out in heaven, and it is Michael and his angels who seem to be instigating the action. The dragon fights back along with his angels, but they are not strong enough (καὶ ὁ δράκων ἐπολέμησεν καὶ οἱ ἄγγελοι αὐτοῦ καὶ οὐκ ἴσχυσεν, 12:7b-8a). If the two units are parallel, as suggested here, then the complication and transforming action of these two plots correspond and refer to the same event, yet from two different perspectives. The attempt to devour—that is, kill or deceive—the child triggers divine intervention through his ascension. This is paralleled with the attack from Michael in heaven. The transforming action is respectively the resurrection/ascension of the Messiah of Plot A and the ejection of Satan in Plot B. The role of Plot C in these matters is to function as an elaboration on the role of the believers in the process of ejecting Satan in Plot B. The beasts of Revelation 13 require worship on pain of death. This death is the proper course of action for the saints, as it gains access to salvation and ushers in the downfall of Satan (12:10-11).

This means that the actions of the three plots are parallel, refer to the same movement (as could be seen from Table 7), and reveal how the Christ event brings about both affliction and salvation to the saints—how the blood of the Lamb and the martyrs is the reason for Satan's expulsion from heaven. When the number of martyrs has reached its full measure (6:9-11), then the end will come. The expulsion of Satan from heaven will usher in a great number of martyrs (13:1-18), that in the

---

[229] Resseguie, *The Revelation of John*, 172, 177; Beale, *The Book of Revelation*, 650.

end will tip the scale of 6:9–11 to the events of 12:7–12. The key event combining the three plot strands is the time element in Rev 12:10–12. Because of the Christ event and the blood of the saints, Satan is being ejected as heavenly prosecutor and salvation is *now* at hand (ἄρτι ἐγένετο ἡ σωτηρία). This is presented as a near future event for the implied reader, depending on the course of action opted for by the saints (6:9–11).[230]

The characterization of Satan as standing behind the beasts of Rome in Revelation 13 intensifies the perspective of πειρασμός as it was presented in Revelation 2–3: the occasional martyr (2:13), as well as the impending threat of imprisonment (2:10), is now increased to certain death unless one yields to the demands of conformity in worship (13:10 and 15). The events of the congregations and that of the saints/dwellers of the earth in Revelation 13 are both experiencing afflictions and threats from the celestial being identified as Satan. The difference is one of perspective and degree, not of nature. The plot and point of view remain the same. This is in line with the earlier mentioned ascending, three-dimensional spiral-shaped plot of the book of Revelation. In other words, Revelation 12–13 is an elaboration of the narrative of Revelation 2–3, yet new information is added and new perspectives are provided as the plot ascends and intensifies.[231] As a part of this intensification, Satan is in Revelation 13 characterized with additional features to the ones presented in Revelation 2–3, of which the hubris, with its claim to be worshipped, is most notable.[232] Furthermore, the heavenly perspective represents a reversal of the earthly point of view: from this perspective, dying at the hands of Roman officials may be considered defeat, but from the heavenly (vertical) perspective, the opposite is the case. The saints are deemed

---

[230] See Barr, *Tales of the End*, 217. In John 12:31, a similar connection is made between the glorification of Jesus and the end of the chief adversarial agent. However, the continued presence of the ruler of this world even after the ascension of Jesus underscores that individual overcoming of this obstacle remains the fate of every believer (John 17:15; cf. 14:30). The key to overcoming is, however, found in the Christ event and the sending of the Paraclete (John 16). See also Stuckenbruck, *The Myth of Rebellious Angels*, 192–4.

[231] This is in line with the conclusions of Gregory K. Beale on the matter when he states, "Just as John retells the conflict of the earlier chapters from the deeper spiritual perspective, so he starts the story again from the perspective of time" and "as will be seen, various sections of the chapter are temporally and thematically parallel and thus tell the story over again from different perspectives" (Beale, *The Book of Revelation*, 623–4). Moreover, his understanding of how the narrative layers of Revelation 12 relate to one another aligns with that of this reading: "Rev. 12:18–13:18 is temporally parallel with 12:13–17 and explains in further detail the nature of Satan's persecution of the church" (ibid., 680); and, "Verses [12:] 7–12 are a narration of the defeat of the devil and his angels in heavenly combat. The actions described are the heavenly counterpart of earthly events recorded in vv 1–6" (ibid., 650). For a similar conclusion, see Resseguie, *Narrative Criticism of the New Testament*, 221 and 230.

[232] According to David L. Mathewson, the choice of verbal aspect signals the level of prominence in Revelation (*Revelation: A Handbook on the Greek Text*, xxvi–xxvii, 178–9). When the present tense is used instead of the aorist, it is "used to indicate foreground information in the narrative … to introduce a new scene, to introduce significant speech or characters, or signal an important transition in the narrative" (ibid., xxvi–xxvii). Since the characterization of the acts of the beast from the earth is done with the use of present tense aspect (13:12–16), whereas the beast from the sea is mainly seen from an aorist tense aspect (13:5–7), this could imply an added emphasis in the text to its narratées. Perhaps this emphasis is done precisely in order to highlight the close relevance of the actions of the false prophet to that of the congregations concerning the propagation of heterodox worship. This would indicate that the false prophet is the most prominent aspect of satanical activity to which the congregations are to expect increased exposure.

victorious by their testimony unto death.²³³ An essential element of this equation is that the antagonists in their various forms are explicitly stated as enabled to do this by God, the architect of history. The words of Rev 17:17 explain how the close connection between the earthly adversaries and their celestial counterparts in these matters came about: ὁ γὰρ θεὸς ἔδωκεν εἰς τὰς καρδίας αὐτῶν ποιῆσαι τὴν γνώμην αὐτοῦ καὶ ποιῆσαι μίαν γνώμην καὶ δοῦναι τὴν βασιλείαν αὐτῶν τῷ θηρίῳ ἄχρι τελεσθήσονται οἱ λόγοι τοῦ θεοῦ (For God has given into their hearts to do his purpose and to be in one accord and give their kingdom to the beast until the words of God will be fulfilled). From this text, along with the frequent use of aorist passives, the characterization of God as the architect of history, and the implications of the cosmology of the throne vision, the God of Revelation is clearly characterized as governing the events, both good and bad, according to his purpose—a purpose presented in the narrative of Revelation 12–13 as a forked road of optional conduct for the people of the earth, displaying two courses of action with their respective destinations, judgment/salvation (12:11; 13:10, 15; 14:12).

Seen from this perspective, the narrative of Revelation 12–13 both aligns with and elaborates on the overarching plot of Revelation as defined in the chapter on method (Section 2.3): the sifting of humankind through inflicted tribulations. From this point of view, Satan is endorsed as a necessary evil. A new element may be discerned in the role assigned to the ejection and downfall of Satan in this plot. Salvation is portrayed as an end of the accusatory activities of Satan in heaven.²³⁴ Salvation is defined among other things by the absence of Satan, an idea familiar from the pseudepigrapha (cf. Jub. 23:29; T. Mos. 10:1). The characterization of the satanical agents as a manifestation of the eschatological antagonists, the eschatological adversary of Michael, and the eschatological advent of Behemoth and Leviathan—all underscore this element of necessary evil, which will eventually be eliminated with time. In short, both the presence and future absence of Satan are described as necessary in the unfolding of the main narrative plot of the book of Revelation.

4.5 Concluding Remarks

In this chapter I found that the plot of Revelation 12–13 consists of three parallel subplots revolving around the death, resurrection, and ascension of Christ on the one hand and the persecution and blood (death) of the saints on the other. The analysis showed that an element of time governs the events revealed in a circular movement, as the Christ event was followed by persecution of the saints, subsequently triggering the downfall of Satan, initiating further persecution. The key verses expressing this were

---

[233] Koester, *Revelation*, 565; Bauckham, *The Theology of the Book of Revelation*, 90.

[234] One does not need to accept the "Satan vs. God/Christ" premise of G. B. Caird to appreciate his points on the legal functions of Satan in Heaven: "In the New Testament and the Rabbinic writings Satan still retains his legal duties as prosecutor … As long as there are human sinners to accuse, Satan's presence in heaven must be tolerated, for God himself recognizes the justice of the indictment" (Caird, *The Revelation of St John the Divine*, 154–5). By the means of the blood of the Lamb and the testimony of the saints, he loses both his case and his job: "There is no more room for him any more in heaven, and it remains only for Michael to drum him out" (ibid., 155).

found to be Rev 12:10-12, as they perceive the fall of Satan to follow both from the blood of the Lamb and the loyalty unto death of the saints. The latter point functions thus as an explanation of how the completion of the number of killed saints of Rev 6:11 could contribute to their vindication and/or retribution. This circular movement is envisioned as both present time and immediate future for the congregations.

The analysis further revealed that the Christ event initiated the eschatological age of salvation and with it a number of expected elements implied by several allusions to the scriptural traditions of the Hebrew Bible. These elements, however extratextual, proved to be important in the narrative analysis of the characterization of Satan in Revelation 12–13, as they fill gaps in the text—gaps that the implied author could assume known to the implied reader. These traditions are found in the utilization of the dragon imagery of the Hebrew Bible, a plethora of allusions to the book of Daniel, and the advent of the characters of Behemoth, Leviathan, Michael, and the eschatological antagonist. All of these elements are found present in the characterization of Satan and his coworkers in Revelation 12–13, yet at no point are they explained. They are simply assumed meaningful by the text. I have therefore argued for an understanding of the characterization of Satan of Revelation 12–13 from both the intratextual and the intertextual angles. The overall impression derived from this analysis is that by associating Satan with several of the dreaded and, with the end of this age, expected characters of the Hebrew Bible, the antagonists of the congregations are presented as something to be dreaded, expected, and in the end persevered unto death, as their advent is ushering in the dawn of salvation by means of their suffering. Events that have been awaited for centuries are now being fulfilled by the hour of trial they are experiencing.

The analysis of the point of view of Revelation 12–13 followed from this, as Satan was found to serve as an important part in (1) bringing about eschatological salvation by being an object of sifting, as well as of his subsequent elimination, and (2) validating judgment and wrath. By his presence and activities, the expected antagonistic characters from the scriptural tradition are fulfilled, and the next step in each of these traditions is eschatological salvation for the faithful and the demise of the antagonist himself after the job is done. It is possible that the seed of his downfall could be found in an element of hubris present in the pursuit of being worshipped. This element is part of both the eschatological antagonist myth as it is found in the book of Daniel as well as the depiction of the fall of Rome in Revelation 17. Yet, as the means of hubris stems from the endorsement from God and thus serves its function to the overarching plot of the book of Revelation to the point, it is hard to see any valid offense, that is, enmity toward God, here. Hence, if we are to assume an implied presence of any conflict at all between God and Satan in Revelation 12–13, it is at best a one-sided as well as implied one.

Overall, the elements of characterization in Revelation 12–13 function as an intensified elaboration of the image of Satan presented to us in Revelation 2–3. It is the same story and plot, yet we perceive the events from a considerably more vertical and intensified angle than in Revelation 2–3. Behind the earthly adversaries of the saints, a Satan characterized as deceiver and accuser is depicted as pulling strings, maneuvering adversaries to challenge their faith in Christ on pain of death. Where Antipas was the only explicit casualty of Revelation 2–3 (2:13), everyone not worshipping the beast will be killed in Revelation 12–13 (13:15). The associations implied suggest that the outcome of the ordeal, the hour of trial about to come upon the saints (2:10), is decisive: one is either written in the book of life or carries the mark of the beast. There is no neutral ground.

We can conclude from this chapter that the activities and ejection of Satan is presented as necessary to usher in eschatological salvation. This eschatological salvation is ordained and governed by the sovereign God presented to us in the throne vision (Revelation 4–5). The cosmology behind the three septets of Revelation 6–16 follows from the theological premises of Revelation 4–5, and provides a context for the reader to interpret the otherwise enigmatic as well as numerous occurrences of the aorist passive in Revelation 12–13: God endorses and enables Satan to carry out his mission, thus making it a "God-given" one. This is why the ancient combat myth falls short as a decisive lens of interpretation of this particular section of the book of Revelation. In a monistic narrative, a dualistic approach cannot suffice in an understanding of its main antagonist. The text itself invites the reader to perceive this otherwise.

Perhaps the most intriguing result from this chapter is the discovery of the possible explanation as to why Satan in the end has to be eliminated after having played his part, a part repeatedly emphasized throughout the narrative as subordinated/confined to the will of God: After the Christ event, Satan's services as accuser are no longer needed in heaven. His function in sifting the population of the earth by constituting the wrong course of action remains, yet it is intensified by the imposed time limit. This restriction results in an intensified ordeal of sifting, through deceiving, threatening, and/or tormenting them into worshipping him. When the 1,260 days are up, his removal will follow. From the traditions alluded to in Revelation 12–13, we found that a part of the eschatological promises of salvation is the future absence of Satan/adversaries. This is a promise we possibly see fulfilled in Revelation 20, to which I now turn.

5

The End of Satan

5.1 Introduction

In the last section of Revelation where Satan appears, he is first bound and thrown into the abyss for a thousand years, and then subsequently released by necessity (δεῖ) for a little while (Rev 20:1–3). Satan spends this interim gathering an army to wage war on the saints and the beloved city, only to be defeated in the end and thrown into the lake of fire. Perceived in light of a cosmological myth of dualistic combat, this interim release does not make sense, but is at best perceived as an unexplainable mystery:[1] Why would the one side of the allegedly continuously warring parties grant its opponent the grace of pardon? Perhaps this back-and-forth movement (i.e., out of heaven, bound and jailed, released and thrown into the lake of fire) relates to the many diverging accounts of the demise of Satan that flourished in this period? According to Jeffrey Burton Russell, the different stories of the fall of Satan in the New Testament inherited from apocalyptic Judaism are thoroughly inconsistent and their tensions irresoluble.[2] Perhaps it is this irresoluble tension we are witnessing at play within the narrative of Revelation when Satan is released after successful incarceration, only to be seized again? I agree with Russell that several elements of the different devil stories within the New Testament are incompatible regarding the nature, geography, and chronology of the fall, yet, as I will argue in this chapter, the release of Satan in Rev 20:3 makes perfect sense within the narrative plot of the book of Revelation itself, but only if one gives up the cosmic conflict paradigm as the main hermeneutical lens.[3] Sigve K. Tonstad argues

---

[1] According to Neil Forsyth,

> The Satan of Revelation, then, represents an ontological dualism that is more extreme than anything we have noticed in the Jewish tradition. True, he is allowed, like his predecessors in Job and Zechariah, to remain in heaven and accuse the saints, at least until the angels expel him. But there is nothing in the Jewish tradition which says that, at the end of the Messiah's Millennium, Satan *must* (*dei*) be released from his chains to stage his final rebellion. The text does not make clear the source of this obligation, or who is bound by it, but Satan seems to enjoy at least a limited measure of independence, and even, what would cause trouble among the church fathers, actual rights, such as could appear to limit the power of God. (Forsyth, *The Old Enemy*, 257)

[2] Russell, *The Devil*, 242–3.
[3] For instance, the rehabilitating Satan of Paul (1 Cor 5:5; 2 Cor 12:7; cf. 1 Tim 1:20) is found side by side with the devil of John, which was considered a murderer, liar, and sinner from the beginning

that the necessity of Satan's release after the thousand-year reign serves to characterize Satan as an important character in the narrative; to isolate him in the end from other malignant agents in order to tell his story; and to elaborate on his role as deceiver by connecting the narrative of his final act in close relation to his first (Genesis 3).[4] I agree with Tonstad in acknowledging the importance of Rev 20:1–3 in understanding the character of Satan within the narrative of Revelation. Too many "irresoluble" solutions have been offered in trying to make sense of this enigmatic δεῖ. An understanding of the function of Satan in Revelation that cannot make sense of his release after the messianic reign is in danger of appearing a stranger to the text.[5] In this chapter, I will argue for an understanding of the character of Satan in light of the defined overarching plot as constituting an important part of the liquidation of the satanic office as a prerequisite to the ushering in of the eschatological salvation of the saints.

I will follow the structure of the previous two analytical chapters. First, I will consider how the story of Satan in Revelation 20 relates to its literary context (Section 5.2). Then I will analyze the literary structure of the text (Section 5.3) and finally analyze the text itself in light of the narrative elements of plot, characterization, and point of view (Section 5.4) in order to conclude on the narrative function of Satan in Revelation 20 (Section 5.5).

5.2 The Literary Context of Revelation 20

As the events of Revelation 20 constitute the final preparations before full-scale salvation is inaugurated (Revelation 21–22), a large part of the pre-context of the text can be perceived as part of these preparations—the elimination of various adversaries being one of them. The demise of Satan in Revelation 20 constitutes the final stage in a chiastic presentation of the introduction and decline of the various adversaries of the saints. This way of structuring both their entrances and their exits from the stage of humankind corresponds with their hierarchical relation to Satan (see Table 8).[6]

This structural pattern points to Satan as encompassing the beginning and end of adversarial acts toward humankind, and as such he is thus designated chief antagonist

---

(John 8:44; 1 John 3:8). That the Son of God was revealed to destroy the works of the Devil (1 John 3:8) could be considered on the edge with the rehabilitating works of the Satan of Paul, or the spiritual-tester kind of Satan encountering Jesus in the desert (Matt 4:1–11; Mark 1:12–13; Luke 4:1–13).

[4] Tonstad, *Saving God's Reputation*, 41–53.

[5] According to David L. Barr, a good ending of a story provides satisfaction to the reader, often by resolving the conflict. This is ideally achieved by an ending that sums up and correlates to earlier moments in the story and resolves the conflict, with an ending that preferably follows "logically and probably from the beginning and the middle actions" (David L. Barr, "Waiting for the End That Never Comes: The Narrative Logic of John's Story," in *Studies in the Book of Revelation*, ed. Steve Moyise [Edinburgh: T&T Clark, 2001], 101–12, 102–3). It is therefore surprising to find a large number of scholars pointing out the suddenness and the unexpectedness of the release of Satan by necessity, yet abstaining from commenting on how such a turn of events can make sense "logically and probably from the beginning and the middle actions" in the closing chapters of the book—or, more importantly, the closure of the story of Satan (see Section 5.4.2.2).

[6] See Koester, *Revelation*, 750; Trafton, *Reading Revelation*, 115.

Table 8 Rise and Fall of Adversaries in Revelation 12-20

Satan is thrown down from heaven to earth (12:1-17)
Beast and false prophet conquer (13:1-18)
Whore rides on the beast (17:1-12)
Whore destroyed by the beast (17:13-18)
Beast and false prophet are conquered (19:11-21)
Satan is thrown down from earth into the abyss and lake of fire (20:1-3, 7-10)

in the book of Revelation. In this way, Satan encapsulates every adversarial agent promoting religious infidelity (beast, prophet, Babylon/Rome), clearly delineating his main function in the narrative as deceiver—something to be shunned. The eschatological trial of the saints and humankind is closely connected to the activities of Satan in Revelation, and it is therefore of no surprise that it ends with him as well. Revelation 20 represents the last and final stage of his career as the adversary, and the final stage of the elimination of the satanic office.

In addition to considering the demise of Satan in light of the earlier mentioned chiastic structure, it is also important to consider its function in light of the other "final" battles of the book of Revelation. The battle of Armageddon (16:14-21) and the battle of the beast and its kings with the heavenly warrior (19:11-21; possible reference in 17:14) are both exceedingly "final" in nature.[7] I therefore agree with David Barr on the matter when he states that these three narrations of war in Revelation "seem more like three ways of telling the story rather than three stages of the same war."[8] The battle of Armageddon marks the end of the third and last of the septets with the concluding formulation γέγονεν (It is done, 16:17). In line with the structure of the preceding septets, the seventh object serves to consolidate the events of the septet (see Table 5)—a denouement of the victory of God—thus making the battle the final event before the consolidation. As mentioned in Section 4.2.2, the septets seem to encompass the plot of Revelation by utilizing the literary tool of recapitulation. As it is the *final* event of the *final* septet, it is possible to perceive the battle of Armageddon as encapsulating both the defeat of the beasts (Revelation 19) and that of the dragon/Satan (Revelation 20). If that is the case, the finality of the war in Revelation 16 makes sense. Furthermore, the structured presentation mentioned earlier and the corresponding defeat of the satanic office may suffice as an explanation as to why the beasts and Satan/the dragon are described in separate battles. The point here is that the battle of Rev 20:7-9 cannot be analyzed in a hermeneutical void but in light of the other battle scenes of Revelation. There is obviously more to be told of these acts of war than mere descriptions of their elimination. The reason for these extra narratives on the respective fall of antagonists will be of particular interest for the scope of this reading.

---

[7] For a survey on the war imagery in the book of Revelation and a discussion of its function to the timeline of the narrative, see Barr, *Tales of the End*, 207-9.
[8] Ibid., 208.

Revelation 20 represents the final stage of the outcome of the trials reported in Revelation 12–13. On the hypodiegetic level, the fundamental question embedded in the interlude of Revelation 12–15 is, on the one hand, whether the saints will respond positively to the call for endurance in the midst of their ordeal (13:10; 14:12) or not.[9] On the other hand, the admonition to fear, worship, and giving glory to God (Rev 14:7) is directed at all humankind, not just the saints. This could indicate the previously mentioned possibility of repentance, thus making the ordeal about not just the fate of the saints but that of all inhabitants of the earth. At the center of Revelation, we find the eschatological ordeal of Revelation 12–13, but scattered across its post context we find rhetorical elements of motivation clearly intended to tip the scale of deliberation in the preferred direction. We saw this literary move at play in the messages to the seven congregations, although at a considerably smaller scale and in a more particularized manner. The events of Revelation 20 thus represent the final stage of the eschatological ordeal unleashed upon the earth—the final preparations before the age of eschatological salvation is inaugurated (Revelation 21–22).

The purpose of the hortative and prohibitive motivators in Revelation 12–20 is thus the same as in Revelation 2–3: to promote repentance and loyalty to Christ in times of affliction. In return, those conquering will receive rest from their labors through death (14:13). They will be singing the song of Moses in heaven with harps in hand (15:1–4). They will be spared from at least some of the impact of the bowls of wrath (16:2, 11). In the end, they will be invited to the wedding feast and partake in a binary status as bride and guests. Those not repentant and/or enduring, and thus not deemed victorious, are to share the fate of the whore/Babylon. Those willing to die for their testimony (Rev 6:9–11; 12:11; 13:10; 14:13; 18:24) will in turn be vindicated (20:4), but those giving in to the works of the false prophet and receiving the mark of the beast will receive wrath and retribution (cf. 14:9–11; 16:5–6, 19; 18:6–8; 19:2, 20). The word pairs whore/bride and vindication/retribution, as well as the antithetical parallelism of the two cities (Babylon/the New Jerusalem), constitute an important part in establishing this rhetorical dichotomy of the final section of the book. Revelation 20 provides a preliminary conclusion to this, preceding the ushering in of eschatological salvation with the descent of the New Jerusalem. In the following, I will consider these word pairs and their relation to Revelation 20 and the overarching plot of the narrative.

5.2.1 The Whore and the Bride

Revelation 18:23 epitomizes the overarching plot of the book of Revelation by introducing wedding imagery within an elaborate description and justification of the judgment of Babylon (Revelation 17–19). The sound of weddings will not be heard in

---

[9] It is in light of the rhetorical thrust of Revelation 12–22 in its entirety that one could say that "Rev 14 acts as a relay for the antithetical parallelism which will pit the whore-city of chapters 17–18 against the bride-city of Rev 21.9–21" (Campbell, *Reading Revelation*, 242). The events of Revelation 12–13 trigger the need for a decision from the inhabitants of the earth. The severity of this decision is foretold and anticipated in Revelation 14, and further elaborated on in detail in Revelation 17–21 as the descriptions of the fate of Babylon, the beasts, and their followers are contrasted with the heavenly rewards of the saints.

this city anymore, "because [ὅτι] your servants were the magnates of the earth, and by your sorcery all nations of the earth were deceived, and in her the blood of prophets and saints was found [εὑρέθη] and of all having been slaughtered on the earth" (Rev 18:23b–24). Because of her trespasses, she will not experience the joy associated with weddings anymore. Instead, she will receive judgment. This imagery represents the diametrical opposition to those invited to the wedding feast of the Lamb. The saints are described in this metaphor both as the bride herself (Rev 19:6–7) and as the guests invited to the wedding supper (Rev 19:9). The saints have earned their right to wear fine linen, bright and pure (βύσσινον λαμπρὸν καθαρόν, Rev 19:8) because these linens are the righteous deeds of the saints (τὰ δικαιώματα τῶν ἁγίων ἐστίν, Rev 19:8). The bright and pure linen of the bride stands in stark opposition to the purple and scarlet clothes of Babylon (Rev 17:4). And the invitation to the wedding supper of the Lamb gravely contrasts the invitation to the birds of heaven to attend the great supper of God in eating flesh from the bodies of the losing side of the battle (19:17–18). These binary word pairs (whore/bride; wedding supper/the great supper of God; wedding feast/war of judgment; Babylon/the New Jerusalem) all seem to revolve around the question of allegiance/affiliation—the sifting of humankind between those proving themselves faithful by their faith in Christ or those giving in to the deception of Satan. From this perspective, the plot presented in Revelation 12–14 (to succumb to or persevere with the trials of the beasts, Rev 13:15–17; 14:9–13) receives its denouement in part by the events described in Revelation 17–20. As already mentioned in Chapters 3 and 4, this is a staged plot. The septets, the events of Revelation 12–13, and the impact of Babylon (cf. Rev 17:17) are all endorsed, directly and/or indirectly, by the sovereign God of the book of Revelation characterized in all his splendor and sovereignty in Revelation 4–5. The purpose of these events does not therefore revolve around the celestial and earthly agents at play but on their objects (saints/dwellers of the earth). Moreover, these objects are now to either be rewarded by attending the wedding supper or share the fate of the followers of the beast (19:21; 20:15). The urban imagery of the two cities continues the dichotomy of the feminine figuration whore/bride (see Table 9).[10]

This dichotomy parallels the one of the woman and the dragon/beasts of Revelation 12–13, establishing a progressive reversal of providence along the present/future axis.[11] In Revelation 12–13, the main exhortation to the objects/victims of the dragon and the beasts is to persevere unto death. The dichotomy of the two cities serves to further motivate this exhortation by revealing the imminent reversal of order.[12] What

---

[10] See also Koester, *Revelation*, 683; Campbell, *Reading Revelation*, 225–6; Bauckham, *Theology*, 131–2; Elisabeth Schüssler Fiorenza, "Babylon the Great: A Rhetorical-Political Reading of Revelation 17–18," in *The Reality of Apocalypse: Rhetoric and Politics in the Book of Revelation*, ed. David L. Barr, SBLSymS 39 (Atlanta, GA: Society of Biblical Literature, 2006), 243–70, 260–1.
[11] Koester, *Revelation*, 683.
[12] W. Gordon Campbell (*Reading Revelation*, 226) makes an interesting observation when stating that this "fusing together of feminine and urban metaphors" is "correlated with one another in the course of the narrative by means of highly sophisticated antithetical parallelism, which makes the former's repudiation correspond to the latter's bridal adornments and wedding." It functions as a parodic play where the former must give way for the coming of the other, and where several of the traits of the former find their strict counterparts in the other. Babylon the Great must be judged and erased before the New Jerusalem can take her place as the great city of the earth.

Table 9 The Two Cities

	Babylon/Rome	New Jerusalem
Connotations from the Hebrew Bible to their names	Historical Babylon represents suppression, tyranny, and false worship	Jerusalem/Zion represents deliverance, true worship, and blessing
Epithets	Her epithets designate her as the archetype of religious promiscuity and the abominations of the earth (17:5)	The gates and foundations of Jerusalem carry the names of the chosen tribes and apostles—the scriptural vehicles of salvation (21:12-1)
Appearances	Adorned as a prostitute (17:4) yet deceitfully amazing (17:6-7)	Adorned as bride (21:2) and the radiance of the glory of God (21:11)
Character	Presented as impure and indecent (17:4-6)	Presented as virtuous and pure (21:27)
Social relations	She dishonorably attracts their attention at first (17:2), yet in the end her allies conspire against her (17:17)	She will bring light to the nations and receive submissive tribute and honor from the kings of the earth (21:24-26)
Metaphors of sustenance	Her wine of fornication has seduced the kings of the earth and made them drunk (17:2)	Water of life and fruit from the tree of life will be made available (22:1-5)
Aftermath	Dwelling place of demons (18:1-3, 9-19)	Dwelling place of God (21:10-22:5)

presently appears to be attractive as well as comfortable will soon be made desolate and afflicted, and vice versa. This is a clear element of motivation by the promise of the rewards of the New Jerusalem, as well as the threat of sharing the fate of Babylon (cf. 18:4). This section of the narrative in turn functions as a powerful elaboration of the rhetorical strategy found embedded within the messages to the seven congregations, firmly backed up by motivation through vindication/retribution.

5.2.2 Vindication/Retribution

The binary word pairs of Revelation 17–19 reveal the dual rhetorical strategy of the narrative at play—the carrot and the stick, so to speak. However, the wording of the cry from those slaughtered for the word of God (Rev 6:9–10) indicates that there is more to the stick than rhetorical motivation or just/mere punishment: ἕως πότε, ὁ δεσπότης ὁ ἅγιος καὶ ἀληθινός, οὐ κρίνεις καὶ ἐκδικεῖς τὸ αἷμα ἡμῶν ἐκ τῶν κατοικούντων ἐπὶ τῆς γῆς; (How long, Lord, holy and true, will you continue to not judge and avenge our blood on the dwellers of the earth?). There is an expectation of vindication in Revelation on behalf of those unjustly abused and killed by the earthly δεσπότης of the congregations/saints. A plea for vindication to the real sovereign δεσπότης of the creation fits the cosmological hierarchy of the narrative perfectly. We saw a similar point being made in chapter 2 where the messages were modeled after an imperial/royal edict. The hierarchical implications of the throne vision add further leverage to this perspective, leaving no doubt that God is the ultimate ruler of the creation—the παντοκράτωρ. The heavenly ruler of the saints surpasses their earthly perpetrators in might and position, and their plea for justice and vindication is therefore rational and, as we will see, arguably just. Apparently, there is some debate among commentators on whether the cry of Rev 6:10 is a cry for justice only or implies retribution and/or vengeance as well.[13] The element of retribution through vengeance is certainly present elsewhere in the narrative (cf. Rev 14:8–11), yet as Craig Koester has pointed out, "the people who have shed the blood of the martyrs will eventually be given blood to drink, which seems just (16:6); yet this is not simple retribution, since those who have killed do not suffer death but are allowed to live so that repentance is still possible (16:8, 11)."[14] In other words, if there is an element of retribution at play in the narrative, it is rehabilitating and not final until the end arrives. However, when the end finally does arrive, there will be no quarter given to those who resisted the rehabilitating element. The severity of retributive punishment spans from a *lex talionis* kind of measurement, where destructors suffer destruction and soldiers suffer death by war (Rev 19:21; cf. 11:18c), to a category of multiplied severity. There is considerable expansion from the formulation ἀπόδοτε αὐτῇ ὡς καὶ αὐτὴ ἀπέδωκεν (give to her as she herself gave, Rev 18:6) to διπλώσατε τὰ διπλᾶ κατὰ τὰ ἔργα αὐτῆς, ἐν τῷ ποτηρίῳ ᾧ ἐκέρασεν κεράσατε αὐτῇ διπλοῦν (give her double according to her deeds, and mix the cup which she prepared twofold, Rev 18:6).[15] "Double according to her deeds" exceeds the implications of "as she herself gave." This increase in impact is a step away from retribution in the direction of vengeance.[16] A similar element of vengeance is probably

---

[13] Koester, *Revelation*, 399–400.
[14] Ibid., 411.
[15] As Meira Z. Kensky has pointed out, the argument of Richard Bauckham for translating the verse alternatively in order to avoid the punishment exceeding the warrant of the crime ("Render to her as she herself has rendered, give her the exact equivalent of her deeds; and in the cup she mixed, mix for her the exact equivalent") does not sufficiently take into consideration the likely reference to Jer 20:29b in the text as well as the possible parallels in Greek literature (Kensky, *Trying Man, Trying God*, 247–8; see also Richard Bauckham, "Judgment in the Book of Revelation," ExAud 20 [2004], 1–24; David E. Aune, *Revelation 17–22*, WBC 52C [Nashville: Thomas Nelson, 1998], 992; Koester, *Revelation*, 700). According to Kensky, the repeated insistence on the worthiness and justice of the judgments of God in the hymnic interludes is inserted precisely to remind and convince the reader that even these oversized judgments are to be considered just. She believes "that the numerous mentions of God's perfect and totally just judgments are designed *to persuade the reader* that God is just and perfect in judgment, in other words, *to justify God*. This is necessary precisely because this claim is not axiomatic" (Kensky, *Trying Man, Trying God*, 243). According to her, this is part of the overall argument of the author of Revelation to show that the justice of God can stand the trial against him, and constitutes a direct response to the accusations of Rev 6:10. Consequently, any translation downplaying the oversized judgment will miss this element in the text (ibid., 244–54). The interpretation of Edmondo F. Lupieri, although depending on an identification of Babylon as Jerusalem, not Rome, argues that the doubling of severity is typically applied to Jerusalem and Israel (Isa 40:2; Jer 16:18; cf. Job 42:10) and "is probably due to the Israelites' awareness that their sins were never 'simple' but always inherently involved betrayal and infidelity and were thus more serious than the sins of other nations and deserving of more severe punishment" (Lupieri, *A Commentary on the Apocalypse of John*, 285).
[16] Grant R. Osborne does not consider this increase in impact when insisting on the just nature of God's judgments in the Apocalypse as a fitting response to the depravity of humanity and its refusal to repent. Moreover, he insists, "It is clear that the judgments of the trumpets and bowls are not just the over-reaction of a vindictive God who wreaks vengeance on all his enemies but a last call to repentance while there is still time." He adds, "Final judgment is not according to the arbitrary

present in the concept of the lake of fire (Rev 19:20; 20:10, 13–15).[17] Finally, Rev 14:8–11 marks what could be described as the pinnacle of vengeance in Revelation as it emphasizes the witnessing of the punishment of those bearing the mark of the beast.[18] Alan E. Bernstein sees this passage as reinforcing "the idea present in Luke 16 that the good will see the torments of the wicked, although here it is the angels and the Lamb who will witness them, not the redeemed humans."[19] This is perhaps also the idea behind the containment of evil outside the New Jerusalem in Rev 22:15. "Evil is not annihilated but contained, and those in its thrall will suffer forever."[20] The torment (τοῦ βασανισμοῦ, Rev 14:11; 18:7, 10, 15) of such texts cannot be stated to be just along the *lex talionis* way of thinking, because in order to do so the crime itself must in some way reflect correspondingly to the torment of the victims of the accused/judged—which is clearly not the case in Revelation. Instead, we should probably perceive the sadism of the grotesque imagery as rhetorical intent.[21] The witnessing of the eternal suffering of one's perpetrators implies a motivational incitement along with the idea of vengeance itself.[22] The rhetorical impact of the idea of eternal suffering is thus twofold: prohibitive and motivating. The latter seems to be given further impact in Rev 20:4 when the victims of Rev 6:10–11 are to be given authority and possibly judge their perpetrators. The narrative being focalized as a message to the congregations on its hypodiegetic level, and not as intimidation to deter outsiders from harassing the saints, adds

whim of an aloof deity but is always based on the individual's actual deeds" (Osborne, "Theodicy in the Apocalypse," 67, 69). In this way he misses out on the rhetorical function of the hyperbolic response to the "actual deeds" of those punished lying outside the scope of both the just nature of God and those envisioned punished: the purpose of deterring the narratées from giving in to the prevalent evil.

[17] According to David E. Aune, this doubling of punishment represents something else than just retaliation (Exod 21:24–25; Lev 24:19–20; Deut 19:21) and "is probably based on Jer 16:18" (Aune, *Revelation 17–22*, 992).

[18] According to David L. Barr, this text is the culmination of a characterization of Christ through a story of contrasts. Through such voyeuristic sadism, a term Barr derives from Chris Frilinigos, Christ is characterized in reverse from the conquered victim to the conqueror: he becomes the divine warrior. Regarding Rev 14:10, this means that he takes the role of the spectator of the Roman arena. See Barr, "The Lamb Who Looks Like a Dragon?," 207–8.

[19] Bernstein, *The Formation of Hell*, 256–7. See 1 En. 27:3–5; 48:9 for attestation of similar expectations.

[20] Bernstein, *The Formation of Hell*, 260.

[21] The element of torture usually relates in some way to the bending through coercion of the resilience of the human will. According to Stephen H. Travis, this connection detaches these sadistic scenes from the idea of retribution: "Although we tend to associate 'torment' or 'torture' with punishment, it rarely refers to a judicial sentence. Rather it is associated with attempts to extract information or confession before (or apart from) any judicial proceedings, or with sheer sadism … 'Torment' should not therefore be seen as a retributive term" (Stephen H. Travis, *Christ and the Judgment of God: The Limits of Divine Retribution in New Testament Thought*, 2nd ed. [Milton Keynes and Colorado Springs: Hendrickson and Paternoster, 2009], 303).

[22] According to Alexander E. Stewart, John is using the rhetorical technique of *ekphrasis* in these vivid descriptions of punishment and reward in order to "direct the hearer's imagination and create the emotion of fear in support of John's rhetorical agenda … Although John likely had not studied classical oratory or rhetoric, the Apocalypse is filled with *ekphrases* (vivid visual description) capable of shaping and stirring the audience's imagination and producing emotional responses in support of his rhetorical agenda" (Alexander E. Stewart, "*Ekphrasis*, Fear, and Motivation in the Apocalypse of John," *BBR* 27, no. 2 [2017]: 227–40, 227 and 238; see also deSilva, *Seeing Things John's Way*, 219).

leverage to such a rhetorical reading of the elements of vindication, retribution, and vengeance.[23] It also fits the overarching plot of the narrative as defined in Section 2.3.

The transition from earthly to otherworldly punishment/rewarding of human merits is a development of the prophetic and later apocalyptic literature and represents a solution to the preceding Deuteronomistic paradigm of justice.[24] The assurance that beyond the end, the people will receive their due and the perpetrators will be punished fits the inherent theodicy of Revelation. Moreover, as such, it constitutes a powerful motivator for the saints when facing the eschatological ordeal. Still, it is important to notice, as Stephen H. Travis has pointed out, that it is primarily from the perspective of a just God that the language of vindication and retribution makes sense in Revelation, because it is "not just the fate of the martyrs, but the reputation of God himself in relation to his faithful people" that is at stake.[25] And it is the just God of Revelation 4–5 who gives judgment *for* the saints *against* Babylon (Rev 18:20), thus reassuring the congregations that in the end everything will be made right. The very plea for a vindication of the blood of the saints is contingent on this premise.

Revelation 17–19 envisions the end of unjust rulers and picks up on the theme of retribution, but this time the rehabilitating element is left out. After the seventh bowl of wrath has been poured out upon the earth, Babylon is split into three parts by an earthquake, and the people suffer giant hailstones while persistently cursing God (Rev 16:19–21). The bowls of wrath thus conclude with the just annihilation of the earthly counterpart of the saints. Still, there is more to be said about Babylon than her justified eradication. A substantial part of the narrative is devoted to an elaboration on the fall of Babylon and its implications (Revelation 17–18, and the elevated [i.e., vertical] point of view in 19:1–10). This large amount of text suggests importance and its literary place within the structure suggests that this is a focal point of this section of the narrative. This prominent position points to an implied function as the ultimate answer to the cry for vindication of the saints (cf. Rev 6:9–11)[26]—the definitive expression of the

---

[23] Stephen H. Travis emphasizes the emotional impact and purpose of these elements as a warning to insiders and not to outsiders in his discussion of the possible doctrinal consequences of such passages in Revelation. This is a reminder of the inherent purpose of the text, which in these cases invites us to perceive the desired impact of such portrayals of judgment on the saints, not the convicted. See Travis, *Christ and the Judgment of God*, 307; see also Elisabeth Schüssler Fiorenza, *Invitation to the Book of Revelation* (New York: Image Books, 1981), 84–5.

[24] Deuteronomistic justice involves rewards in this life (rich crops, long lifespan, to live in the land of the fathers, and to leave this earth with a great name) for those keeping the covenant and commandments of the Lord, and punishment (i.e., swift death, sickness and poor health, loss of property and land) for those who do not. With the exilic period comes a challenge to this paradigm since keeping the covenant and commandments did not seem to alter the conditions of the people. According to Alan Bernstein, it is here that the minority voice of messianism starts to replace the Deuteronomistic perception of justice. Instead of divine intervention in everyday life, a future Messiah would arrive in time "to establish an invincible and just regime whose law would enlighten the world" (Bernstein, *The Formation of Hell*, 153). A third option was to expect vindication after death (ibid., 146–53). The first reference to vindication in the afterlife in the Hebrew Bible is found in Dan 12:2, along with the added reference to the future resurrection of Job in LXX 42:17. From here on, "the old Deuteronomic view yielded to belief in personal immortality and reward in heaven" (Russell, *A History of Heaven*, 29).

[25] Travis, *Christ and the Judgment of God*, 309.

[26] As Richard Bauckham has pointed out, the answer to the cry for vengeance in Rev 6:10 is indicated in 16:5–7 by reference to the same altar and is explicitly found in 19:2, where we find the only

justice of God (cf. 18:23–24; 19:1–3). With its counterpart of the New Jerusalem, it establishes an elaborate rhetorical manifestation of the two potential outcomes of the overarching plot of the narrative.[27] In the following, I will consider Revelation 17–19 and its characterization of Babylon in light of the overarching plot of the narrative. I will argue that Babylon is to be perceived as an earthly manifestation of the beast, and as such, her characterization and function indirectly reflect the characterization and function of Satan. Moreover, as the elimination of Satan receives little if any explanation (Rev 20:1–10), the substantial elaboration of the judgment of Babylon may provide relevant information on the background and function of the demise of Satan.

5.2.3 Babylon the Great

The visions of Babylon (Rev 17:1–19:10) bridge the section of the three septets to the final section of the narrative by constituting what Elisabeth Schüssler Fiorenza refers to as double intercalation.[28] It functions both as an interlude to the bowl septet (cf. 16:19 and 17:1) and as the first element of the sandwiching of the Parousia and judgment section between the two cities in an A-B-A pattern. In this way it functions as a diptych tying the septets to the final section, similar to the way in which the throne vision tied the opening section to the septets. Where the throne vision introduces the septets, the vision of Babylon closes it. In light of the overarching plot of Revelation, the visions of Babylon could be perceived as the final element of the eschatological ordeal. This leaves us with the outline of the major parts of the narrative of Revelation in light of the overarching plot (i.e., who will make it through the unfolding eschatological ordeal?) as shown in Table 10.

The visions of Babylon can be subdivided into two parts: 17:1–18, which presents an elaborate presentation of the identity of the woman sitting on the scarlet beast, and 18:1–19:10, which consists of a hymnic section interpreting the meaning of her judgment. The judgment of her is not explicitly part of this section but only referred to as envisioned future and prophetic past.[29] However, the judgment of Babylon is

---

other use of ἐκδικέω in Revelation, "forming a kind of *inclusio* linking the prayer with its answer" (Bauckham, "Judgment in the Book of Revelation," 66).

[27] This resonates well with the conclusions of W. Gordon Campbell (*Reading Revelation*, 226, 243) when he states, "The double metaphor [i.e., feminine-urban imagery] is a means of exhorting believers, who live out their Christian faith in the Churches and cities of Ephesus and its hinterland, to stand firm in the human city and to resist apostasy." He finds the best explanation for the expansiveness of the development of the "Babylon" theme in its correlation to the New Jerusalem section. The space obtained by the Babylon/New Jerusalem dichotomy is substantial because it encapsulates the entire rhetorical thrust of the narrative. It relates directly to the overarching plot, and thereby fittingly concludes the book.

[28] Fiorenza, *Justice and Judgment*, 172–3.

[29] The use of prophetic past tense is mixed with descriptions of her judgment as a future event across the entire section. Babylon *has* fallen and *received* her judgment (18:2, 10, 16–17, 19) and God *has* judged her (18:20; 19:2), yet she *will* be betrayed by her allies (17:16); the angelic voice pleads for (future) divine intervention upon her (18:6–7); the kings, merchants, and seafarers of the earth *will* mourn her (18:10, 15); and the angel reveals that Babylon *will* receive severe judgment (18:21–24). The meaning of the use of prophetic past tense is probably to emphasize that the decisions of God are irrevocable. The verdict is so certain that it can be seen as having been accomplished. The future tense is then used as it is elsewhere in Revelation—reassuring the imminence of future

Table 10 Outline of the Major Parts of Revelation in Light of the Overarching Plot

Introduction, 1:1–20

    Messages to the seven congregations—local contextualization (microcosm) of the eschatological ordeal, 2:1–3:22

        Throne vision introducing, explaining, and interpreting the eschatological ordeal, 4:1–5:14

            Three septets constituting the eschatological ordeal (macrocosm), 6–16 (cf. Figure 3).

    Visions of Babylon concluding the eschatological ordeal and preannouncing the final judgment and salvation, 17:1–19: 9

    Judgment and salvation—outcome of the eschatological ordeal, 19:11–22:7

Epilogue, 22:8–21

mentioned in the aftermath of the seventh bowl of wrath (16:19). The identification of the judged and the purpose of judgment thus seem to be the major issue here—and not so much the execution or the nature of the judgment itself.

The answer to her identity is provided in a twofold manner: 17:1–6 describes her, whereas 17:7–18 explains the vision. Her many names and epithets convey key aspects of her identity and will in the following be my starting point in analyzing her characterization. The importance of such an approach becomes clear when considering that several of her traits and actions toward the saints overlap with the ones of Satan elsewhere in the narrative. The interrelation between the two is further enhanced by the hierarchy of adversaries in Revelation characterizing her as an extension of his office (her reign rests upon the beast [17:3, 9–14], which in turn receives its authority from the dragon [13:2]).

The reference to her as τῆς πόρνης τῆς μεγάλης (the great whore, Rev 17:1) and ἡ μήτηρ τῶν πορνῶν καὶ τῶν βδελυγμάτων τῆς γῆς (mother of whores and abominations of the earth, Rev 17:5) is part of the offensive sexual language of Revelation, which is used as a metaphor for religious promiscuity. This element of characterization makes her the center of a verbal thread of seven "porn-words" in the section (πόρνη, 17:1, 5, 15, 16; πορνεύω, 17:2, πορνεία, 17:2 and 4) that epitomize and encapsulate similar references elsewhere in the narrative (the fornication of Pergamum, 2:14; the beguiling deception of Jezebel of Thyatira, 2:20; as well as her acts and status as fornicator mentioned elsewhere in the narrative, 14:2; 18:3, 9; 19:2).[30] Of all religious fornicators, Babylon is here portrayed as the archetype. This, along with the shedding of the blood of the saints, is presented as her gravest offense (cf. 18:23–24).[31]

---

    vindication and salvation for the congregations/saints. See Prigent, *Commentary on the Apocalypse of St. John*, 499.

[30] See Resseguie, *The Revelation of John*, 218.

[31] According to Elisabeth Schüssler Fiorenza, Rev 18:24 must be understood as the hermeneutical key to the whole Babylon series of judgments because here "the legal claim of the persecuted victims against Babylon is now granted. The powerful capital of the world is destroyed not just because it has persecuted Christians but also because it has unlawfully killed many other people" (Elisabeth

As γυναῖκα (woman, Rev 17:3, 4, 6, 7, 9, 18), she is attached through both gender and the promiscuous language to Jezebel of Thyatira (2:20). They are both characterized as mothers of religious infidelity and as representing the path to judgment by fostering religious promiscuity. Her antithesis is the woman clothed in the sun, fostering the Messiah—the path to salvation. As a woman-city, Babylon is cast as the counterpart to the New Jerusalem, thereby completing the moral dichotomy of the promiscuous whore and pure bride (see Section 5.2.1).

As ἡ πόλις ἡ μεγάλη ἡ ἔχουσα βασιλείαν ἐπὶ τῶν βασιλέων τῆς γῆς (The great city ruling the kings of the earth, Rev 17:18), she is characterized as having a major impact on the dwellers of the earth. The many waters represent peoples, multitudes, nations, and languages (17:15). Waters are known as a common metaphor for inhabitants in the Hebrew Bible (Isa 8:7; 17:12-13; Jer 46:7-8; 47:2) and is a formula of universality derived from Daniel that occurs throughout Revelation.[32] According to Gregory K. Beale, the act of "sitting" (κάθημαι) connotes sovereignty elsewhere in Revelation. "That she 'sits' both here and in vv 3, 9, and 15 connotes that she is able to control the multitudes and the beast because of her powerful influence" (cf. 18:7).[33] In light of the reference to her sitting as a queen in 18:7 being expressed as a justification for judgment, one might assume an element of hubris at play implied in the reference of sitting. If so, the whore sitting upon her throne as ruler might be a deliberately ironic description of her attempt to usurp the place and authority of the Godhead.[34]

The sitting upon many waters could also be a probable allusion to the description of historical Babylon in Jer 51:13. The choice of a name so laden/saturated with scriptural meaning suggests that it is not an arbitrary but rather a deliberate symbolical reference. The explicit identification of the woman as Βαβυλὼν ἡ μεγάλη (Babylon the Great) in Rev 17:5 (cf. 14:8; 16:19; 18:2, 10, 21) is therefore a highly probable characterization by association to the Babylon of the Hebrew Bible.[35] The expression itself (i.e., Babylon *the Great*) occurs only in Dan 4:30, where it is part of an expression of the Babylonian king's (Nebuchadnezzar's) self-glorification. Because of this, judgment would descend upon him. As a foreign ruler of the land of the fathers who is dominating its inhabitants socially, politically, and economically; who is responsible for the destruction of the temple; and who is promoting self-deification and religious temptation in order to compromise one's faith, historical Babylon represents the ideal symbol to interpret the situation of believers under Rome.[36]

Schüssler Fiorenza, "Babylon the Great: A Rhetorical-Political Reading of Revelation 17–18," in *The Reality of Apocalypse: Rhetoric and Politics in the Book of Revelation*, ed. David L. Barr, SBLSymS 39 (Atlanta, GA: Society of Biblical Literature, 2006), 243–70, 260).

[32] Osborne, *Revelation*, 625; Beale, *The Book of Revelation*, 882.
[33] Beale, *The Book of Revelation*, 848.
[34] Smalley, *The Revelation to John*, 427.
[35] The name Babylon is an obvious case where a strictly intratextual interpretation of the text would lose apparent implied meaning if ignoring the intertextual reference in the term (see Section 2.5 in this reading).
[36] According to Gregory K. Beale, "Rome came to be called 'Babylon' in some sections of Judaism because it also destroyed the temple in Jerusalem and exiled Israel," see Midr. Rab. Num 7.10; Midr. Pss 137.1, 8; cf. Tg. Lam 1:19; as well as 2 Bar. 11:1; 33:2; 67:7; 79:1; 1 Pet 5:13; Midr. Rab. Lev 6.6; 4 Ezra 3:2, 31; and possibly Sib. Or. 4:119, 138–139; 5:140–143, 434 (Beale, *The Book of Revelation*, 755).

The description of Babylon as sitting on a beast reminiscent of the dragon and the beast of Revelation 12–13 serves to emphasize her relation to the activities of these. She sits upon the beast, thus implying mutual contingency up to the point where, by divine intervention, the beast and the kings turn on her (17:16–17). I therefore agree with Gregory K. Beale when stating that the amount of space taken up with the beast in Revelation 17 suggests that in order to understand the woman, one has to understand the beast.[37] She being seated upon seven mountains (17:9) as well as being designated ἡ πόλις ἡ μεγάλη ἡ ἔχουσα βασιλείαν ἐπὶ τῶν βασιλέων τῆς γῆς (the great city that rules over the kings of earth, Rev 17:18) both suggest Rome as an additional point of reference in a narrative of the first century AD, which may constitute an active element of characterization implied within the narrative.[38] The use of ἑπτὰ ὄρη (seven mountains) instead of the more commonly used ἑπτάλοφος (seven-hilled) could suggest an added element of self-deification. Physically, the mountain represents the boundary as well as the area of contact between heaven and earth in biblical traditions such as Gen 11:1–9; Exod 3:1–4:17; 19:9–25; 1 Kgs 18:19–46, and is traditionally considered to be the residence of the gods as well as the place of the encounter between gods and men (cf. Rev 14:1; 16:16).[39] The combination of mountains and unwarranted self-deification is reminiscent of the Babel tradition of Genesis 11, but our attention is drawn in particular toward Isa 14:13–15, where the king of Babylon is charged with hubris for attempting to usurp the throne of God on the mountain of God by making himself like El Elyon:[40] "You said in your heart: I will ascend to Heaven, above the stars of God I will lift my throne, and I will sit on the mount of assembly on the heights of Saphon. I will ascend over the top of the clouds and make myself like El Elyon. But to Sheol you are brought down, into the depths of the pit."

This taunt is about the rise and fall of the King of Babylon (Isa 14:4) and is a poetic elaboration of the just consequences of hubris. A distinct feature of the God of the Hebrew Bible is his use of the neighboring nations of his people as instruments to bless,

---

[37] Beale, *The Book of Revelation*, 847.
[38] For references to texts from writers following the mid-first century BC referring to Rome by the phrase "seven hills," see Aune, *Revelation 17–22*, 944–5; and Osborne, *Revelation*, 617.
[39] In the Hebrew Bible, Mount Saphon/Zion is the mountain of the chief god and is where Yahweh will take up the battle (Joel 3:9–17, 19–21; Zech 14:4; 2 Esd 13:35). According to Mark S. Smith,

> the biblical motif of the divine mountainous abode derives primarily from the North Semitic tradition of divinely inhabited mountains ... this dependency of language connected with Sapan in Ugaritic tradition is especially manifest in the identification of Mount Zion as *yarkĕtê ṣāpôn*, 'the recess of the north,' in Psalm 48:3 (cf. Isa. 48:3) and the MT's apparent substitution of Zion for *ṣpn* in the Aramaic version of Psal 20:3 written in Demotic. (Mark S. Smith, *The Early History of God: Yahweh and the Other Deities in Ancient Israel*, 2nd ed. [Grand Rapids, MI: Eerdmans, 2002], 88–9).

A similar point is made by Walther Zimmerli when stating that "Zion becomes the world mountain, Zaphon (צָפוֹן *ṣāpôn*) in the north, which was referred to at Ugarit as the dwelling place of Baal (Ps. 48:3) ... Now Zion becomes the site where Yahweh destroys the weapons of the attacking nations" (Walther Zimmerli, *Old Testament Theology in Outline*, trans. David E. Green [Edinburgh: T&T Clark, 1978], 77). To Zimmerli, the association of Yahweh with the mountain of God is a "heritage from the early period of the tribes" and the association of Yahweh and his mountains (Zion/Horeb/Zaphon) is an important part in expressing the presence of Yahweh among his people (ibid., 71, see 70–7).

[40] Resseguie, *The Revelation of John*, 220–1.

motivate, punish, or even annihilate them (the northern kingdom). In 1 Kgs 11:14 and 23 we read, "And the Lord raised an adversary to Solomon: Hadad the Edomite, he was of the royal house in Edom"—"And God raised to him an adversary, Rezon, son of Elyadah, who had fled from his master King Hadadezer of Soboah."

The raising of adversaries to Solomon is linked with the apostasy of Solomon due to his foreign wives (cf. 1 Kgs 11:1–13). This also seems to be the case when Yahweh raises Rezin as an enemy of King Ahaz in Isa 9:11–13 (cf. 2 Kgs 16:1–9):

> And Yahweh raised enemies against them, Rezin, and stirred up their enemies the Arameans from the east, and the Philistines from the west, and they devoured Israel with open mouth. Despite all of this he (Yahweh) did not turn his anger away, and his hand is stretched out still. The people did not turn to the one who struck them, and they did not turn to Yahweh of Hosts.

In Isaiah 10 we see a similar act from Yahweh against his own people, motivated by their apparent apostasy, but this time it is the Assyrian king who is raised as the hand of Yahweh's fury (Isa 10:5–19). This text introduces us to an additional element to the sequence of punishment: the rod of anger is struck by hubris—the king wants more than he is intended to have. He is therefore to be dethroned and punished for this. The pattern can be mapped out as follows:

1. The people suffer from apostasy (Isa 10:5, 8–11).
2. A foreign king is raised to punish and cause them to repent (10:6).
3. The foreign king is struck by pride and wants more than he signed up for (10:12, 15).
4. Penalty is measured out (10:16–18).
5. The people (or some of them) repent and are vindicated through retribution (10:20–27).

This pattern is found elsewhere in the Hebrew Bible, used on, among others, the Babylonian king in Jer 27:1–7; Dan 2:37; Ezek 26:7–21; 29:17–21. It is precisely this king who is taunted in Isa 14:4–21.

My point here is that in Revelation 17, Babylon seems to have been given a similar function with relation to the eschatological ordeal and that this is part of the reason for utilizing the association to historical Babylon. In Revelation 17–18, Babylon has served her purpose in sifting the population of the earth and is targeted as the object of divine wrath on accounts of hubris—pretending to be godlike by demanding worship. She is initially raised as an adversary to serve a function toward the people but is in the end disposed of. In Revelation as in the prophetic literature of the Hebrew Bible, kings and empires rule at the mercy of God. This is made explicit in Rev 17:17. This fits well with my conclusions so far because the sovereign παντοκράτωρ of Revelation is very much akin to the sovereign God of Isa 45:7 (I form light and create darkness, I make peace and create woe; It is I, Yahweh, who do all this). In light of the possibility of having here encountered a similarly typical way of portraying the pedagogical, judging, and testing hand of God behind the apparently sovereign kingdoms of the earth, the probability of having a historical empire as a baseline reference for the characterization in Rome makes sense in a narrative reading.[41]

As the element of hubris was found in Chapter 4 of this book to be potentially present in the characterization of Satan in Revelation 12–13, it is highly relevant to find it effecting the fall of the earthly manifestation of the beast—that is, the reign of Rome. Perhaps the revealing of the identity of the woman and her close relation to the beast in Revelation 17 being followed by a taunt similar to that of Isaiah 14 in Revelation 18 could be seen to further underscore this impression. The relation between the woman and the beast of Revelation 17 and the dragon and other beasts of Revelation is made explicit by her being seated on a scarlet beast that shares the traits and characteristics of the beasts and the dragon:[42] seven heads and ten horns (17:3, 7, 9; 12:3; 13:1); the epithet θηρίον (17:3; 11:7; 13.1–18; 16:13); the characteristics of blasphemy (17:3; 13:1, 5, 6; cf. 2:9); the acts of war (17:14; 11:7; 13:7; 16:13–16; cf. 19:19; 20:7–9); marvelous impact (17:3; 13:6); and as fellow residents of the abyss (17:8; 11:7; cf. 20:1, 3). The woman herself is the great city that rules over the kings of the world. The relation between the woman and the beast is complex. Perhaps James L. Resseguie is right when he states, "While the woman is the beguiling face of evil, the beast is evil's ugly reality."[43] Still, the unity seems fractured when the kings of the beast are stated to hate the whore, and subsequently act on these feelings in Rev 17:16–17. The identification of the empire/beast and the woman is now blurred, which suggests that Rome is to be perceived as a manifestation, a temporary incarnation of its being.[44] The beast turns from being an instrument of sustenance to one of punishment in these verses, and it is all orchestrated by the sovereign God. In 17:17 we see the repetition of the motif of giving in order to emphasize that God is in absolute control, overseeing the outcome of events at play:[45] ὁ γὰρ θεὸς ἔδωκεν εἰς τὰς καρδίας αὐτῶν ποιῆσαι τὴν γνώμην αὐτοῦ καὶ ποιῆσαι μίαν γνώμην καὶ δοῦναι τὴν βασιλείαν αὐτῶν τῷ θηρίῳ ἄχρι τελεσθήσονται οἱ λόγοι τοῦ θεοῦ (for God gave into their hearts to act according to his purpose, to act as one mind, and give their kingdom to the beast until the word of God will be fulfilled). As the beast itself *was given* (ἐδόθη) to act in Revelation 13, the kings are given directions from God

---

[41] According to Elisabeth Schüssler Fiorenza, "to understand the symbolic representation not in historical but in archetypal or philosophical terms does not avoid its interpretation as 'representation' of something which the interpreter is able to name" (Fiorenza, *Justice and Judgment*, 185). In other words, it is equally important not to reduce the symbolism of Babylon by equating it with historical Rome as it is not to deny the implications of Rome being the historical representation of the transhistorical archetype of Babylon in Revelation. In Revelation, the Roman Empire is the historical actualization of an archetypical symbol of power, Babylon, known from the Hebrew Bible and pseudepigrapha. Still, it remains to be seen if this actualization contributes anything else to my literary reading of its narrative besides confirming the presence of the apocalyptic tradition of demonizing one's foreign rulers by theriomorphic imagery, a probable geographical reference to ἑπτὰ ὄρη (seven mountains), and the intratextual implications of the messages of Revelation 2–3 being formed as imperial decrees.

[42] See Aune, *Revelation 17–22*, 941–4, for a synoptic comparison of the biographical material of the beast of Revelation.

[43] Resseguie, *The Revelation of John*, 223.

[44] Prigent, *A Commentary on the Apocalypse of St. John*, 496.

[45] Osborne, *Revelation*, 627.

regarding their ambivalent relation to Babylon. They hate her, but their power, wealth, and luxury seem to depend on her (17:16; 18:9).

The application of the symbolical name of Babylon to the antagonist of the congregations allows the implied reader to perceive the fall of eschatological Babylon (Rome) in light of the prophetic message of historical Babylon.[46] The fate of eschatological Babylon can be expected to be like the historical one, as it is literarily associated with the reliable integrity of the God of the Hebrew Bible: God will act in the same way as he always has done.[47] Having pointed out how various elements of the characterization of Rome in Revelation 17 correspond to the messages to the seven churches in various ways, Craig Koester concludes, "Rhetorically, John's goal is to give readers incentive to resist the beguiling social and economic forces represented by the whore."[48] As a rhetorical incentive, the fate of Babylon is meant to discourage the following of her example of conduct and to motivate conquering by death, knowing that her violent deeds will be subjected to divine justice.

The first part of the poetic section of Rev 18:1–19:8 is constituted by a funeral dirge on the future fall of Rome laden with allusions to the Hebrew Bible.[49] The angelic proclamations of her fall (18:1–8) are followed by the lamentations of kings (18:9–10), merchants (18:15–17a), and the sailors (18:17b–19). The second part (18:20–19:8) is an admonition to the heavens, saints, apostles, and prophets to rejoice over her fall, and can be perceived as a direct/final response to the cry of Rev 6:9–11. A hallelujah thus follows the dirge.[50] The two parts clearly reflect the two potential outcomes of the eschatological ordeal. According to Elisabeth Schüssler Fiorenza, "the hymns and acclamations serve as a commentary on the apocalyptic action of Rev. Their

---

[46] It is possible to argue for a more abstract and less historically dependent definition of Babylon. Stephen Smalley concludes that "the city should not be aligned directly with the imperial power of Rome" and "'Babylon' is more than a city; she stands for any organized power group which denies freedom to the individual, and tries to seduce secular society, already rebelling against God, into further doom-laden acts of impious, unjust oppression and wickedness" (Smalley, *The Revelation to John*, 442 and 429). Although such a reading is possible within the parameters of narrative criticism, I find Rome to be the most likely point of reference of an implied reader situated in this area in the late first century AD (see argumentation above). For a similar understanding of the point of reference of the symbol of Babylon in Revelation to this one, see Aune, *Revelation 17–22*, 959; Koester, *Revelation*, 683; Mounce, *The Book of Revelation*, 307–8; and Osborne, *Revelation*, 608–9, 628. W. Gordon Campbell, on the other hand, argues for understanding Babylon as a complex literary symbol/theme too multifaceted and complex to be the object of simple decoding (Campbell, *Reading Revelation*, 235). He argues at length for an interpretation in which Jerusalem is the historical and literary basis for the imagery of Babylon the Great—not Rome (ibid., 231, 234, 236; see also Lupieri, *A Commentary on the Apocalypse of John*, 223–7, 248–53.) Elisabeth Schüssler Fiorenza argues similarly yet arrives at a less assertive conclusion when she too argues against an oversimplification of the symbolism behind the Babylon/whore imagery in light of the prostitution metaphors used on Jerusalem in the Hebrew Bible. In the end, she concludes on Rome as the primary point of reference (Fiorenza, "Babylon the Great: A Rhetorical-Political Reading of Revelation 17–18," 260–1). However, no matter how one identifies Babylon the Great, identifying her function in the narrative through the structural elements of the dichotomies of the whore/bride, Babylon/New Jerusalem imagery is essential to any narrative reading of Revelation, because it corresponds directly to its overarching plot.

[47] See also Koester, *Revelation*, 695.
[48] Ibid.
[49] Especially Isaiah 13–14; 34; Jeremiah 51; Ezekiel 26–28; Nahum 3.
[50] Barr, *Tales of the End*, 237.

contribution to its structure is interpretation and comment. Thus they function in a manner similar to the chorus in the Greek tragedy which commented and explained the actions of the principals in the drama."[51] What, then, is the comment provided by this rather substantial poetic passage of Rev 18:1–19:8? Aside from the general rhetorical effect of perceiving judgment to have been enacted, the section consists predominantly of a series of ὅτι sentences providing an explanation of why she is being judged and the severity of the punishment. The reasoning behind the punishment of a manifestation of the beast, which in turn is endorsed by both dragon and God in his function as a sifter of the world, is important to this reading since the liquidation of the office of Satan in Rev 20:1–10 is given no such thing. Revelation 18:1–19:8 is the most elaborate explanation in the book of Revelation of its severe punishment of agents of evil, and could therefore be relevant in understanding the final scene involving Satan in Rev 20:10.

Firstly, Babylon is fallen because of her part in promoting religious infidelity: ὅτι ἐκ τοῦ οἴνου τοῦ θυμοῦ τῆς πορνείας αὐτῆς πέπωκαν πάντα τὰ ἔθνη καὶ οἱ βασιλεῖς τῆς γῆς μετ' αὐτῆς ἐπόρνευσαν καὶ οἱ ἔμποροι τῆς γῆς ἐκ τῆς δυνάμεως τοῦ στρήνους αὐτῆς ἐπλούτησαν (Because all of the nations have drunk from the wine of the wrath of her fornication, and the kings of the earth have committed fornication with her, and the merchants of the earth have grown rich from the power of her luxury, Rev 18:3).

Secondly, the people of God are to distance themselves from her because of her many sins and transgressions (the most severe of these are explained as her main offense in 18:23–24, as discussed below): ὅτι ἐκολλήθησαν αὐτῆς αἱ ἁμαρτίαι ἄχρι τοῦ οὐρανοῦ καὶ ἐμνημόνευσεν ὁ θεὸς τὰ ἀδικήματα αὐτῆς (because her sins have been piled up unto heaven and God remembered her iniquities, Rev 18:5). The context of this explanation is that anyone in her proximity is likely to take part in her transgressions and experience her plagues.

Thirdly, the woman will be repaid double for her deeds because of her boastful claim as prostitute claiming to be queen. This personification of the boasting of Babylon/Rome is an ironic expression of her hubris with an obvious intratextual parallel in the message to Laodicea (Rev 3:17):[52] ὅτι ἐν τῇ καρδίᾳ αὐτῆς λέγει ὅτι κάθημαι βασίλισσα καὶ χήρα οὐκ εἰμὶ καὶ πένθος οὐ μὴ ἴδω (because in her heart she says: I rule like a queen, no widow I am, and mourning I will never see, Rev 18:7). As was the case with Laodicea, she is ignorant of the reality being the opposite of how she perceives it.

Fourthly, she will be judged violently and laid barren because of her acts of deceiving the rulers of the earth and leading them astray (religiously). According to 13:10–15, capital punishment was dealt to anyone not adhering to her deceptions. This leads in turn to the shedding of the blood of the people of God: ὅτι οἱ ἔμποροί σου ἦσαν οἱ μεγιστᾶνες τῆς γῆς, ὅτι ἐν τῇ φαρμακείᾳ σου ἐπλανήθησαν πάντα τὰ ἔθνη, καὶ ἐν αὐτῇ αἷμα προφητῶν καὶ ἁγίων εὑρέθη καὶ πάντων τῶν ἐσφαγμένων ἐπὶ τῆς γῆς (Because

---

[51] Fiorenza, *Justice and Judgment*, 171–2.
[52] David E. Aune (*Revelation 17–22*, 995) refers to this as an allusion to Isa 47:9–11 as an example of a "*hybris soliloquy*, a short literary form that occurs several times in the OT and early Jewish and early Christian literature, as well as in Greco-Roman literature." He refers to Ezek 28:2; Jer 5:12; Sib. Or. 5:173; Rev 3:17; Tg. Esth II, 1.1 as other examples of this literary form (see also Osborne, *Revelation*, 643).

your [= her] merchants were the magnates of the earth, and by your [= her] sorcery all nations were led astray and in her the blood of prophets and the saints was found and of all having been slaughtered on the earth, Rev 18:23–24).

Fifthly, it is because of the gravity of her transgressions that her punishment will be executed violently and fast. The severity and swiftness are explained and rooted in the superior power of God: διὰ τοῦτο ἐν μιᾷ ἡμέρᾳ ἥξουσιν αἱ πληγαὶ αὐτῆς, θάνατος καὶ πένθος καὶ λιμός, καὶ ἐν πυρὶ κατακαυθήσεται, ὅτι ἰσχυρὸς κύριος ὁ θεὸς ὁ κρίνας αὐτήν (Because of this, in one day her plagues will come, death, mourning, and famine, and in fire she will burn up, for strong is the Lord God judging her, Rev 18:8). The same rhetorical point is made by the threefold chorus of the laments of the kings, merchants, and those trading at sea: ὅτι μιᾷ ὥρᾳ ἦλθεν ἡ κρίσις σου (because in one hour your judgment came, Rev 18:10) and ὅτι μιᾷ ὥρᾳ ἠρημώθη (because in one hour she was laid waste, Rev 18:17, 19).

All in all, Babylon being guilty of promoting religious infidelity, deceiving the rulers of the earth, contagious conduct demanding the saints to distance themselves from her, and exhibiting hubris in her unrightful claim to rule is all highly relevant to the scope of this reading in light of her close relation to the beasts and the dragon of Revelation 12–13. In light of the "raising an adversary" pattern found of the Hebrew Bible mentioned above, Babylon becomes the adversary raised and used in the divine ordering of things. In this hierarchy, Satan/the dragon functions as an inserted agent— the one raising the beast from the sea/earth (Rev 12:18–13:1, 4, 11–12, 14) from which Babylon in turn derives her power and constitutes her reign (17:3, 17). As with the pattern found in the Hebrew Bible, here too the adversarial function is utilized according to divine purposes (17:17; see Section 4.4 on the subordinated function of the dragon). Hence, the fate of Babylon can be perceived as following in the literary footsteps of similar adversarial kings and kingdoms overstepping their boundaries due to hubris found in the Hebrew Bible. The hubris of Babylon and the beasts is clearly associated with the works of Satan. Yet, at the same time, it is both explicitly given (13:5) and regulated by God (17:17), and constitutes an important means to an end in light of the eschatological ordeal.

The concluding section (19:9–10) is another focalizing element to secure the ethos of John to the implied reader by reminding him/her of John's role in the mode of revelation. The angel is not to be worshipped, because he too is but another medium of the testimony of Jesus—the spirit of prophecy of God.

5.2.4 The Two Suppers

In Rev 19:7 we read χαίρωμεν καὶ ἀγαλλιῶμεν καὶ δώσωμεν τὴν δόξαν αὐτῷ, ὅτι ἦλθεν ὁ γάμος τοῦ ἀρνίου καὶ ἡ γυνὴ αὐτοῦ ἡτοίμασεν ἑαυτήν (Let us rejoice and exult, and give glory to him because the wedding day of the Lamb has come, and its bride has made herself ready). The day of salvation has finally arrived, yet we are still two chapters away from its culmination.[53] Before the New Jerusalem can arrive, the score

---

[53] Koester, *Revelation*, 741.

has to be settled—the overarching plot of Revelation must reach its denouement. The preliminary event for judgment and vindication to commence was the rise and fall of Babylon the Great. According to Gregory K. Beale, "the existence of Babylon was a necessary factor in the bride's preparation for the marriage ... Babylon's oppression and temptation was the fire ultimately used by God to refine the saints' faith to prepare them to enter the heavenly city."[54] Babylon's presence among the people of the earth, saints and dwellers, was the ultimate test of loyalty. The righteous deeds that the bride of the Lamb is given to wear (19:8) are the reward of the righteous deeds of the saints for their conquest through faithful testimony unto death (19:7–8; cf. 3:5–6). Their refusal to compromise with Babylon's norms, values, and beliefs has earned them the right to wear these fine garments (cf. 2:10, 13; 13:10; 14:12; 17:14).[55] The sifting of the earth has now come to its end, and conclusions are now being drawn: "The imagery of the wedding on the one hand, and the illicit affair with the whore on the other, accentuate the two choices of the Apocalypse: to follow the Lamb and to participate in the Lamb's wedding feast, or to follow the beast and Babylon."[56] It is from this perspective that we must approach the battle of 19:11–21. The saints are vindicated by enduring the afflictions imposed on them by agents, who are in turn governed and/or endorsed by God (cf. 17:17). In return for their perseverance they get to partake in their own vindication as fellow combatants in the armies of heaven (19:14; cf. 17:14 and white garments worn by the saints in 3:4–5, 18; 4:4; 6:11; 7:9, 13–14) and later to reign and possibly judge with Christ (20:4).[57] The rhetorical thrust of the dichotomy of Rev 19:11–21 is obvious: in light of the envisioned outcome of the battle (19:21), the wedding supper of the Lamb (τὸ δεῖπνον τοῦ γάμου τοῦ ἀρνίου, 19:9) is preferable to that of the great supper of God (τὸ δεῖπνον τὸ μέγα τοῦ θεοῦ, 19:17). Both the rise *and* fall of Babylon were thus necessary in order to get the "invitations" to the wedding supper in place and to usher in the coming of the kingdom of God (cf. 18:1–19:6).[58] However, the continued activity of the beast in 19:11–21, following the aftermath of the demise of Babylon, supports the cosmological scope of the sifting activity of the beast, as it targets all of humankind, not only those connected to Babylon the Great. Four elements of the battle scene of Rev 19:11–21 seem important to the following analysis of the narrative function of Satan in Revelation 20.

Firstly, as many commentators have pointed out, the battle of Rev 19:11–21 functions as a comment on the battle mentioned in Rev 16:12–21 and 17:14.[59] The overlapping details are many (the gathering of the kings of the earth to wage war/lay siege, the presence of the beast, the one-sided character of the battles, and a swift but devastating defeat), yet it is the differences that must in some way be the reason for the many references to the same event. Mere repetition would be superfluous. The reference in 16:12–21 seems emblematic as it encompasses the final removal of the adversaries of the saints in total (including the

---

[54] Beale, *The Book of Revelation*, 934.
[55] Resseguie, *The Revelation of John*, 235.
[56] Ibid.
[57] Beale, *The Book of Revelation*, 960
[58] Ibid., 934.
[59] Prigent, *Commentary on the Apocalypse of St. John*, 535; Witherington, *Revelation*, 242; Barr, *Tales of the End*, 208–13.

dragon of Revelation 20). The reference in 17:14 anticipates the dual function of the beast within the hand of God—to usher the rise and fall of Babylon, and to deceive the kings of the earth into waging war on the rider on the white horse and his armies. The battle of Rev 19:11–21 serves primarily to highlight the role of the rider in this event, as half of the text is carefully composed to his presentation (19:11–16).[60] In light of these references to a final battle, the battle of the dragon (20:7–10) also seems to be encompassed by the emblematic reference of 16:12ff., and serves to highlight the role and removal of Satan in this event.

Secondly, at this stage the conflict is no longer between the saints and their adversaries but between Christ and those adhering to the opposite side of the dichotomy.[61] Both 17:14 and 19:19 explicitly state that the purpose of the armies of the beast is to wage war on the Lamb/the white rider. By comparison, the purpose of the armies in which the dragon is involved is to gather them for battle on the great day of the Lord Almighty (16:15) and to besiege the camp of the saints and the beloved city (20:9). To avoid anticipating the analysis of Revelation 20 below, it will suffice for now to note that the dragon is not stated as the adversary of Christ/God in the battle scenes of Revelation, while the beast clearly is cast as such. That the rider can be identified as Christ follows from several of his names and epithets.[62] The πιστὸς καὶ ἀληθινός (faithful and true, 19:11) is reminiscent of the reference to Jesus Christ as the faithful and true witness in 1:5, as well as being an epithet of the voice of the seven messages in 3:14. His eyes being like a φλὸξ πυρός (a flame of fire, Rev 19:12) points back to the description of one like a son of man in 1:13–14 and the Son of God in 2:18. In 19:15 he is called ὁ λόγος τοῦ θεοῦ (the word of God, Rev 19:13), which is fitting for a celestial agent carrying out the just judgment of the God Almighty (cf. 19:15).[63] The title also fits the aspect of focalization within the narrative, where Christ functions as the revelation of God, both as medium and message. According to James L. Resseguie, there might also be something of the powerful testimony of Christ as a means of conquest at play in the title: "The 'Word of God' wages and wins the war with the powerful weapon of his

---

[60] Whether the events of Rev 19:11–21 and 20:7–15 are to be considered temporally parallel (Beale, *The Book of Revelation*, 976, 1031) or not seems to be outside the purpose of the texts since the emblematic reference in Rev 16:12ff. seems to refer to them both as one singular event. I agree with Craig Koester in that the best way of making sense of the two scenes is to approach them as two battles that "are part of the same plotline, which concerns God's defeat of evil, even though the two scenes play distinctive literary roles" (Koester, *Revelation*, 789). Their common point of reference (the final battle) and their diverging literary functions make this another probable example of the device of recapitulation we saw at play in the three septets of Revelation 6–16—describing the same event twice, yet with alternate information and literary purpose.

[61] The characterization of Christ as the white rider is the third of Revelation's three major characterizations of Christ. The first is the one like a son of man of 1:13–20; the second the slaughtered and risen Lamb of 5:1–14 (Resseguie, *The Revelation of John*, 236; Barr, "The Lamb Who Looks Like a Dragon?" 214–15).

[62] The extratextual connotations of the names and epithets of the rider are overwhelming, yet as the purpose of this section is only to argue for an identification of the rider as Christ, and not a full-fledged analysis of the narrative characterization of him, the intratextual references will suffice. See Pierre Prigent: "The presentation of the rider is made in terms that are judiciously chosen because they are steeped in tradition. Nearly every word, as we shall see in explaining the text, refers either to prophecies of the OT, or to names that are titles destined to describe minutely the being and function of the Messiah" (Prigent, *Commentary of the Apocalypse of St. John*, 535).

[63] Mounce, *The Book of Revelation*, 345–6; see also Witherington, *Revelation*, 243.

testimony."⁶⁴ After all, the sole medium of the conquering of adversaries in Revelation is through the word of testimony (Rev 12:11). This testimony is closely related to the idea of Christ being the acting word of God (see the juxtaposing of the titles ὁ λόγος τοῦ θεοῦ and τὴν μαρτυρίαν Ἰησοῦ Χριστοῦ [the testimony of Jesus] in 1:2, 9; 6:9; 20:4). The identification of the rider as Christ is further confirmed by the parallel reference to him as τὸ ἀρνίον (the Lamb) in 17:14.⁶⁵

Thirdly, despite the grotesque violence of the scene, its main rhetorical thrust seems to rely on the nonviolent nature of the battle itself. The armies of the beasts and kings of the earth are gathered to wage war on the rider on the white horse (19:19), but the beasts are captured, and the armies are killed by the sword coming out from the mouth of the rider (19:21)—the word of his true and faithful testimony. By using the graphic imagery of the Holy War of the Hebrew Bible,⁶⁶ the argument of conquest by enduring suffering is repeated: the power of the death of the Lamb has the power to overcome one's adversaries (cf. 12:11).⁶⁷ This element is emphasized through the blood present on the garments of the rider, even before the battle has begun. The blood probably serves a dual symbolic function by anticipating the imminent carnage and treading of the winepress, as well as reminding of the worthiness of its executor and the means by which he carries out the verdict.⁶⁸ According to James L. Resseguie, both the bloodied

---

⁶⁴ Resseguie, *The Revelation of John*, 238.
⁶⁵ The titles Βασιλεὺς βασιλέων καὶ κύριος κυρίων (Rev 19:16; cf. 17:14) are titles used of God in the Hebrew Bible and pseudepigrapha ("King of kings": 2 Macc 13:4; 3 Macc 5:35; Philo, *QG* 4.76; "Lord of lords": Deut 10:17; Ps 136:3; both: 1 En. 9:4; Dan 4:37 LXX), and conforms thus to the high Christology of Revelation (see Koester, *Revelation*, 759).
⁶⁶ See David Barr: "We have all the paraphernalia of Holy War, but no war" (Barr, "The Lamb Who Looks Like a Dragon?," 215).
⁶⁷ Barr, *Tales of the End*, 241-2. Although Barr presents good arguments for the nonviolent manner of the means of conquest of the rider on the white horse, I disagree with his arguments for perceiving the whole section not as an expectation of imminent future events within the narrative but rather as symbolic presence (Barr, "The Lamb Who Looks Like a Dragon?," 215, 218; Barr, *Tales of the End*, 241-2). This is mainly because the literary function of the battle scene of Rev 19:11-21 seems primarily to be to emphasize the instrumental aspect of the same event reported in Revelation 12, 16, 17, and 20. This is also supported by the presence of the adversaries of the congregations that suggests that their removal remains to be effectuated and its literary place in the narrative next to the final judgment (cf. 19:11).
⁶⁸ The origin of the blood on the rider's garments is debated. The main arguments for perceiving this as anticipating the blood of enemies are the allusion to Isa 63:1-4 and the military context of the scene. (Aune, *Revelation 17-22*, 1057; Beale, *The Book of Revelation*, 957-9; Mounce, *The Book of Revelation*, 345; Osborne, *Revelation*, 682-3; Prigent, *Commentary on the Apocalypse of St. John*, 543-4; Witherington, *Revelation*, 243-4). Counterarguments, viewing the blood as the blood of Christ himself, emphasize the sequence of the narrative and the habit of transforming older images in light of Jesus's death and resurrection elsewhere in the narrative (Koester, *Revelation*, 755-6; see also Barr, *Tales of the End*, 241-2; Campbell, *Reading Revelation*, 316). Perhaps Stephen S. Smalley's conclusion, while considering arguments from both sides, constitutes the reading closest to the text when stating,

> The picture is that of a triumphant warrior, rather than a sacrificial victim. The 'blood' associated with the robes of the victorious Messiah, therefore, is not primarily that of the crucified Jesus … Nevertheless, the sacrificial dimension of Christ's 'blood' would not have entirely escaped the Christian sensitivities of the seer and his audience at this point … But at 19.13 these links are secondary. Christ is presented here as avenging judge and triumphant warrior, not as the Redeemer. (Smalley, *The Revelation to John*, 491-2)

garments of the rider (suggesting a reference to the victory having already been won, cf. 5:6, 9, 12; 7:14; 12:11; 13:8) and the position of the sword are "emblematic of God's counterintuitive way of conquering. Victory is achieved not through traditional warfare but through the testimony of the Lamb."[69] The divine warrior is the manifestation of God's judgment upon the world, but his weapon further suggests his dual function as both medium and impact.

Fourth and finally, there is a differentiation in fate between the objects of the eschatological ordeal and the divine agents effectuating it. From the context of Rev 19:11–21 we may deduce that the beast and the false prophet are not "invited" to the great supper of God. They are relocated to the lake of fire before the birds are to feast on the bodies of their armies (19:20; see the anticipation of the event in 17:8, 11). The divine banquet does not concern them (19:21). They are in this way separated from the supper/female-city dichotomies, and are clearly to be seen not as objects of the cosmological sifting of Revelation but rather as agents facilitating it. This corresponds to the related differentiation of the dragon (20:10) and those not written in the book of life (20:15).

The battle of Rev 19:11–21 envisions the just judgment of the former allies of Babylon as part of the vindication of the saints.[70] They are to suffer the same fate as they granted Babylon (17:17)—swift death, followed by being eaten and burned (19:21; cf. 20:15). This fate of public humiliation and postmortem disgrace exceeds the just punishment for even killing the saints, but carries within it the seed of vindication/retribution as discussed above (Section 5.2.2). The time for rewarding the saints and destroying those destroying the earth has come by means of wrath and judgment as anticipated in 11:18 (see the considerable overlapping of victims of 19:18 and 6:15, where the opening of the seventh seal follows as a direct response to the cry for vindication of the saints). The removal of anything adversarial is imperative, in order for the imminent paradise to arrive. The removal of Babylon, the beasts, the kings of the earth, and their armies is preliminary for the envisioned features of the New Jerusalem to manifest (21:3–4). The removal of the negations of its splendor defines the "newness" of the New Jerusalem (3:12; 21:2)—the newness of everything (21:1, 5). It is here, at the brink of the ushering in of the long-awaited eschatological salvation, that the narration of the elimination of the archetypical adversary of Satan is inserted.

5.2.5 Preliminary Conclusion on the Literary Context of Revelation 20

Revelation 20 is the third and final phase of preparations before eschatological salvation is inaugurated at full scale (Revelation 21–22). These preparations seem to revolve around the removal of adversarial agents, vindication of the saints through retribution and reversal of fortune, and judgment upon the portion found wanting in the process of sifting humankind.

> In this way both the instrumental function of the rider on the white horse and the full scale of his identity receive their implied narrative attention in a scene primarily as well as predominantly occupied with just judgment through war.

[69] Resseguie, *The Revelation of John*, 238.
[70] Beale, *The Book of Revelation*, 949.

The adversarial agents of the section function within a larger frame of events that constitute the overarching plot of Revelation. Their function is described both implicitly and explicitly as governed by and/or endorsed by the sovereign God of the narrative.

These adversarial agents are not considered as objects of the eschatological ordeal but rather as a means to its ends. Their fates are separated from that of the saints/dwellers of the earth primarily by the lack of an interim period of trial and "custody." Consequently, an explanation of the grounds for their fate in the lake of fire is nowhere to be found, compared to the elaborations on the fate of those not written in the book of life/receiving the mark of the beast and worshiping its image.

Babylon the Great functions as something in between the celestial agents of adversity and humankind as objects of the eschatological ordeal. As an earthly manifestation of the activities of the beast, central to the plot of the narrative, she fits neither category. Her fate and characterization function literarily as the culmination and end of the eschatological ordeal for the saints. The function of her character is similar to that of the empires of the Hebrew Bible—utilized by the Almighty God according to his purposes, in the end to be dethroned and judged on the charge of hubris. The element of hubris is further emphasized through her epithet Babylon, which revokes the archetypical symbol of hubris derived from the historical Babylon of the Hebrew Bible. The rhetorical thrust of the substantial section on Babylon the Great is backed up by the fact that her might, fate, and apportioned time of rule are subject to the will of the sovereign God. In the narrative of Revelation, her function aligns with its overarching plot as a means to sift humankind.

Revelation 17–19 introduces the element of retribution/vindication in a language unique to the New Testament. Its rhetorical intent of motivating endurance when facing afflictions is established through a string of binary oppositions: bride/whore; vindication/retribution; the supper of God/the wedding supper of the Lamb; and Babylon the Great/the New Jerusalem. Among these, the fate of Babylon was found to serve a twofold function. On the one hand, it is clearly functioning as rhetorical deterrence for the saints—to motivate them in their perseverance and resisting compliance to the demands of the beasts. On the other hand, the death and humiliation of the former executioner of the saints is described as a message of joy and celebration, suggesting a function of vindication through retribution. Of particular relevance for the analysis of Revelation 20 is the absence of such elements in the briefly reported fate of the beast and false prophet (Rev 19:20–21). Their fate appears to lack both the elements of deterrence and vindication/retribution and seems to be removed simply because of their purpose of deceiving is deemed no longer necessary. Seen from such a perspective, the elimination of adversaries follows the literary progression suggested by the analysis of Revelation 12–13: when the agents of sifting have fulfilled their purpose, their removal is needed as a prerequisite to the inauguration of eschatological salvation. Perhaps this is also the case with the dragon of Revelation 20?

The relation between the beasts and Babylon seems blurred as they all encompass the earthly adversarial reality of the congregations. Still, the events of Rev 19:11–21 clarify that the beasts exceed the historical actualization of the archetypical adversarial empire in historical Rome. This makes it a generic reference encompassing any empire at the service of God and his eschatological ordeal. (The implications of perceiving an open-ended symbolism behind the epithet Babylon—i.e., a "the whore is Rome, yet more than Rome" way of thinking—fits the general eschatological outlook of the narrative.[71]) To this hierarchy the function of the dragon is that of a celestial puppeteer. It summoned the beasts from the sea and the earth to serve its purpose. Babylon in turn resides and rules upon the foundation of the beast. Throughout the narrative, this whole string of control and power is continuously portrayed as subordinate to the control and will of God. To the adversarial agents, the eschatological ordeal appears to be a "rigged game" (cf. 17:17) because it is not around them that the plot revolves, but around the people of the earth. Their function and fate are subordinate to the divine will.

The battle scene of Rev 19:11–21 was seen to be part of a larger string of "final battles" within the narrative of Revelation, emphasizing different aspects of the liquidation of adversarial forces before the inauguration of the age of eschatological salvation. Here the role of Christ and the removal of the beasts are emphasized. The battle of Revelation 20 must be interpreted as part of this string of battle scenes with a keen eye on its emphasized particulars—the final removal of the role and character of Satan.

5.3 The Literary Form and Function of Revelation 20

According to Pierre Prigent, in light of the considerable amount of attention given to the thousand-year reign and the judgment of Revelation 20, commentators "have lost sight of what constitutes both the internal unity of the chapter and its logical tie to the preceding developments: the end of Satan."[72] Therefore, it is important to perceive the narrative of Satan here as the final scene of a longer narrative with many ties stretching outside this particular textual unit. I agree that Satan is the focal point of a development we saw unravel in the preceding chapters, thereby closing off the events that started in Revelation 12–13. Yet this is not the main drive of the narrative, but a rhetorically laden sidetrack. He is not maintained as the subject of the plot after Revelation 12–13, but again reduced to being a secondary character. In other words, Satan is best perceived in Revelation as the explanation and elaboration on the trials of the saints primarily, and humankind in general secondarily. In my opinion, this is also the case of Revelation 20. The action here revolves around the saints reigning and possibly judging with Christ, whereas Satan represents the negation of these. The concluding judgment reveals the purpose and closure of adversarial activities in the narrative of Revelation. The literary structure of this part of the narrative concurs with this point of view as it reveals the status of this scene as an intermediary stage between the closure of the eschatological ordeal and its consequences. This is also reflected in the literary structure of Revelation 20, which falls into four parts in the following manner:[73]

---

[71] Koester, *Revelation*, 684.
[72] Prigent, *Commentary of the Apocalypse of St. John*, 554.
[73] Resseguie, *The Revelation of John*, 243–4.

A: The binding and imprisonment of Satan, 20:1–3
B: The thousand-year reign of the saints, 20:4–7
C: The release of Satan, 20:7–10
D: The final judgment, 20:11–15

The reign of a thousand years (B) is sandwiched between two narrative units about Satan (A and C)—clearly implying the two to be interpreted in light of each other. The final part of this section is the scene of judgment (D). Together these parts contribute to the elimination of anything incompatible with salvation. After this follows the age of eschatological salvation (Revelation 21–22).

Parts A, B, and D are initiated with the revelatory formula εἶδον, which frequently occurs throughout the book.[74] Each part constitutes a separate scene in the last chapter of the unfolding narrative of the liquidation of the adversarial office (see Section 5.2). As the narrative approaches the final stage of the visionary journey of John, and with it, the eschatological unfolding of salvation to those conquering in Christ, the stage in Revelation 20 is set for removal of the final adversary—Satan. As the primary adversarial agent, he is saved for last. In light of the conclusion of Section 5.2.5, we again notice the separation of the fate of the adversarial agent who is instigating the events of the section from those considered the object of it as part of the eschatological ordeal. Satan is removed and eliminated, whereas those not written in the book of life are judged according to their works, thereby continuing the tendency found in Revelation 17–19.

In Revelation 20 the two main plotlines of Revelation intertwine in the rewards of the conquerors and removal of adversaries—the vindication of God's people and the downfall of adversarial enemies.[75] As the removal of Satan concludes the abovementioned three-stage downfall of Satan (heaven → earth; earth → abyss; abyss → lake of fire) and the liquidation of the adversarial office (Babylon, beasts, dragon), a new level of vindication is envisioned in the possible judging and reigning with Christ for a thousand years.

One could compare the function of Revelation 20 with a forked road, where the left-hand path turns into a dead-end road, whereas the right-hand path takes you safely to your preferred destination. Revelation 20 functions as both a period and a punctuation mark, which is reflected in its content and structure. Both the structure and function of the scenes of Revelation 20 will be of considerable importance in detecting a probable narrative reading of it.

---

[74] As εἶδον also occurs in 20:12, this structural analysis is not only based on the presence of this formulation but also reflects the different themes present in the chapter. The formulation appears sometimes to be used to introduce new scenes in the narrative, yet other times not. It is probably this varied use of the formulation that challenges the often-suggested division of the vision of 19:11–22:5 into seven smaller parts (Koester, *Revelation*, 750).

[75] Koester, *Revelation*, 751.

5.4 Analysis

5.4.1 Plot

As mentioned above, the narrative of Revelation is not a narrative about Satan (see Section 2.3). It is a narrative within which he occurs with a given function in relation to its main characters—the saints/humankind. He is part of the eschatological event often referred to as the eschatological ordeal, which is the age of God sifting and dividing humankind into two antithetical categories (cf. Rev 3:10): those loyal to their faith in Christ and those not, those who have their names written in the book of life and those who do not, those resisting the demands of worshipping the beast and receiving its mark, and those who are not.

Revelation 20 is not a self-contained unit like the messages to the congregations or Revelation 12–13. Its content is tied closely to other related events of the narrative. It functions in part as the closing section of the overarching plot (the eschatological ordeal), but with an outlook to the final fate of those loyal to Christ. Treating it as a separate narrative unit with a self-contained plot would thus be forced. Yet, taking into consideration the various ties to the narrative in general, in the following I will try to discern a plot as seen from (1) the perspective of a "narrative of Satan"; (2) the function of Revelation 20 as a micronarrative (episode); and (3) how this functions within the overarching plot of Revelation. (By the term "narrative of Satan," I refer to the way Revelation 20 could be perceived as finding its culmination in light of the actantial structure of Revelation 12–13, where Satan was cast as subject.) By approaching the text in this manner, a "perspective of Satan" is established where there is none in order to emphasize the role and function of Satan within the plot of the episode as well as in the overarching plot.

Paul Ricoeur once defined the plot as "the set of combinations by which events are made *into* a story ... The Plot mediates between the event and the story."[76] Following such a train of thought, the events of Revelation 20 are mediated by the overarching plot of Revelation into the grand story of Revelation (see Table 11, column 3). It follows from this that if we are to decipher the function of Satan within this grand narrative of Revelation, any established perspective and plotline/strand of Satan in Revelation 20 must align with the overarching one. It is my view that Plots 1 and 2 as defined in columns 1 and 2 relate well to Plot 3 in Table 11, thus providing a basis for a best possible reading of the section. It is a reading that extends "our understanding, both comprehensively to the whole work and specifically to other aspects of the work."[77] In other words, it makes sense in light of the minor plot of the section from the perspectives of both the saints and Satan per se, as well as to the events of the narrative in general. Therefore, the plot in column 1 as defined in Table 11 will be my baseline

---

[76] Paul Ricoeur, *From Text to Action: Essays in Hermeneutics II*, trans. Kathleen Blamey and John B. Thompson (New York: Continuum, 2008), 4.
[77] See David Barr's method of discerning wrong from worse interpretations of a work of literature in Barr, "The Lamb Who Looks Like a Dragon?," 219.

Table 11 Perspectives on the Plot of Revelation 20

	(1) Plot seen from the perspective of a "narrative of Satan"	(2) Episodical function (perspective of the saints/humankind)	(3) Function of episode to the overarching narrative of Revelation
Initial situation	Intensively pursuing the rest of the woman's kind knowing he has little time (12:12–17)	Saints reigning and judging with Christ for a thousand years (20:4–6)	Implied: Congregations existing and working within a challenging sociocultural environment
Complication	An angel seizes Satan and locks him up in the abyss (20:2–3)	Satan released for a little while engaging acts of war toward the saints (20:3, 7)	Revelation 2–3; 6–16: God unleashing the eschatological ordeal upon the earth (cf. 3:10b)
Transforming action	Satan is released for a little while (20:3, 7)	Fire from heaven concluding the siege by consuming the deceived nations (20:9)	Saints enduring or giving in. Humankind is repenting or being deceived (2:5, 10, 13, 21; 3:3, 8, 10, 19; 12:11; 13:10; 14:12–13; 20:4–6)
Denouement	Continued activity of deception leading up to final battle (20:8–9)	Satan eliminated in the lake of fire (20:10)	Revelation 20: Judgment according to the outcome of the eschatological ordeal
Final situation	End of eschatological ordeal. Final liquidation of the adversarial office (20:9–10)	Judgment or salvation (20:11–15)	Revelation 21–22: Eschatological salvation

for analyzing the character of Satan in Revelation 20 as well as for delineating the point of view of the section.

5.4.2 Characterization

5.4.2.1 Introduction

The narrative function of Satan in Revelation 20 revolves around the inauguration of the thousand-year reign and the judgment of those not having their names written in the book of life.

Having defeated the armies of the beast and the kings of the earth (19:11–21), Christ now turns to establish his reign on earth. A decisive feature in the establishing of this interim kingdom is the removal of Satan. His initial removal, absence, and subsequent return serve to express both the reasons for and the essence of salvation/judgment—both of which are contingent on the unrivaled power of God/Christ. It is therefore of no surprise that even in the final stage of the career of the satanic office,

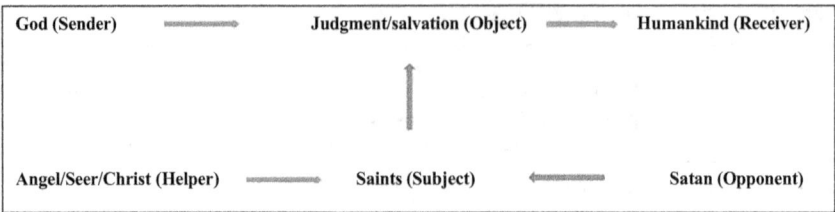

Figure 5 The actants of Revelation 20

it is soaked in a language of divine power, control, and sovereignty. In the following, I intend to argue that the characterization of Satan in Revelation 20 functions as a natural closure of what we have seen of him elsewhere in the narrative as a subordinate agent in the eschatological ordeal of God. Revelation 20 constitutes the liquidation of the office and function of Satan after having run its course in light of the overarching plot of the narrative. I will analyze the characterization of Satan of Revelation 20 in light of the actantial function he is assigned in the section (see below) and the three main events relating to him: the temporary binding (Section 5.4.2.2), the deceiving of the nations in the interim between release and demise (Section 5.4.2.3), and his end (Section 5.4.2.4).

In Revelation 20, the actantial positions as they appeared in Revelation 2–3 are now reestablished (see Section 3.4.1).[78] Thus in Revelation 20 the actantial positions are structured and govern the action of the narrative in the manner shown in Figure 5.

God is unleashing his eschatological ordeal upon the earth, thereby ushering the possibility of both salvation and judgment. That it is God who is characterized as the ultimate authority and power behind the events of the scene is made clear from the related descriptions of him sitting on a throne in Rev 4:2; 5:7; 19:4; and probably 21:5. God is characterized as the one sitting upon a *great* throne, indicating "the majesty of its influence,"[79] and *white* throne, a description that "connotes holiness and vindication."[80] Still, the overlapping characterization of Christ with that of God found elsewhere in the narrative is also present in this text. The thrones seen in Rev 20:4 are probably the thrones upon which the saints are to reign with Christ, being priests of God and Christ (20:6). The κρίμα ἐδόθη αὐτοῖς (judgment was given in their favor, Rev 20:4) probably refers to the scene of judgment in 20:11–15, where the saints are notably absent.[81] Αὐτοῖς refers to the saints, both those beheaded and those faithful in other ways (20:4), and follows the habit of mentioning a throne first and then identifying who sits on it

---

[78] Fiorenza, *The Book of Revelation Justice and Judgment*, 174–5.
[79] Resseguie, *The Revelation of John*, 249.
[80] Beale, *The Book of Revelation*, 1032.
[81] I follow the arguments of Craig R. Koester in interpreting the dative here as a dative of interest (*dativus commodi*), because of it being a probable response to the cry for vindication and vengeance in Rev 6:10, functioning antithetically to the unfavorable judgment of Babylon (18:8, 20; 19:2, 11) and those whose name was not found written in the book of life (20:15). This reading is supported by the fact that it constitutes a likely allusion to the favorable judgment given to the saints of the Most High, which in turn gave them reign over the kingdom (Dan 7:22). See Koester, *Revelation*, 772; see also Beale, *The Book of Revelation*, 996–7; Smalley, *The Revelation to John*, 506.

(4:2, 4; 14:14, 20; 20:11).[82] God judges the saints favorably but leaves it to Christ to carry out its implications—to reign with Christ. This concurs with the promise to those conquering in Laodicea: to sit with Christ upon the throne of his Father (Rev 3:21). A string of aorist passives (ἐκρίθησαν, Rev 20:12, 13; ἐβλήθησαν, Rev 20:14, 15) agrees with the identification of God as the ultimate *sender* in control of events in this section.

The roles of Christ and God intertwine in Revelation 20, even though the function of Christ is clearly subordinate to that of the judging God, in that it is because of the faithfulness to Christ and the word of God that the saints are able to conquer. As Christ constitutes the means for the subject to reach its object, he is primarily functioning in actantial position of *helper*, though his status as coregent makes him function partly as object as well. This roundness to the character of Christ makes him difficult to position in the actantial scheme, and hints at a deep level of complexity in terms of characterization.

It follows from the arguments above that the primary *subject* of Revelation 20 is the saints. They have been the main subject of the narrative all along, although indirectly in the rhetorical roundabout of Revelation 12–13 (see Section 4.4.2). Having said that, we must also acknowledge the prominent yet secondary position of those *not* written in the book of life (20:15). The rest of humankind, the dwellers of the earth, mainly serve as a rhetorical incentive to the saints of the congregations throughout the narrative. Their fate works here, as with Babylon the Great, to dissuade the saints from straying from the path of loyalty. This function also makes them objects of judgment, even if this is not the primary purpose of the text (i.e., their function is not to show how to get judged, but to repel those considering idolatry). Both saints and dwellers of the earth constitute the *receiver* to which God sends his *object*, the eschatological ordeal of salvation and judgment.

Finally, the function of *helper* is complex as it encompasses several elements of the text. The angel binding Satan, God judging favorably, and Christ having implicitly provided the means to conquer and subsequently reign—all contribute to this function. Moreover, the vision is focalized as a vision to the saints in order to help them endure the ordeal. The vision reveals all of these positive and encouraging elements and itself thus functions also as a *helper* by means of its revelation. The vision is given as *help* to the *subject* by the angel/Christ, mediated by the seer, John. I will now turn to the opponent of Revelation 20, Satan. Note that the string of names and epithets characterizing Satan in 20:2 is an almost verbatim repetition of the one found in 12:9, which is probably done to connect the two events to the reader. The identification of the opponent in this manner characterizes the events of Revelation 20 as the closing section of the narrative about the adversary of Revelation 12 (see Table 10 earlier). For the exegetical remarks on these names and epithets, please confer Section 4.4.2.[83]

---

[82] Aune, *Revelation 17–22*, 1085; Koester, *Revelation*, 771; Resseguie, *The Revelation of John*, 246.

[83] As W. Gordon Campbell (*Reading Revelation*, 47, 62) and Pierre Prigent (*Commentary on the Apocalypse of St. John*, 565) have suggested, the unusual use of nominatives in the adjectival phrases (ὁ ὄφις ὁ ἀρχαῖος, ὅς ἐστιν Διάβολος καὶ ὁ Σατανᾶς) rather than agreeing with the accusative case of the object (τὸν δράκοντα), could emphasize the antithetical relation to God/Christ—the sole deity to worship in Revelation (see Rev 1:1–5, where God and Christ are characterized in a similar manner with nominatives despite the presence of the preposition ἀπὸ, which usually requires the

5.4.2.2 The Temporary Binding of Satan

The vision of Revelation 20 is introduced with an angel descending from heaven with a great chain, ἔχοντα τὴν κλεῖν τῆς ἀβύσσου (having the key to the abyss, Rev 20:1). The imagery of the κλεῖς and the subsequent locking and releasing of the abyss relate to the other "keys" of the narrative in expressing sovereignty (1:18; 3:7; 9:1).[84] In 1:18 Christ holds τὰς κλεῖς τοῦ θανάτου καὶ τοῦ ᾅδου (the keys to Death and Hades), probably obtained as a result of his own merit of conquering death (1:18a). In 3:7 Christ is the wielder of τὴν κλεῖν Δαυίδ (the key of David), which is closely related to the door that he has put before the congregation of Philadelphia and no one is able to shut (3:8). The context connects this key/door imagery with Christ's ability to spare the congregation of Philadelphia from the coming hour of testing (τῆς ὥρας τοῦ πειρασμοῦ, Rev 3:10) and the humbling of the adherents of the synagogue of Satan before their feet (3:9). In Rev 9:1 a star is given (ἐδόθη) the ἡ κλεὶς τοῦ φρέατος τῆς ἀβύσσου (the key to the shaft of the abyss). The giving of the key, the unleashing of the locusts, and the instructions allowing and forbidding their conduct (9:4–5) all connote the wielding of the key to the sovereignty of God (see Section 4.2.2 for the function of the three septets in relation to God).[85] It is therefore reasonable to interpret the angel with the key to the abyss of Revelation 20 as similarly expressing the same divine sovereign authority when binding and incarcerating Satan for a thousand years. This clearly characterizes Satan as subordinate to God. However, the interesting question here is how this subordination functions in this particular text. The binding and locking away of Satan is explained with an explicit purpose: ἵνα μὴ πλανήσῃ ἔτι τὰ ἔθνη ἄχρι τελεσθῇ τὰ χίλια ἔτη (so that he would no longer lead astray the nations until the thousand years have ended, Rev 20:3). A parallel statement is found in 20:8, which may help us grasp why he must be released after the thousand years: λυθήσεται ὁ σατανᾶς ἐκ τῆς φυλακῆς αὐτοῦ καὶ ἐξελεύσεται πλανῆσαι τὰ ἔθνη τὰ ἐν ταῖς τέσσαρσιν γωνίαις τῆς γῆς (Satan will be released and go out to deceive the nations at the four corners of the earth, Rev 20:7–8).[86] In itself, the reason for his release is not apparent, but according to 20:3, he *must* (δεῖ) be released after this limited period. As we saw in Sections 4.2.2.1 and 4.2.2.2, δεῖ is used elsewhere in Revelation to express divine

---

genitive case). Whether one ought to agree with Campbell's claim that this should be seen as "a hugely significant phenomenon" (*Reading Revelation*, 62) is debatable, but it clearly emphasizes the link of the events of this passage with the ones of Rev 12:9, as well as establishes the destructive path of the Devil/Satan in diametrical opposition to the salvific one of God/Christ (see Wiriya Tipvarakankoon, *The Theme of Deception in the Book of Revelation: Bringing Early Christian and Contemporary Thai Culture into Dialogue* [Claremont: Claremont Press, 2017], 231–5).

[84] Beale, *The Book of Revelation*, 984–5; Smalley, *The Revelation to John*, 504–5.
[85] Possibly connected to the same sphere of imagery is the authority of sealing and unsealing visionary material, depending on the worthiness of the one opening (5:3–5) as well as divinely ordained secrecy (10:4; cf. 22:10).
[86] The argument of Thomas, following Smalley, that ἐξελεύσεται is "a term closely associated with deception and betrayal" does not add up in light of the larger context of the narrative of Revelation. It is true that whenever divine agents are described as "going out" using this term, it refers to afflictions of humankind as part of the eschatological ordeal (Rev 6:2, 4; 9:3; 14:15, 17–18; 15:6; 20:8), but as the agents in and below heaven clearly operate within the boundaries of God's bidding, the description seems out of place (Thomas, *The Apocalypse*, 608; Smalley, *The Revelation to John*, 511–12).

sovereignty and control through the course of history.[87] There is no reason to read the δεῖ of Rev 20:3 otherwise.[88] The same argument could also be made about the time limitation of χίλια ἔτη, which is mentioned no less than six times in this passage (Rev 20:2–7). We saw in Section 4.2.2.2 that time limitations within the apocalyptic genre in general, as well as in the book of Revelation per se, are an expression of divine control by the characterization of God as the architect of history. It follows from the presence of this string of elements expressing divine control in Rev 20:1–8 that just as the incarceration of Satan is done with the purpose to pause his deception temporarily, his release is done in order to achieve the opposite.[89] As the release of Satan in Rev 20:3 and 7 has proven difficult for scholars to interpret sufficiently within the context of the narrative,[90] in the following I will explore a different approach in arguing that the text narrates this act as a divine necessity, instigated and controlled by God.[91]

---

[87] See also Beale, *The Book of Revelation*, 987; Smalley, *The Revelation to John*, 505; Trafton, *Reading Revelation*, 186–7.

[88] Frederick J. Murphy rightly points out that the use of δεῖ here is part of presenting God's plan as inevitable—it *must* happen. Despite having located the release of Satan in God's plan by necessity, Murphy still finds in this formulation an author that "uses this opportunity to assert once again the resilience of Satan and the difficult and complicated process by which he is annihilated … The binding of Satan is a victory for Christ, but the fact that it is temporary emphasizes that Satan is powerful and can reemerge, even after the messiah's reign" (Frederick J. Murphy, *Fallen Is Babylon: The Revelation to John* [Harrisburg, PA: Trinity International, 1998], 395–6). The main problem with Murphy's reading is, in my opinion, in his location of the necessity of releasing Satan within the might and power of Satan—thus, not in the sovereign plan of God, which is usually expressed through the use of δεῖ in Revelation. The two explanations are mutually exclusive.

[89] See also Trafton, *Reading Revelation*, 186, 191–2.

[90] G. B. Caird finds some of the explanation for the unexpected release of Satan in the prophecy of Ezekiel, but does not seem to find this explanation strong enough to carry the burden of interpretation alone:

> The simple but inadequate answer is that he found this event prophesied in Ezekiel xxxviii–xxxix, and prophecies must have their fulfilment. It is inadequate because there has already been one fulfilment of this prophecy in the banquet of the birds, and there was no need to introduce another, unless John had found in Ezekiel some truth of ultimate and abiding significance. (Caird, *The Revelation of St John the Divine*, 256)

> Ian Boxall offers a different, but in my opinion equally insufficient, explanation for the necessity of Satan's release: "Satan must be released because his imprisonment has not dealt with evil definitively. Evil is still lurking, albeit chained; the fiery, glassy sea before the throne has been a reminder of this almost from the beginning of the book (4:6; 15:2)" (Boxall, *The Revelation of Saint John*, 286). This explanation is problematic in light of the cosmological implications if not from its lack of inherent logic: If God wanted to deal with evil—why imprison Satan if it was not sufficiently dealing with the problem? Furthermore, how is release a good way of dealing with evil? Would it not be more efficient to throw him in the lake of fire instead of releasing him? The demise of Satan does not follow from the battle he instigates, so it cannot be as Boxall comments that "John sees the irony inherent in that release: for its freedom paradoxically brings about its downfall" (ibid.)—it does not explain why the lake of fire must happen after the battle rather than before. I will therefore argue below for divine purposes governing the demise of Satan, rather than self-inflicted misery on behalf of Satan.

[91] Sigve Tonstad (*Saving God's Reputation*, 41–8) makes a good argument when considering the many interpretations of the necessity of releasing Satan after the thousand years have ended: interpretations of Revelation often fail "to give the peculiar ending its due," and he subsequently argues extensively to show how the traditional ways of dealing with its ending (textual editing, necessity to the nature of free will, demonstrating the sovereign divinity of God, etc.) are left wanting. I agree with him that we cannot be content with a reading unable to sufficiently make sense of this element

The temporary release of Satan after his imprisonment marks a distinct deviation from the more traditional scriptural expectation of antagonists, who are usually imprisoned until final eschatological judgment.[92] According to Craig Koester, "one purpose of prison was to hold people until a sentence could be imposed. This function fits the accounts of the evil watchers, who are imprisoned until the final judgment … but Revelation is unique in envisioning the Devil's temporary release before the end."[93] The imprisonment of Satan in Rev 20:1-7 contains several parallels to these traditions,[94] and it is precisely because of these parallels that a release of Satan, a surprising yet deliberate exception from these traditions, constitutes a key factor in understanding the function of this incident within its plot.[95]

---

in the narrative. Still, contrary to the reading presented here, Tonstad's own interpretational contribution on the passage suggests that Satan *must* be released in the end to stand alone on the stage to be judged, thus forming a full circle back to Eden where he first appeared—also alone (see Section 1.2.2). Peter J. Leithart also argues for the necessity of Satan's release as reflecting the divine orchestration of history, but goes even further than Tonstad in finding symmetry in this passage to various parts of the Bible. He answers his own question of why God would release the Devil after confinement by retorting to an alleged symmetry of apocalyptic history ("the end of the premillennial first creation anticipates the end of the millennial second creation"), symmetry between the beginning and the end of the Bible, and (contrasting) symmetry between the end of Jesus and that of Satan (Leithart, *Revelation 12–22*, 328-9).

[92] Azazel is bound and thrown into a hole in the desert, and lies there waiting, beneath rugged and sharp rocks, to be sent into the fire on the great day of judgment (1 En. 10:4-7). Semyaza and the rest of the Watchers are to suffer a similar fate when Michael binds them

> for seventy generations underneath the rocks of the ground until the day of their judgment and their consummation until the eternal judgment is concluded. In those days they will lead them into the bottom of the fire—and in torment—in the prison (where) they will be locked up forever. And at the time when they will burn and die, those who collaborated with them will be bound together with them (1 En. 10:11-15).

According to 1 En. 54:1-6, these characters are working as "messengers of Satan, leading astray those who dwell upon earth." A similar expectation is also found in the book of Jubilees, where the angels of Gen 6:1-5 are said to be "bound in the depths of the earth forever, until the day of great judgment in order for judgment to be executed upon all of those who corrupted their ways and their deeds before the Lord" (Jub. 5:1-11). These expectations connected to Gen 6:1-5 are reflected in 2 Pet 2:4; Jude 6; and possibly Isa 24:21-22 and 2 Bar. 56:13. As in 1 En. 54:1-6, the Satan/Mastema of Jubilees, too, is considered as a separate entity from the angels/Watchers/sons of God of Gen 6:1-5 (cf. Jub. 10:1-14).

However, it is in the character of Mastema/Satan of Jubilees that we find the adversarial equal of the Satan of Revelation: (1) his deception falls into the divine order of creation, as an indicator of the evil ways of men (Jub. 10:7-9); (2) the age of eschatological salvation is defined partly by his absence (Jub. 23:29); and (3) his binding and incarceration with subsequent release is done according to the divine control of things (Jub. 48:15-18).

[93] Koester, *Revelation*, 770-1.

[94] For a literary analysis of the similarities, see Aune, *Revelation 17–22*, 1078-9.

[95] Margaret Baker suggests that the release of the ancient serpent in Revelation 20 derives from the ancient New Year rituals. According to her, "every year, Azazel was banished and, as the story is told in *1 Enoch*, imprisoned in a pit in the desert until the last judgement (1 En. 10.4-6). Since this was enacted every year, there must have been some account of his release/escape and reimprisonment" (Baker, *The Revelation of Jesus Christ*, 358). It is unclear from her argument which New Year ritual she refers to that involves banishment of Azazel each year. However, the text of 1 En. 10:1-12 refers to the incarceration of Azazel, Semyaze, and their minions as lasting unto "the day of their judgment and of their consummation." Moreover, the only reference to Azazel in the Hebrew Bible (Lev 16:1-10) refers not to a banishment *of* Azazel, but to a goat being sent *into* the desert carrying

Of the sparse number of narrative analyses that have been conducted on this section of Revelation, few if any have proven helpful in coping with the unexpected release of Satan.[96] David L. Barr admits that the text is silent as to why Satan *must* be released, yet he finds part of its possible function in the presence of an allusion to Ezekiel 37–48 and the theme of overcoming/conquering like Christ on the part of the saints.[97] James L. Resseguie does not comment on the divine necessity of the δεῖ in 20:3, but he holds to a mere description of the release of Satan as part of divine pardon succeeded by justified punishment.[98] Within the motif of temporary binding of the antagonist, Michael Labahn has correctly identified an association, if not an allusion, to Jub. 38:15–18. Therefore, I find it strange that he fails to appreciate the implications of this allusion or association when insisting on perceiving Satan as a defeated enemy deprived of his powers.[99] In Jub. 38:15–18, Mastema is bound and released according to the will and purpose of God in order to show his strength by killing the Egyptians in the sea (Jub. 38:17; cf. Exod 15:17). As we have seen from the earlier allusions to the Exodus traditions in Revelation, the rhetorical point revolves not around the Egyptians but around the hand of God. In the book of Jubilees, the more shady business of this hand is referred to as Mastema. In Revelation 20 as in Jub. 38:15–18, it is not the deception of Satan that is in focus but those deceived/not deceived (Satan is removed to make way for the thousand-year reign of 20:4–6 and the results of his deception culminate in the judgment scene of 20:1–15). It is my distinct impression that Labahn fails to appreciate the subordinate function of Satan within the text and instead comes close to assume something of a subjective agenda of Satan when

---

the sins of the people *to* Azazel. Andrei A. Orlov has shown that the scapegoat ritual of Leviticus 16, later explored and developed in the Enochic traditions, is further reinterpreted and enhanced in early Christian and Mishnaic writings of the first centuries of the Common Era (Andrei A. Orlov, "The Demise of the Antagonist in the Apocalyptic Scapegoat Tradition," in *The Open Mind: Essays in Honour of Christopher Rowland*, ed. Jonathan Knight and Kevin Sullivan [London: T&T Clark, 2015], 201–23). A part of this enhancement is the blurring of the function of the goat and the receiver (Azazel) and/or the means of destruction (ibid., 214, 222–3). The apparent parallels to the Watcher traditions in the binding and incarceration of Satan in Rev 20:1–3 suggest that this development is relevant to one's understanding of the incarceration itself. However, as these texts do not mention any release of Azazel and his likes, and due to the general lack of any expiatory language in the characterization of Satan in Revelation, such a reading seems to be outside the scope of the text.

[96] See also Shane J. Wood and his insightful survey on how commentators have dealt inadequately with the release of Satan, often blindsided by theological bias or neglecting the issue altogether (Shane J. Wood, "God's Triumphal Procession: Re-examining the Release of Satan in the Light of Roman Imperial Imagery," in *The Book of Revelation: Currents in British Research on the Apocalypse*, ed. Garrick V. Allen, Ian Paul, and Simon P. Woodman, WUNT II/411 [Tübingen: Mohr Siebeck, 2015], 209–24, 209–10; Wood, "The Alter-Imperial Paradigm: Empire Studies and the Book of Revelation" [PhD diss., University of Edinburgh, 2014], 224–8).

[97] Barr, *Tales of the End*, 244–5. A similar conclusion is found in the commentary of Jürgen Roloff: "Why is Satan released from his prison? ... And how is such deception at all possible if the earth is directly subordinate to the dominion of Christ and his own? These questions remain unanswered" (Roloff, *The Revelation of John*, 228). Having said as much, he conclusively points out that the scene must be understood from the point of view of its central concern, which he finds to be God's cleansing of enemies and resistance from the cosmos (ibid.). In my opinion, this latter perspective does not contribute to our understanding of why Satan must be released after imprisonment.

[98] Resseguie, *The Revelation of John*, 244–5, 248.

[99] Labahn, "The Dangerous Loser," 168–9.

stating, "Satan escapes from prison one last time (ἐξελεύσεται), again a caricature that prepares ultimately for his decisive defeat."[100] It would seem that Labahn falls prey to his own preconceived misconception of Satan as "a powerless figure who was rendered impotent by God's power" or "one that can be described as 'the absolute anti-divine power'" in his encounter with Revelation 20.[101] I find no such "impotent" Satan within this text, or in Revelation in general, but a highly efficient tool of deception that has to be locked up in order to pave the way for the thousand-year reign, and released in order to usher in the final eschatological conflict. Furthermore, I find it hard to trace any element of autonomy, let alone subjective agenda, at play here—only divine distribution of the forces at hand. That being said, the severity of the fate of Satan *could* imply an element of punishment for his transgressions—the potential reference of hubris in Rev 12:4 is a probable candidate. The possible purpose behind the events of 20:10b will therefore be considered below.

Sigve K. Tonstad dedicates practically his entire chapter on discerning the storyline of Revelation from the perspective of the end of the narrative to the enigmatic δεῖ of Rev 20:3.[102] He points out how several readings of the text struggle to make sense of this surprising turn of events.[103] I agree with his assessment that interpretations of Revelation have often failed to give its peculiar ending its due, yet I find that his reading of Revelation 20 partly exceeds the text.

Tonstad initially argues that Satan is singled out for special attention by the events narrated in Revelation 20 on literary and narrative terms alone.[104] I agree with Tonstad on this point as it concurs with the points I made earlier on the presence of a chiastic structure in the presentation and removal of adversarial forces within Revelation 12–20. Satan is introduced first with the same clustering of names and epithets (12:9) as he is as the last of the three antagonists that are taken away (20:2), thereby forming an *inclusio* of antagonists presented and eliminated. Tonstad further argues that "Satan is made to stand alone on stage at the end of Revelation's narrative in order to place him in a separate category that is distinct from the human drama."[105] He is separated from the beasts and Babylon by his endeavors in Revelation 20 compared to their abrupt fate in 19:19–20. It is hard to disagree with this, yet at this point, Tonstad takes on an intertextual detour in order to support his argument that "as evil comes to an end, his role corresponds to the part he is assumed to have played from the beginning."[106] And by "from the beginning" Tonstad means from the day Satan deceived Eve in Eden. He

---

[100] Ibid., 169.
[101] Ibid., 168 and 157.
[102] Tonstad, *Saving God's Reputation*, 41–54.
[103] The list of Tonstad (*Saving God's Reputation*, 41–8) reveals how different commentators have tried to get around this interpretational obstacle by employing various reading strategies: it is a result of later additions to the text or a loss of interest/focus in his own text by the author; it is inserted to enhance the role of Satan in order to fit the mythical imagery of the scene; or it is included to demonstrate the sovereignty of God. Georg S. Adamsen represents a different category of interpretation with his neglect of the δεῖ of Rev 20:3 altogether (Adamsen, *Johannes' Åpenbaring*, 400–5).
[104] Tonstad, *Saving God's Reputation*, 48–9.
[105] Ibid., 49.
[106] Ibid., 48.

was the first deceiver to appear; therefore, he must receive special attention as the last villain standing. By identifying Satan with the fallen star of Rev 9:1, he can combine the two, a falling star with the throwing of Satan into the abyss (20:3), and thereby find in Isa 14:15 and 24:22 the allusions needed to further support his idea that the Satan of Revelation is derived primarily from the narrative of the Hebrew Bible, and only secondarily in later historical manifestations. In short, Satan is singled out for special attention because of his role as deceiver since the Garden of Eden, which implies "the significance of Satan above other characters on the losing side of the drama."[107]

In my opinion, it is possible and preferable to accept Tonstad's point of Revelation 20 singling out Satan for special attention on narrative terms without accepting this rather (textually speaking) excessive reading of the necessity of intertextual cosmic conflict coming full circle in Revelation 20. This is important in order not to lose sight of the narrative focus of Revelation 20—the sifting of humankind. If we perceive the text and its plot to reach its denouement by the event of salvation/judgment (Revelation 20–22), it becomes clear that someone else is left upon the stage alone—the saints (20:4-6; 21–22) and humankind (20:11-15)—not Satan. In fact, Satan has to be preliminarily removed—twice—in order for humankind to receive proper attention. In Rev 20:11-15, Satan is eliminated, and the objects of his deception are emphasized as standing alone on the stage, strongly suggesting their functions as main/lead characters of the plot. Satan plays an important role in effectuating the final judgment of humankind, yet his own elimination barely gets attention in comparison. His release and presumably his removal are presented as mere necessity. As argued above, there is no need to accept an assumed presence of a cosmological combat paradigm running throughout the biblical narrative in order to grasp the antagonistic features of Satan in Revelation. The subordinating monistic elements of the narrative are too many to render such a reading credible (see Section 4.4.2.1.1). This aspect of divine government is in fact derived from prophetic traditions of the Hebrew Bible, among which we find the oracle against the king of Babel (Isaiah 14). I agree that this tradition constitutes a probable implied background to the characterization of adversarial agents in Revelation (such as Babylon the Great, see Section 5.2.3), yet it does not warrant a dualistic interpretation of the function of Satan in the narrative. On the contrary, it supports the subordination of every adversarial encounter of humankind under God's sovereign rule as an expression of divine superiority (cf. 9:11-13; 10: 5-19; Isa 45:7).[108]

---

[107] Ibid., 53.

[108] Part of Tonstad's argument for attaching Isaiah 14 to the characterization of Satan involves the identification of the fallen star in Rev 9:1 with Satan (Tonstad, *Saving God's Reputation*, 50–2). Although stated in a different context, the conclusions of Stuckenbruck and Mathews as to why 1 En. 86:1, 3 is to be considered conceptually different from the falling star of Rev 9:1 seem valid here as well: According to them, "at the sounding of the fifth trumpet blast, the 'star' in Revelation falls, as a divine emissary, to whom a key is given for unlocking 'the bottomless pit' in order to unleash the destructive locusts (9:3; cf. 'the angel' with a similar function in 20:1–2)" (Stuckenbruck and Mathews, "The Apocalypse of John, 1 Enoch, and the Question of Influence," 211). I agree with this reading of Rev 9:1, identifying the star as "a divine emissary," as it concurs with the analysis earlier on the function of intermediary agents in the three septets of Revelation 6–16 (Section 4.2.2.2). This perspective in the text makes the rebel/hubris reading of Tonstad in light of Isaiah 14 unfitting to the overall context of Rev 9:1.

In the end, I find myself acknowledging Tonstad's own modified conclusions when stating that "the binding and release of Satan at the very least makes him an important character in the narrative."[109] He *is* literally singled out for special attention by the adversarial *inclusio* mentioned earlier, thus making this an intratextual feature. To elevate this to an intertextual level is in my opinion excessive and, furthermore, unwarranted by the text.

Although Steven Grabiner builds his narrative analysis within the hermeneutical frame of cosmic conflict derived from Sigve K. Tonstad, he makes a point related to the release of Satan that I have not considered yet. He argues that the ὀλίγον καιρόν (little time, Rev 12:12) and the μικρὸν χρόνον (little time, Rev 20:3) are not identical (contrary to the arguments of Beale and Aune), but argues rather that the reasons for the extension of Satan's time to wage war and his unexpected release probably overlap.[110] James L. Resseguie, on the other hand, suggests that the little time after his release (20:3) is the last section of the little time of the work of Satan on earth in 12:12.[111] In any case, the purposes of the two seem to overlap. Steven Grabiner argues that "time is allotted to Satan in both contexts in order that his character may be more fully contrasted with the character of Christ."[112] However, as the plot analysis earlier revealed, the conflict of Revelation 20 is not one of Christ/Satan or God/Satan, but humankind/Satan. Siege is laid upon the beloved city and the saints, deliberately excluding the element of Christ found present in 19:19. The character of Satan does indeed contrast Christ in Revelation 20, but not by the theme of conflict. Satan represents the path to judgment (cf. 20:12, 15; 21:8) compared to that of Christ, which represents vindication (20:4-6) and salvation (21:6-7). According to Craig Koester, the two contrasting periods of the latter half of Revelation, the three and a half years allotted to Satan on earth (12:6, 7; 13:5-7) and the thousand-year reign of the saints (20:4-6), "fit the pattern of presenting readers with contrasting pairs of visions."[113] It is a contrast from small to large functioning as a rhetorical incentive of choice. The wrong choice is motivated by three and a half years of Satan wielding his authority while the faithful are imprisoned and suffer affliction. The right choice is motivated by reigning a thousand years with Christ, while the main adversary is imprisoned and the beheaded are resurrected.[114] That the vindication of the saints is the focus of the section also seems to be the conclusion of Richard Bauckham when deducing from the contrast between the earthly kingdoms of the saints and the beasts/kings that "the theological point of the millennium is solely to demonstrate the triumph of the martyrs."[115] In light of the many imageries of contrast at play in the section, all of which fit better with the contrasts mentioned in Section 5.2 rather than the one suggested by Grabiner (i.e., Satan vs. Christ), the abruption of the thousand-year period serves to

---

[109] Tonstad, *Saving God's Reputation*, 44.
[110] Grabiner, *Revelation's Hymns*, 171; see also Aune, *Revelation 6-16*, 704; Beale, *The Book of Revelation*, 668.
[111] Resseguie, *The Revelation of John*, 175.
[112] Grabiner, *Revelation's Hymns*, 172.
[113] Koester, *Revelation*, 783.
[114] Ibid., 782-3.
[115] Bauckham, *The Theology of the Book of Revelation*, 107-8.

separate the vindication of the saints from the age of eschatological salvation. Earthly vindication of the saints is a necessary response to the cry of the blood of the saints (6:10–11), but it is not the age of salvation.[116] It is the release of Satan and his continued act of deception that serve to separate these entities—thus deeming it necessary (δεῖ) in the divine ordering of the events of history.[117]

Lastly, I will consider a more intriguing and bold explanation as to why Satan *must* be released in Shane J. Wood's concept of the Alter-Imperial Paradigm.[118] According to Wood, the release of Satan in Rev 20:1–3, 7–10 is not the result of a prison break or other unforeseen events, but a direct result of divine intervention. Satan is released by divine necessity (δεῖ), an event that is orchestrated by God (λυθήσεται). The purpose of this "does not surface in Old Testament allusions or theological schemas; instead, the picture is found in points of conversation with the Roman Empire," and more specifically, "Rev 20.7–10 depicts the release of Satan through a key conduit of the Flavian 'foundational myth': the Roman triumphal procession."[119] According to Wood, Rev 19:11–21 represents the starting point of the procession, whereas 20:7–10 constitutes the final part of the parade where the chief enemy leader is led in chains to reenact his own defeat.

A key element in Wood's interpretation is his insistence of Satan being released from only his prison, and not his chains.[120] The scene functions thus as a public display and humiliation of the leader of an already defeated enemy, culminating in his execution. Perceived this way, the release of Satan is the climax of a cosmic victory of God. It forms the centerpiece of the combat in the entire narrative. If the thesis can be proved solid, then he has solved the issue of narrative dissonance regarding Rev 20:1–10 to proponents of reading Revelation in light of a cosmic conflict between God and Satan. Yet, in my opinion, there are several problems connected with his reading as it is mainly based on arguments from silence. He invites the reader into a world of "ifs," gravely endangering his reading to the pitfalls of eisegesis.

---

[116] See also Culy, *The Book of Revelation*, 237–8. According to Martin M. Culy, Satan must be bound in order for God to keep his promise to the saints to rule the nations on earth (Rev 2:26–27), and released due to divine grace granting a second chance to humankind.

[117] A divinely imposed interim rule of various lengths occurring before the age of eschatological salvation is known from Ezekiel 33–39; 1 En. 91:12–14; 93; 4 Ezra 7, 28–35; 2 Baruch 29, 40. Robert H. Mounce seems to agree with Robert H. Charles's notion of the millennium as "really a late and attenuated form of the old Jewish expectation of an eternal Messianic Kingdom on the present earth" when stating, "The origin of the idea seems to stem from the eschatological expectations of late apocalyptic Judaism. In earlier times Jews pictured a messianic kingdom which would last on the present earth forever" (Mounce, *The Book of Revelation*, 357; see Robert H. Charles, *A Critical and Exegetical Commentary on the Revelation of St. John, Vol. 2*, ICC [Edinburgh: T&T Clark, 1920], 142). It functions thus as a mediation between the earlier eschatological hope of an earthly kingdom and the later idea of a transcendental kingdom. According to Richard Bauckham, the thousand-year reign depicts the meaning rather than the manner of the vindication of the martyrs by utilizing the idea of a temporary messianic reign on earth before the final judgment, derived from Jewish apocalyptic tradition (Bauckham, *The Theology of The Book of Revelation*, 108).

[118] Wood, "God's Triumphal Procession," 209–23; Wood, "The Alter-Imperial Paradigm," 223–56.

[119] Wood, "God's Triumphal Procession," 211–12. The term "foundational myth" refers to the narrative of victory of the Flavians displayed through means of enacted and static propaganda in order to "remind the empire of their justifiable claim to the throne" (ibid., 216–17).

[120] Wood, "The Alter-Imperial Paradigm," 233–4.

Firstly, his hermeneutical paradigm works only *if* we assume that the Roman victory parade is the particular background implied in the narrative. This is in itself problematic as the central elements of the Roman triumphal procession (as defined by Wood)[121] are not present in the narrative (the quadriga, the parade, the cheering audience,[122] the bound leader, the [explicit mention of] enacting of warfare, the final destination of the parade in the "emergence of the triumphant general,"[123] etc.). Moreover, we have some narrative elements present in the text explicitly tugging the reader in the opposite direction: the description of war activities in the midst of the "parade," and the climax of the whole scene, its final event, not being the "execution of Satan," but rather the final judgment of humankind (20:11–15).

Secondly, the implied background of the paradigm can only be seen as probable *if* we perceive the war imagery of 20:8–9 (and 19:11–21) not as a description of Satan's defeat but only as a reenactment of it, despite it being narrated as such and despite this being the first time Gog and Magog are described in the book.[124]

Thirdly, it is probable only *if* we assume that λυθῆναι (20:3) and λυθήσεται (20:7) do not literally mean untie, loose, and set free. Moreover, *if* one is to ignore the possible effects of the binding and releasing of Satan (deceiving/not deceiving) on the meaning of his binding/release: the total of verbs relating to his confinement is done in order for him *not* to deceive (Rev 20:3a), whereas his release is followed by his apparent ability to deceive (20:7–9). His resumption of his "pre-incarceration activity" upon his release indicates that this is a genuine release.[125]

---

[121] See the list of key features in the Roman triumphal procession in Wood, "The Alter-Imperial Paradigm," 237–41.

[122] If we are indeed to assume an implied reference to this being a reversed Roman triumphal procession, one would expect the element of public humiliation on part of the defeated leader to be emphasized explicitly. Keeping in mind that the public humiliation and judgment of Babylon the Great is granted the vast section of Rev 17:1–19:10, it seems out of proportion to consider an implied humiliation and execution of Satan as "the climax of God's triumphal procession" (Wood, "God's Triumphal Procession," 210).

[123] Wood rightly points out that "immediately after this context is the magnificent procession of the 'one on the throne' in 20.11–21.4" (ibid., 222). However, the introduction of the scene of judgment with the typical Καὶ εἶδον indicates that this is not to be perceived as additional detail to the previous climactic scene, but rather as introducing a self-sufficient part of the narrative on its own. I will argue that this part constitutes the real climax of this section of the narrative.

[124] See Steve Moyise, "A Response to *Currents in British Research on the Apocalypse*," in *The Book of Revelation: Currents in British Research on the Apocalypse*, ed. Garrick V. Allen, Ian Paul, and Simon P. Woodman, WUNT II/411 (Tübingen: Mohr Siebeck, 2015), 281–8, 283–4.

[125] The binding and incarceration of Satan are explicitly (20:3) done in order for him not to deceive the nations during the thousand years. Moreover, he immediately resumes these activities upon his release in 20:8. Clearly, deception is the primary purpose of Satan at this point, and I therefore find it strange that a dissertation solely devoted to the theme of deception in the book of Revelation as that of Wiriya Tipvarakankoon does not consider the reason for the deceiver being released and thereby reinstated into the service of deception (Tipvarakankoon, *The Theme of Deception in the Book of Revelation*, 77–8, 237–41). This becomes a problem of consistency in his reading when taking into consideration his numerous—and mostly textually unwarranted—explicit characterizations of Satan and related epithets as "God's enemy," "adversary," or "antagonist" (cf. ibid., 3, 33, 35, 36, 40, 43, 44, 48, 49, 59–61, 68, 85–6, 90, 122, 229–30, 239–40, and 247). His repeated emphasis on the ἐδόθη formula as constituting divine control and allowance in relation to the deceiving activities of the dragon and the two beasts should, in my opinion, warrant an investigation of the nature of this alleged enmity. For instance, Tipvarakankoon states that "the Sea-Beast is under divine

Fourthly, it is probable only *if* we assume that the apparent allusion to Ezekiel 38–39 in the reference to Gog and Magog carries no significance to the events of 20:7–10 other than "a banner announcement conjuring up images of a great Jewish battle with cosmic implications" as a reenactment of their defeat.[126] There is nothing in the narrative suggesting that the envisioned battles of Rev 16:12–16; 19:11–21; 20:7–10 are not to be perceived as visions of the last eschatological battle but rather as reenactments of an earlier victory. The language of these three battles is clearly derived from the scriptural traditions expecting a solid eschatological battle at the end of history (Ezek 38:1–6; Zech 14:2; Joel 3:1–17; 4 Ezra 13:33–34; 1QM XV, 1; XVI, 1),[127] not a reenactment of envisioned prophecy. Moreover, I think Wood neglects the "cosmic implications" of the Gog and Magog reference too easily (see Section 5.4.2.3). In all three final battle sections in Revelation, divine agents gather humans to fight the last battle, as is also the case with Ezekiel 38–39. It is hard to see how these strong scriptural expectations are not confirmed and described as eschatological fulfillment in Revelation but rather as implied reenactments of the victory Christ achieved on the cross.

Fifth and finally, the Alter-Imperial Paradigm as presented by Wood is probable only *if* one assumes God and Satan as cosmic enemies in the narrative of Revelation. This final "if" separates his reading from that of mine to such a degree that it deems them obviously incompatible.

However intriguing and bold this solution to interpreting the necessity of releasing Satan from prison after his incarceration is, it is simply contingent upon too many "ifs" to make the reading probable.[128]

This little survey of various hermeneutical options leaves us with at least three probable reasons as to why it is necessary to release Satan after his imprisonment. Firstly, it serves to convey the idea of God being in absolute control of the ordeal humankind is experiencing, by setting time and spatial limitations for the activities of divine agents. As an expression of divine control through binding and releasing of human adversaries, Jub. 38:15–18 rather than the Watcher myth serves as possible implied allusion. Secondly, it serves to separate Satan from the other adversarial agents by the literary device of *inclusio*, thus isolating him as the archetypical adversary of humankind. The names and epithets of 12:9 are repeated to leave no possibility of

control" and, quoting Roloff, "Even God's adversary can do nothing without God's tolerance and permission" (ibid., 122). About the beast from the earth, he writes that its signs were "allowed by God ... a great power that God allows," but still the seer does allegedly "expose that this power cannot be legitimated as that of God. Rather, this power is used as a parody of that of God and his prophets" (ibid., 171–2). If Satan and related agents are indeed the enemies of God through their deception of humankind, why does God allow, permit, and give them the means to do so? Moreover, why does God release the deceiver unless the activity is in some sense necessary? These issues are not sufficiently dealt with in the otherwise comprehensive study of Tipvarakankoon.

[126] Wood, "God's Triumphal Procession," 222 (cf. the analysis of the Gog and Magog reference in 5.4.2.3 below).

[127] According to Craig Koester, the use of the definite article (τὸν πόλεμον) "fits a context that recalls the well-known tradition of a specific battle with the nations at the end of the age" (Koester, *Revelation*, 659).

[128] I have not commented upon the presence of imperial imagery in the characterization of the rider on the white horse in Rev 19:11–21, despite it being a central feature of Wood's argument, simply because its presence in itself does not necessitate the presence of a triumphal procession.

mistake regarding the identity of the character in question. Seen from this perspective, the beasts and Babylon become mere earthly manifestations of Satan's works, which is fully in line with the hierarchy as described in Revelation 12–13. The dragon summons the beasts upon which Babylon derives its rule and authority. Thirdly, it is important in order to separate the time of vindication of the saints from that of eschatological salvation. All of these three functions can be deduced from the literary context of Revelation 20 in relation to the macrostructure of the narrative, but we have not yet considered the actual events of the extra interim themselves.

The third point above is achieved by the thousand-year reign (Rev 20:4–6), which constitutes the vindication of the saints (contingent upon the absence of Satan) being separated from the eschatological salvation (Revelation 21–22) by the final judgment (Rev 20:11–15), to which Satan functions as instigator and facilitator. In the narrative reading of Joseph L. Trafton, a fourth reason for the release of Satan in Rev 20:7 is found and explored in the actions of Satan: he is released in order to gather the nations for war.[129] Ezekiel 37–38 and Zech 14:2 (cf. Sib. Or. 3:663–668) are probable allusions behind the description of these events of the interim, suggesting that God is using Satan in order to achieve his grand finale. I will argue extensively below for the implications of this to the characterization of Satan.

When the thousand years have ended, Satan will be released from his prison (τῆς φυλακῆς αὐτοῦ, Rev 20:7). The term φυλακή is used in the message to the congregation of Smyrna to prepare them for the coming test. The Devil will throw some of them into prison (2:10). The presence of both the act of throwing (βάλλω) and prison (φυλακή) in both 2:10 and 20:3, 7, could suggest a motif of vindication by retribution present in the text (see Section 5.2.2). If this is so, then the focus of the reversal of roles is here being addressed rhetorically to the saints in order to motivate their endurance. The motivational force of knowing that one day the roles will be reversed is a powerful one in itself, but when the impact is enlarged from ten days to a thousand years, both intent and the symbolical nature of the text come to surface. This rhetorical element alerts us not to read any subjective function on behalf of Satan in this reference.[130] The focus of the thousand years is not the rehabilitation of Satan but the reign of the saints—an interim in which his services are no longer needed. The function of the abyss serves elsewhere in the narrative to separate the spatial sphere of the underworld below from the earth in a manner equal to the boundaries of heaven above (see Section 4.4.2.3.1). Movement across these spatial borders always has consequences for humankind. In Rev 20:7 the release of Satan from his φυλακή therefore functions in the same manner as a storage room where he is relegated to when inactive (cf. 9:1–21; 11:7; 17:8). After all, the whole purpose of Satan's imprisonment is to render him inactive. The notion of φυλακή as a reference to natural habitat, in agreement with one's characteristics,

---

[129] Trafton, *Reading Revelation*, 191–2; see also Thomas, *The Apocalypse*, 598–9.

[130] Craig R. Koester interprets the incarceration as an effort to rehabilitate Satan. However, his continued acts of deception upon his release indicate no change of heart, and he must therefore be brought to an end by the lake of fire (Koester, *Revelation*, 784, 788; see also Mounce, *The Book of Revelation*, 361; and Osbourne, *Revelation*, 711, for a similar approach to the necessity of Satan's incarceration and release).

is found three times in Rev 18:2. At this point in the narrative, the natural habitat of Satan is no longer heaven (cf. 12:8) but that of the abyss. Perhaps one can sense here the contours of involuntary dethronement of the accuser as his nature struggles against divine restrictions. Knowing he has little time left, he tries to make the best of it—perhaps his aspirations turned out a little too ambitious. Perhaps he had to be restrained by incarceration to fit better within the divine eschatological plan. The text says nothing of this, but such a reading could be perceived as plausible in light of the sudden shift in natural habitat.

Before we leave the incarceration of Satan, I will consider the possibility of the prison imagery (chains, lock, seal, and prison) as adding an element of autonomy to the characterization of Satan in addition to being a prerequisite to the reign of the saints. From such a cluster of items of restraint, one gets the sense of a prisoner not willing to step down from his office voluntarily, thus possibly indicating a conflict of interests. Initially, one has to consider the possibility of whether this too is a rhetorical expression of the vindication through retribution of the saints. However, the imprisonment alone would suffice to reflect the fate of the prisoners of Smyrna. The chains, in particular, seem to be reflecting a strong sense of zealous purpose in need of being contained by force in order for the agent not to cross the divinely imposed boundaries of its purpose. Such a function would be similar to that of the four "killer" angels who are also bound (δεδεμένους) to restrict their killing activity until the appointed time (9:14).[131] Furthermore, these items of restraint could also be indicating a personal refusal to accommodate the divinely imposed will/control. If so, then we would have another possible autonomous trait associated with the character of Satan, along with the possible hubris of Revelation 12. The strength of such a reading is that we would be better equipped to interpret the eternal torment of 20:10 by providing us with a just reason for it. The drawback is that the reading is derived from assumptions *about* and not *from* the text itself. Moreover, it creates a much bigger hermeneutical problem in making sense of the narrative in light of the cosmological implications of such a reading. How does the narrative make sense of a God endorsing[132] and collaborating[133]

---

[131] Such a zealous nature as a trait of the character of Satan can certainly be discerned in the eager accuser of Job 1–2 and Zechariah 1. In both of these texts, the zeal of the adversary seems both to be expected and to be exceeding that of God. A similar trait seems to be at work in Luke 22:31–34, where Satan is demanding to sift the disciples. The response of Jesus validates the legitimacy of the claim, as he prays for their success in these ordeals, not their avoidance from it.

[132] See the ἐδόθη arguments above and the release of Satan in 20:3, 7. The aiding of adversarial forces in Revelation is in my opinion best understood in light of the monistic cosmology of the prophetic traditions of the Hebrew Bible and pseudepigrapha, due to the many allusions to these texts and this being a common feature of the apocalyptic genre.

[133] With "collaborating," I refer to the function of Satan in the eschatological ordeal where he performs groundwork leading up to the denouement of the overarching plot of the narrative, discerning who is to be saved and judged. This is also the case with the septets in general where "good/evil" agents serve alike toward a common purpose. The comments above regarding 16:14 make a good example in displaying this feature. The adversarial trio gathers the participants on the judged side to face their destiny at Armageddon. On the other hand, the angel acts to dry up the river of Euphrates to make their goal accessible. The reference to this event as the τῆς ἡμέρας τῆς μεγάλης τοῦ θεοῦ τοῦ παντοκράτορος ([on] the great day of God the Almighty) makes the event antithetical to the drying up of the sea of Reeds (Exod 14:21–22), Jordan (Josh 3:13–17; 4:23), and the eschatological escape route of the faithful remnant (Isa 11:15–16; 44:27; 50:2; 51:10; cf. Jer 51:36; Zech 10:11; 4

with such an agent of affliction, if the nature of their relationship is antithetical, and God intends to punish him for this work in the end?[134] It fits better with the general rationale of the narrative that the binding of Satan in Rev 20:2-3 is done to restrict his force of nature (cf. 9:14) and is confined to a place fitting of said nature (cf. 18:2), until his services are needed again. As this is a preliminary conclusion derived from what appears to be the natural reading within its context, it will have to be reconsidered in the conclusions in Chapter 6.

5.4.2.3 Deceiving the Nations, from Gog and Magog

After his release, Satan will go out to deceive the nations from the four corners of the earth. This is the purpose of his release and reveals the central function of Satan within the eschatological ordeal of God. As Pierre Prigent puts it, "he is necessary in order for Christians to avoid the temptation of evasion, of musing about angels, of a theology centered on glory."[135] And, we should add, he is necessary in order for the nations to be deceived.[136] In short, for the ancient deceiver of humankind there is still much to be done. This continuing of affairs after the end of the thousand-year reign concurs with the comments of Richard Bauckham (quoted above) that the interim reign is a symbolical intermission, the primary function of which is to emphasize the vindication of the saints. The activities of Satan are thus to be perceived as the continuing and final stage of the "short time" of 12:12, coinciding with the events of the emblematic activities of war in 16:12-16.

An important detail added in Rev 20:8 is the epexegetical reference to Gog and Magog in relation to the nations deceived. These are names assumed known to the implied reader of the narrative and are therefore not explained any further. What could the deceiving and gathering of Gog and Magog add to the characterization, and thus the function, of Satan in this text? What is the symbolic point of reference of these names attached to the last eschatological battle scene of Revelation?

According to Sverre Bøe in his comprehensive study of the use of the Gog and Magog traditions in Revelation, its use corresponds directly to Ezekiel 38-39, albeit somewhat altered.[137] The alterations are in line with the overarching plot of the narrative of Revelation and present Gog and Magog as the eschatological, although human, enemies of the universal people of God. Both Revelation 20 and Ezekiel 38-39

Ezra 13:39-47). The point here is that despite the reversal of function (aiding the enemy rather than the people), the purpose (judgment) and the function, as an expression of divine intervention, are the same (see Osborne, *Revelation*, 590).

[134] The literary reading provided by John Christopher Thomas appears incompatible in these matters as he rightly identifies the divine hand behind the δεῖ and the events of Rev 20:3, 7, but at the same time clings to a characterization of Satan as the (arch-)enemy of God (Thomas, *The Apocalypse*, 27, 597, 607-9, 611-13). In his reading the divine necessity of the testing of the nations (ibid., 599) represents a stark contrast to his elaborate descriptions of Satan being judged rightfully in the lake of fire for such actions (ibid., 612; see also 595).

[135] Prigent, *Commentary on the Apocalypse of St. John*, 567.

[136] See also Thomas, *The Apocalypse*, 599.

[137] For a survey on the corresponding elements as well as the altered ones, see Sverre Bøe, *Gog and Magog: Ezekiel 38-39 as Pre-text for Revelation 19,17-21 and 20,7-10*, WUNT II/138 (Tübingen: Mohr Siebeck, 2001), 342-3.

lack the mention of assistance from any human or celestial agent when describing the defeat of Gog and Magog, attributing the action solely to the intervention of God.[138] (The descending fire from heaven is probably an element derived from 2 Kgs 1:10–14, which fits the general use of fire in Scripture as "the principal agent of divine wrath"; cf. Gen 19:24; Ezek 38:22; 39:6; Zeph 3:8; Sib. Or. 3:672–673; Luke 9:54; cf. 1 Kgs 18:38.)[139] This aspect separates the use of Gog and Magog traditions of Ezekiel and Revelation from other ones. It also separates the allusion to this tradition in Revelation 20 from the one of Rev 19:11–21, thereby suggesting that we have here a theological alteration to make a point: God is the one sending the fire. This theocentric alteration (from the Christocentric one of Revelation 19) could be the key to unlocking the implied meaning connected to the specific mentioning of Gog and Magog of Rev 20:8. According to Ezekiel 38–39, God uses Gog and Magog to prove a point by utilizing the imagery of the eschatological antagonist. The text is similar to the examples from the prophetic tradition mentioned in Section 5.2.3, where God raises an adversary to rehabilitate his people and proclaim his sovereignty to the nations. We have here an elaborate monologue—a violent display of power in the veins of the Exodus motif (see Section 4.2.2). As the similarities in context and situation in the two texts are substantial, the relevant issue here is to consider the possible function this reference is given in Revelation 20. What connotations does the hypotext of Ezekiel 38–39 carry over to the characterization of Satan in the hypertext of Revelation 20? The following elements of Ezekiel 38–39 seem to be of importance to the characterization of Satan by association in Revelation 20 in light of the competence of the implied reader as defined in Chapter 2 earlier.[140]

Firstly, according to 38:16 God uses Gog to his purposes: "In the last days I will bring you against my land in order for the nations to know me through you, I display my holiness to their eyes in you, Gog" (cf. 38:4, 8–9, 22; 39:2, 21–24). In this scenario Gog and the land of Magog are used as the vehicle of God's anger (see Section 5.2.3), in order to rehabilitate his people (39:21–29), display his glory to the nations (38:16, 23; 39:7, 21) and reassure his people of his might as well as the severe nature of their relation (39:21–29).

Secondly, the humiliating defeat of Gog and his armies is presented as an act of vindication for the people (39:9–20). They will receive retribution both through the physical harm (39:10)[141] and through the public humiliation of birds feeding off the bodies of their enemies (39:17–21). The zeal of the Lord for the sake of his name leads

---

[138] Bøe, *Gog and Magog*, 244, 347.
[139] Koester, *Revelation*, 779; see also Beale, *The Book of Revelation*, 1027.
[140] I write "seem" as there is no way of pinpointing with certainty the implied meaning carried over from the hypotext to the hypertext. However, it is a probable reading in light of the scope of this study. It is what David L. Barr refers to as an opportunity occurring in the gap that is always present between the signifier and the signified—a place where the reader can find a place to stand (David L. Barr, "Women in Myth and History: Deconstructing John's Characterizations," in *A Feminist Companion to the Apocalypse of John*, ed. Amy-Jill Levine and Maria Mayo Robbins [London: T&T Clark International, 2009], 55–68, 65).
[141] וְשָׁלְלוּ אֶת־שֹׁלְלֵיהֶם וּבָזְזוּ אֶת־בֹּזְזֵיהֶם (They will despoil those who despoiled them and plunder those who plundered them).

to the vindication of his people, as these entities are considered closely connected (38:19; cf. Ezek 36:20–23).[142]

Thirdly, God's utilization of Gog is expressed as something Gog must be punished for. Ezekiel 38:21–22 anticipates this with God entering into the process of judging Gog with, among other things, fire and sulfur. The transition from 39:2 to 39:3–6 emphasizes the dual function of Gog: as disciplinary rod of God to his people, and as the object on which he makes his name, glory, and holiness known to humankind. Perhaps a touch of hubris can be discerned in the high thoughts he thinks to himself (38:11–14), as his intentions will seem obviously incredible to those around him (38:13). Ezekiel 39:7 seems to interpret the actions of Gog as at least partly guilty of profaning the name of the Lord, as it is inserted in the context of God waging war on his homeland, Magog. The fate of Gog is thus much akin to the one of the Pharaoh of the Exodus, a motif we also saw present earlier in the septets of Revelation 6–16 (see Section 4.2.2).

The reason for these elaborations on the Gog and Magog traditions of Ezekiel 38–39 is to look for possible meaning behind the reference to Gog and Magog in Rev 20:8. An allusion to this tradition within the context of Revelation 20 seems to associate the fate of Gog and Magog here with that of Ezekiel 38–39. If this is the case, then here we again have an element of characterization by association present in the text. The important question is, then, what part does Satan fulfill in this allusion? If the cosmology of Ezekiel 38–39 is used to interpret Rev 20:7–10, then Satan equals the hand of Yahweh—the voice of hubris in the head of Gog (cf. Ezek 38:10–12)—forcing his hand to go to war against his people. This is tantamount to what the beast from the sea experienced (see Section 4.4.2.3.1), as it was given a mouth speaking blasphemous words (13:5) and authority to wage war against the saints in victory (13:7).

What we have in Rev 20:7–10 and Ezekiel 38–39 is a similar situation in which humankind is divided into two camps and God himself intervenes in battle with fire. Moreover, the people of God are vindicated by the defeat of the vast enemy, and the defeat is subsequently justified.[143] The purpose of such acts of divine intervention is complex, yet in both texts the elements of salvation to God's people and judgment of their trespassers are present along with the element of magnifying the name of and giving glory to God.[144] The function of Gog and Magog in these texts is to be the

---

[142] Leslie C. Allen, *Ezekiel 20–48*, WBC 29 (Dallas: Word Books, 1990), 207.

[143] The urban metaphor for the community of the saints is picked up again here, where the beloved city is protected and defended by divine intervention (cf. 14:20). Urban imagery is elsewhere in Revelation used in 11:2; the Babylon motif (17:18; 18:18) and the New Jerusalem (21:29), to emphasize the dichotomy between the two categories of people. Within this imagery, the defeat of those besieging the beloved city in Rev 20:9 represents another act of vindication on behalf of the city of the saints (see Koester, *Revelation*, 790). An element of justification of the fate of the armies of Gog and Magog can probably be discerned in the subsequent scene of judgment in 20:11–15, but also in the manner of their fate—fire from heaven and lake of fire being reminiscent of the fate of Sodom and Gomorrah (Gen 19:24–28).

[144] In Revelation this is not stated explicitly, but texts such as 11:13; 14:7; 16:9; 19:1 and 7 indicate that to give God glory is the proper response to such acts. Moreover, the eschatological ordeal seems to be paving the way for the glory of God, making his name known and his presence felt among humankind in Revelation 21–22.

vessel of God's purpose.¹⁴⁵ In Revelation, Satan is inserted between the arm of God and Gog and Magog, thus making him the prolonged arm of God. This is in line with the development of the character of Satan from the prophetic tradition of the Hebrew Bible into the unpleasant servant of God found in the pseudepigrapha and parts of the New Testament (see Chapter 1). The insertion of Satan within the tradition of Ezekiel 38–39 functions thus much like that of the transition from 2 Sam 24:1 to 1 Chr 21:1 and the function of Mastema in the book of Jubilees.

Unlike the beast of 19:19, the Satan of 20:7 is probably only facilitating the war, not taking part in it himself. The *inclusio* established by the references to the actions of Satan in 20:7 and 10 seems to imply a differentiation of Satan from those deceived/gathered in light of the them/they phrases in between (συναγαγεῖν αὐτοὺς εἰς τὸν πόλεμον—to gather *them* for war, Rev 20:8; ὧν ὁ ἀριθμὸς αὐτῶν ὡς ἡ ἄμμος τῆς θαλάσσης. καὶ ἀνέβησαν—*their* number being as numerous as the sands of the sea, *they* marched up, Rev 20:8-9; ἐκύκλευσαν τὴν παρεμβολὴν τῶν ἁγίων—*they* surrounded the camp, Rev 20:9; and finally, κατέφαγεν αὐτούς—[fire from heaven] consumed *them*, Rev 20:9).¹⁴⁶ This focus on his function as instigator and deceiver rather than aggressor is supported by a similar focus on the deceitful gathering rather than the violent intentions of war in anticipation of the same event in 16:12-16. In light of the implications of the characterization of Satan derived from the Gog and Magog reference in the text (see above), this separation in the action and fate of Satan from the humans involved (see Section 5.4.2.4) diminishes any alleged anti-divine function or intention associated with Satan in the scene.

5.4.2.4 *The Death of Satan*

After the battle, we encounter the final scene involving the Satan of Revelation. According to Rev 20:10, καὶ ὁ διάβολος ὁ πλανῶν αὐτοὺς ἐβλήθη εἰς τὴν λίμνην τοῦ πυρὸς καὶ θείου ὅπου καὶ τὸ θηρίον καὶ ὁ ψευδοπροφήτης, καὶ βασανισθήσονται ἡμέρας καὶ νυκτὸς εἰς τοὺς αἰῶνας τῶν αἰώνων (and the devil deceiving them was thrown into the lake of fire and sulfur, where the beast and the false prophet were. And they will be tormented day and night forever and ever, Rev 20:10). There are at least two aspects of this verse that seem to be of considerable relevance for determining the narrative function of Satan in this section of the text: the question of whether this is narrated as a judgment of the Devil and the meaning/function of eternal suffering *in*, as well as the nature *of*, the lake of fire. I will consider these in the following.

Are we invited to perceive the throwing of Satan into the lake of fire as *judgment* for his transgressions? This seems to be a given assumption for several commentators of this verse.¹⁴⁷ However, this almost unison perspective is challenged by the notable

---

¹⁴⁵ See also Gregory K. Beale when arguing that the scriptural prophecies behind the idea of a gathering of nations against God's people (i.e., Ezekiel 38–39; Zechariah 12–14, and Zephaniah 3) present in Rev 20:8; cf. 16:14 and 19:19, all "foretell that *God* will gather the nations together in Israel for the final war of history" (Beale, *The Book of Revelation*, 1022, see also 835 and 967).

¹⁴⁶ See also Trafton, *Reading Revelation*, 191.

¹⁴⁷ Adamsen, *Johannes' Åpenbaring*, 394, 411; Aune, *Revelation 17–22*, 1065–7, 1104; Beale, *The Book of Revelation*, 1028–31; Koester, *Revelation*, 782–3; Osborne, *Revelation*, 715–17; Thomas,

absence of such prejudicial hermeneutics in the two narrative commentaries that have been published on Revelation.[148] I dare to deem it prejudicial because the text is silent on the matter. The most important objection to seeing it as judgment is found in the singling out of Satan in 20:10 in a similar manner to that of the beast and the prophet of 19:20. In both texts, the adversarial agent is initially singled out to be thrown into the lake of fire. After this removal, the human combatants are killed by the sword of the rider on the white horse (19:21), whereas in 20:11 meticulous preparations are made for judgment. In both instances, the people rather than the celestial agents are singled out for special attention by being saved for last. This structuring of events indicates that the fate of the people is the primary focus of the text—the denouement of the plot. In other words, Satan is removed before the real action is about to commence. His fate is not of central concern here, but the fate of humankind is. This perspective is further emphasized by the place of confinement of the judged being the exact same location as Satan—the lake of fire (20:15). The main difference between the narration of the two fates is that the fate of Satan is expedited as mere routine (as also the beast and prophet of 19:20), whereas the fate of humankind is narrated as judgment.[149] In the presence of the white throne, everyone who has ever lived is judged according to the books of human merits and the book of life (20:12–13). Here at the end of the narrative, the presence of God is once more narrated by use of the throne motif, reminiscent of the vision of Revelation 4 (cf. 4:2). This resolution brings the overarching plot of the narrative full circle—a resolution devoid of elements of combat myths and anti-divine characteristics of Satan. Instead, we find a full-blown judicial scene emphasizing the purpose of the messages to the congregations. It is a moment of reckoning—a rhetorical incitement to the saints—reminding them of the severity of the trial that lies

---

The Apocalypse, 611–13; Witherington, *Revelation*, 245. Although the notion of the lake of fire as judgment is the predominant perspective in these commentaries, the judicial language is often accompanied by terms and formulations evoking the notion of elimination, destruction, cessation, and removal. See Campbell (*Reading Revelation*, 99–100): "finished off," "abolition of the triad of monsters"; Koester (*Revelation*, 782–3): "brought to an end" yet, still, "receiving his final sentence"; Prigent (*Commentary on the Apocalypse of St. John*, 577): "he is removed from the world forever," "no more place for him," and "eternity without resurrection." This could indicate an attempt to come to terms with the obvious tensions residing in the symbolic language of the section, where dragons, death, Hades, and abstract symbols of earthly empires are thrown into a lake of fire to prove a point.

[148] James L. Resseguie (*The Revelation of John*, 248–9) prefers the "imprisonment" reference of Rev 19:20 in his rather brief description on the matter. David Barr describes the event but does not elaborate on its meaning (Barr, *Tales of the End*, 244–6). The literary commentary of Joseph Trafton, on the other hand, raises the question of whether Satan is released in order to be punished (Trafton, *Reading Revelation*, 187) only to conclude that he was released in order to gather the nations for war (ibid., 191–2). In the end, he twice describes the fate of Satan and the beast and false prophet as both judgment and punishment (ibid., 193).

[149] One might add to this the words of W. Gordon Campbell, "Death, and not the Satan (20.14), is a curse afflicting fallen humanity from start to finish; as such *it* is the last enemy" (W. Gordon Campbell, "Facing Fire and Fury: One Reading of Revelation's Violence in the Context of Recent Interpretation," in *The Book of Revelation: Currents in British Research on the Apocalypse*, ed. Garrick V. Allen, Ian Paul, and Simon P. Woodman, WUNT II/411 [Tübingen: Mohr Siebeck, 2015], 147–74, 168).

ahead.¹⁵⁰ Who will remain faithful when facing the hour of trial that is about to come upon the whole world to test the inhabitants of the earth (Rev 3:10)? This is the hour of judgment, the outcome of the trial, and Satan is not part of it.¹⁵¹ He has played his part and has been disposed of prior to the scene of judgment. His disposal leads to the question of the manner of disposal—τὴν λίμνην τοῦ πυρὸς (the lake of fire).

The lake of fire is defined in 20:14 and 21:8 as ὁ θάνατος ὁ δεύτερός (the second death). There is no mention of a first death in Revelation; we encounter, however, θάνατος several times (6:8; 9:6; 18:8; 20:13; 21:4). The reference in 20:13 to death and Hades giving up their dead for judgment suggests that the term θάνατος represents a first and preliminary death. The second death thus represents the end of everything incompatible with the age of salvation, including the first death and Hades (20:14; cf. 21.4). The lake of fire is also the final destination of those not persistent in faith or repentant from idolatry. It represents the final judgment for those marked by the beast (20:15), but for those taking part in the first resurrection there will be no second death (20:6). This makes the lake of fire the antithesis to the age of salvation, but not in a dualistic (i.e., radical dualistic) way. It is the divinely sanctioned antithesis to the fate of the saints. This connotation of fire to the divine concurs with the use of fire (πυρός) elsewhere in the narrative, where it is used either directly or indirectly as a trait of the divine (1:14; 2:18; 3:18; 4:5; 8:5, 7, 8; 14:10; 15:2; 19:12; 20:9) or as a trait of celestial agents carrying out the eschatological ordeal (8:8; 9:17-18; 10:1; 11:1; 14:18; 16:8).¹⁵² Moreover, making fire come down from heaven is part of the signs that the beast from the earth performs in order to deceive the inhabitants of the earth (13:13). If fire is a trait of the divine in the narrative, such actions of the beast can be seen as part of the comprehensive imitation of the divine similar to the "aspiring trio hypothesis" mentioned above (see Section 4.4.2.3.2). Fire in Revelation thus signifies divinity, but also purification, and the imposition of judgment and/or wrath, in addition to referring to natural fire. If fire can be said to be a divine trait in Revelation, what then is the function of the lake of fire? Here our understanding of the symbolic language of Revelation is put to the test. As David Barr once aptly put it, "in what kind of lake do you burn a dragon anyway?" and moreover, "I note that within the story four characters are consigned to this fate: the two beasts (19:20), the devil (20:10), Death and Hades (20:14), and all those not written in the Lamb's book of life (20:15). What these four share is their utter incompatibility with the followers of the Lamb who shares his testimony."¹⁵³ The symbolism behind the dragon imagery

---

¹⁵⁰ See Culy, *The Book of Revelation*, 240-3, for a similar view on the fate of the damned functioning as a powerful rhetorical incitement to the saints.
¹⁵¹ Note how the aspect of the present participle ὁ πλανῶν αὐτοὺς (he who is [continuously] deceiving them), the aorist passive of ἐβλήθη (he was thrown), and the subsequent judgment of 20:11-15 indicate that the impact of the eschatological ordeal corresponds and overlaps considerably with the intensified presence and activities of Satan and that its outcome is measured out immediately after his removal.
¹⁵² Note how the reference to the intentions of the beast and the ten horns to burn the whore (17:16) are ultimately characterized as an act of divine judgment (18:8) (see also Ureña, "The Book of Revelation: A Chromatic Story," 419).
¹⁵³ Barr, "The Lamb Who Looks Like a Dragon?," 218.

along with the tossing of abstract entities like Death and Hades into the lake of fire suggests a symbolic function rather than a literal place of torment. Stephen S. Smalley suggests in his comments on how to perceive the dragon and its epithets that "John is referring to the devil's representative office as the *figurative agent of wickedness*, more than to his person" (my italics).[154] This is not the place to discuss the dogmatic problem of annihilation versus eternal, sentient suffering, but the idea of Smalley's fits what seems to be the main conceptual function of the lake of fire: it is the symbolical end of the prosecuting office—the mandate of Satan. Satan, along with Death, Hades, and all those not conforming to the new reign of God, represents something that there can be no place for in the coming age of salvation.[155] In Rev 20:10–15 we see the elimination of all things incompatible with the notion of salvation present in Revelation. Thus, there is no need for the satanic office in terms of deception and testing. The plot is resolved and a new era is about to begin. Intertextually, this is the envisioned fulfillment of a possibly assumed known scriptural expectation of an age of salvation without the presence of a Satan (Jub. 23:29 and T. Mos. 10:1; cf. 1QS IV, 15–19; 1QM I, 3–5; 11Q13 I, 13–15).[156] His removal by means of fire is possibly an allusion to the burning of the beast in Dan 7:11 and Beliar/l in T. Jud. 25:3; 11Q13 III, 7.[157] Despite fire being a common symbol of judgment in biblical, Jewish, and Greco-Roman literature, there is no precedence there of a "lake" of fire.[158] Still, the epexegetical reference to it as the second death (20:14; 21:8; cf. 2:11; 20:6), along with the tossing of abstracts entities into it, seems to indicate a symbolic transition from reality to a nonentity, rather than sentient suffering.[159] The latter would indicate judgment/retribution, whereas

[154] Smalley, *The Revelation to John*, 502.
[155] As Richard Bauckham aptly states regarding the tossing of Death and Hades into the lake of fire, which he defines as the opposite of eternal life: "Having surrendered all their dead, the dead they have held in safekeeping until the judgment (20.13), they have no further function in God's purpose ... they belong in the old order of things, with its mortality, rather than in the new order of eternal life" (Bauckham, "Judgment in the Book of Revelation," 76).
[156] The cosmology present in the book of Jubilees, the Community Rule, and the War Scroll all fit the suggested cosmology of Revelation as presented in this reading: In Jubilees, Mastema/Satan is allotted a tenth of the host of demons to be able to do his work, because the evil of the sons of men is great (Jub. 10:7–12). In the War Scroll, Belial is the angel of malevolence, who was created for the pit and rules in darkness, and whose purpose is to bring about wickedness and iniquity (1QM XIII, 10–13). According to the Community Rule, God "has appointed for him two spirits in which to walk until the time of his visitation: the spirits of truth and injustice ... The Angel of Darkness leads all the children of righteousness astray, and until his end, all their sin, iniquities, wickedness, and all their unlawful deeds are caused by his dominion in accordance with the mysteries of God" (1QS III, 18–23). My point here is to emphasize that my reading of Rev 20:10 regarding the instrumental function of Satan is neither unusual nor without precedence concerning cosmology. On the contrary, it fits well with the monistic approach to such agents of evil as explained in Section 1.1.1 of this reading.
[157] According to David L. Barr, the lake of fire is "a heightening of the vision of Daniel (7:11) by interpreting the fire that destroys the beast in conjunction with the Greek idea of hell as a place of fiery suffering" (Barr, *Tales of the End*, 247).
[158] Travis, *Christ and the Judgment of God*, 305.
[159] Stephen H. Travis argues convincingly with David J. Powys (*"Hell": A Hard Look at a Hard Question—the Fate of the Unrighteous in New Testament Thought* [Carlisle: Paternoster, 1998], 392–3) against Beale (*The Book of Revelation*, 1036–7) that the use of the term "second death" in light of its use in targums and rabbinic literature suggests "a state of non-being rather than a state of conscious torment" (Travis, *Christ and the Judgment of God*, 307; see also Wood, "God's Triumphal Procession," 221).

the former would indicate the liquidation of divinely ordained institutions no longer required. Moreover, the result of tossing ὁ θάνατος into the lake of fire (Rev 20:14) is that it will be no more (ὁ θάνατος οὐκ ἔσται, 21:4). This suggests annihilation rather than eternal containment.[160] Still, the context is more ambiguous than this. Even if the kings of the earth are killed in 19:19, and most probably are to be counted among those raised to life, judged, and thrown into the lake of fire in 20:13–15, they are later narrated as subdued, loyal subjects bringing glory into the New Jerusalem (21:24). In order to make sense of this dichotomy inside/outside the holy city, the lake of fire functions as the antithetical fate to that of salvation. According to Alan Bernstein, "for whatever reason, evil remains to the very end of the tour of the New Jerusalem. The symmetrical tradition conceives of bliss in contrast to suffering, the city and its garden in contrast to the surrounding plane, the new heaven in contrast to the lake of fire."[161] It seems that the main function of the lake of fire is rhetorical, and its purpose is to motivate the saints. This makes sense when taking into consideration that the vision itself is part of a grand narrative communicated to the congregations by John in order to prepare them for the ordeal that is coming upon the earth. Moreover, a reading of the lake of fire as negative motivation fits the vindication/retribution motifs we saw earlier dominating the pre-context of the text (see Section 5.2).[162] As such, the lake of fire becomes a symbol of dethronement/liquidation in terms of everything not compatible with the age of salvation, and one powerful rhetorical message of future separation and eternal death to the congregations not enduring the ordeal to come.

If we understand the lake of fire as both the closure of everything negative in this age as well as encompassing the possibility of not accessing the fruits of salvation to come—and if we understand the destruction of Satan as the liquidation of the "devil's representative office" and "the figurative agent of wickedness"—then the βασανισθήσονται (they will be tormented, 20:10) and its longevity (εἰς τοὺς αἰῶνας τῶν αἰώνων) must in some way be interpreted along the same lines.

Firstly, it is when encountering such rhetorically laden texts (20:10; 14:11) that it is important to remember the epistolary frame of Revelation. It is written as a message *to* somebody in order to promote desired conduct (holding fast to faith in Christ when facing prosecution and death). I believe it is from the perspective of these "somebodies" that the meaning behind the symbolism can be discerned to an implied reader. This means that the torment of Satan, the beasts, and those marked by the beast is intended as meaningful from the perspective of the narratées to whom the narrator narrates.

---

[160] See also Bauckham, "Judgment in the Book of Revelation," 76–7.
[161] Bernstein, *The Formation of Hell*, 260; see also Travis, *Christ and the Judgment of God*, 319–20.
[162] Stephen H. Travis argues with the words of Eugene Boring for a less doctrinal and more rhetorical reading of these texts when stating, "John's language does not deliver a doctrine about the fate of outsiders; it functions to warn insiders, who ponder the question 'Is it such a terrible thing to participate in Roman Worship?' John regards this worship as making a this-worldly substitute for the one Creator and Lord and answers, 'More terrible than you can imagine!'" (Travis, *Christ and the Judgment of God*, 307; see also Bauckham, "Judgment in the Book of Revelation," 79). To avoid misquotation, I find it important to state that Travis prefers a judicial reading of these texts to that of vindication/retribution (Travis, *Christ and the Judgment of God*, 308–10).

Secondly, it is the final answer to the cry for vindication from the blood of the saints for divine justice (κρίνεις καὶ ἐκδικεῖς, "judge and avenge," Rev 6: 10). The dwellers of the earth have shed the blood of the saints, and justice can be expected from a just God.

Both the fate of the abstract entities (Rev 19:2–3; 20:10) and their human counterparts (14:11; cf. 20:15) are described in the same language (eternal torment) and serve the same purpose. The same function is present in the fate of Babylon the Great. She has received her judgment from God, and smoke from her will go up forever. This calls for a fourfold hallelujah and praise of God (19:1–6) because ἐξεδίκησεν τὸ αἷμα τῶν δούλων αὐτοῦ ἐκ χειρὸς αὐτῆς (He [God] has avenged the blood of his servants from her hands, Rev 19:2). The eternal judgment of God upon the adversaries of the saints is retributive and worthy of rejoicing. A similar function can be discerned in the language of Rev 14:11, where the smoke of the torment of those marked by the beast will go up forever and ever in the presence of the holy angels and the Lamb.[163] They will have no rest from their torments (14:11), which contrasts with the eternal rest of the saints (14:13). This repetition of phrases (torment, smoke going up, eternity) ties the texts of Rev 14:10–11; 19:3; and 20:10 thematically together and adds to the conveyed meaning of these by the literary technique of cross-reference. According to Richard Bauckham, "a remarkable feature of the composition of Revelation is the way in which very many phrases occur two or three times in the book, often in widely separated passages, and usually in slightly varying form. These repetitions create a complex network of textual cross-reference, which helps to create and expand the meaning of any one passage by giving it specific relationships to many other passages."[164] If these three passages create and expand each other's meaning, then it makes sense to read them as conveying or

---

[163] The possible sacrificial overtones of the imagery of smoke going up from the carcasses of those tormented by fire in the presence of the Lamb and the holy angels add another possible rhetorical element to the vision: that the divine feels similarly about the enemies of the saints as they do (cf. Rev 2:6) (see Koester, *Revelation and the End of All Things*, 138). A similar combination of smoke, torment, and sacrifice (altar) is found in the introduction of the septet of trumpets (Rev 8:4), and adds leverage to this idea of torment by fire as both justified and perhaps pleasing (cf. 19:1–5) to a just and sovereign God. Here the smoke from incense and the prayers of the saints rising before God from the altar in heaven results in the pouring out of torment (9:5–6) and death (9:15), and serves in part to testify to the corrupted state of humankind (9:20–21)—thus reflecting some of the functions of Rev 14:10–11. Violent expressions of the idea of God taking pleasure in the torment and destruction of the enemies of his people through sacrificial imagery is a known feature of the holy war traditions of the Hebrew Bible, and constitutes a major component in the concept of the West Semitic ban (חרם, Josh 6:17–20; 8:26; Judg 1:17; 21:11; 1 Sam 15; Isaiah 34; cf. the Ugaritic *KTU 1.3 II*; *KTU 1.13*; and lines 10–12 of the Moabite Mesha Stela). In this concept, the annihilation of enemies was considered an act of dedication and worship to the national deity. The combination of חרם (Isa 34:2,5); violent death envisioned as sacrificial pleasing to God (34:6–7); torment and warfare described as both vengeance and vindication of the people upon its enemies (34:8); the presence of fire, sulfur resulting in smoke rising from the enemies forever (34:9–10); and the description of the entire event as the judgment of God (34:5)—all suggest Isaiah 34 as providing scriptural precedent and thereby a highly relevant hermeneutical lens for sacrificial language present in the imagery of war, violence, and torment connected with the acts of judgment as pleasing God in Revelation (see Gerhard von Rad, *Holy War in Ancient Israel*, trans. John H. Yoder and Marva J. Dawn [Grand Rapids, MI: Eerdmans, 1991], 49–50; Mark S. Smith, "Anat's Warfare Cannibalism and the West Semitic Ban," in *The Pitcher Is Broken: Memorial Essays for Gösta W. Ahlström*, ed. Steven W. Holloway and Lowell K. Handy [Sheffield: Sheffield Academic, 1995], 368–86, 379–83).

[164] Bauckham, *The Climax of Prophecy*, 22, see also 28–9.

elaborating on the same topic. If this is so, then the eternal torment of Satan conveys the same meaning as the eternal suffering of those marked by the beast, and of the beasts themselves. Furthermore, if the eternal suffering of those marked by the beast primarily functions to prove a rhetorical point for the congregations, then we should probably look for a similar rhetorical meaning in the eternal suffering of Satan and his colleagues as well. This makes the eternal suffering of Satan (and the beasts) a rhetorical thrust for the members of the congregations—another motivational element along the axis of vindication and retribution. As such, it adds to the already broad palette of adversarial necessity in the characterization of Satan in this text. This implies that the severe fate of Satan constitutes more a message to the congregations than deserved punishment for assumed crimes. Such a reading fits the function of (adversarial) necessity ascribed to Satan elsewhere in Revelation. Moreover, it is a reading that fits the monistic cosmology of Revelation in a better way than readings perceiving Satan as being punished for doing what he is (God-)given to do throughout the narrative.

Thirdly, the phrase εἰς τοὺς αἰῶνας τῶν αἰώνων (forever and ever, Rev 20:10) is used elsewhere in Revelation to describe the attributes of the divine (God lives forever, 4:9–10; 10:6; 15:7; Christ lives forever, 1:18; God is to receive glory forever, 1:6; 7:12; Christ is to receive glory forever, 5:13; God and Christ will reign forever, 11:15). The longevity of the rewards and punishments of Revelation bears this trait of the divine as an imprint emphasizing both source and severity: the saints are to reign forever in the light of the Lord and the Lamb (22:5); the smoke of those worshipping the beast and receiving its mark will go up forever (14:11); the smoke of Babylon will go up forever (19:3); and Satan, the beast, and the false prophet will be tormented forever (20:10). Alan E. Bernstein makes a good point when stating that "any fire that is long lasting, on a scale somehow conceived as comparable in duration to God, should also be eternal like God, though, strictly, nothing can be compared to him."[165] In Revelation, only God and the Lamb are "forever." When their rewards and punishments are described with the same trait, it is not to elevate the status of the rewarded/punished to the level of "forever," but rather to reflect the origin and contingency of the fate in question.[166] The element of severity and certainty surfaces when we take into consideration the

---

[165] Bernstein, *The Formation of Hell*, 258–9.
[166] This concurs well with the conclusions of Simon P. Woodman, who views the presence of fire imagery in Revelation as a sign of divine presence, divine judgment, and divine purification (Simon P. Woodman, "Fire from Heaven: Divine Judgment in the Book of Revelation," in *The Book of Revelation: Currents in British Research on the Apocalypse*, ed. Garrick V. Allen, Ian Paul, and Simon P. Woodman, WUNT II/411 [Tübingen: Mohr Siebeck, 2015], 175–92, 181–91). However, Revelation only describes humankind as explicitly sentenced by judgment into the lake of fire (Rev 20:11–15), whereas Woodman seems to conclude the other way around by insisting that the lake of fire is "the fitting end to those forces which seek to enslave humanity" (ibid., 183), and "the ultimate destination of the beast, the false prophet, the devil, Death and Hades" (ibid., 186). He only interprets fire as purification or cleansing on part of the humans envisioned suffering the lake of fire (ibid., 186–90). Moreover, Woodman fails to mention the aspect of hyperbole in Rev 18:6 as well as the voyeuristic element of 14:9–11 in his argument regarding fire as a fitting judgment. It seems, then, as if Woodman's hermeneutical premise—interpreting the violence of Revelation through a tradition of nonviolence—is forced. I will instead argue for a reading perceiving the fate of the lake of fire as divine cleansing of everything incompatible with the coming age of salvation, characterized with elements of vengeance, retribution, and judgment, collectively constituting a rhetorical thrust in order to exhort the saints to be faithful to the testimony of Christ unto the pain of death.

common denominator of the ones punished: those not willing to give God his due (glory, worship, honor, and reign), those shedding the blood of the saints, those testing the fidelity/loyalty of humankind, and the heavenly accuser. The very definition of the coming age of salvation (Revelation 21–22) reveals the redundancy of these characters. If we include the other inhabitants of the lake of fire, Death, and Hades, this becomes even more obvious. There is no need for death, much less afterlife incarceration such as Hades if the eternal future is devoid of death, suffering, tears, and so forth. In the age of salvation ὁ θάνατος οὐκ ἔσται ἔτι οὔτε πένθος οὔτε κραυγὴ οὔτε πόνος οὐκ ἔσται ἔτι, [ὅτι] τὰ πρῶτα ἀπῆλθαν (death will be no more, and mourning, crying or pain will be no more, Rev 21:4). The tossing of abstract entities like Death and Hades into the lake of fire as a means of extinction could be stating the obvious: Death and Hades are gone—forever. This mixing of abstract entities with human characters in the lake of fire makes sense as a mode of transition: from being to not being.[167] The salvific nature of salvation demands their absence, and as salvation is eternal, so must the absence of its antithesis be eternal. However, this does not explain the eternal state of the suffering of Satan, beast, prophet, and those worshipping the beast. As suggested above, this element can only make sense from the perspective of retribution/vengeance on behalf of those the promise of such is given to (i.e., the congregations/saints). This seems very much in line with the suggestions of John Sweet when concluding that the language of this phrase is liturgical, and

> Abstractions like the dragon and beasts can hardly be tortured, though those who build their lives on them may (14¹⁰). If Satan symbolizes freedom to sin and its consequences, this may be to say that the human drama is not an episode in the divine plan which can be simply transcended. If the blood of the Lamb's victory is eternal, so must be the smoke of Satan's defeat.[168]

The focus remains, even in the description of the severe fate of Satan and the beasts, forever on the human side of the drama.

From the perspective of this reading, the elimination of the satanic office concurs with the eschatological expectation of the prophetic voice of the Hebrew Bible and related pseudepigrapha. There is no further need for a tester of humankind, a heavenly accuser, or a deceiver to prove the evil nature of humankind. He is therefore removed *before* the final judgment, having fulfilled his purpose. The eternal torment of Satan, and that of his semi-abstract coworkers and those humans proved unworthy of salvation, makes sense from the perspective of those expecting vindication through

---

[167] The satanical characters of Revelation function as abstract entities (kingdoms/empires, clergy, typologies, etc.) characterized as singular characters, thus constituting some sort of middle ground between the abstract nature of death and individuals worshipping the beast. We saw earlier that the beast from the sea is characterized as the sum of all four beasts of Daniel 7 (see Section 4.4.2.3.1), and Babylon the Great in turn was seen to function as an earthly manifestation of the beast (see Section 5.2.3). Behind these entities, we have the dragon sharing the visual traits of the beast, clearly functioning as instigator pulling the strings. Finally, the false prophet reflects a promotional/marketing function that probably encompasses more than one person as a point of reference.

[168] Sweet, *Revelation*, 292.

vengeance (6:10–11) as well as assurance of their absence in the age of salvation—forever and ever.

5.4.3 Point of View

As Revelation 20 constitutes the very denouement of the overarching plot of Revelation—God's own plot as revealed to John—I have subdivided the point of view section of this chapter in order to emphasize the subjugated function Satan is given to that of God in this section.

5.4.3.1 *God's Point of View*

A reasonable question related to the resolving of the plot posed by both John Sweet and Sigve K. Tonstad is why Satan is not eliminated in one blow, and why not earlier in the narrative, instead of isolating him, binding him, and incarcerating him, then unexpectedly releasing him, ultimately to toss him in the lake of fire?[169] Why the extra roundabouts and elaborate detours? If Revelation 4–5 revealed the purpose and nature of God's eschatological plan, and Revelation 20–22 its fulfillment, why the many repetitions, detours, and elaborations of Revelation 6–20? "Why could this not have been depicted (why could Satan not have been liquidated) in one comprehensive scene? Because John is concerned not primarily with the end but with the swaying conflict of free choice in the present."[170] If Revelation were indeed a narrative about the life and fall of Satan, then its contents would seem excessive; yet as Sweet rightly points out, it is a narrative concerned with the choices of men. This is the primary point of view of the narrator focalized as God's point of view (see Section 3.2), and it explains why Satan disappears abruptly (Rev 20:10) before the thrones and books of judgment appear (Rev 20:11–15). It is not *his* judgment that marks the grand finale of the eschatological ordeal, but the fate of *men*.[171] As the denouement of the overarching plot of the entire narrative (see Table 11), Revelation 20 represents the climax of intent behind the ordeal of testing that is about to be unleashed upon the earth (3:10). The very presence of rhetorical incitement in the messages to the congregations witnesses the uncertainty as to who in the end will reign as conquerors with Christ, and who will perish in the lake of fire. This uncertainty is resolved in Revelation 20. The final judgment is the definitive answer to the question that constitutes the overarching plot of Revelation, thereby God's point of view. It is only in relation to this question and its answer that the narrative function of Satan can be discerned in the manner the text invites us to.

---

[169] Tonstad, *Saving God's Reputation*, 42; Sweet, *Revelation*, 293–4.
[170] Sweet, *Revelation*, 293–4.
[171] See also Gordon D. Fee's comments. Even though he argues for the lake of fire as punishment for Satan after having lost the eschatological battle against God, he emphasizes that this is not the focus of the text: "The judgment of Satan is not the whole story; indeed it is not the primary concern of the story at all. Rather, John's concern is with people; first with those who belong to Christ, and then with all the rest—those who have chosen to go the way of Satan" (Fee, *Revelation*, 286).

Satan's function in God's eschatological ordeal in Revelation 20 is presented to us in a language of subjugation. He is taken, bound, and locked away for a thousand years in order to restrict his deceiving activities (Rev 20:1-3). After this, he *must* be released for a little while in order to deceive once again (Rev 20:3, 7-8). Moreover, Satan, after having been released, deceives the nations with a specific purpose in mind: συναγαγεῖν αὐτοὺς εἰς τὸν πόλεμον (to gather them for war, Rev 20:8). This purpose is a verbatim repetition of 16:14, which provides us with the necessary cosmological context of the event. The angel pours the sixth bowl of (God's) wrath upon the great river Euphrates to make way for the kings gathered for war. The war itself is scheduled to take place on the great day of the Lord Almighty.[172] This characterizes the events of 16:12-16; 19:11-21; and 20:7-10 as a joint feature between several divine agents—beasts, dragon, angel, white rider, and God—orchestrating the eschatological carnage of Armageddon. In light of the apparent allusion to Ezekiel 38-39 (see Section 5.4.2.3), Satan functions here as the vehicle of God's will in preparing the final battle (Rev 20:8).[173] The satanic deception is thus controlled and subdued in order to fulfill its divine purpose in relation to the great day of judgment.

That Satan must be let loose for a little while is according to David L. Barr "a surprising idea that seems to undermine the idea of complete victory over evil; such surprises should cause us to reevaluate our interpretations."[174] This is common (hermeneutical) sense. However, in light of the overarching plot as defined in this reading and the cosmology derived from Revelation 4-5, this is not as much of a "surprising idea" as it is expected to be in light of its anticipation (cf. 16:12-16). It is deemed surprising and unfitting from a reading following a dualistic combat paradigm, yet it fits the monistic approach of this reading. From God's point of view, Satan is both the instigator of deception and in part the means to unleash wrath and destruction by leading the nations up to the camp of the saints and the beloved city (20:9; cf. 16:12-16; 19:19). The verb πλανάω (20:8, 10) suggests that even at this point there is an element of choice, thus sifting, at play. It is by such works of choice, probably in the veins of worship and loyalty, that humankind is to be judged (20:12-13)—to give in to the deceiving acts of Satan and his affiliated, or to endure/conquer.[175]

Still, the scene of Rev 20:8-9 also carries connotations of the pouring of divine wrath upon the enemies of God's people (Ezek 39:6; 1QM XI, 16-17; cf. 2 Kgs 1:10-14).[176]

---

[172] According to Gregory K. Beale, the background of the imagery and language of the gathering for war by God in Rev 16:12-16 is found in Zech 12:3-4; 13:2; 14:2, whereas a more general reference to the gathering for the eschatological war, as found in Revelation 16, 19, and 20, can be found in several texts: Ezekiel 38-39; Joel 4:2, 9, 12; Mic 4:11-12; Ps 2:1-2; cf. 4 Ezra 13:8-11, 34-35; 1 En. 56:5-8; 90:16-19; 2 Bar. 70:7-10; Sib. Or. 3:663-668; 1QM I, 10-11; XV, 2-3 (Beale, *The Book of Revelation*, 835-6; Aune, *Revelation 6-16*, 896).

[173] See also David L. Barr when locating the meaning behind the mysterious δεῖ of Rev 20:3 in the succeeding allusion to Ezekiel: "Why Satan *must* be released from prison (20:3) and why once released Satan again takes up this futile war and why nations still gather to his side are questions not taken up in this story. Part of the answer probably rests with the prototype of this scene, found in Ezekiel 37-48" (Barr, *Tales of the End*, 244).

[174] Ibid., 248.

[175] According to Pierre Prigent, "he [Satan] is necessary in order for Christians to avoid the temptation of evasion, of musing about angels, of a theology centered on glory. The threat of the monster still hovers over the world" (Prigent, *Commentary on the Apocalypse of St. John*, 567).

[176] See Beale, *The Book of Revelation*, 1027.

This adds to the function of Satan as not only the instigator of transgressions but also a contributor to the succeeding conviction and execution.

5.4.3.2 Evaluative Point of View

The narrative function of Satan in Revelation 20 contributes to the evaluative point of view of Revelation by utilizing the familiar rhetorical dichotomy of the carrot and the stick. On the one hand, to reign with Christ for a thousand years and not to experience the second death is the reward for conquering adversity in the manner of the Lamb (Rev 20:4-6). It is the reward for keeping the testimony to Christ unto death. The ones found doing so are to be kept from the activities of Satan (cf. 3:10) during the thousand-year reign—both through his incarceration and by the distinct separation of the resurrection and judgment of the saints (20:4) from that of those not written in the book of life (20:11-15). On the other hand, we have those marked by and worshipping the beast. These are to suffer both death by fire (20:9; cf. 19:21) and eternal torment in the lake of fire (20:15; cf. 14:10-11). The implied reader is guided toward momentary affliction followed by eternal bliss, and away from momentary conformity followed by eternal torment.

In light of such an evaluative point of view, the fate of Satan, the beast, and the false prophet (20:10; cf. 19:20) functions as a rhetorical deterrent. As the testimony of Christ leads to everlasting joy, the worship of the beast leads to everlasting horror. The rhetorical thrust of the section is hard to miss, yet as argued above, many commentators still perceive Revelation 20 as primarily the climax of combat between good and evil—between Satan and God. We must therefore ask ourselves what evidence there is to support such a claim. What anti-divine elements can be seen at play in Revelation 20?

Firstly, we must consider the possibility of the unwillingness of Satan to accept his fate, as suggested by the prison props of Rev 20:1-3, 7, which could be hinting at an autonomous will to oppose the divine restrictions. Yet as argued above (see Section 5.4.2.2), such binding could equally imply a zealous nature in the vein of the four "killer angels" of Rev 9:14-16 (cf. Job 1-2; Zechariah 1; Luke 22:31). Thus δέομαι (to bind) in Revelation does not equal enmity by necessity, although the possibility remains.

Secondly, we have the possible trace of divine enmity in the act of war itself. Waging war against the saints and the beloved city is in other parts of the Scripture bound to unleash the wrath of God on behalf of his people. As argued in Section 5.4.2.3 above, the allusion to Ezekiel 38-39 emphasizes and elaborates on several cosmological ideas by its presence in Revelation 20: God is controlling the course of events, Gog/Magog is used to prove a point related to disciplining/motivating his people and displaying his might to the nations (Ezek 38:16; 39: 7, 21-22), and anyone attacking the people of God will suffer his wrath. In this allusion, Satan functions in the same manner as the hand of God by constituting the very means of deception in order to facilitate war (the hooks in the jaws of Gog, Ezek 38:4; inciting voice, 38:9-10, 14; the direct control of God on Gog, 39:2).[177] In sum, the allusion to Ezekiel 38-39 in Revelation 20

---

[177] In the book of Job, the adversary is given a similar function—functioning as the extended hand of the Lord—when all of the misfortune bestowed upon Job, executed by the adversary, is described as the doings of the Lord (Job 42:11).

suggests that the act of war instigated by Satan is not expressing enmity toward God, but rather divine control. This perspective in turn provides us with a probable lens to interpret the necessity of releasing Satan from his prison, while the lens of enmity/combat does not. It also establishes precedent for the elimination of divine instruments of discipline after having fulfilled its purpose: both Gog of Ezekiel 38-39 (38:22) and the besieging army of Rev 20:8-9 are judged for their deeds (Rev 20:11-15 as well as the connotations of judgment in the raining of fire from heaven).

Thirdly, the everlasting torment of Satan could imply punishment, and since it is God who is ultimately responsible for his fate (i.e., ἐβλήθη, "was thrown," is probably another divine passive), any punishment from him could imply transgression toward him or his will. But, as argued in Section 5.4.2.4, the everlasting torture (by fire) of dragons, emblematic symbols such as the beast and the prophet, or abstract entities such as Death and Hades make no sense unless perceived from the literary function of the event. I suggested the rhetorical impact of everlasting torture as a hope of vengeance/vindication as the most promising lens of interpretation of this passage (similar to the one found in 14:10-11), rather than literal, sentient torture. This is supported by the initial removal of Satan *before* the thrones and books of judgment are presented for the implied reader in the grand scene of judgment of Rev 20:11-15. That being said, the scriptural connotations of judgment in the very imagery of fire, along with the possible reference to hubris in Rev 20:4 mentioned earlier (see Section 4.4), opens up for the possibility of an implied reference of Satan being judged for overstepping his divinely set boundaries.

Fourth and finally, if hubris is part of the characterization of the dragon of Revelation 12-13 (see Section 4.5), one could expect to find some trace or version of it here at the end of the earthly function of Satan. The element of hubris is present in the characterization of the beast from the sea, modeled after the fourth beast of Daniel 7, yet it was given to do so by God. In the taunt of Babylon (Revelation 18), hubris is the main reason for her judgment. Her hubris made her capable of transgressing toward the saints and believing she could go on doing so unpunished (18:5-8; 19:2). Yet, the power and impact of Babylon rest upon the beast of Revelation 17, which in turn relates its deceiving conduct to the dragon/Satan (12:18; 13:2, 12). In light of the messages to the seven congregations, the inclination toward religious conformity and possible apostasy is triggered and challenged by the presence of the imperial cult and its embedded threat of persecution. The hubris of the beasts and Babylon functions in light of the overarching narrative as an important element of the coming hour of testing (cf. Rev 3:10). They are abstract concepts encompassing the people harassing the saints. The apparent grandeur of the Roman Empire is thus portrayed as hubris—unwarranted self-confident human authority—the rival authority and path to that of Christ/God. The very purpose of the revelation of Revelation is to proclaim the one sovereign authority—the truth behind the reality as it appears. In light of this revelation, the evaluative point of view is to follow the path of Christ. The elements of hubris can therefore *not* be seen as a trait of Satan in Revelation 20 directly, but indirectly as a trait of several of his coworkers. The hubris element in the case of the beasts is something given in order to be able to deceive the dwellers of the earth—those not written in the book of life, but marked by the beast (13:8). It is logical to assume that the hubris of Babylon, which derives her reign from and rules "upon" this beast (Rev 17:1-2, 16-18), is somehow related to the hubris of the beast, in function if not in origin. Also, it is in function that it aligns with Satan, as the purpose of both is to test and deceive humankind. Any trace of hubris on the part of Satan in Revelation 20 can therefore arguably be interpreted as implied within the judgment of him in the lake of fire. It follows from the analysis above that this possibility is beside the narrative focus of Revelation, but it remains part of the semantical plethora of possible meanings behind the rich symbolic language and imagery of the narrative.

In light of this understanding of hubris as an efficient way of establishing a credibly zealous alternative to the path of Christ, and in light of the prominent language of divine control in Revelation 20, the idea of hubris somehow being the reason for the ejection of Satan from heaven as punishment seems far-fetched, yet possibly peripheral. Instead, we should probably understand this event in light of divine necessity. Several commentators have pointed out the possibility of Rev 12:12 and 20:3 as describing the same, or at least partly overlapping, period of time—a small temporal interim in which Satan accentuates his activities on earth before the final judgment arrives (see discussion in Section 5.4.2.2).[178] Although the texts in question are too ambiguous to conclude with any certainty on the matter, both events seem to be governed by divine necessity according to their relation to the overarching plot of the narrative. Any further overlap between the two sections would thus add to this conclusion, as the ejection of Satan of Revelation 12 then would be the object to the δεῖ of Rev 20:3.

Seen from the evaluative point of view, the function of the Satan of Revelation 20 corresponds directly with the overarching plot by deceiving and dividing up humankind until the day of judgment arrives. This function is clearly intended to evoke antipathy in the implied reader against Satan and the course of action advocated by him. He is not functioning as an enemy of God, but one of humankind. He clearly represents the wrong course of action (20:15; cf. 14:10–11) as opposed to that of being faithful to the testimony of Christ unto death (20:4–5).

5.5 Concluding Remarks

Revelation 20 contains the last explicit references to Satan in the narrative. He is removed from the stage before the grand finale of the narrative hits the reader: the eschatological division of humankind into the categories of judged and saved. Up to this point, Satan has functioned as instigator, facilitator, and tempter/deceiver, but after having fulfilled these purposes, his office is liquidated; left upon the stage are the real stars of the drama. As the function of Satan appeared more and more subjugated to the will and plan of God, the main issue in the question of the analysis was whether his characterization revealed any degree of autonomy or not. Could Revelation 20 reveal an oppositional subjective will behind the character of Satan that could explain the

---

[178] Aune, *Revelation 6–16*, 704; Beale, *The Book of Revelation*, 668, 993; Prigent, *Commentary on the Apocalypse of St. John*, 567; Resseguie, *Revelation of John*, 175.

concept of what Henry Ansgar Kelly refers to as a "retrofitted understanding" of Satan as the enemy of God?[179]

In the analysis of the literary context of Revelation 20, we saw several binary word pairs constituting a rhetorical dichotomy aimed at influencing the loyalty of the narratées: whore/bride, vindication/retribution, the two suppers, and the antithetical parallelism of the two cities (Babylon/the New Jerusalem). Revelation 20 constitutes a preliminary conclusion to this tension, preceding the ushering of eschatological salvation and the descent of the New Jerusalem. In Revelation 20, we are presented with the preliminary rewards of holding on to the faith in Christ, and the punishment awaiting those giving in to the temptations of momentary bliss.

As opposed to Revelation 12–13, the Satan of Revelation 20 is *not* the center of attention. True, he is the common denominator tying the various parts of the chapter together, and the chapter concludes his narrative that starts in the messages to the congregations.[180] However, the two main events that clearly constitute the main issues at stake in the chapter are the vindication of the saints by reigning with Christ for a thousand years (20:4–6) and the judgment of the dwellers of the earth (20:11–15). This is the denouement of the plot of the entire narrative of Revelation—the outcome of the eschatological ordeal by the sifting of humankind. To this event, the function of Satan is twofold: to abstain from deceiving during the reign of the saints, and then to resume deceiving again unto the final judgment.

The binding and incarceration of Satan are done prior to the establishing of the reign of the saints on earth. The binding and release respectively precede and succeed the reign, thus indicating the absence of Satan as a prerequisite to the establishing of the thousand-year kingdom. The prison imagery indicates an element of unwillingness, similar to the anger of the zealous dragon of Revelation 12 knowing that he has little time. This unwillingness was seen as the best explanation for the necessity of binding and restraining a celestial agent in order to contain its activity for a limited period, and not necessarily a sign of anti-divine enmity. The angels of destruction bound at the river Euphrates (9:14–15) and the confinement of Abaddon/Apollyon and his armies (9:1–11) represent other celestial agents in need of restriction in light of their function in the divine plan—possibly due to their zealous nature.[181] A similar expression of control through binding and releasing of a celestial adversarial character was found

---

[179] Kelly, *Satan: A Biography*, 2.
[180] Prigent, *Commentary on the Apocalypse of St. John*, 554.
[181] Sverre Aalen argues convincingly regarding the abyss not referring to a demonic or devilish sphere, but rather as being seen as part of the divine creation, and hence, its distribution of it: "I og for seg er ikke avgrunnens krefter onde, men de er farlige når de slippes løs. Men det er Gud som er herre over avgrunnen og som derfor bestemmer om den skal åpnes ... Det som kommer fra avgrunnen, er ikke i og for seg demonisk, men i høyden mektig og farlig, krefter som *kan* misbrukes" (In and of itself the forces of the abyss are not evil, but they are dangerous when unleashed. But it is God that is Lord of the abyss and thereby decides whether it shall be opened ... That which comes from the abyss is not in itself demonic, but at best powerful and dangerous, forces that *can* be misused) (Sverre Aalen, "Helveteslæren i Bibelen og i religionshistorisk sammenheng," in *Bakenfor Inferno*, ed. John Nome [Oslo: Lutherstiftelsen, 1955], 7–32, 29–31). Consequently, neither Apollyon, his army of locusts, nor the beast from the abyss are in themselves evil, but rather dangerous forces that can be used by both God and the Devil (ibid., 30–2).

in the character of Mastema in the book of Jubilees. This provided us with a highly relevant precedent for our reading and supports its probability in light of the implied reader as defined in Chapter 2.

In light of the overarching plot, the somewhat unexpected temporarily release of Satan (20:3) was found to have several functions: Firstly, it concludes the chiastic structure of the entrance and exit of adversarial agents related to Satan. Satan is separated from other agents as the last adversary of humankind to be eliminated, before the inauguration of eschatological salvation. Secondly, it separates the vindication of the saints from the age of eschatological salvation by inserting just reasons for the final judgment as facilitated by Satan in the deception of the nations. Thirdly, it reveals the sovereignty of God in relation to that of adversaries in the narrative. In the allusion to the Gog and Magog tradition in Rev 20:8, Satan functions as the voice of hubris by being the device deceiving them into besieging the saints and the beloved city. Finally, the temporary release of Satan enhances his function as constituting the wrong course of action. The final judgment succeeds his deception of the nations, suggesting the events preceding the judgment as the reasons for judgment following them (cf. 19:11–21). This element is concluded by the fate of the judged, which is to share the fate of their deceiver. The difference is slight but important: Satan is removed, whereas those who fail the eschatological test are judged.

We saw in the analysis and concluding remarks of Chapter 4 that the removal of Satan was seen as a precondition to the ushering in of the age of salvation. In both the Hebrew Scriptures as well as in Revelation, the very nature of salvation is defined by his absence. Still, the violent nature of the demise of Satan (and beasts), accompanied by the apparent lack of explanation, prompted the question of whether this is to be considered as punishment for certain trespasses or not. Revelation 20 gives no explicit answer to this and leaves us to contextual deduction and the uncertainty of possible intertextual allusions as the basis for our reading. The results of the analysis boiled down to two possible readings as to why Satan had to be removed in such a violent way: punishment for his acts of hubris and/or rhetorical impact to the addressees of the narrative. The former reading is supported by the indirect association to Satan by the hubris of Babylon the Great, which in turn would support the hubris thesis as the reason for the ejection of Satan in Revelation 12 (see Section 4.5). Both could explain the severity of the fate as well as provide us with an explanation as to why Michael waged war on the dragon in the first place. The main weakness with such a reading is that the liquidation of Satan in Revelation 20 is not only devoid of judicial language and imagery, but his fate is explicitly separated from the judicial scene of the chapter (Rev 20:11–15). Moreover, the strong language of subjugation of the satanic office under divine authority in Revelation in general, present in the binding and subsequent release of Satan of Revelation 20, indicates a cosmology diverging from the dualistic, anti-divine element that would follow from a prisoner/judged/condemned characteristic of Satan. This is further supported by the Gog and Magog reference, in which Satan functions as the voice of hubris in Gog rather than the rebellious kings besieging the beloved city and the saints. According to the allusion to Ezekiel 38–39 and the emblematic presentation of his event in Rev 16:12–16, the purpose of Satan is to gather the nations for war. When this is done, the rest is mere formalities. In Rev

16:17 the outcome is of no interest, thus not narrated, thereby suggesting the gathering itself as the main issue. In Revelation 20 the Devil is tossed into the lake of fire, to leave the center of attention to the fate of those gathered. The war party is initially killed by fire from heaven and then revived in order to be judged (20:9, 11–15). A similarly explicit separation of fates was also found present in the war scene of Rev 19:11–21, whereas the fate and possibly the inclination (see Section 4.2.2.2) of celestial agents of deception/gathering are neglected in the emblematic reference of the scene in 16:17–21.[182]

The special attention given to the fate of humankind in these scenes of war aligns with the overarching plot of Revelation and constitutes the main perspective of the narrative. This is also the case with Revelation 20, as the main events of this chapter are the vindication of the saints and the judgment of the dwellers of the earth—*not* the eternal torment of Satan. Seen from this perspective, rhetorical necessity represents a more probable explanation for the violent nature of the exit of Satan. The end of Satan coincides with the consummation of the eschatological ordeal. The judgment of the dwellers of the earth and the inauguration of the age of eschatological salvation are the final events of the narrative, in both of which Satan is deemed unnecessary. The violent nature of the liquidation of the satanic office, eternal torment in the lake of fire, is given no explanation in itself, but seen from the perspective of the suffering saints it conveys a rhetorical incentive as well as the definitive answer to the cry for vengeance in Rev 6:10–11.

The Satan of Revelation 20 is thus removed by mere necessity in order for salvation to be devoid of his presence, while the violent nature of his removal is best understood as rhetorical. If this is the case, then Satan has been used and subsequently removed like Gog from the land of Magog in Ezekiel 38–39, and thus functions as a pawn in the game concerning the main objects of the text—humankind. This leads to the preliminary conclusion that due to the subordinated function he is given, there is no obvious anti-divine autonomy present in the characterization of Satan in Revelation 20.

---

[182] Note how the focus of the effects of the events are exclusively concerned with the great city of Babylon (16:19) and the people suffering and blaspheming because of the earthquake and the hailstones (16:18, 21), whereas the dragon, the beast, and the false prophet indirectly responsible for assembling the kings and nations at Armageddon (16:13) go unnoticed.

6

Conclusion

According to Adam Kotsko, of the three paradigms developed in the Hebrew Bible in dealing with the problem of evil in changing historical circumstances, the hostile earthly ruler of what he refers to as the apocalyptic paradigm is identified as Satan, God's cosmic enemy.[1] This is a bold conclusion, and Kotsko later finds himself in need of modifying his own premise when stating, "to the extent that he relieves God of responsibility for unjust suffering, he also diminishes God's power and control. Yet insofar as the devil's wickedness is inscribed into God's mysterious plan as a necessary element, it becomes more and more difficult to avoid attributing his deeds directly to God, undermining God's goodness."[2] As theodicy, the apocalyptic paradigm, as defined by Kotsko above, is worthless, or could even be stated to be counterproductive, in that it diminishes God's character and sovereignty rather than relieves him of responsibility for unjust suffering.[3] In the analytical chapters of this reading, I have found such a paradigm to be foreign to the book of Revelation. The literary function assigned to Satan in Revelation is a subordinate one, much more akin to the prophetic paradigm of Kotsko than his so-called apocalyptic one. This should not come as a surprise to anyone aware of the close affinity of Revelation to the Hebrew Bible in general, and the prophetic literature in particular. The Satan of Revelation functions as a divine agent participating in the eschatological ordeal of the sovereign Lord God almighty, resembling in many ways the raising of adversaries by Yahweh in the Hebrew Bible. He is the most prominent of the adversaries of the congregations, presented as something to be dreaded, expected to be working in their midst, and in the end persevered with

---

[1] Kotsko sees in the Hebrew Bible three paradigms of dealing with evil: The Deuteronomistic paradigm identifies the earthly ruler as a potential rival of God (for instance, the Pharaoh of the Exodus tradition) and sees the suffering of the people as God's punishment. The prophetic paradigm sees the hostile earthly ruler as the unwitting tool of God (for instance, Nebuchadnezzar of Jer 25:9 and the Assyrians of Isa 10:5) and the suffering of the people as purification. In the apocalyptic paradigm, the earthly ruler is identified as God's cosmic enemy (for instance, Antiochus Epiphanes in the book of Daniel) and suffering is an unjust but necessary part of the divine plan. The unjust suffering excludes the ruler from absolution even if repentant, as could be seen from Antiochus's terrible fate (2 Maccabees 9). According to Kotsko, the apocalyptic enemy, between the Maccabean and early Christian periods, came to be "clearly identified as our familiar figure of Satan or the devil" (Kotsko, *The Prince of This World*, 44–5).

[2] Ibid., 45–6.

[3] See also Ryan E. Stokes's comments on how the transition from 2 Sam 24:1 to 1 Chr 21:1 does not detach God from the census plan (Stokes, "The Devil Made David Do It," 99–100).

unto death. Moreover, his increased activity toward the end time is an important part of the ushering in of the dawn of salvation by the means of the suffering of the saints. Events that have been awaited and expected for a long time are now being fulfilled by and through the hour of trial they are experiencing.

In the chapter on the messages to the seven congregations, I found that the messages function both as an introduction as well as a frame of interpretation to the rest of the book. They constitute a microcosm of the visionary world of Revelation. The Satan found in this section is thus reflected in the visionary section of the book, and vice versa. The initial position of this section suggests its primary function as a lens of interpretation as it constitutes the first encounter with the reader of the plot of the narrative of Revelation. Accordingly, this reading perceives the cosmology of Revelation 2–3 as governing the one of chapters 12–13 and 20, rather than (as Michael Labahn, Sigve Tonstad, and Steven Grabiner suggest) allowing the possible presence of cosmic conflict in the vein of the ancient combat myth in Revelation 12 to define the plot of the narrative. Perceiving Revelation 12 as an elaboration of the problem of the seven congregations defines the problem of the narrative in the human sphere rather than the celestial. Accordingly, the subject, protagonist, and main contestant to the problem at hand becomes humankind, and not Christ, Michael, or God. In Revelation 2–3, the opponent is Satan—the tester and adversary in and of the congregations. The challenge of the saints is to prevail and endure the hour of affliction and testing that God/Christ is about to send upon this earth (Rev 3:10). Satan forms a natural part of this ordeal (cf. 2:10). Furthermore, he represents the more convenient alternative of both internal challenges of diverging religious parties (2:6, 14–16, 20–25) and external ones imposed directly or indirectly by representatives from local government (2:9–10, 13). The subjugated function of Satan to that of God/Christ is essential in the humiliation of the local adversaries of the congregation of Philadelphia. They will be forced to humble themselves to the congregation in order for them to understand that God/Christ loves the saints (3:9). Because of their faithful endurance, the congregation of Philadelphia will be spared from the coming hour of trial (3:10), in which Satan is playing a considerable part. Here we have a disciplining, punishing, and rewarding utilization of human adversaries closely associated with Satan as well as a clear-cut example of the subjugation of the eschatological ordeal as something orchestrated by the firm hand of God/Christ. The God/Christ of the messages is characterized in monistic terms, an element further emphasized in the throne vision (Revelation 4–5), and controls every power at its disposal in reproving and disciplining humankind in order to motivate the right choice of conduct (3:19). The cosmological implications of the messages to the seven congregations to the rest of the book is monumental and leaves little or no room for perceiving Satan as the enemy of God, but rather as a means to an end. This was further confirmed by the interchangeability of divine actants of adversity, affliction, and punishment in the messages. Their oppositional function is subjugated to their function to the plot—it does not constitute the plot itself. In other words, the main question of the narrative is how the saints and humankind in general respond to the hour of trial, not whether or not Satan will succeed in usurping the throne of God.

The Christological predications introducing each message serve to underscore who is revealing, controlling, and orchestrating this coming hour of trial. Similarly, the closing references to the final section of the book regarding punishment and rewards signal the purpose of revelation: a rhetorical incitement to its implied readers in order for them to make the right choice by exhibiting affiliation through loyalty. This is the microcosm of the book of Revelation—this is what revelation is all about. Subsequently, when bringing this as a starting point of the interpretation of Revelation 12–13, the element of cosmic conflict is downplayed in favor of a transcendental interpretation of a local conflict. In this core section of the book, I found three parallel subplots revolving around the death and vindication of Christ and the saints. The key element combining the three was found to be time, as the events of the vision were simultaneously present and near future for the saints in question. The afflictions of the saints in the present contribute directly to the liquidation of the satanic office (Rev 12:10–12), which in turn constitutes the main rhetorical incitement of the section. The events of Revelation 12–13 correspond directly to the concept of the hour of trial in Rev 3:10, and the function of Satan is thus the same. This subjugated function of Satan resonates in Revelation 12–13 through the characterization of him by several allusions to various traditions of the Hebrew Bible (the book of Daniel, the dragon imagery, Michael as the eschatological warrior, and the coming of the eschatological antagonist). This is further supported by the consistent use of the aorist passive and divinely imposed time limitations on the actions of the beasts in Revelation 13. Finally, the subjugation of Satan and related forces align with the function of opponent to the overall plot of the narrative, in the same manner found in a smaller scale in the messages to the seven congregations. This is the eschatological test of loyalty. However, as Antipas was the only reported casualty in the messages (2:13), we see in Revelation 12–13 a more severe situation in that anyone not worshipping the beast will be put to death (13:15). The vision is intensified and it is reported from a gradually more vertical angle. The reader is presented with a transcendental perspective on the present as well as anticipated future of the congregations. This perspective allows for a more elaborate characterization of the adversaries of the saints. The vision is more elaborate and intensified from that of the messages to the congregations, yet the function of the opponents is the same. They represent earthly adversaries, perceived from a vertical perspective, to be overcome by the saints. The plot is the same, and the potential outcome remains equally decisive: one is either written in the book of life or carries the mark of the beast.

The repeated admonition to conquer found in the messages is further explained in 12–13, and 12:10–12 in particular. Not only is perseverance through affliction the main vehicle of salvation, but it is also the means of defeating one's adversaries. This defeat is anticipated in the ejection of the dragon from heaven but is to be fully accomplished in Revelation 20. When Satan has fulfilled his function, and humankind has either passed or failed the eschatological ordeal, his services are no longer needed, and he is removed from office.

In Revelation 20, Satan is singled out for last by his incarceration during the earthly thousand-year reign of the victors. His subsequent release can appear as unexpected when perceived from a God/Christ versus Satan point of view, but it fits well with this reading's point of view. Firstly, Satan is separated from other adversarial agents and given special attention, as he is the main antagonist of the protagonists of the narrative—the last adversary to be removed before the age of salvation is ushered in. Secondly, he serves as an inserted wedge, separating the vindication of the saints from the eschatological judgment/salvation. Thirdly, his function in the intermission of deception between his imprisonment and elimination is closely associated with the Gog and Magog traditions of Ezekiel 38-39—an association that casts him as the punitive and chastening hand of God. Fourthly, the binding, releasing, and elimination of Satan are highly suggestive of a subjugated function—inferior to the God in charge of the action. Fifth and finally, his removal *before* the final judgment, combined with his function to the overarching plot of the narrative, exposes his secondary function to that of the main character of the narrative—humankind.

It follows from all of the above that my initial hypothesis of approaching the narrative function of Satan in Revelation from a "servant of God" perspective, and as such constituting the wrong course of action, seems to ease several of the many ambiguities created by the more common hermeneutical approach of cosmic conflict. It is a reading that explains the element of theodicy by offering good reasons as to why the saints and humankind in general must endure the ordeals described. It is a reading that makes sense of the divine control, endorsement, and utilization of the afflictions in question. It is a reading that fits well with the majority of the traditional functions attributed to the character of Satan in Second Temple Judaism and early Christian Scriptures. It is a reading that fits well with a narrative soaked in allusions to certain parts of the Hebrew Bible, which are predominantly monistic in their cosmological outlook. It is a reading that makes sense of the unexpected release of Satan after his binding and incarceration. It is a reading of the individual passages explicitly mentioning Satan that fits naturally with their literary context. In short, it is a highly probable reading that makes sense within the text itself in light of the assumed competence of the implied reader. Moreover, it is a reading with a less degree of tension in the characterization of Satan in light of the presentation in the introductory chapter, and thus a preferable one.

Having concluded that the servant, or divine agent, aspect of Satan is a probable function of Satan in Revelation, it remains to be seen whether there was any trace of the enemy of God perspective at all. Regarding the element of autonomy, and with it the possibility of hubris, it seems to rely largely on an assumed allusion to texts like Isa 14:12-14 and Ezek 28:14-18 present in the character of Satan itself. Without this assumption, the element seems to be missing in the text. I opt for "seems" because it is possible to interpret an implied presence of autonomy in the very mode of the elimination of Satan—the lake of *fire*. I have argued above for a rhetorically inclined reading of the burning of Satan in the lake of fire, but perceived from a dualistic point of view this could obviously be seen as punishment. Moreover, since the nature of the crime committed is not explicitly stated, this could as easily be thought to be hubris as anything else. Thus, it remains a possible reading of the text, but it is not a central element to the overarching plot of the narrative. The same could be argued about the attempt of the dragon to devour the child in Revelation 12. If interpreted in light of an assumed presence of hubris in the dragon, this could be perceived as the very reason why Michael and his angels wage war on the dragon in heaven. On the other hand, if interpreted as the continuous effort of the dragon to put to the test both the source and adherents to any seed of hope erupting from the messianic community—the people of God—in the veins of Abraham on Mount Moriah or Jesus in the desert, then it is a natural part of the divine ordering of things and not a sign of enmity between God/Christ and Satan. The attempt to devour the boy instigates the eschatological ordeal, and thus explains the parallel storyline of the ejection of Satan (see Table 7), regardless of the degree of autonomy in the characterization of Satan. Moreover, the incident provides the saints with the means through the example of Christ on how to prevail and conquer their adversaries. These means are in turn closely connected to the increased activity of Satan in the little time he has, in that their numbers and conquests ushers in the age of salvation preceded by the liquidation of his office.

The point being made is that the text is silent on the issue of satanic autonomy, and what the reader makes of such gaps or ambiguities in the text is largely governed by what assumptions one approaches the text with. The conclusion here must be, in light of the analysis of Revelation 12–13 and 20, that satanic autonomy is neither explicit nor essential to the plot of the narrative—the antagonism of Satan is not contingent on hubris. However, due to the rich symbolic language and imagery of Revelation, it may still be considered a possible part of the semantical plethora of possible meanings. Still, accepting the possibility of rebellious satanic autonomy does not demand divine enmity in return. On the contrary, due to the continuously divine endorsing, allowing, tolerating, and orchestrating of Satan and related agents, God can never be stated to be the enemy of Satan in the book of Revelation in any ordinary sense of the word. Thus, in any attempt to read cosmic conflict into the narrative of Revelation, one is most certainly left with a one-sided one. This reading has argued for a more monistic approach to the text rather than the customary dualistic one. The result is a reading with less narrative tension regarding the narrative function of Satan, especially in relation to the imagery of God, but also one that creates new questions of ambiguity. Thus, this reading is not to be considered as final, but rather as part of a continuous process.

Bibliography

Aalen, Sverre. "Helveteslæren i Bibelen og i religionshistorisk sammenheng." Pages 7–32 in *Bakenfor Inferno: Oppgjør med tradisjonelle forestillinger om helvete*. Edited by John Nome. Oslo: Lutherstiftelsen, 1955.

Abbott, H. Porter. *The Cambridge Introduction to Narrative*. Cambridge, NY: Cambridge University Press, 2008.

Abrahams, M. H. *A Glossary of Literary Terms*. 7th ed. Fort Worth, TX: Harcourt Brace College, 1999.

Adamsen, Georg S. *Johannes Åpenbaring: En indledning og fortolkning*. Credo Kommentaren 23. Fredericia: Lohse, 2010.

Alkier, Stefan. "New Testament Studies on the Basis of Categorical Semiotics." Pages 223–48 in *Reading the Bible Intertextually*. Edited by Richard B. Hays, Stefan Alkier, and Leroy A. Huizenga. Waco, TX: Baylor University Press, 2009.

Allen, Leslie C. *Ezekiel 20–48*. Word Biblical Commentary 29. Dallas: Word Books, 1990.

Almond, Philip C. *The Devil: A New Biography*. London: I.B. Tauris, 2014.

Alter, Robert. *The Art of Biblical Narrative*. Rev. ed. New York: Basic Books, 2011.

Aune, David E. "Apocalypse Renewed: An Intertextual Reading of the Apocalypse of John." Pages 43–70 in *The Reality of Apocalypse: Rhetoric and Politics in the Book of Revelation*. Edited by David L. Barr. Society of Biblical Literature Symposium Series 39. Atlanta, GA: Society of Biblical Literature, 2006.

Aune, David E. *Apocalypticism, Prophecy, and Magic in Early Christianity: Collected Essays*. Grand Rapids, MI: Baker Academic, 2006.

Aune, David E. *Prophecy in Early Christianity and the Ancient Mediterranean World*. Grand Rapids, MI: Eerdmans, 1983.

Aune, David E. *Revelation 1–5*. Word Biblical Commentary 52A. Dallas: Word, 1997.

Aune, David E. *Revelation 6–16*. Word Biblical Commentary 52B. Nashville: Thomas Nelson, 1998.

Aune, David E. *Revelation 17–22*. Word Biblical Commentary 52C. Nashville: Thomas Nelson, 1998.

Aune, David E. *The Westminster Dictionary of New Testament and Early Christian Literature and Rhetoric*. Louisville, KY: Westminster John Knox, 2003.

Baker, Margaret. *The Revelation of Jesus Christ: Which God Gave to Him to Show to His Servants What Must Soon Take Place (Revelation 1.1)*. Edinburgh: T&T Clark, 2000.

Bal, Mieke. *Narratology: Introduction to the Theory of Narrative*. 3rd ed. Toronto: University of Toronto Press, 2009.

Barr, David L. "Choosing between Readings: Questions and Criteria." Pages 163–72 in *Reading the Book of Revelation: A Resource for Students*. Edited by David L. Barr. Atlanta, GA: Society of Biblical Literaure, 2003.

Barr, David L. "The Lamb Who Looks Like a Dragon? Characterizing Jesus in John's Apocalypse." Pages 205–20 in *The Reality of Apocalypse: Rhetoric and Politics in the Book of Revelation*. Edited by David L. Barr. Society of Biblical Literature Symposium Series 39. Atlanta, GA: Society of Biblical Literaure, 2006.

Barr, David L. *Tales of the End: A Narrative Commentary on the Book of Revelation*. 2nd ed. Salem, OR: Polebridge, 2012.

Barr, David L. "Using Plot to Discern Structure in John's Apocalypse." *Proceedings of the Eastern Great Lakes and Mid-West Biblical Societies* 15 (1995): 23–33.

Barr, David L. "Waiting for the End That Never Comes: The Narrative Logic of John's Story." Pages 101–12 in *Studies in the Book of Revelation*. Edited by Steve Moyise. Edinburgh: T&T Clark, 2001.

Barr, David L. "Women in Myth and History: Deconstructing John's Characterizations." Pages 55–68 in *A Feminist Companion to the Apocalypse of John*. Edited by Amy-Jill Levine and Maria Mayo Robbins. London: T&T Clark International, 2009.

Barthes, Roland. "The Death of the Author." Pages 1322–6 in *The Norton Anthology of Theory & Criticism*. 2nd ed. Edited by Vincent B. Leitch, William E. Cain, Laurie A. Finke, Barbara E. Johnson, John McGovan, T. Denean Sharpley-Whiting, and Jeffrey J. Williams. New York: W. W. Norton, 2010.

Bauckham, Richard. *The Climax of Prophecy: Studies on the Book of Revelation*. Edinburgh: T&T Clark, 1993.

Bauckham, Richard. "Judgment in the Book of Revelation." *Ex Auditu* 20 (2004): 1–24.

Bauckham, Richard. "Judgment in the Book of Revelation." Pages 55–80 in *The Book of Revelation: Currents in British Research on the Apocalypse*. Edited by Garrick V. Allen, Ian Paul, and Simon P. Woodman. Wissenschaftliche Untersuchungen zum Neuen Testament II/411. Tübingen: Mohr Siebeck, 2015.

Bauckham, Richard. *The Theology of the Book of Revelation*. Cambridge: Cambridge University Press, 1993.

Beale, Gregory K. *The Book of Revelation: A Commentary on the Greek Text*. New International Greek Testament Commentary. Grand Rapids, MI: Eerdmans, 1999.

Bell, Richard H. *Deliver Us from Evil: Interpreting the Redemption from the Power of Satan in New Testament Theology*. Wissenschaftliche Untersuchungen zum Neuen Testament 216. Tübingen: Mohr Siebeck, 2007.

Bennema, Cornelis. *A Theory of Character in New Testament Narrative*. Minneapolis: Fortress, 2014.

Bernstein, Alan E. *The Formation of Hell: Death and Retribution in the Ancient and Early Christian Worlds*. Ithaca, NY: Cornell University Press, 1993.

Bøe, Sverre. *Gog and Magog: Ezekiel 38–39 as Pre-text for Revelation 19,17–21 and 20,7–10*. Wissenschaftliche Untersuchungen zum Neuen Testament II/138. Tübingen: Mohr Siebeck, 2001.

Boring, Eugene M. "Narrative Christology in the Apocalypse." *Catholic Biblical Quarterly* 54 (1992): 702–23.

Boxall, Ian. *The Revelation of Saint John*. Black's New Testament Commentaries. London: A & C Black, 2006.

Brand, Miryam. Evil Within and Without: The Source of Sin and Its Nature in Second Temple Literature. Journal of Ancient Judaism Supplements 9. Göttingen: Vandenhoeck & Ruprecht, 2013.

Branden, Charles Robert. *Satanic Conflict and the Plot of Matthew*. Studies in Biblical Literature 89. New York: Peter Lang, 2006.

Brown, Derek. *The God of This Age: Satan in the Churches and Letters of the Apostle Paul*. Wissenschaftliche Untersuchungen zum Neuen Testament II/409. Tübingen: Mohr Siebeck, 2015.

Brown, Raymond E. *The Birth of the Messiah: A Commentary on the Infancy Narratives in the Gospels of Matthew and Luke*. Anchor Bible Reference Library. New York: Doubleday, 1993.

Caird, G. B. *The Revelation of St John the Divine*. 2nd ed. Harper's New Testament Commentaries. London: A & C Black, 1984.

Campbell, W. Gordon. "Facing Fire and Fury: One Reading of Revelation's Violence in the Context of Recent Interpretation." Pages 147–74 in *The Book of Revelation: Currents in British Research on the Apocalypse*. Edited by Garrick V. Allen, Ian Paul, and Simon P. Woodman. Wissenschaftliche Untersuchungen zum Neuen Testament II/411. Tübingen: Mohr Siebeck, 2015.

Campbell, W. Gordon. *Reading Revelation: A Thematic Approach*. Cambridge: James Clarke, 2012.

Canoy, Robert W. "Time and Space, Satan (Devil, Ancient Serpent, Deceiver, and Accuser), and Michael in Revelation." *Review and Expositor* 114 (2017): 254–65.

Carey, Greg. "The Apocalypse and Its Ambiguous Ethos." Pages 163–80 in *Studies in the Book of Revelation*. Edited by Steve Moyise. Edinburgh: T&T Clark, 2001.

Carey, Greg. "A Man's Choice: Wealth Imagery and the Two Cities of the Book of Revelation." Pages 147–58 in *A Feminist Companion to the Apocalypse of John*. Edited by Amy-Jill Levine and Maria Mayo Robbins. London: T&T Clark International, 2009.

Casey, John. *After Lives: A Guide to Heaven, Hell, and Purgatory*. New York: Oxford University Press, 2009.

Chambers, Andy. *Exemplary Life: A Theology of Church Life in Acts*. Nashville, TN: B&H, 2012.

Charles, Robert H. *The Book of Jubilees or the Little Genesis*. London: SPCK, 1917; San Diego, CA: Book Tree, 2003.

Charles, Robert H. *A Critical and Exegetical Commentary on the Revelation of St. John*. Vol. 1. International Critical Commentary. Edinburgh: T&T Clark, 1920.

Charles, Robert H. *A Critical and Exegetical Commentary on the Revelation of St. John*. Vol. 2. International Critical Commentary. Edinburgh: T&T Clark, 1920.

Charlesworth, James H., ed. *The Old Testament Pseudepigrapha*. Vol. 1. Peabody, MA: Hendrickson, 1983.

Charlesworth, James H., ed. *The Old Testament Pseudepigrapha*. Vol. 2. Peabody, MA: Hendrickson, 1983.

Chatman, Seymour. *Story and Discourse: Narrative Structure in Fiction and Film*. Ithaca, NY: Cornell University Press, 1978.

Clark-Soles, Jaime. *Death and the Afterlife in the New Testament*. New York: T&T Clark, 2006.

Collins, John J. *The Apocalyptic Imagination: An Introduction to Jewish Apocalyptic Literature*. 2nd ed. Grand Rapids, MI: Eerdmans, 1998.

Collins, John J. "What Is Apocalyptic Literature?" Pages 1–18 in *The Oxford Handbook of Apocalyptic Literature*. Edited by John J. Collins. New York: Oxford University Press, 2014.

Culpepper, R. Alan. *Anatomy of the Fourth Gospel: A Study in Literary Design*. Philadelphia: Fortress, 1983.

Culy, Martin M. *The Book of Revelation: The Rest of the Story*. Eugene, OR: Pickwick, 2017.

Danker, Frederick W., Walter Bauer, William F. Arndt, and F. Wilbur Gingrich. *Greek-English Lexicon of the New Testament and Other Early Christian Literature*. 3rd ed. Chicago: University of Chicago Press, 2000.

Darr, John A. *On Character Building: The Reader and the Rhetoric of Characterization in Luke-Acts*. Louisville, KY: Westminster John Knox, 1992.

Day, John. *Yahweh and the Gods and Goddesses of Canaan*. London: Sheffield Academic, 2000.

Day, Peggy L. *An Adversary in Heaven: Satan in the Hebrew Bible*. Harvard Semitic Monographs 43. Atlanta, GA: Scholars Press, 1988.

deSilva, David A. *Seeing Things John's Way: The Rhetoric of the Book of Revelation*. Louisville: Westminster John Knox, 2009.

Dochhorn, Jan. *Schriftgelehrte Prophetie: Der eschatologische Teufelsfall in Apc Joh 12 und seine Bedeutung für das Verständnis der Johannesoffenbarung*. Wissenschaftliche Untersuchungen zum Neuen Testament 268. Tübingen: Mohr Siebeck, 2010.

Duff, Paul B. "'The Synagogue of Satan': Crisis and Mongering and the Apocalypse of John." Pages 147–68 in *The Reality of Apocalypse: Rhetoric and Politics in the Book of Revelation*. Edited by David L. Barr. Society of Biblical Literature Symposium Series 39. Atlanta, GA: Society of Biblical Literaure, 2006.

Duff, Paul B. *Who Rides the Beast? Prophetic Rivalry and the Rhetoric of Crisis in the Churches of the Apocalypse*. New York: Oxford University Press, 2001.

Egger, Wilhelm. *How to Read the New Testament: An Introduction to Linguistic and Historical-Critical Methodology*. Translated by Peter Heinegg. Peabody, MA: Hendrickson, 1996.

Eidevall, Göran. "The Role of the Enemies of YHWH in the Book of Isaiah and in the Psalms." Pages 27–40 in *L'Adversaire de Dieu—Der Widersacher Gottes*. Edited by Michael Tilly, Matthias Morgenstern, and Volker Henning Drecoll. Wissenschaftliche Untersuchungen zum Neuen Testament 364. Tübingen: Mohr Siebeck, 2016.

Ellis, Nicholas J. "A Theology of Evil in the Epistle of James: Cosmic Trials and the *Dramatis Personae* of Evil." Pages 262–81 in *Evil in Second Temple Judaism and Early Christianity*. Edited by Chris Keith and Loren T. Stuckenbruck. Wissenschaftliche Untersuchungen zum Neuen Testament II/417. Tübingen: Mohr Siebeck, 2016.

Fee, Gordon D. *Revelation*. New Covenant Commentary. Eugene, OR: Cascade Books, 2011.

Finamore, Stephen. *God, Order and Chaos: René Girard and the Apocalypse*. Milton Keynes: Paternoster, 2009.

Fiorenza, Elisabeth Schüssler. "Babylon the Great: A Rhetorical-Political Reading of Revelation 17–18." Pages 243–70 in *The Reality of Apocalypse: Rhetoric and Politics in the Book of Revelation*. Edited by David L. Barr. Society of Biblical Literature Symposium Series 39. Atlanta, GA: Society of Biblical Literaure, 2006.

Fiorenza, Elisabeth Schüssler. *The Book of Revelation: Justice and Judgment*. 2nd ed. Minneapolis: Augsburg Fortress, 1998.

Fiorenza, Elisabeth Schüssler. *Invitation to the Book of Revelation: A Commentary on the Apocalypse with Complete Text from the Jerusalem Bible*. New York: Image Books, 1981.

Fiorenza, Elisabeth Schüssler. *Revelation: Vision of a Just World*. Minneapolis: Augsburg Fortress, 1991.

Fletcher, Michelle. "Apocalypse Noir: How Revelation Defined and Defied a Genre." Pages 115–34 in *The Book of Revelation: Currents in British Research on the Apocalypse*. Edited by Garrick V. Allen, Ian Paul, and Simon P. Woodman. Wissenschaftliche Untersuchungen zum Neuen Testament II/411.Tübingen: Mohr Siebeck, 2015.

Fludernik, Monika. *An Introduction to Narratology*. Translated by Patricia Häusler-Greenfield and Monika Fludernik. New York: Routledge, 2009.

Fontaine, Piet F. M. "What Is Dualism and What Is It Not?" Pages 266-76 in *Light against Darkness: Dualism in Ancient Mediterranean Religion and the Contemporary World*. Edited by Armin Lange, Eric M. Meyers, Bennie H. Reynolds III, and Randall Styers. Journal of Ancient Judaism Supplements 2. Göttingen: Vandenhoeck & Ruprecht, 2011.

Forsyth, Neil. *The Old Enemy: Satan & the Combat Myth*. Princeton, NJ: Princeton University Press, 1987.

Forsyth, Neil. *The Satanic Epic*. Princeton, NJ: Princeton University Press, 2003.

Frey, Jörg. "Apocalyptic Dualism." Pages 271-94 in *The Oxford Handbook of Apocalyptic Literature*. Edited by John J. Collins. New York: Oxford University Press, 2014.

Frey, Jörg. "Dualismus: Zur frühjüdischen Herausbildung und zur neutestamentlichen Rezeption dualistischer Weltdeutung." Pages 3-46 in *Dualismus, Dämonologie und diabolische Firguren*. Edited by Jörg Frey and Enno Edzard Popkes. Wissenschaftliche Untersuchungen zum Neuen Testament II/484. Tübingen: Mohr Siebeck, 201.

Friesen, Steven J. "Sarcasm in Revelation 2-3: Churches, Christians, True Jews, and Satanic Synagogues." Pages 127-46 in *The Reality of Apocalypse: Rhetoric and Politics in the Book of Revelation*. Edited by David L. Barr. Society of Biblical Literature Symposium Series 39. Atlanta, GA: Society of Biblical Literature, 2006.

Gallusz, Laszlo. *The Throne Motif in the Book of Revelation: Profiles from the History of Interpretation*. Library of New Testament Studies 487. London: T&T Clark, 2014.

Genette, Gérard. *Narrative Discourse Revisited*. Translated by Jane E. Lewin. Ithaca, NY: Cornell University Press, 1988.

Genette, Gérard. *Narrative Discourse: An Essay in Method*. Translated by Jane E. Lewin. Ithaca, NY: Cornell University Press, 1980.

Goff, Matthew. "Enochic Literature and the Persistence of Evil: Giants and Demons, Satan and Azazel." Pages 43-58 in *Das Böse, der Teufel und Dämonen—Evil, the Devil, and Demons*. Edited by Jan Dochhorn, Susanne Rudnig-Zelt, and Benjamin G. Wold. Wissenschaftliche Untersuchungen zum Neuen Testament II/412. Tübingen: Mohr Siebeck, 2016.

Grabiner, Steven. *Revelation's Hymns: Commentary on the Cosmic Conflict*. Library of New Testament Studies 511. London: T&T Clark, 2015.

Graves, Kersey. *The Biography of Satan or a Historical Exposition of the Devil and His Fiery Dominions: Disclosing the Oriental Origin of the Belief in a Devil and Future Endless Punishment*. Montana: Kessinger, 1865.

Greimas, Algirdas Julien. *Structural Semantics: An Attempt at a Method*. Lincoln: University of Nebraska Press, 1984.

Gunn, David M. "Narrative Criticism." Pages 201-29 in *To Each Its Own Meaning: An Introduction to Biblical Criticisms and Their Application*. Rev. and exp. ed. Edited by Steven L. McKenzie and Stephen R. Haynes. Louisville, KY: Westminster John Knox, 1999.

Hallo, William W., and K. Lawson Younger, eds. *The Context of Scripture, Vol. 1: Canonical Compositions from the Biblical World*. Leiden: Brill, 1997.

Hemer, Colin J. *The Letters to the Seven Churches of Asia in Their Local Setting*. Grand Rapids, MI: Eerdmans, 2001.

Herman, David. *Story Logic: Problems and Possibilities of Narrative*. Lincoln: University of Nebraska Press, 2002.

Horton, Fred L. "Dualism in the New Testament: A Surprising Rhetoric and a Rhetoric of Surprise." Pages 186-208 in *Light Against Darkness: Dualism in Ancient Mediterranean Religion and the Contemporary World*. Edited by Armin Lange, Eric M. Meyers,

Bennie H. Reynolds III, and Randall Styers. Journal of Ancient Judaism Supplements 2. Göttingen: Vandenhoeck & Ruprecht, 2011.

Iser, Wolfgang. "The Reading Process: A Phenomenological Approach." *New Literary History* 3 (1972): 279–99.

Johnson, M. D. "Life of Adam and Eve." Pages 249–95 in *The Old Testament Pseudepigrapha. Vol. 2*. Edited by James H. Charlesworth. Peabody, MA: Hendrickson, 1983.

Kahl, Brigitte. "Gaia, Polis, and Ekklēsia at the Miletus Market Gate: An Eco-Critical Reimagination of Revelation 12:16." Pages 111–50 in *The First Urban Churches 1: Methodological Foundations*. Edited by James R. Harrison and Larry L. Wellborn. Atlanta, GA: Society of Biblical Literature Press, 2015.

Kalms, Jürgen U. *Der Sturz des Gottesfeindes: Traditionsgeschichtliche Studien zu Apokalypse 12*. Wissenschaftliche Monographien zum Alten und Neuen Testament 93. Göttingen: Vandenhoeck & Ruprecht; Neukirchener Verlag, 2001.

Keel, Othmar. "Schwache alttestamentliche Ansätze zur Konstruktion einer stark dualistisch getönen Welt." Pages 211–36 in *Die Dämonen: die Dämonologie der israelitisch-jüdischen und frühchristlichen Literatur in Kontext ihrer Umwelt*. Edited by Armin Lange, Herman Lichtenberger, and K. F. Diethard Römheld. Tübingen: Mohr Siebeck, 2003.

Kelly, Henry Ansgar. *The Devil, Demonology, and Witchcraft: The Development of Christian Beliefs in Evil Spirits*. Rev. ed. Eugene, OR: Wipf & Stock, 2004.

Kelly, Henry Ansgar. *Satan: A Biography*. New York: Cambridge University Press, 2006.

Kelly, Henry Ansgar. *Satan in the Bible: God's Minister of Justice*. Eugene, OR: Cascade Books, 2017.

Kensky, Meira Z. *Trying Man, Trying God: The Divine Courtroom in Early Jewish and Christian Literature*. Wissenschaftliche Untersuchungen zum Neuen Testament II/289. Tübingen: Mohr Siebeck, 2010.

Klutz, Todd. *The Exorcism Stories in Luke-Acts: A Sociostylistic Reading*. Society for New Testament Studies Monograph Series 129. Cambridge: Cambridge University Press, 2004.

Knibb, Michael A. *Essays on the Book of Enoch and Other Early Jewish Texts and Traditions*. Studia in Veteris Testamenti Pseudepigraphica 22. Leiden: Brill, 2009.

Koester, Craig R. "The Image of the Beast from the Land (Rev 13,11–18): A Study in Incongruity." Pages 333–52 in *New Perspectives on the Book of Revelation*. Edited by Adela Yarbro Collins. Bibliotheca Ephemeridum Theologicarum Lovaniensium 291. Leuven: Peeters, 2017.

Koester, Craig R. *Revelation and the End of All Things*. Grand Rapids, MI: Eerdmans, 2001.

Koester, Craig R. *Revelation: A New Translation with Introduction and Commentary*. Anchor Bible 38A. New Haven, CT: Yale University Press, 2014.

Kotsko, Adam. *The Prince of This World*. Stanford, NC: Stanford University Press, 2017.

Labahn, Michael. "The Dangerous Loser: The Narrative and Rhetorical Function of the Devil as Character in the Book of Revelation." Pages 156–80 in *Evil and the Devil*. Edited by Ida Frölich and Erkki Koskenniemi. Library of New Testament Studies 481. London: T&T Clark, 2013.

Lange, Armin, Eric M. Meyers, Bennie H. Reynolds III, and Randall Styers. "Introduction." Pages 7–18 in *Light against Darkness: Dualism in Ancient Mediterranean Religion and the Contemporary World*. Edited by Armin Lange, Eric M. Meyers, Bennie H. Reynolds III, and Randall Styers. Journal of Ancient Judaism Supplements 2. Göttingen: Vandenhoeck & Ruprecht, 2011.

Larivaille, Paul. "L'analyse (morpho)logique du récit." *Poétique,* 19 (1974): 368–88.
Leithart, Peter J. *Revelation 12–22.* International Theological Commentary. London: T&T Clark, 2018.
Leonhardt-Balzer, Jutta. "Evil at Qumran." Pages 17–33 in *Evil in Second Temple Judaism and Early Christianity.* Edited by Chris Keith and Loren T. Stuckenbruck. Wissenschaftliche Untersuchungen zum Neuen Testament II/417.Tübingen: Mohr Siebeck, 2016.
Lupieri, Edmondo F. *A Commentary on the Apocalypse of John.* Grand Rapids, MI: Eerdmans, 1999.
Margolin, Uri. "Character." Pages 66–79 in *The Cambridge Companion to Narrative.* Edited by David Herman. Cambridge: Cambridge University Press, 2007.
Marguerat, Daniel, and Yvan Bourquin. *How to Read Bible Stories.* London: SCM, 1999.
Martínez, Florentino García. "Apocalypticism in the Dead Sea Scrolls." Pages 162–92 in *The Encyclopedia of Apocalypticism. Vol 1.* Edited by John J. Collins. New York: Continuum, 1998.
Mathewson, David L. *Revelation: A Handbook on the Greek Text.* Waco, TX: Baylor University Press, 2016.
Maxwell-Stuart, P. G. *Satan: A Biography.* Gloucestershire: Amberley, 2008.
Mayo, Philip L. *"Those Who Call Themselves Jews": The Church and Judaism in the Apocalypse of John.* Pittsburgh Theological Monograph Series 60. Eugene, OR: Pickwick, 2006.
McKnight, Edgar V. "Reader-Response Criticism" Pages 230–52 in *To Each Its Own Meaning: An Introduction to Biblical Criticisms and Their Application.* Rev. and exp. ed. Edited by Steven L. McKenzie and Stephen R. Haynes. Louisville, KY: Westminster John Knox, 1999.
Meier, John P. *A Marginal Jew Volume II: Mentor, Message, and Miracles.* New York: Yale University Press, 1994.
Messadié, Gerald. *A History of the Devil.* New York: Kodansha, 1996.
Miola, Robert S. "Seven Types of Intertextuality." Pages 13–25 in *Shakespeare, Italy and Intertextuality.* Edited by Michele Marrapodi. Manchester: Manchester University Press, 2004.
Mischel, Walter. *The Marshmallow Test: Mastering Self-Control and How to Master It.* London: Corgi Books, 2014.
Mobley, Gregory, and T. J. Wray. *The Birth of Satan: Tracing the Devil's Biblical Roots.* New York: Palgrave Macmillan, 2005.
Moloney, Francis J., SDB. *The Resurrection of the Messiah: A Narrative Commentary on the Resurrection Accounts in the Four Gospels.* New York: Paulist, 2013.
Moore, Stephen D. "Hypermasculinity and Divinity." Pages 180–204 in *A Feminist Companion to the Apocalypse of John.* Edited by Amy-Jill Levine and Maria Mayo Robbins. New York: T&T Clark International, 2009.
Morton, Russell S. *Recent Research on Revelation.* Recent Research in Biblical Studies 7. Sheffield: Sheffield Phoenix, 2014.
Mounce, Robert H. *The Book of Revelation.* New International Commentary on the New Testament. Grand Rapids, MI: Eerdmans, 1977.
Moyise, Steve. "Genesis in Revelation." Pages 166–80 in *Genesis in the New Testament.* Edited by Maarten J. J. Menken and Steve Moyise. London: T&T Clark, 2012.
Moyise, Steve. *The Old Testament in the Book of Revelation.* Journal for the Study of the New Testament Supplement Series 115. Sheffield: Sheffield Academic, 1995.

Moyise, Steve. "A Response to *Currents in British Research on the Apocalypse.*" Pages 281–8 in *The Book of Revelation: Currents in British Research on the Apocalypse*. Edited by Garrick V. Allen, Ian Paul, and Simon P. Woodman. Wissenschaftliche Untersuchungen zum Neuen Testament II/411. Tübingen: Mohr Siebeck, 2015.

Murphy, Frederick J. *Fallen Is Babylon: The Revelation to John*. Harrisburg, PA: Trinity International, 1998.

Nickelsburg, George W. E., and James C. VanderKam. *1 Enoch: The Hermeneia Translation*. Minneapolis: Fortress, 2012.

Nielsen, Kirsten. *Satan: Den fortabte søn?* Frederiksberg: ANIS, 1991.

Ogden, Daniel. *Drakōn: Dragon Myth and Serpent Cult in the Greek and Roman Worlds*. Oxford: Oxford University Press, 2013.

Oldridge, Darren. *The Devil: A Very Short Introduction*. New York: Oxford University Press, 2012.

Orlov, Andrei A. "The Demise of the Antagonist in the Apocalyptic Scapegoat Tradition." Pages 201–23 in *The Open Mind: Essays in Honour of Christopher Rowland*. Edited by Jonathan Knight and Kevin Sullivan. London: T&T Clark, 2015.

Osborne, Grant R. *Revelation*. Baker Exegetical Commentary on the New Testament. Grand Rapids, MI: Baker Academic, 2002.

Osborne, Grant R. "Theodicy in the Apocalypse." *Trinity Journal* 14 (1993): 63–77.

Page, Sydney H. T. *Powers of Evil: A Biblical Study of Satan & Demons*. Grand Rapids, MI: Baker Books, 1995.

Page, Sydney H. T. "Satan: God's Servant." *Journal of the Evangelical Theological Society* 50 (2007): 449–65.

Pagels, Elaine. *Adam, Eve, and the Serpent*. New York: Random House, 1988.

Pagels, Elaine. *The Origin of Satan*. New York: Random House, 1995.

Popović, Mladen. "Apocalyptic Determinism." Pages 255–70 in *The Oxford Handbook of Apocalyptic Literature*. Edited by John J. Collins. New York: Oxford University Press, 2014.

Powell, Mark Allen. *What Is Narrative Criticism? A New Approach to the Bible*. Minneapolis: Augsburg Fortress, 1990.

Powys, David J. *"Hell": A Hard Look at a Hard Question—the Fate of the Unrighteous in New Testament Thought*. Carlisle: Paternoster, 1998.

Prigent, Pierre. *Commentary on the Apocalypse of St. John*. Tübingen: Mohr Siebeck, 2004.

Reed, Annette Yoshiko. *Fallen Angels and the History of Judaism and Christianity: The Reception of Enochic Literature*. New York: Cambridge University Press, 2005.

Resseguie, James L. *Narrative Criticism of the New Testament: An Introduction*. Grand Rapids, MI: Baker Academic, 2005.

Resseguie, James L. *The Revelation of John: A Narrative Commentary*. Grand Rapids, MI: Baker Academic, 2009.

Rhoads, David, Joanna Dewey, and Donald Michie. *Mark as Story: An Introduction to the Narrative of a Gospel*. 2nd ed. Minneapolis: Fortress, 1999.

Ricoeur, Paul. *From Text to Action: Essays in Hermeneutics II*. Translated by Kathleen Blamey and John B. Thompson. New York: Continuum, 2008.

Rollston, Christopher A. "An Ur-History of the New Testament Devil: The Celestial שׂטן (śāṭān) in Zechariah and Job." Pages 1–16 in *Evil in Second Temple Judaism and Early Christianity*. Edited by Chris Keith and Loren T. Stuckenbruck. Wissenschaftliche Untersuchungen zum Neuen Testament II/417. Tübingen: Mohr Siebeck, 2016.

Roloff, Jürgen. *The Revelation of John: A Continental Commentary*. Translated by John E. Alsup. Minneapolis: Fortress, 1993.

Rudnig-Zelt, Susanne. "Der Teufel und der alttestamentliche Monotheismus." Pages 1–20 in *Das Böse, der Teufel und Dämonen—Evil, the Devil, and Demons*. Edited by Jan Dochhorn, Susanne Rudnig-Zelt, and Benjamin G. Wold. Wissenschaftliche Untersuchungen zum Neuen Testament II/412. Tübingen: Mohr Siebeck, 2016.

Russell, David Syme. *Divine Disclosure: An Introduction to Jewish Apocalyptic*. London: SCM, 1992.

Russell, Jeffrey Burton. *The Devil: Perceptions of Evil from Antiquity to Primitive Christianity*. Ithaca, NY: Cornell University Press, 1977.

Russell, Jeffrey Burton. *A History of Heaven: The Singing Silence*. Princeton, NJ: Princeton University Press, 1997.

Russell, Jeffrey Burton. *Lucifer: The Devil in the Middle Ages*. Ithaca, NY: Cornell University Press, 1984.

Russell, Jeffrey Burton. *Mephistopheles: The Devil in the Modern World*. Ithaca, NY: Cornell University Press, 1986.

Russell, Jeffrey Burton. *The Prince of Darkness: Radical Evil and the Power of Good in History*. Ithaca, NY: Cornell University Press, 1988.

Russell, Jeffrey Burton. *Satan: The Early Christian Tradition*. Ithaca, NY: Cornell University Press, 1981.

Schreiber, Stephan. "The Great Opponent: The Devil in Early Jewish and Formative Christian Literature." Pages 437–58 in *Deuterocanonical and Cognate Literature—Yearbook 2007—Angels: The Concept of Celestial Beings—Origins, Development and Reception*. Edited by Friedrich V. Reiterer, Tobias Nicklas, and Karin Schöpflin. Berlin: Walter deGruyter, 2007.

Skinner, Christopher W. "Overcoming Satan, Overcoming the World: Exploring the Cosmologies of Mark and John." Pages 101–21 in *Evil in Second Temple Judaism and Early Christianity*. Edited by Chris Keith and Loren T. Stuckenbruck. Wissenschaftliche Untersuchungen zum Neuen Testament II/417. Tübingen: Mohr Siebeck, 2016.

Skjærvø, Prods Oktor. "Zoroastrian Dualism." Pages 55–76 in *Light against Darkness: Dualism in Ancient Mediterranean Religion and the Contemporary World*. Edited by Armin Lange, Eric M. Meyers, Bennie H. Reynolds III, and Randall Styers. Journal of Ancient Judaism Supplements 2. Göttingen: Vandenhoeck & Ruprecht, 2011.

Smalley, Stephen S. *The Revelation to John: A Commentary on the Greek Text of the Apocalypse*. London: SPCK, 2005.

Smit, Peter-Ben. "Sadomasochism and the Apocalypse of John: Exegesis, Sensemaking and Pain." *Biblical Interpretation* 26 (2018): 90–112.

Smit, Peter-Ben, and Toon Renssen. "The *Passivum divinum*: The Rise and Future Fall of an Imaginary Linguistic Phenomenon." *Filología Neotestamentaria* 17 (2014): 3–24.

Smith, Mark S. "Anat's Warfare Cannibalism and the West Semitic Ban." Pages 368–86 in *The Pitcher Is Broken: Memorial Essays for Gösta W. Ahlström*. Edited by Steven W. Holloway and Lowell K. Handy. Sheffield: Sheffield Academic, 1995.

Smith, Mark S. *The Early History of God: Yahweh and the Other Deities in Ancient Israel*. 2nd ed. Grand Rapids, MI: Eerdmans, 2002.

Smith, Mark S. *The Genesis of Good and Evil: The Fall(out) and Original Sin in the Bible*. Louisville, KY: Westminster John Knox, 2019.

Smith, Mark S. *The Memoirs of God: History, Memory, and the Experience of the Divine in Ancient Israel*. Minneapolis: Fortress, 2004.

Smith, Mark S. *The Origins of Biblical Monotheism: Israel's Polytheistic Background and the Ugaritic Texts*. New York: Oxford University Press, 2001.

Stanford, Peter. *The Devil: A Biography*. London: Arrow Books, 2003.
Stewart, Alexander E. "*Ekphrasis,* Fear, and Motivation in the Apocalypse of John." *Bulletin for Biblical Research* 27 (2017): 227–40.
Stokes, Ryan E. "The Devil Made David Do It … or Did He? The Nature, Identity, and Literary Origins of the *Satan* in 1 Chronicles 21:1." *Journal of Biblical Literature* 128 (2009): 90–106.
Stokes, Ryan E. "What Is a Demon, What Is an Evil Spirit, and What Is a Satan?" Pages 259–72 in *Das Böse, der Teufel und Dämonen—Evil, the Devil, and Demons*. Edited by Jan Dochhorn, Susanne Rudnig-Zelt, and Benjamin G. Wold. Wissenschaftliche Untersuchungen zum Neuen Testament II/412. Tübingen: Mohr Siebeck, 2016.
Stuckenbruck, Loren T. *The Myth of Rebellious Angels: Studies in Second Temple Judaism and New Testament Texts*. Grand Rapids, MI: Eerdmans, 2014.
Stuckenbruck, Loren T., and Mark D. Mathews. "The Apocalypse of John, 1 Enoch, and the Question of Influence." Pages 191–234 in *Die Johannesapokalypse: Kontexte—Konzepte—Rezeption*. Wissenschaftliche Untersuchungen zum Neuen Testament 287. Edited by Jörg Frey, James A. Kelhoffer, and Franz Tóth. Tübingen: Mohr Siebeck, 2012.
Sweet, John. *Revelation*. TPI New Testament Commentaries. London: SCM, 1990.
Synnes, Martin. *7 profetiske budskap til menighetene: En gjennomgåelse av sendebrevene i Johannes' åpenbaring*. Oslo: Verbum, 1996.
Talbert, Charles H. *The Apocalypse: A Reading of the Revelation of John*. Louisville, KY: Westminster John Knox, 1994.
Thomas, John Christopher. *The Apocalypse: A Literary and Theological Commentary*. Cleveland: CPT Press, 2012.
Thomas, John Christopher. *The Devil, Disease and Deliverance: Origins of Illness in New Testament Thought*. Cleveland: CPT Press, 2010.
Thompson, Leonard L. *The Book of Revelation: Apocalypse and Empire*. New York: Oxford University Press, 1990.
Tipvarakankoon, Wiriya. *The Theme of Deception in the Book of Revelation: Bringing Early Christian and Contemporary Thai Culture into Dialogue*. Claremont: Claremont, 2017.
Tonstad, Sigve. *Saving God's Reputation: The Theological Function of* Pistis Iesou *in the Cosmic Narratives of Revelation*. Library of New Testament Studies 337. London: T&T Clark, 2006.
Trafton, Joseph L. *Reading Revelation: A Literary and Theological Commentary*. Macon, GA: Smyth & Helwys, 2005.
Travis, Stephen H. *Christ and the Judgment of God: The Limits of Divine Retribution in New Testament Thought*. 2nd ed. Milton Keynes and Colorado Springs: Hendrickson and Paternoster, 2009.
Twelftree, Graham H. *In the Name of Jesus: Exorcism among Early Christians*. Grand Rapids, MI: Baker Academic, 2007.
Ulrich, Eugene. "Our Sharper Focus on the Bible and Theology, Thanks to the Dead Sea Scrolls." *Catholic Biblical Quarterly* 66 (2004): 1–24.
Ureña, Lourdes García. "The Book of Revelation: A Chromatic Story." Pages 393–419 in *New Perspectives on the Book of Revelation*. Edited by Adela Yarbro Collins. Bibliotheca Ephemeridum Theologicarum Lovaniensium 291. Leuven: Peeters, 2017.
VanderKam, James C. "The Demons in the *Book of Jubilees*." Pages 339–64 in *Die Dämonen: die Dämonologie der israelitisch-jüdischen und frühchristlichen Literatur in Kontext ihrer Umwelt*. Edited by Armin Lange, Herman Lichtenberger, and K. F. Diethard Römheld. Tübingen: Mohr Siebeck, 2003.

Vermes, Geza. *The Complete Dead Sea Scrolls in English*. London: Penguin Books, 1998.
Von Rad, Gerhard. *Holy War in Ancient Israel*. Translated by John H. Yoder and Marva J. Dawn. Grand Rapids, MI: Eerdmans, 1991.
Waltke, Bruce K., and Michael Patrick O'Connor. *An Introduction to Biblical Hebrew Syntax*. Winona Lake, IN: Eisenbrauns, 1990.
Wassén, Cecilia. "Engler og demoner." Pages 341–54 in *Dødehavsrullene: Deres innhold, historie og betydning*. Edited by Årstein Justnes. Kristiansand: Norwegian Academic Press, 2009.
Wengst, Klaus. "The Devil in the Revelation of St John." Pages 68–74 in *The Problem of Evil and Its Symbols in Jewish and Christian Tradition*. Edited by Henning Graf Reventlow and Yair Hoffman. Library of Hebrew Bible/Old Testament Studies 366. London: T&T Clark International, 2004.
Wheelwright, Philip. *Metaphor and Reality*. Bloomington: Indiana Fortress, 1962.
Wimsatt, William K., and Monroe C. Beardsley. "The Intentional Fallacy." *Sewanee Review* 54 (1946): 468–88.
Wink, Walter. *Unmasking the Powers: The Invisible Forces That Determine Human Existence*. Philadelphia: Fortress, 1986.
Witherington, Ben, III. *Revelation*. New Cambridge Bible Commentary. Cambridge: Cambridge University Press, 2003.
Wold, Benjamin G. "Apotropaic Prayer and the Matthean Lord's Prayer." Pages 101–12 in *Das Böse, der Teufel und Dämonen—Evil, the Devil, and Demons*. Edited by Jan Dochhorn, Susanne Rudnig-Zelt and Benjamin G. Wold. Wissenschaftliche Untersuchungen zum Neuen Testament II/412. Tübingen: Mohr Siebeck, 2016.
Wood, Shane J. "The Alter-Imperial Paradigm: Empire Studies and the Book of Revelation." PhD diss., University of Edinburgh, 2014.
Wood, Shane J. "God's Triumphal Procession: Re-examining the Release of Satan in the Light of Roman Imperial Imagery." Pages 209–24 in *The Book of Revelation: Currents in British Research on the Apocalypse*. Edited by Garrick V. Allen, Ian Paul, and Simon P. Woodman. Wissenschaftliche Untersuchungen zum Neuen Testament II/411. Tübingen: Mohr Siebeck, 2015.
Woodman, Simon P. "Fire from Heaven: Divine Judgment in the Book of Revelation." Pages 175–92 in *The Book of Revelation: Currents in British Research on the Apocalypse*. Edited by Garrick V. Allen, Ian Paul, and Simon P. Woodman. Wissenschaftliche Untersuchungen zum Neuen Testament II/411. Tübingen: Mohr Siebeck, 2015.
Wright, Archie T. *The Origin of Evil Spirits: The Reception of Genesis 6:1–4 in Early Jewish Literature*. Minneapolis: Fortress, 2015.
Wright, Nicholas Thomas. *Jesus and the Victory of God*. London: SPCK, 1996.
Wright, Nicholas Thomas. *The New Testament and the People of God*. London: SPCK, 1992.
Yarbro Collins, Adela. *The Combat Myth in the Book of Revelation*. Missoula, MT: Scholars Press for Harvard Theological Review, 1976.
Yarbro Collins, Adela. *Cosmology and Eschatology in Jewish and Christian Apocalypticism*. Supplements to the Journal for the Study of Judaism 50. Leiden: Brill, 1996.
Yarbro Collins, Adela. *Crisis and Catharsis: The Power of the Apocalypse*. Philadelphia: Westminster, 1984.
Yarbro Collins, Adela. "The Power of Apocalyptic Rhetoric—Catharsis." Pages 73–94 in *The Revelation of St. John the Divine*. Edited by Harold Bloom. New York: Chelsea House, 1988.
Yarbro Collins, Adela. "Vilification and Self-Definition in the Book of Revelation." *HTR* 79 (1986): 308–20.

Yeates, Paul Henry. "Blaspheming Heaven: Revelation 13:4–8 and the Competition for Heaven in Roman Imperial Ideology and the Visions of John." *Novum Testamentum* 59 (2017): 31–51.

Zimmerli, Walther. *Old Testament Theology in Outline*. Translated by David E. Green. Edinburgh: T&T Clark, 1978.

Zumstein, Jean. "Intratextuality and Intertextuality in the Gospel of John." Pages 121–35 in *Anatomies of Narrative Criticism: The Past, Present, and Futures of the Fourth Gospel as Literature*. Edited by Tom Thatcher and Stephen D. Moore. Resources for Biblical Study 55. Atlanta, GA: Society of Biblical Literature, 2008.

Zurawski, Jason M. "Separating the Devil from the Diabolos: A Fresh Reading of Wisdom of Solomon 2.24." *Journal for the Study of the Pseudepigrapha* 21 (2012): 266–399.

Index

Aalen, Sverre 226
Abaddon/Apollyon 18, 109, 226
Abbott, H. Porter 54
abyss 147, 150, 151, 169, 198, 203, 208, 226
actantial scheme 37, 38, 67, 122, 196, 197
Adam books 132
Adamsen, Georg S. 202
adversarial agents 8, 15, 133, 165, 171, 190, 191, 192, 193, 203, 207, 214, 227, 231
adversarial forces 9, 10, 43, 146, 156, 192, 202
adversaries 4, 6, 13, 20, 77, 86, 96, 105, 128, 136, 140, 166, 167, 182, 188, 189, 191, 218, 223, 227, 229, 230, 231, 233
  and demonization 124
  rise and fall of 170
Ahab, King 81
Ahaz, King 182
Ahura Mazdâ 19
allegiance/affiliation 173
allusions 39, 40, 51, 52, 72, 91, 94, 111, 125, 196
Almond, Philip C. 21
Alter, Robert 53
Alter-Imperial Paradigm 205, 207
anachronistic reading 45
Ancient Near Eastern Combat Myth 138–43, 139, 140, 143, 168, 230
Angel of Darkness 7, 9, 12
Angel of the Lord 149
anti-divine trait, of Satan 16, 23, 25, 214, 223–25, 226, 227
Antiochus Epiphanes IV, 5, 134, 151, 152, 153, 229
Antipas, death of 73, 74, 75, 76, 167, 231
antipathy, towards characters 72, 73, 78, 82, 86, 89, 92, 94, 124, 163–64, 163, 225
antithetical agency 9
aorist passives 71, 101, 113, 114, 142, 144, 151, 155, 156, 159, 166, 168, 197, 231

apocalypse 34, 175, 187
apocalyptic paradigm 229
apocalyptic, definition of 43
Apocalypticism 44
apostles 88
apostles, false 88, 89, 90
apotropaic prayer 10–11, 71
Arendt, Hannah 28
Aristotle 37
Armageddon 8, 47, 117, 171, 188, 192, 207, 209, 222
Arp, Thomas R. 99
Asia Minor 1, 32, 37, 42, 45, 46, 47, 158
Aune, David E. 34, 57, 62, 63, 70, 71, 94, 124, 139, 149, 152, 155, 156, 161, 176, 185
Austin, John 58
Azazel 10, 14, 127, 200

Babel 83, 181, 203
Babylon the Great 173, 178–86, 184, 187, 191, 218, 224
  battles 187–90
  and beasts 191, 208
Babylon/New Jerusalem dichotomy 173, 226
Baker, Margaret 4, 200
Bal, Mieke 51–52, 60
Balaam 74, 77–78, 78, 81, 125
Barr, David L. 25, 33, 66, 69, 88, 142, 165, 170, 171, 176, 189, 201, 211, 214, 215, 216, 222
Barthes, Roland 55
battle, the final. *see* Armageddon
Bauckham, Richard 49, 66–67, 103, 110, 111, 113, 140, 175, 177, 204, 205, 210, 216, 218
Beale, Gregory K. 48, 57, 64, 65, 70, 71, 101, 107, 113, 116, 131, 134, 140, 147, 165, 180, 181, 187, 213, 216, 222
Beardsley, Monroe C. 50

beast(s) 75, 112, 118
   and Babylon 191, 208
   from the earth. *see* the beast from
      the earth
   from the sea. *see* the beast from the sea
   time limitations on the actions of 231
   worship of 76, 152, 157
the beast from the earth
   antipathy 163–64
   characterization of 150, 157–62
   evaluative point of view 163–64
   God's point of view 162–63
   horizontal point of view 164–66
   plot analysis 120–22
   sympathy 163–64
   vertical point of view 164–66
the beast from the sea 81, 114, 154, 155,
      158, 159, 161, 165, 186, 212, 220, 224
   antipathy 163–64
   characterization of 150–57
   evaluative point of view 163–64
   God's point of view 162–63
   horizontal point of view 164–66
   plot analysis 120–22
   sympathy 163–64
   vertical point of view 164–66
Behemoth 161–62, 163, 166, 167
Belial 7, 8, 9, 12, 216
Beliar 8, 9
Bell, Richard H. 11
Ben Sira 15
Bennema, Cornelis 39, 53, 54, 55
Bernstein, Alan E. 5, 176, 177, 217, 219
blasphemy 69, 151, 154
Bøe, Sverre 210
book of life, 18, 47, 70, 76, 90, 152, 156,
      168, 190, 191, 193, 194, 195, 197, 214,
      215, 223, 224, 231
Boring, Eugene 34, 217
Bourquin, Yvan 37, 58, 121
Boxall, Ian 112, 117, 137, 199
Brand, Miryam T. 6, 8, 10
Branden, Robert Charles 2, 11
Brown, Derek R. 9, 22, 130
Brown, Raymond E. 135

Caird, G. B. 73, 135, 136, 166, 199
Campbell, W. Gordon 44, 64, 65, 66, 71,
      137, 173, 178, 184, 197, 214

Canaanite mythology 126, 127, 139
Canoy, Robert W. 136
Carey, Greg 102
Celsus 3
characterization 36–42
   beasts of earth and sea 150–62
   the dragon and the woman 122–38
   Ephesus congregation 88–89
   Laodicea congregation 93–94
   Pergamum congregation 74–78
   Philadelphia congregation 85–86
   Sardis congregation 90–92
   Satan's fall 195–221
   Smyrna congregation 67–72
   Thyatira congregation, 80–82
   war in heaven 137–38, 143–50
Charles, Robert H. 121, 143
Chatman, Seymour 68
Collins, John J. 43–45, 131
Collodi, Carlo 11
combat myth. *see* Ancient Near Eastern
      Combat Myth
Corinthians 80
cosmic conflict 26, 27, 28, 30, 140, 141,
      142, 143, 169, 203, 204, 205, 230, 231,
      232, 233
cosmic dualism 13, 17, 18, 156
Culpepper, R. Alan 35, 53
cultural point of view 29, 43, 76, 81
Culy, Martin M. 70, 205

Dante Alighieri 45
Darr, John 39
de Saussure, Ferdinand 55
death 137, 215, 216, 220, 224
   of Ahab 81
   angel of 84
   of Antipas 73, 74, 75, 76, 167, 231
   first death 215
   of Lamb 106, 136, 147, 164, 189
   of saints 166
   of Satan 213–21
   second death 66, 215, 216, 223
demons 6, 7, 9, 12, 13, 14, 216
   and God 13
deSilva, David A. 82, 115
Deuteronomistic justice 177
Deuteronomistic paradigm, of evil 229
Devil 2, 14–16, 21, 45, 48, 70

deceptive nature of 14
publications on 21–24
Dewey, Joanna 34
dispositio 62, 74, 77
divine assembly 104–5
divine determinism 105, 108, 109, 112, 113
divine governing 6, 16, 19, 20, 108, 137
divine necessity (δεῖ) 112, 169, 170, 199, 201, 202, 205, 222, 225
divine ordering 11, 13, 186, 205, 233
divine passive 113, 144
Dochhorn, Jan 17, 132
dragon 75, 121, 122–23, 123, 158, 163, 167, 231, 232
  as ὁ ὄφις 129–30
  actions of 134–38
  epithet 146
  eradication in the end 128
  in Judaism 126
  number of heads, diadems, and horns, as symbolism 128–29
  representation of 127
  and Satan 120
  and sovereignty of God 126, 127–28
  time limitations 127
the dragon and the woman 109, 112, 118, 121, *see also* dragon
  antipathy 163–64
  characterization of 122–38
  evaluative point of view 163–64
  God's point of view 162–63
  horizontal point of view 164–66
  intercalation. *see* war in heaven
  plot analysis 120–22
  sympathy 163–64
  vertical point view 164–66
dragon/beasts dichotomy 40, 47, 49, 173
dualism 8, 11–16, 17–20, 105
Duff, Paul B. 85, 124
dwellers of the earth 47, 93, 114, 165, 180, 191, 197, 218
  and the beasts 81, 89, 150, 224
  and dragon 123
  judgment of 226, 228
  suffering imposed on 47
  testing of 48

Eden, 14, 131
  Adam, 130, 133

Eve 130, 133, 202
  fall 130, 132
  serpent 28, 45, 130–34, 130, 133
Eidevall, Göran 126
ekphrases 176
El Elyon 181
empathy, towards characters 72, 78, 87, 92, 163
Ephesus congregation 64
  characterization of 88–89
  plot analysis 88
  point of view 89–90
eschatological ordeal 1, 2, 46, 47, 122, 172, 177, 192, 194, 196, 215, 228, 229, 231
  objects of 190, 191
eschatological prophecy 44
eschatological salvation 8, 14, 67, 74, 145, 167, 168, 170, 172, 190, 191, 192, 193, 205, 208, 226, 227, 228
eternal suffering 176, 213, 219
ethical dualism 8, 18
evaluative point of view 42–43, 61, 103, 105, 116
  beasts of the sea and the earth 163–64
  the dragon and the woman 163–64
  Ephesus congregation 90
  Pergamum congregation 78
  Philadelphia congregation 87
  Satan's fall 223–25
  Smyrna congregation 72
  Thyatira congregation 83
  war in heaven 163–64
the evil one 11, 14, 15, 19
evil, paradigms of 229
exorcisms 11–14, 11, 12, 13
extratextual references 39, 50–55, 129
Ezekiel prophecy 199

faithfulness 1, 148, 197
fall of Satan. *see* Satan, fall of
false apostles 88, 89, 90
false prophet 157, 158, 172, 220
false teaching 79
Fee, Gordon D. 221
final battle. *see* Armageddon
final judgment 13, 14, 110, 111, 116, 193, 203, 206, 208, 215, 220, 221, 224, 225, 226, 227, 232
Finamore, Stephen 111

Fiorenza, Elisabeth Schüssler 69, 102, 122, 178, 179, 183, 184
fire 215
fire imagery 219
Fletcher, Michelle 44
Fludernik, Monika 33, 60
focalization of narrative 42, 57
Fontaine, Piet F. M. 17, 19
Forsyth, Neil 2, 15, 23, 120, 130, 138, 139, 140, 143, 144, 148, 151, 169
Frey, Jörg 8
Frilinigos, Chris 176

Gadreel 14
Gallusz, Laszlo 75, 102
gematria 160
Genette, Gérard 42, 60
Gnosticism 131
God 28, 61, 62, 63, 68, 74, 76, 80, 85, 158, 164, 230
  adversarial enemies 193
  adversarial forces of 156
  agents of 18, 91, 95, 105, 190, 207, 222, 229, 232
  authority and powers of 95, 103, 106, 196
  and demons 13
  eschatological endgame 128
  evaluative point of view 78
  faith on 1
  faithfulness in Christ 28
  glorification of 47, 116, 212
  great supper of 173, 186–90
  just God 177
  just judgments 175
  justice of 1
  sovereignty of 103, 105, 106, 108, 126, 142, 155, 198, 227
  superiority of 203
  supremacy of 71
  upon the throne 102–6
  will of 105, 108, 112, 117, 137, 168, 192
  wrath of 46, 172, 182, 223
Goff, Matthew 14
Gog and Magog 152, 206, 207, 210–12, 210–12, 212, 223, 227, 232
Grabiner, Steven 26, 27, 28, 38, 130, 140, 141, 142, 143, 204
great supper of God 173, 186–90, 226

Green, Thomas 41
Greimas, A. J. 37, 38

Hades 150, 151, 215, 216, 220, 224
Hays, Richard B. 51
heads, of dragon 123, 128–29, 152, 153
heaven 101
heavenly assembly 4, 26, 104, 106, 114, 146
Hell 9, 46, 64, 128
Herman, David 38
hermeneutical circle 45
Herodotus 91
hidden manna 74, 78
hope 46
horns, of dragon 123, 128–29, 153
horsemen 112, 117
Horton, Fred L. 17, 18
hubris 20, 71, 80, 124, 135, 137, 151, 152, 153, 167, 180, 183, 186, 191, 224–25, 224, 227, 232, 233
hymnic passage 26, 120, 122, 141, 142, 149

ignorance 90, 93, 94
implied author 34, 36, 39, 42, 44, 45, 63, 68, 70, 72, 73, 75, 76, 78, 81, 94, 125, 163, 167
implied reader 3, 26, 28, 29, 34, 36, 38, 39, 40, 41, 43, 44, 49, 52, 53, 61, 69, 72, 77, 78, 81, 82, 86, 91, 101, 111, 115, 124, 125, 126, 127, 128, 129, 140, 146, 163, 165, 167, 184, 186, 210, 211, 217, 223, 224, 225, 227, 231, 232
intermediary agents 5
  in the septets 112–18, 118, 151
intertextual references 125
intratextual references 145
Iser, Wolfgang 53

Jesus Christ 28, 62, 63, 68, 74, 80, 83, 85, 88, 90, 91, 93, 94, 96, 136, 158, 159, 164, 166, 176, 187, 195, 197, 198, 230
  authority and powers of 97
  as avenging judge and triumphant warrior 189
  faithfulness of 27
  as the Lamb 27
  messianic kingship 113
  promise to eat with 93
  as rider on the white horse 188, 189

share a place on the throne with 93
Jews 85, 86
Jezebel 77, 79, 80, 81, 82, 83, 85, 157
Johnson, M. D. 132
judgment 1, 196
judgment, the final 13, 14, 110, 111, 116, 193, 203, 206, 208, 215, 220, 221, 224, 225, 226, 227, 232
Jung, Carl Gustav 21
just God 177
just judgments 175

Kafka, Joseph 28
Kahl, Brigitte 127
Kalms, Jürgen U. 130
Karamazov, Ivan 21
Keel, Othmar 5
Kelly, Henry Ansgar 2, 23–24, 23, 24, 45, 120, 132, 141, 226
Kensky, Meira Z. 1, 175
Kingsbury, Jack D. 42
Koester, Craig R. 39, 57, 65, 73, 93, 95, 100, 137, 147, 163, 175, 184, 188, 196, 200, 204, 207, 208
Kotsko, Adam 23, 229

Labahn, Michael 24–25, 123, 129, 201, 202
lake of fire 16, 17, 47, 48, 70, 89, 147, 151, 169, 176, 190, 191, 213, 214, 215–17, 220, 221, 225, 228, 232
Lamb 61, 103, 106–8, 112, 118, 223
    death of 106, 136, 147, 164, 189
    resurrection of 152
Laodicea congregation 64
    characterization of 93–94
    plot analysis 92–93
    point of view 94–95
Larivaille, Paul 36
Leibniz, Gottfried 21
Leithart, Peter J. 154, 199
Leviathan 161–62, 163, 166, 167
lex talionis 176
life-giving spirit 19
Lord of Hosts 105
Lord of Spirits 162
Lord's Prayer 12
loyalty 137, 172, 194, 231
Lucifer, Satan as 83
Lupieri, Edmondo F. 148, 175

lying Spirit 81, 84, 133

Marguerat, Daniel 37, 58, 121
Martínez, Florentino García 7
Martyr, Justin 14
martyrs 37, 46, 113, 147, 164, 165
    vindication of 205
Mastema 6, 9, 71, 131, 149, 200, 201, 216, 227
Mathews, Mark D. 144
Mathewson, David L. 165
Maxwell-Stuart, P. G. 21
Meier, John P. 12
Messadié, Gerald 23
messages to the seven congregations. *see* seven congregations
Messiah 83, 121, 137
metaphors 52
Michael 6, 16, 43, 137, 139, 143, 144, 145, 146, 147, 149, 163, 164, 167, 200, 232
Michie, Donald 34
Milton, John 45
Miola, Robert S. 41
Mischel, Walter 2
monism 4–11, 17–20, 105, 107
    and dualism, tension between 2–20
monotheism 11, 104
Moore, Stephen D. 49
Morningstar 28, 80, 83
Mounce, Robert H. 77, 110, 205
mountain(s) 181
mouths 155
Moyise, Steve 41, 51, 133
Murphy, Frederick J. 199

narratio 62, 74, 75
narrative criticism 33–35, 125
    characterization of 36–42
    extratextual references in 50–55
    extratextual references in 39
    and historical criticism 52
    intertextuality in 40–42
    plot analysis 35–36
    point of view 42–45
narrative, definition of 33
narratology 51
Neo-Assyrian empire 104
New Criticism 34, 50
New Jerusalem 173, 178, 190

New Year rituals 200
Nicolaitans 74, 77, 78, 85, 88, 89, 90
Nielsen, Kirsten 37
number of the beast 159
numbers, symbolic 159–61
   number seven 128–29
   number ten 129
   triune number 159, 161

Oldridge, Darren 120
Orlov, Andrei A. 200
Osborne, Grant R. 95, 112, 148, 158, 161, 175
overarching plot of Revelation 45–48, 166

Page, Sydney H. T. 23
Pagels, Elaine 4, 17, 26, 28, 131, 146
Passivum Divinum 113, *see* divine passive
Pergamum congregation
   characterization of 74–78
   plot analysis 73–74
   point of view 78–79
Philadelphia congregation 64, 96, 136, 198, 230
   adversaries in 86
   characterization of 85–86
   plot analysis 84–85
   point of view 86–88
plagues 72, 76, 95, 111, 115, 116
Plato, 59
plot analysis 35–36
   beasts of the earth and the sea 119
   the dragon and the woman 120–22
   Ephesus congregation 88
   fall of Satan 194–95, 194
   Laodicea congregation 92–93
   Pergamum congregation 73–74
   Philadelphia congregation 84–85
   Sardis congregation 90
   Smyrna congregation 65–67
   Thyatira congregation 79–80
   war in heaven 120–22
point of view 42–45
   conceptual 42
   cultural 29, 43, 76, 81
   evaluative 42–43, 61, 163–64, 223–25
   first-person perspective 42
   horizontal 164–66
   vertical 164–66

Popović, Mladen 108
Powell, Mark Allen 36, 42, 44, 52
Prigent, Pierre 33, 57, 121, 154, 188, 192, 197, 210, 222
prophetic paradigm, of evil 229
Propp, Vladimir 37
punishments 2, 32, 61, 162, 164, 175, 177, 182, 183, 185, 202, 219, 224, 227
   just punishment 5, 190
   justification of 46, 201

Quinary scheme 36, 120
   beasts from the earth and sea story 120
   Ephesus congregation 88
   Laodicea congregation 66
   Pergamum congregation 73–74
   Philadelphia congregation 84–85
   Sardis congregation 90
   Satan's fall 194
   Smyrna congregation 66
   the woman and the dragon story 120
   Thyatira congregation 79–80
   war in heaven story 120
quotations 40

radical dualism 19, 20
Rahab 126, 127
recapitulation 110
red dragon. *see* dragon
Reed, Annette Yoshiko 14, 132
references 40
religious compromise 62, 72, 73, 77, 79, 80, 81, 94, 96
repentance 46, 74, 89, 90, 91, 92, 93, 94, 115, 116, 172, 175
Resseguie, James L. 25, 27, 35, 45, 53, 66, 67, 72, 81, 94, 99, 102, 113, 128, 149, 152, 153, 159, 183, 188, 189, 201, 204, 214
retribution 109, 110, 118, 147, 167, 172, 174–78, 190, 191
retrofitted reading 23, 45, 142
rewards 1, 46, 83, 164, 219, 223
Rhoads, David 34
Ricoeur, Paul 194
Roloff, Jürgen 201
Roman triumphal procession 205, 206
Rome 40, 49, 78, 126, 153, 160, 167, 180, 181, 183, 184, 191

Rudnig-Zelt, Susanne 16
ruler of the this world 83
Russell, David Syme 108
Russell, Jeffrey Burton 2, 169

saints 5, 28, 75, 122, 129, 139, 147, 164, 165, 173, 187, 191, 197, 230
   death of 166
   persecution of 166
   thousand-year reign of 193
   tribulation of 76
   urban metaphor 212
   vindication of 86, 96, 190, 205, 208, 226, 228
salvation 1, 145, 146, 147, 148, 166, 167, 186, 196, 212, 227, 231, 233
   coming age of 220
   and suffering 167
Sardis congregation 96
   characterization of 90–92
   plot analysis 90
   point of view 92
Satan 1, 6, 119, 120, 131, 200, 216
   ambiguity 2–20
   anti-divine trait of 16, 23, 25, 214, 223–25, 226, 227
   autonomy 233
   binding of 193, 206, 226, 232
   characterization of 36–42
   death of 213–21
   as a deceiver and stumbling block 9
   deception of nations 210–13
   deep things of 80, 81, 82
   as divine agent 13, 23, 229
   dragon as. *see* the dragon and the woman
   end of 147, 168, 169, 170–72, 170, 228, 232
   as enemy of God 16, 20, 232
   eternal suffering of 219
   function in God's eschatological ordeal 222
   function of deceiving and dividing up humankind 225
   as God's cosmic enemy 229
   as God's sifting device 2
   imperial presence as presence of 78
   incarceration of 206, 208, 231
   as an intermediary agent 5
   as Lucifer 83
   names and epithets 119, 145
   narrative function of 194, 195
   non-generic references to 4
   as Opponent 77, 96
   Peter as 72
   prison imagery 209, 226
   publications on 21–24
   removal before the final judgment 232
   removal of 227
   role in final judgment effectuation 203
   as servant of God 13, 16, 17, 23, 30, 105, 232
   sifting and testing traits 79
   subordinate function of 201
   temporary binding of 198–210
   as tester 4, 73, 90, 92, 96, 135, 220, 230
   throne of 75, 76
   time limitation 204
   war in heaven 16, 28
Satan, fall of 12, 28, 144, 167, 193, 221, 231
   and Babylon 178–86
   characterization of 195–221
   evaluative point of view 223–25
   God's point of view 221–23
   and great supper of God 186–90
   plot analysis 194–95
   plot, perspectives on 194
   primeval 134, 141, 148
   and vindication/retribution dichotomy 174–78
   and wedding supper of the Lamb 186–90
   and whore/bride dichotomy 101–2
Satan, release of 169, 193, 205–6, 207–9, 232
   as divine necessity 199
   temporary release 200, 227
Satan's character
   construct of 39
   definition of 21
   dualistic approach 11–16
   monistic approach 4–11
scarlet beast 124, 151, 154, 178, 183
Schreiber, Stephan 7
second death 66, 215, 216, 223
Semyaza 14, 127, 200
septets. *see* three septets
serpents 131
   and dragons 130–34

Eden serpent 45, 130–34, 130
sea serpent 126, 127, 130, 161
seven congregations 57, 99, 107, 119, 121, 164, 172, 230
  Christ and God, blurred distinction between 97
  diegetic levels 59–62, 66, 107
  Ephesus 88–90
  hypodiegetic level of 60, 66, 107
  interpolated frame 60
  Laodicea 92–95
  literary form and function of 62–65
  literary frame 58–62
  multiple framing 60
  Pergamum 73–79
  Philadelphia 84–88
  Sardis 90
  Smyrna congregation 65–73
  Thyatira 79–84
seven messages 188
  stereographical categories of 62
seven mountains 40, 181
Sheol 181
sifting 47, 187
Skinner, Christopher W. 11
slandering 3, 70
Smalley, Stephen S. 134, 184, 189, 198, 216
Smit, Peter-Ben 118, 147
Smith, Mark S. 104, 105, 181
Smyrna congregation 64, 136
  adversaries in 86
  characterization of 67–72
  plot analysis 65–67
  point of view 72–73
Solomon, adversaries to 182
Son of God 13, 14, 83, 86, 139, 169, 188
son of man 60, 61, 188
Spirit of Darkness 9
Spirit of Injustice 12
spirit of prophecy 114, 158, 159, 161, 164, 186
stars, interpretation of 134
Stewart, Alexander E. 176
Stokes, Ryan E. 5, 104
Stuckenbruck, Loren T. 9, 13, 15, 144
stumbling block 9, 77, 89
subordinated function 228
suffering 46, 47
  eternal suffering 176, 213, 219
  imposed on dwellers of the earth 47
  as just punishment or chastisement 5
  personification as Satan 21
  and salvation 167
  and trust 1
Sweet, John 153, 220, 221
symbolism 3, 40, 44, 52, 53, 121, 122, 125, 133, 183, 184, 192, 215, 217
sympathy, towards characters 72, 82, 92, 94
synagogue of Satan 69, 72, 75, 85, 86, 154, 198

Talbert, Charles H. 106, 158
Tannin 126, 127
tensions, in Revelation 16–17
tester, Satan as 4, 73, 90, 92, 96, 135, 220, 230
testing 88
  of believers 2
  methods of 48
  in seven congregations 70, 96
Thomas, John Christopher 25, 41, 198, 210
Thompson, Leonard L. 64, 95, 124
thousand-year reign 17, 145, 169, 170, 192, 193, 195, 198, 201, 202, 204, 208, 210, 222, 223, 226, 231
three septets 65, 95, 102, 105, 108–18, 109, 116, 168, 171, 173
  common structure of progression 109
  intermediary agents in 112–18, 118, 151
  limitations 114
  and plague traditions of Exodus 114–16
  progressively repeating 109
  and Rev 4–16, 109–12
  and sovereignty of God 116–17
  and will of God 117
throne of Satan 75, 76
throne vision 100–101, 142, 163, 174, 230
  ethos of John 101–2
  God upon the throne 102–6, 111
  and the Lamb 106–8
  and septets 110–12
Thyatira congregation 96
  characterization of 80–82
  plot analysis 79–80
  point of view 82–84
time 70, 110, 113, 231
Tipvarakankoon, Wiriya 206

Tonstad, Sigve K. 25, 27, 28, 99, 103, 125, 142, 143, 169, 199, 202, 203, 204, 221
torture 176
Trafton, Joseph L. 25, 122, 134, 135, 137, 148, 208, 214
Travis, Stephen H. 176, 177, 216, 217
Treatise of the Two Spirits 7
tribulation of the saints 76
triumphal procession, Roman 205, 206
triune number 159, 161

VanderKam, James C. 6
Venus 83
vertical point of view 99
vindication 109, 110, 118, 147, 167, 172, 174–78, 187, 191, 193, 204
   of God's people 145
   of the saints 86, 96, 190, 208, 226, 228
vindication/retribution dichotomy 226

war in heaven 119, 143, 171, 232
   antipathy 163–64
   characterization of 137–38, 143–50
   evaluative point of view 163–64
   God's point of view 162–63
   horizontal point of view 164–66
   plot analysis 120–22
   sympathy 163–64
   vertical point of view 164–66
War scroll 8, 216
Watchers 9, 13–14, 14, 131, 132, 135, 149, 151, 200
   fall of 144
waters 180
wedding supper of the Lamb 186–90, 226

Wengst, Klaus 156
white stone with the new name inscribed 74, 78
whore of Babylon 81
whore/bride dichotomy 101–2, 226
Wimsatt, William K. 50
Witherington, Ben 89
Wold, Benjamin 10, 12
woman
   clothed with the sun 127, 180
   sitting on scarlet beast 178–81
Wood, Shane J. 201, 205, 206, 207
Woodman, Simon P. 219
Word of God 174, 183, 188, 189, 197
worship, act of, 100, 101, 106, 152, 165, 182, 217
worthiness 106
Wright, Archie T. 8, 9

Yahad 9, 12
Yahweh 5, 20, 77, 81, 84, 97, 104, 182, 212, 229
   enemies of 126
   self-presentation 47
   sovereignty of 71
   unrivaled power 103
Yahweh of Hosts 104, 106
Yarbro Collins, Adela 1, 25, 61, 63, 64, 78, 81, 110, 128, 138, 139, 140, 142, 143
Yeates, Paul Henry 154

Zimmerli, Walther 181
Zumstein, Jean 40
Zurawski, Jason M. 132

www.ingramcontent.com/pod-product-compliance
Lightning Source LLC
Chambersburg PA
CBHW072136290426
44111CB00012B/1889